Digital SAT® Workbook

5001 Cordell Avenue
Bethesda, MD
20814

6731 Curran Street
McLean, VA
22101

4646 40th St. NW
Washington, DC
20016

www.prepmatters.com • 301-951-0350
© PrepMatters, Inc., 2023

ACKNOWLEDGMENTS

Author: Rachel Jones

With special thanks to Ned Johnson for his leadership and vision

With additional special thanks to Ana Laura Carignani, Michael DePalatis, Susan Dykeman, Aaron Golumbfskie, John Jones, Daniela Manopla, Laura Moore, and many other past and present PrepMatters employees who made this project possible

TM and © 2023 by PrepMatters, Inc. PREPMATTERS is a registered trademark of Prepmatters, Inc. All rights reserved.

College Board, SAT, and the acorn logo are registered trademarks of the College Board, which is not affiliated with, and does not endorse, this product.

Student Assignment Sheet

Date	Next Appt.	Homework
4/7		send ss of test one report to tutor pg. 424-462 multiple choice (odd #s)
4/13	Zoom	Circle problems pg 221-296
4/14		Practice test 2 math only do test corrections
4/20		Practice test 3 math
4/21		pg 297-366
4/27		Practice test 4 math
4/28		pg 367-423; test 6; 269-423 *anything in blue*
week of test		- eating healthy, stay hydrated, good sleep schedule, print out ticket, laptop charged, take charge w/ me, charged calculator, ID, pencil, snack, drink, wear comfy clothes
May 4th	TEST	

Student Assignment Sheet

Date	Next Appt.	Homework

TM and © 2023 PrepMatters, Inc. All rights reserved.

Table of Contents

Introduction to the SAT

Test Overview	7
Scoring	8
Percentiles	9
Computer-Based Testing	10
SAT vs. ACT	12
General SAT Strategies	14
How to Use this Book	15

Reading and Writing

Section Overview	17

Reading: Information, Ideas, and Structure

Words in Context	20
Central Ideas and Details	30
Structure and Purpose	44
Compare and Contrast	57

Reading: Evidence and Logical Reasoning

Command of Evidence – Illustrate the Claim	71
Command of Evidence – Strengthen/Weaken	82
Command of Evidence – Quantitative	95
Logical Inferences	109

Writing: Standard English Conventions

Sentence Structure	120
Commas	132
Semicolons, Colons, Dashes, and Apostrophes	148
Verbs	167
Pronouns	179
Misplaced Modifiers	188

Writing: Expression of Ideas

Transitions	193
Rhetorical Synthesis	206

Math

Section Overview	219
Strategy in Brief	
Back-Solving and Substitution	221
Mastering the Calculator	232
Approximating and Measuring	244
Algebra	
Algebra Essentials	247
Word Problems	259
Coordinate Geometry	269
Systems of Equations	279
Inequalities and Absolute Value	289
Advanced Math	
Exponents and Roots	297
Factoring, FOILing, and Fractions	306
Function Essentials	321
Linear Functions	333
Quadratic Functions	341
Polynomial, Exponential, Radical, and Rational Functions	351
Problem Solving and Data Analysis	
Data Interpretation	367
Ratios, Proportions, and Unit Conversions	380
Percentages	391
Mean, Median, and Mode	399
Probability	409
Statistics	417
Geometry and Trigonometry	
Area and Volume	424
Angles, Lines, and Triangles	437
Right Triangles and Trigonometry	452
Circles	463

Introduction to the SAT
Test Overview

Here's what to expect when you arrive at the testing center to take the SAT.

**Check-in and test instructions
at least 30-60 minutes**

After presenting your ID, you'll be directed to a testing room where you can set up your laptop or tablet (you can bring your own or use one provided by College Board). Expect to spend some time listening to instructions and filling in your basic information before the test begins.

**Reading and Writing, Module 1
27 questions, 32 minutes**

Each question in this module will present you with a brief standalone passage, which may or may not be accompanied by a chart, graph, or other figure. You'll be asked to analyze the passage, pick the best version of a sentence, or make logical deductions based on what you've read.

**Reading and Writing, Module 2
27 questions, 32 minutes**

This module includes the same types of questions as those found in the first module, but you may notice a change in the difficulty level. Depending on how well your first module went, the test will adjust your second module to be either somewhat easier or somewhat harder than the first.

**Break
10 minutes**

During this break in testing, you'll be allowed to leave the room, stretch your legs, get a snack, and so on. You may not use your cell phone or any other electronic device.

**Math, Module 1
22 questions, 35 minutes**

The content you'll see tested will include algebra, data interpretation, ratios, percentages, geometry/trig, and some "advanced" math such as quadratic and exponential functions. Both multiple-choice questions and "student-produced response" questions (fill-ins) are included.

**Math, Module 2
22 questions, 35 minutes**

Just as with the verbal section, the difficulty level of the second math module will be determined based on your performance on the first math module. The content and question types remain the same.

Total testing time: **about 2½ – 3 hours.**

TM and © 2023 PrepMatters, Inc. All rights reserved.

Scoring

When you sit for the SAT, you'll see four "modules" of questions, as discussed on the previous page. The test will calculate your two section scores (one Reading and Writing score and one Math score) based on the number of questions you got right on the corresponding modules. Each of the two sections is scored on a scale of 200 to 800. The two section scores are then added together, so your final SAT score is on a scale of 400-1600.

However, not all questions are treated equally. The reason that the sections are separated into two modules each is that the SAT is now an **adaptive** test, meaning its difficulty level is set based on your performance. That is, if you do well on the first math module, you'll see a harder set of questions in the second math module—and the opportunity for a higher score. The same is true on the Reading & Writing side: the difficulty level of the second module is based on the number of questions you answered correctly on the first one. This means if you score poorly on the first module, there is a limit to how high your section score will be—even if you get every question in the second module right.

On the other hand, this means if you're seeing a lot of tough questions in your second module, that's good news! It means you aced the first module, and you've put yourself in the best position for a high overall score.

> ***TIP:***
> There is no "guessing penalty" on the SAT—you do not lose points for incorrect answers. So there's no reason to ever leave anything blank.

Percentiles

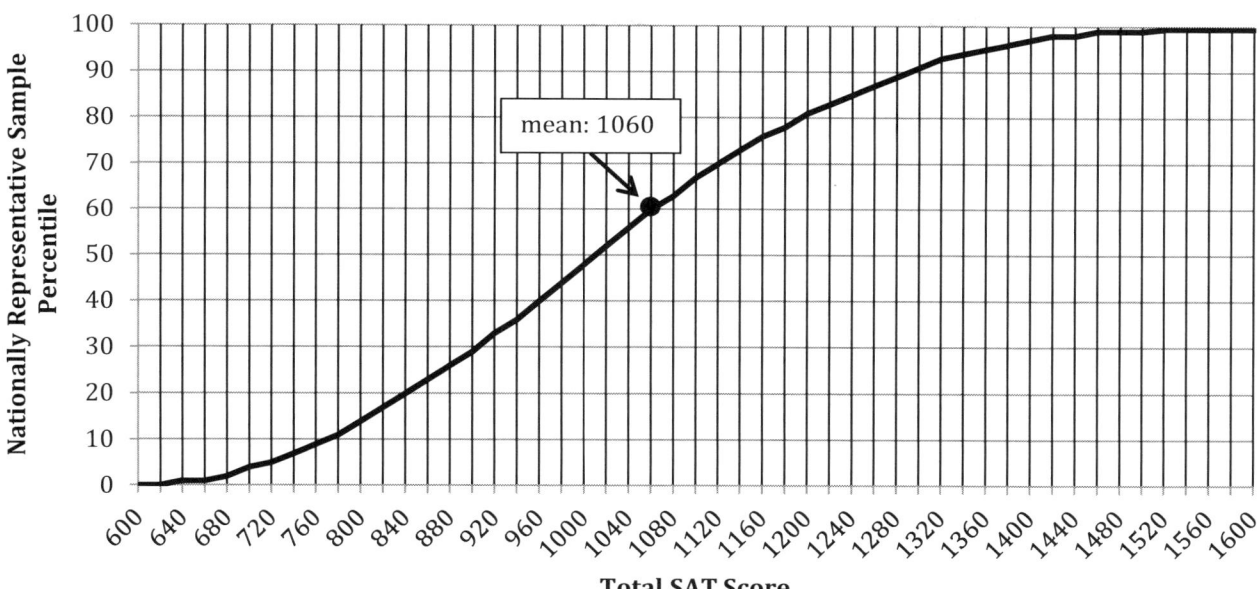

Curious how your score stacks up to those of other students? The graph above shows the 2021-2022 SAT percentiles based on a nationally representative sample of US students in the 11th and 12th grades.

Percentile ranks represent the percentage of students who score equal to or below that score. For example, according to this graph, a total score of 1120 was at about the 70th percentile for this time period: this means that if you scored an 1120, your score was greater than or equal to the scores of approximately 70% of students.

Although these percentiles are based on the previous (written) version of the SAT rather than the current (digital) version, approximately the same curve should apply. The College Board, the company that makes the SAT, asserts that the scoring on the digital test has been carefully formulated so that an 1120 on the new test is equivalent to an 1120 on the old: roughly the same proportion of students should earn that score either way.

Computer-Based Testing

One of the most important ways you can prepare yourself for the digital SAT is to familiarize yourself with the testing software you'll be using. If you haven't already, go to the College Board website and download Bluebook, the testing app you'll use to take the SAT.

In the Reading and Writing sections, you'll see a format like this:

Section 1: Reading and Writing   0:00   Annotate More
Directions v   (Hide)

Many scientists believe that the universe is made up of dark matter, a mysterious substance that does not interact with light or other forms of electromagnetic radiation and is therefore invisible to telescopes. While the existence of dark matter has been _____ from its gravitational effects on visible matter, the precise nature of dark matter is still not understood.

1 ☐ Mark for Review   [ABC]

Which choice completes the text with the most logical and precise word or phrase?

A. insinuated
B. denied
C. construed
D. inferred

1 of 27   Next

The left side of the screen contains a brief passage, usually no more than one paragraph long. The right side of the screen contains the question and answer choices. Click on an answer to choose it; click the [Next] button on the bottom right to move to the next question. Immediately above the question, there's a little ☐ symbol with "Mark for Review" written next to it: click that to flag a question to remind yourself to return to it later. Click on the [ABC] button to the right of that if you want to eliminate answer choices.

Now look at the top row, above the question. Up in the middle is a timer which will count down the number of minutes you have remaining in the section; click the (Hide) button below it if you don't want this staring at you. In the top right, note the important [Annotate] button! This is what allows you to mark up the text on the screen as you go. To use it, select some text, then click that button. A pop-up menu will allow you to highlight the text, underline it, or even type a quick note to yourself.

The [More] button in the top right corner is for assistive technology, IT help, and emergency tools to exit the exam early or take an unscheduled break. Most students won't use this button at all.

TM and © 2023 PrepMatters, Inc. All rights reserved.

The format of the Math questions is very similar.

Section 2: Math
Directions ⌄

0:00
(Hide)

Calculator Reference More

1 ☐ Mark for Review   ABC

If $0 < c < d < 1$, then which of the following has the greatest value?

- A. d^2
- B. cd
- C. c
- D. d

1 of 22   Next

This time, the question and answer choices are presented right in the middle of the screen. You no longer have the ability to highlight or underline text, but you now have two other important tools. Click on the $\boxed{\text{Reference } x^2}$ button to see a list of geometry formulas that you can access at any time. Click on the $\boxed{\text{Calculator}}$ button to access the built-in graphing calculator, which you definitely should use. All the other buttons are the same as in the Reading and Writing modules.

> **TIP:**
> Take some time to get comfortable with the built-in calculator. It can be an incredibly powerful tool for your math score.

SAT vs. ACT

Both the SAT and the ACT are well-established standardized tests accepted by all colleges and universities in the US. How can you decide which test is right for you? Here's a breakdown of how they differ.

Digital format	As of 2024, the SAT can only be taken in digital format (on a computer or tablet). Depending on when and where you're testing, the ACT may still be a traditional paper test, or you may have a choice between paper and digital versions. Unlike the SAT, however, the ACT will not be an *adaptive* digital test: the difficulty level of a section will not depend on your previous performance.

Reasoning	Questions on the ACT tend to be more straightforward, with a focus on assessing your knowledge of actual content. SAT questions are often more focused on testing your reasoning ability. The test rewards creative thinking more than subject matter mastery, and a tough problem often presents more like a logic puzzle than a familiar math question out of your textbook.

Reading pace and difficulty	The ACT reading passages are longer, and you have much less time to get through them. On the other hand, the passages are also easier than SAT passages, and the questions are more straightforward.

Science	The ACT includes a Science section, which the SAT does not. However, neither test is actually testing your science expertise. The ACT Science section is really just a test of quickly reading and interpreting charts and graphs in a science context. That task is also included on the SAT, just spread throughout the sections instead of concentrated in one place.

FROM THE BLOG

There's no reason to take *both* the SAT and the ACT. One, I don't know what you do with your Saturday mornings, but you must have more creative/worthwhile/fulfilling ways to spend those hours than in taking every test available to you. Two, grades remain the most important criterion of college admissions. Less time on test prep means more time for school (or friends, sports, sleep, you name it). Three, because the tests are different, the preparation for one is similar to but also meaningfully different than that for the other. It should be. They are different tests. Trying to study for or take both tests at once is akin to trying to switch between shortstop and left field and back, or the roles of Romeo to Juliet on subsequent nights (talk about heartbreak!). Lastly, no college asks for both. They ask for one or the other. Never both. Please choose. Trust me, you will be happy you did.

SAT to ACT Concordance Tables

SAT to ACT:						ACT to SAT:	
SAT Total	ACT Composite	SAT Total	ACT Composite	SAT Total	ACT Composite	ACT Composite	SAT Total
1600	36	1260	27	920	17	36	1590
1590	36	1250	26	910	16	35	1540
1580	36	1240	26	900	16	34	1500
1570	36	1230	26	890	16	33	1460
1560	35	1220	25	880	16	32	1430
1550	35	1210	25	870	15	31	1400
1540	35	1200	25	860	15	30	1370
1530	35	1190	24	850	15	29	1340
1520	34	1180	24	840	15	28	1310
1510	34	1170	24	830	15	27	1280
1500	34	1160	24	820	14	26	1240
1490	34	1150	23	810	14	25	1210
1480	33	1140	23	800	14	24	1180
1470	33	1130	23	790	14	23	1140
1460	33	1120	22	780	14	22	1110
1450	33	1110	22	770	13	21	1080
1440	32	1100	22	760	13	20	1040
1430	32	1090	21	750	13	19	1010
1420	32	1080	21	740	13	18	970
1410	31	1070	21	730	13	17	930
1400	31	1060	21	720	12	16	890
1390	31	1050	20	710	12	15	850
1380	30	1040	20	700	12	14	800
1370	30	1030	20	690	12	13	760
1360	30	1020	19	680	11	12	710
1350	29	1010	19	670	11	11	670
1340	29	1000	19	660	11	10	630
1330	29	990	19	650	11	9	590
1320	28	980	18	640	10		
1310	28	970	18	630	10		
1300	28	960	18	620	10		
1290	27	950	17	610	9		
1280	27	940	17	600	9		
1270	27	930	17	590	9		

Adapted from "2018 ACT/SAT Concordance Tables," a joint publication of The College Board and ACT, Inc.

TIP:

The best way to tell which test is best suited for you is to take a practice test in each. Use these tables to compare your results.

TM and © 2023 PrepMatters, Inc. All rights reserved.

General SAT Strategies

The SAT is an intellectual marathon in which stamina is a key determinant of success. In order to succeed, you must prepare yourself physically, emotionally, and mentally. Although many students abandon the physical and emotional elements of preparation and focus solely on the mental aspect, they may find it difficult to do their best without the energy, alertness, and focus that physical and emotional preparation supply.

Physical preparation	Be sure to get enough sleep. When you are well rested, you will be more alert, less likely to make careless errors, and better able to devote your attention to the test. Similarly, regular exercise will help you feel more alert for the test and train your body to better handle stress. Nutrition also plays an important role in reaching optimal performance: healthy foods give you energy without leading to a crash later.
Emotional preparation	The best way to be emotionally prepared for the test is to feel in control of it, which comes from the knowledge that you have all the tools and information that you need to succeed. Also, practice a strategy for calming yourself down should you find yourself panicking during the test. Deep breathing is surprisingly effective; talk to a tutor or trusted teacher about other methods that may work for you.
Mental preparation	The best way to prepare for this test—and to lower your stress surrounding it at the same time—is to PRACTICE, PRACTICE, PRACTICE. Continue reviewing topics and doing practice problems until you thoroughly understand each section and have made each topic and strategy your own. Practice will also help you to know the pace at which you need to work.

How to Use This Book

While you're certainly welcome to start this book at page one and make your way in order through all the sections, many students will be better served by a more tailored approach. A good place to begin is the Table of Contents. Which math topics are areas of strength for you, and which ones are you less confident about? Are there any Reading question types that seem completely mysterious? How about topics of Writing mechanics on which you know you could use a refresher?

Each chapter begins with a Preview Quiz that gives you a glimpse of what topics the chapter will cover. Use these to help triage the sections for you. If you can breeze through a quiz with no effort, that's a chapter that's probably not a top priority for your studying time. If the quiz stumps you, focus on that chapter earlier rather than later.

Following the Preview Quiz, you'll see several pages of instruction that walk you through the topic and discuss both content and strategy, starting with the basics and building toward the more difficult content. The answers to all the Preview Quiz questions will be explained along the way. Most chapters also include "Try It" questions so you can test your understanding. You'll also see some "From the Blog" boxes every once in a while: these include excerpts from the PrepMatters blog about important elements of non-academic preparation, such as stress management and the importance of sleep.

After you finish reading the chapter and answering the Try It questions, you're ready to move on to the Practice Sets. Each chapter has two: one with easy to medium level problems, and the other with medium to difficult problems. Depending on your confidence, skill level, and goals, you may want to attack only the first set, only the second, or both.

You're ready for this! It's time to turn to the Table of Contents, pick a topic, and dive in.

FROM THE BLOG

Some years ago, before we all carried GPS-equipped cell phones in our pockets, a friend of mine called to tell me he was lost. In the panicked, disoriented voice of a person who has lost all perspective, he gasped, "I thought I knew how to get there, because I went once with Derek, and I only have 65 cents and I remember being on a road with a roundish-even-numbered-route like 8 or 80 or 36 or maybe 22 and I'm at a pay phone and I don't know how much gas is left and please help me."

"Take a deep breath," I said. "What do you see?"

Knowing the area well, or having a map handy, is a nice way to keep from getting lost. But telling my friend facts about the area or the map would have been completely useless. What was helpful was being able to imagine how the world looked to him: following his wrong turns or embracing his errant logic. Only after empathizing with how he saw the world could I be helpful in getting him to take inventory of what he knew and helping him to reorient himself.

That panicked, disoriented tone of voice is exactly the same one I hear from my students. They don't know how SAT questions connect to their Algebra II class, or how comma rules relate to semicolons. Their minds race, but they only get more confused, more lost. They worry they don't have enough time. They worry they won't live up to expectations, or that they're inferior to their friends. They resent the test for measuring such inane, uninteresting skills.

Knowing how to test well, and the rules of grammar, and tricky facts of quadratic equations are necessary to help my students. But if they're lost enough, they don't even know how far they are from where they want to be. Telling them the best route is useless unless I know where they are and how they view things. Only then can we gain some perspective and reorient. Take a deep breath, I say. What do you see?

Most of the time, my students find their way, relieved to have the confusion behind them. More exciting, though, is when they learn to orient themselves. When they can retrace their steps and be aware of how their mental routes lead them away from where they want to go. Then, getting a little lost isn't as scary as they feared. Then, getting lost is an interesting side effect of going somewhere new.

Reading & Writing Section Overview

The two modules that make up the SAT's Reading and Writing section will test your proficiency with the written word. In each module, you'll have 32 minutes to answer 27 standalone questions. Unlike on other standardized tests, you will not need to answer multiple questions based on the same lengthy passage. Here, each question is self-contained, based on a passage no more than about one paragraph long.

The topics of the passages will vary. Some will cover history, social studies, the humanities, or science. Others will be fiction passages, often excerpts from a novel or short story. Occasionally, you may be asked to analyze poetry as well.

Roughly half of the questions focus on your skills in **reading** comprehension and analysis. Many of these are familiar types that you've seen before: find the meaning of a word in context, identify the most likely purpose of a particular sentence, state the main idea of a passage, and so on. Other questions will emphasize your logical reasoning skills. For example, for some questions, you'll be asked to demonstrate that you can choose the relevant information from a chart or graph in order to strengthen an author's argument. This requires a fairly advanced understanding of both the chart/graph and the argument, as well as the ways that the two relate to each other.

The other half of the questions are designed to test your **writing** skills. You'll be asked to choose the best version of a sentence, weighing considerations of English mechanics (punctuation, verb agreement, etc.) as well as style (for example, choosing a clean, concise sentence rather than a wordy, awkward one). For a few questions, you'll be given a set of facts and asked to choose the sentence that most effectively incorporates the relevant information to accomplish some specific goal.

These question types may seem unfamiliar, but they all get easier with practice. Helpfully, the SAT Reading & Writing section is very, very predictable. The more you practice it, the more you'll know exactly what to expect on test day.

Section Breakdown

Reading: Information, Ideas, and Structure
17-20 per section
≈ 33%

Reading: Evidence and Logical Reasoning
10-13 per section
≈ 21%

Writing: Standard English Conventions
11-15 per section
≈ 25%

Writing: Expression of Ideas
8-12 per section
≈ 21%

Reading: Information, Ideas, and Structure

These questions test your ability to read and analyze various kinds of texts. After reading a brief passage, you'll answer a single question designed to test your understanding. Some questions are about the details: you may be asked how a particular sentence fits into the passage as a whole, or what specific word best fits into a sentence. Other questions are about the bigger picture, asking you to summarize the main idea or compare one author's viewpoint to another's. For all of these questions, what matters most is the *context* of the passage. Be sure to limit your answers to what the passage explicitly tells you—never rely on your own outside knowledge of the topic, and try to avoid making any big assumptions about what the author is trying to say.

> ***TIP:***
>
> In an average SAT Reading and Writing section, about a third of the questions will come from this category. More than half of those will be Words in Context questions.

Strategy in Brief

Unlike in the math portion of the SAT, for which we all agree on the criteria for correct answers, the distinction between two answer choices in the Reading and Writing section can sometimes appear quite subtle. As a result, students sometimes believe this section to be "subjective" or impossible to prepare for. **This is not the case.** Every question has one right answer and three wrong ones. The right answer is right because it has the most evidence *in the text*. Here are a few general principles to keep in mind to help you identify it.

Prediction is key.	We can spend a lot of energy thinking hard about why the answers "might..." "sort of..." "in a way..." "kind of..." work. Comparing answers only to each other is a great way to frustrate ourselves. Instead, the most crucial strategy is—whenever possible—to have an answer to the question **before** looking at the answer choices presented. It's a lot easier to find something if you know exactly what you're looking for.
Put it in your own words.	Have you ever gotten to the end of a passage and realized that you have no idea what you just read? It's easy to do. To keep that from happening, keep your reading **active**. As you go, summarize complex ideas into simple statements. What did the author just tell me? How does it relate to what they told me before? What are they probably going to tell me next?
Weaker is better.	If you're torn between two answer choices, the one using weaker language (e.g., words like "sometimes" or "at least a few") is more likely to be right than one that uses stronger language (such as "always" or "never"). Although some wrong answer choices overtly contradict or distort information in the passage, many are wrong simply because they are too extreme. Be wary, and make sure that the ENTIRE answer is correct.
Make intentional choices.	Depending on your goals, it may make sense to answer the questions out of order. In general, you may want to do fast, easy tasks before difficult, irritating ones. Or you may want to save the fun questions as an incentive to stay on task halfway through the section—managing your energy is another factor, after all. The passage's content and topic are considerations, as is the question type. As with many things on the test, just remember your options and that ***you're* in charge of your approach.** Take charge of the section and handle it the way that works best for you.

Words in Context

Preview Quiz

What do the following signify?

	contrast	continuation of thought
1) the word *however*	_____	_____
2) the word *moreover*	_____	_____
3) a colon	_____	_____

In each of the following, which choice completes the text with the most logical and precise word or phrase?

4) Janice is an optimistic person with a positive outlook on life. Although she is usually happy, today she seems quite _____

   A) fortunate.
   B) surprising.
   C) sad.
   D) unusual.

5) Bugs Bunny is a _____ character; people around the world recognize his face and his line, "What's up, Doc?"

   A) striking
   B) legitimate
   C) humorous
   D) well-known

6) Insider trading scams would not have flourished in the 1980s, as they clearly did, had regulators not been _____ to crack down on white-collar crime.

   A) motivated
   B) swift
   C) disinclined
   D) predisposed

These questions focus on our understanding of the subtle meanings of individual words, and how those meanings can change with context. In most cases, you'll be presented with a brief passage that has a word missing from one of its sentences, and you'll be asked to choose the word that fits the blank best. Occasionally, you'll see a variation where there is no blank—instead, you'll be asked to analyze an underlined word in the passage and choose the synonym that could best take its place.

The key to getting the correct answer is to understand the natural rhythm and context of the given sentence. Once you understand how the sentence "feels," you ought to be able to fill in the blank with a word of your choosing. Your first instinct will usually be "in the ballpark," if not exactly correct. Understanding, practicing, and adhering to the process described below will ensure that you master the idea of each sentence and that you do not get fooled by incorrect answer choices.

Read.	Cover the answer choices with your hand and read through the text, just saying the word "blank" to yourself when you hit the blank. It is important *not* to look at those answer choices yet so that they don't lead you astray.
Predict.	If no answer choices had been provided, what word would *you* choose to fill this blank? Use all the clues that the text has supplied, and feel free to **reuse the words already in the sentence**.
Evaluate the choices.	Remove your hand and compare the answer choices to the word you predicted. Which one is the best match?
Re-read.	This is a crucial final step! Re-read the text with your choice plugged into the blank to make sure it works.

The right answers to these questions do *not* necessarily involve difficult vocabulary words. In fact, for most of these questions, you will already know the definitions of the words in all four answer choices. The trick is to understand the **context** and make smart use of the **evidence** provided in the text.

> *TIP:*
>
> Avoid the temptation to automatically pick the "fanciest" word as the answer. The only factors that matter are the meanings of the words and the context of the sentence.

Reading: Information, Ideas, and Structure

The text will always supply **clue words** that help you understand the relationship between the ideas expressed and help you find the correct answer.

Words that indicate a **CONTINUATION** of thought:

and	as well	similarly	furthermore
also	too	moreover	additionally

Words that indicate a **CONTRASTING** ideas:

yet	although	but	rather than
however	even so	in spite of	nevertheless
instead	despite	alternatively	on the other hand

Words that indicate a **CONCLUSION**:

in short	therefore	accordingly	as a result
thus	consequently	hence	in other words

Words that indicate a **CAUSE** or **MOTIVATION**:

because	since	for	to these ends

TIP:

For much more detail about these connecting words and phrases, see the Transitions section on p. 193.

Use these clue words to **predict** a word or phrase that logically would fill the blank. Remember, you can **reuse the words already in the text** to make this step simpler and more accurate.

Example: *Janice is an optimistic person with a positive outlook on life. Although she is usually happy, today she seems quite* _____

Focus on the clue word "although." What does it tell you about the word we're looking for? It indicates a contrast, meaning we're looking for a word that's the opposite of "happy." A simple word like "unhappy" would be a good prediction here. Now look at the choices:

A. *fortunate.*
B. *surprising.*
C. *sad.*
D. *unusual.*

The answer is **C**.

- 22 -

TM and © 2023 PrepMatters, Inc. All rights reserved.

Try It — Which choice completes the text with the most logical and precise word or phrase? First cover the answer choices with your hand and write in your prediction. Then pick the best match from the choices.

1) Many New Yorkers like to escape their crowded cities by visiting the Adirondack Mountains so that they may experience rare moments of _____ when they are truly alone and undisturbed.

   Prediction: _____

   A. solitude
   B. companionship
   C. loneliness
   D. cosmopolitanism

2) Thomas Kuhn's theories on the method of structural change within science were _____ when Kuhn first proposed them, but now they are universally respected and accepted.

   Prediction: _____

   A. well-established
   B. ridiculed
   C. praised
   D. endorsed

Another good source of clues is the **punctuation** of the original text. In general, semicolons and colons link two independent clauses that express similar ideas. On the SAT, semicolons and colons will be used to restate an idea. Similarly, three phrases or words strung together with commas will also express the same idea.

Example: *Bugs Bunny is a _____ character; people around the world recognize his face and his line, "What's up, Doc?"*

The clue here is the semicolon, which tells us that the second clause is intended to express the same idea as the first. So, according to the second clause, what kind of character is Bugs Bunny? Make it simple and reuse a word from the text: *recognizable* is a great prediction for this one.

A. striking
B. legitimate
C. humorous
D. well-known

The answer is **D**.

TIP:
Notice that some of the incorrect choices may create sentences that are *true*. Many of us do find Bugs Bunny to be a humorous character, after all. But only one choice gives us a sentence that is backed up by the **evidence** in the rest of the text.

Reading: Information, Ideas, and Structure

Try It   Which choice completes the text with the most logical and precise word or phrase?

3) Most people think of diamonds as rare gems, but they are actually quite _____; the diamond supply has to be tightly restricted or the value of the gems would drop dramatically.

   Prediction: _____

   A. uncommon
   B. exquisite
   C. common
   D. expensive

4) The photographer was best known for his revealing _____ photographs: he never posed his subjects for fear that the artificiality would ruin the end result.

   Prediction: _____

   A. candid
   B. unnatural
   C. theatrical
   D. brilliant

CHALLENGE:

When these questions get difficult, it is usually due to the twisty structure of the sentence rather than the difficulty of the vocabulary. Be sure to read all the way to the end of the text before making your prediction (or choosing an answer) so that you know exactly where the writer is headed.

Example: *Insider trading scams would not have flourished in the 1980s, as they clearly did, had regulators not been _____ to crack down on white-collar crime.*

   A. *motivated*
   B. *swift*
   C. *disinclined*
   D. *predisposed*

Don't move too fast. What's the author's overall point? Scams flourished in the 1980s, and this wouldn't have happened if regulators had cracked down. But there's a "not" in front of the blank, so we need a word that expresses what the regulators did *not* do. Like this: if the regulators had not been so useless, the scams wouldn't have flourished. We need a word that expresses the regulators *not* acting. Choices A, B, and D all go the wrong way. Choice **C** is the only one that works.

Chapter Answer Key

Try It	1)	A
	2)	B
	3)	C
	4)	A

FROM THE BLOG

Under stress, most people speed up. This is especially true on tests, because students have been conditioned by school to fear not finishing. But on the SAT, answering fewer than all the questions does not spell doom, so panicking over unanswered questions is not called for. And it's a lot easier to accurately answer what you *do* know how to do if you don't rush to answer everything.

Reading: Information, Ideas, and Structure

Practice Set 1: Easy-Medium

Recycled plastics go through a process called reclamation, where they are collected, sorted, cleaned, melted, and then _____ into new plastic products. During this process, the properties of the plastic can be affected, which can result in some changes in the material's characteristics.

1

Which choice completes the text with the most logical and precise word or phrase?

A. completed
B. embodied
C. formed
D. originated

Mary Oliver was an acclaimed American poet known for her contemplative, lyrical style. Oliver's work often explores themes of the _____ between humans and nature, urging us to deepen our relationship with the world around us.

2

Which choice completes the text with the most logical and precise word or phrase?

A. interconnections
B. articulations
C. fusions
D. illuminations

Many scientists believe that the universe is made up of dark matter, a mysterious substance that does not interact with light or other forms of electromagnetic radiation and is therefore invisible to telescopes. While the existence of dark matter has been _____ from its gravitational effects on visible matter, the precise nature of this fascinating substance is still not well understood.

3

Which choice completes the text with the most logical and precise word or phrase?

A. insinuated
B. denied
C. construed
D. inferred

The simple insight behind graphology is that handwriting is connected in a very deep and very real way to our true selves. Kathi McKnight's take on this idea is that "hand writing is brain writing," and she's so clearly right.

4

As used in the text, what does the word "take" most nearly mean?

A. steal
B. end
C. perspective
D. agenda

The idea of "terraforming" Mars—modifying the planet's environment to make it habitable for humans—has tantalized scientists for years. Some proposed methods include _____ greenhouse gases to warm the planet, melting the polar ice caps to provide water, and introducing genetically engineered plants to produce oxygen.

5

Which choice completes the text with the most logical and precise word or phrase?

A. inflicting
B. asserting
C. suggesting
D. releasing

TM and © 2023 PrepMatters, Inc. All rights reserved.

The practice of traveling over long distances on a seasonal basis is thought to be an important element of the success of a wide variety of species, though scientists still debate the exact mechanism behind this behavior. It is not _____ that the evolution of migratory behavior remains a topic of active research and investigation, as it is a complex and multifaceted phenomenon that is likely influenced by a range of factors.

6

Which choice completes the text with the most logical and precise word or phrase?

A. outstanding
B. surprising
C. unremarkable
D. conspicuous

Recent research has uncovered several magma storage regions under Hawaii's volcanoes. The magma there is located in pockets of partially molten rock at various depths, which allows the magma to move easily and quickly to the surface, leading to more explosive and effusive eruptions. These magma reservoirs are connected through a system of dikes and sills that act as "plumbing systems," _____ magma to move from the deep reservoirs to the surface.

7

Which choice completes the text with the most logical and precise word or phrase?

A. transporting
B. rendering
C. allowing
D. bestowing

Witchweed (*Striga*) is a parasitic plant that reduces the yield of maize grown in infected fields. The impact of witchweed on maize is particularly severe in sub-Saharan Africa, where it is considered one of the major biotic constraints to maize production. Research by C. Li et. al. found that reduction of a single enzyme, ZmCYP706C37, could significantly reduce *Striga* germination and infection, suggesting that it may be possible to breed a strain of maize that is _____ to witchweed.

8

Which choice completes the text with the most logical and precise word or phrase?

A. resistant
B. adverse
C. insubordinate
D. tenacious

For certain types of crystalline materials, a history of exposure to high-energy radiation can instill a hidden superpower known as thermoluminescence. As a result of the electronic excited states trapped in the crystal lattice, these materials emit light when heated. The older an object is, the more light is produced, and in fact the proportion is so well understood that this phenomenon is routinely used to _____ ancient artifacts dug out of the earth after tens of thousands of years.

9

Which choice completes the text with the most logical and precise word or phrase?

A. predict
B. date
C. accompany
D. disinter

Reading: Information, Ideas, and Structure

Practice Set 2: Medium-Hard

Wildlife biologist Jonathan Slaght has devoted much of his career to the study of the Blakiston's fish owl (*Bubo blakistoni*), an endangered species found in the Russian Far East and in northeastern China. The bird is remarkable not only for its size—with a wingspan of over six feet, it is the largest living owl species—but also for the unusual physiology of its head: it _____ the disk-shaped face characteristic of other owls.

1

Which choice completes the text with the most logical and precise word or phrase?

A. requires
B. lacks
C. maintains
D. distinguishes

It is commonly believed that character motivation in ancient Greek dramas had little to do with individual autonomy. Professor Mellich, for example, argues that even when characters are explicitly faced with a "choice," the situation is crafted by deistic forces who also heavily influence, or in some cases completely control, the outcome. The character _____ the dilemma and his decided course of action as a compulsion, such that any amount of "debating" over the resolution of his problem is nothing more than an agonizing awareness of the tragic situation he finds himself in and the acts he'll have to take as a result. The choice is therefore almost entirely external to the character, lying instead in the hands of the supernatural beings who dominate the story.

2

Which choice completes the text with the most logical and precise word or phrase?

A. sustains
B. develops
C. experiences
D. resolves

If Hollywood is to be believed, Anne Sullivan gave Helen Keller the gift of communication with the outside world. In the famous movie account of the relationship between Keller and her teacher (_____ titled *The Miracle Worker*), Sullivan is hailed as something approaching a saint. By contrast, the film portrays young Keller as a wild, violent child given to fits of uncontrollable rage as she vents her frustration. Sullivan is idealized as the kind soul who refuses to back down, who battles her way past Keller's defenses through stubborn, persistent love.

3

Which choice completes the text with the most logical and precise word or phrase?

A. tellingly
B. artfully
C. proficiently
D. durably

The assumption underlying our reluctance to move proactively into international conflicts that seem poised to escalate to full-scale war is that the risks entailed by all bold actions are not outweighed by the potential dangers inherent to _____.

4

Which choice completes the text with the most logical and precise word or phrase?

A. aggression
B. imperialism
C. hostility
D. inaction

The primary driver behind many dystopian scenarios is the notion that science *must* do all that it *can* do. Those who advocate subsuming scientific inquiry to public discourse and ethical inquiry are often dismissed as reactionary moralists bent on holding back human progress with <u>set</u> worldviews.

5

As used in the text, what does the word "set" most nearly mean?

A. fixed
B. group
C. win
D. collection

In the 1940s, Elizabeth Stern was working at the Los Angeles County Hospital when she noticed a high incidence of cervical cancer in Mexican-American women. She began investigating the cause and discovered a strong association between the human papillomavirus (HPV) and cervical cancer. It is difficult to _____ the importance of this discovery: it was the first time that a virus had been identified as the cause of a human cancer, and it paved the way for the development of HPV vaccines that have saved countless lives.

6

Which choice completes the text with the most logical and precise word or phrase?

A. downplay
B. overstate
C. ascertain
D. evaluate

A recent study investigated the chemical composition and genetic variation of cumin, a spice widely used in food and traditional medicine. The researchers found that cumin contains various bioactive compounds such as essential oils, phenolic compounds, and flavonoids, which contribute to its medicinal properties. Additionally, the study examined the use of somatic embryogenesis, a technique used to produce clones of plants, to _____ cumin. The researchers observed that the somatic embryogenesis technique was effective in producing healthy cumin plantlets, but also noted the occurrence of somaclonal variation, which can result in genetic changes in the plants.

7

Which choice completes the text with the most logical and precise word or phrase?

A. circulate
B. diffuse
C. propagate
D. publicize

Central Ideas and Details

Preview Quiz

Fill in your answer:

1) What should you read first, the passage or the question?

2) As a general rule, an answer choice that uses weak language is (more / less) likely to be right than an answer choice that uses strong language.

3) To help decide on the right answer, it is a (good / bad) idea to rely on your own knowledge of the subject from outside the passage.

Choose the best answer:

4) Elephants are taught to reproduce specific brushstrokes, explains Desmond Morris, a noted naturalist who spent time at Nong Nooch elephant center in Thailand observing the phenomenon. Morris confirmed that the brush strokes are well executed and the result of meticulous training. His research led him to conclude, however, that the paintings are more a product of muscle control than artistic talent.

Based on the text, which of the following is a belief held by Desmond Morris about artistic talent?

A) It is an innate skill.
B) It is less useful than other pursuits.
C) It consists of more than muscle control.
D) It is the only thing that separates humans from other animals.

Some of these questions will ask about a specific detail from one part of the passage, while others will ask you to state the main idea of the text as a whole. You do *not* have to "read between the lines" for these questions. The correct answer is typically just a restatement of what the author literally said.

Read the question.	It's best to start with the question so that you know exactly what you'll be looking for. Is there a detail to find? A general idea to summarize?
Read the text.	Read the *entire* passage. Do not skim. Helpfully, these passages are quite short, so you have time to read it all.
Predict.	Come up with your own answer to the question before looking at the answer choices. Stay as literal as possible, basing your answer only on what is contained in the text. Do *not* base your answer on your own outside knowledge of the subject.
Evaluate the choices.	Analyze the answers carefully to find the best match for your prediction. Be wary of any choices that use strong, extreme language or take a step beyond what the text literally says. Generally, a correct answer is a bland, wishy-washy reworking of the information in the passage.

Watch out for **tempting wrong answers** that

- rely on outside knowledge
- are *probably* true but don't have specific support in the text
- slightly mischaracterize something from the passage
- are only half-right, half-wrong
- simply go too far (are too extreme)

> **TIP:**
>
> Keep in mind the author's **tone**. Was the passage making an argument? Or was it more a neutral description that didn't take sides? Does it read like a persuasive speech or like a textbook?

Reading: Information, Ideas, and Structure

A key step in the process is to **predict** your answer *before* you look at the answer choices. This makes spotting the right answer much easier, and it makes the wrong answers much less tempting. Plus, in general, it's just easier to find something if you have a clear idea of what you're looking for.

> *Try It*   Write in your own answer.
>
> 1) In Europe during the Middle Ages and Renaissance, paper production relied heavily on discarded textiles, such as linen and cotton rags. Rags were collected, sorted, and washed to remove impurities. The fibers were then beaten, mixed with water, and formed into sheets. This method, known as rag papermaking, remained common until the introduction of wood pulp in the 19th century. By then, the limited supply of rags was struggling to meet the increased demand for paper arising from the Industrial Revolution, and the process of collecting and processing them required significant resources. Meanwhile, technological advances had made the processing of wood pulp much more efficient and cost-effective.
>
>   Based on the text, what was a primary reason that European papermakers switched from rag papermaking to the use of wood pulp?
>
> 2) The ghazal is a poetic form originating in Arabic literature and subsequently embraced by Persian, Urdu, and other languages. It consists of independent couplets called *bayts*, with each *bayt* functioning as a complete poem. The ghazal follows a specific structure, with a repeating word or phrase (*radif*) appearing at the end of the second line in each couplet, creating a distinctive rhyme scheme. The first line of each couplet often ends with a similar or identical word or phrase (*qafia*) to further contribute to the rhyme pattern. The final *bayt* is typically more personal than the other couplets and often contains the poet's *takhallus*, or pen-name.
>
>   Based on the text, which two elements of a ghazal contribute most directly to the rhyme scheme?

Next, find the answer choice that is the best match for your prediction. If you can't decide between two tempting choices, there are a few reliable tiebreakers to keep in mind.

Weaker is better than stronger. The general rule is that the language of the correct answer choice can be no stronger than the language of the passage. So, all else being equal, a less extreme answer choice (for example, one using words like "sometimes" or "at least a few") is more likely to be right than a more extreme one (for example, one using words like "always" or "never"). It's just easier to support.

General is better than specific. Similarly, it's easier to support a general answer choice than a more specific one. This is true by logical necessity—if you're guessing what object an opaque box contains, you're better off guessing that the object is "red" than that the object is "red and round." An even likelier answer would be that the box contains "something." Answers need not be fulfilling to be correct.

Consider the main idea. Choose the answer that's more in line with the main idea of the passage. For example, if the passage as a whole is about Native American language acquisition projects, an answer that focuses on "Cherokee linguistic techniques" is more likely to be correct than an answer that discusses funding for schools in a state that was only briefly mentioned.

Be a prosecutor, not an advocate. If you find yourself arguing on behalf of your answer choice—trying to build the best case for why it's a good interpretation of what the author said—then you're probably going down the wrong path. Instead, attack each tempting answer choice with a critical eye, doing your best to build the strongest case *against* it. Then choose the answer that best holds up to scrutiny.

> **TIP:**
>
> If a choice is 50% right and 50% wrong—or even 90% right, 10% wrong—it is WRONG.

Reading: Information, Ideas, and Structure

Of all of these factors, language strength is the most important tiebreaker.

Try It   Practice evaluating choices without a passage. For each of the below, first **underline** any words or phrases in the answers that affect the overall language strength of the choice. Then **select** the choice that's most likely to be the right answer.

3) Which choice best states the main idea of the (absent) text?

   A) Researchers have developed a revolutionary new method for refining zirconium.
   B) Chlorination is the most important step in the zirconium refining process.
   C) A recent experiment has proven the criticisms of the new zirconium refining method to be completely unfounded.
   D) A new method of refining zirconium appears to be a promising alternative to the traditional approach.

   What is the most likely answer? _____

4) According to the (absent) text, what does Alfred do on Friday?

   A) He reads at least part of the reference book.
   B) He starts on his homework to avoid an inevitable confrontation.
   C) He uses the reference book to complete his entire assignment three days early.
   D) He asks for help in using the reference book after trying and failing to understand it.

   What is the most likely answer? _____

5) [a text consisting only of dialogue between two characters]

   Based on the text, what is true about Susan?

   A) She regrets her life choices.
   B) She thinks her children ought to visit her more.
   C) She sometimes argues with her family members.
   D) She privately believes that the picnic is sure to be a disaster.

   What is the most likely answer? _____

Let's put it all together by walking through an example question.

Example: *Elephants are taught to reproduce specific brushstrokes, explains Desmond Morris, a noted naturalist who spent time at Nong Nooch elephant center in Thailand observing the phenomenon. Morris confirmed that the brush strokes are well executed and the result of meticulous training. His research led him to conclude, however, that the paintings are more a product of muscle control than artistic talent.*

Based on the text, which of the following is a belief held by Desmond Morris about artistic talent?

A) It is an innate skill.
B) It is less useful than other pursuits.
C) It consists of more than muscle control.
D) It is the only thing that separates humans from other animals.

Don't be distracted by all the extraneous detail in this passage. Focus on the question: what do we actually know about *artistic talent* specifically? That was only mentioned in the last sentence. We don't know whether this guy thinks artistic talent is an innate skill, or how useful it might or might not be. We certainly don't know anything as extreme as the idea expressed in choice D. But we do know that Morris distinguishes artistic talent from muscle control: if paintings are more about muscle control than artistic talent, then those two things can't just be the same. Choice C is the only one of these choices that *has* to be true. The answer is **C**.

Reading: Information, Ideas, and Structure

Try It Now let's return to the passages you read earlier. Use the predictions you made and consider the strength of language of the answer choices to help you pick the best answer.

6) In Europe during the Middle Ages and Renaissance, paper production relied heavily on discarded textiles, such as linen and cotton rags. Rags were collected, sorted, and washed to remove impurities. The fibers were then beaten, mixed with water, and formed into sheets. This method, known as rag papermaking, remained common until the introduction of wood pulp in the 19th century. By then, the limited supply of rags was struggling to meet the increased demand for paper arising from the Industrial Revolution, and the process of collecting and processing them required significant resources. Meanwhile, technological advances had made the processing of wood pulp much more efficient and cost-effective.

Based on the text, what was a primary reason that European papermakers switched from rag papermaking to the use of wood pulp?

A) People were concerned about the potential hygiene risks posed by using discarded textiles.
B) The papermaking technology that became available during the Industrial Revolution could only be used with natural materials.
C) Fewer rags were available due to a change in popular fashion tastes.
D) Using wood pulp had become less expensive than using rags.

7) The ghazal is a poetic form originating in Arabic literature and subsequently embraced by Persian, Urdu, and other languages. It consists of independent couplets called *bayts*, with each *bayt* functioning as a complete poem. The ghazal follows a specific structure, with a repeating word or phrase (*radif*) appearing at the end of the second line in each couplet, creating a distinctive rhyme scheme. The first line of each couplet often ends with a similar or identical word or phrase (*qafia*) to further contribute to the rhyme pattern. The final *bayt* is typically more personal than the other couplets and often contains the poet's *takhallus*, or pen-name.

Based on the text, which two elements of a ghazal contribute most directly to the rhyme scheme?

A) The bayt and the qafia.
B) The radif and the takhallus.
C) The radif and the qafia.
D) The bayt and the takhallus.

Central Ideas and Details

Chapter Answer Key

Try It

1) Wood pulp was cheaper.

2) The radif and the qafia.

3)
   A) Researchers have developed a <u>revolutionary</u> new method for refining zirconium.
   B) Chlorination is <u>the most important step</u> in the zirconium refining process.
   C) A recent experiment has <u>proven</u> the criticisms of the new zirconium refining method to be <u>completely unfounded</u>.
   D) A new method of refining zirconium <u>appears to be</u> a <u>promising</u> alternative to the traditional approach.

   Most likely answer: <u>D</u>

4)
   A) He reads <u>at least part</u> of the reference book.
   B) He starts on his assignment to avoid an <u>inevitable</u> confrontation.
   C) He uses the reference book to complete his <u>entire assignment</u> three days early.
   D) He asks for help in using the reference book <u>after trying and failing to understand it</u>.

   Most likely answer: <u>A</u>

5)
   A) She <u>regrets</u> her life choices.
   B) She <u>thinks</u> her children ought to visit her more.
   C) She <u>sometimes argues</u> with her family members.
   D) She <u>privately believes</u> that the picnic is <u>sure</u> to be a disaster.

   Most likely answer: <u>C</u>

6) D

7) C

Reading: Information, Ideas, and Structure

Practice Set 1: Easy-Medium

Tryptophan is an essential amino acid, meaning it is necessary for the body's functioning but cannot be produced by the body and must come from the diet. When tryptophan is transported across the blood-brain barrier into the brain, it is converted into 5-hydroxytryptophan (5-HTP) and then into the neurotransmitter serotonin.

1

Based on the text, what is true about serotonin?

A. It is synthesized outside the brain.
B. The body cannot function without it.
C. It is a derivative of a substance obtained from food.
D. It is an amino acid transported across the blood-brain barrier.

The following text is adapted from John Burroughs' 1881 essay "An Idyl of the Honeybee."

A colony of honey bees, with its neatness and love of order, its division of labor, its public-spiritedness, its thrift, its complex economies, and its inordinate love of gain, seems as far removed from a condition of rude nature as does a walled city or a cathedral town. Our native bee, on the other hand, the "burly, dozing humblebee," affects one more like the rude, untutored savage. He has learned nothing from experience. He lives from hand to mouth. He luxuriates in time of plenty, and he starves in times of scarcity.

2

Based on the text, what is the primary difference between the honey bee and the native bee?

A. The native bee is less common.
B. The honey bee is more industrious.
C. The native bee is smaller in size.
D. The honey bee is more apt to be imported.

As Heike Kamerlingh Onnes first discovered in 1911, certain materials have the ability to conduct electricity with zero resistance and zero energy loss. This "superconductivity" was at first of only theoretical interest, because the property appeared to exist only in conditions of extreme cold—more specifically, at approximately 4.2 K, a temperature that was highly impractical to maintain. However, in 1986, scientists at IBM's Zurich Research Laboratory dramatically changed that picture. Their experiments showed that some ceramic materials made from copper and oxygen exhibited superconductivity at a much higher temperature point, a breakthrough that paved the way for real-world applications in such varied fields as medical imaging, electronics, and power transmission.

3

Based on the text, which of the following best describes the significance of the 1986 experiments at the Zurich Research Laboratory?

A. They demonstrated that superconductivity was possible at temperatures that were more practical to maintain than was previously believed.
B. They proved that ceramic materials were better superconductors than non-ceramic materials.
C. They suggested that colder temperatures might improve the efficiency of superconductivity.
D. They indicated that Heike Kamerlingh Onnes's discoveries were limited by the inferior materials available to him in 1911.

The following text is from Claude McKay's 1922 poem "When I Have Passed Away."

When I have passed away and am forgotten,
And no one living can recall my face,
When under alien sod my bones lie rotten
With not a tree or stone to mark the place;

Perchance a pensive youth, with passion burning,
For olden verse that smacks of love and wine,
The musty pages of old volumes turning,
May light upon a little song of mine,

And he may softly hum the tune and wonder
Who wrote the verses in the long ago;
Or he may sit him down awhile to ponder
Upon the simple words that touch him so.

4

The "pensive youth" described in the second and third stanzas is best characterized as which of the following?

A. a distant relative of the poet who barely remembers him
B. a hypothetical future student who might ask the poet for advice
C. a stranger who the poet imagines discovering his work after the poet's death
D. a lover of poetry who is a great fan of the poet

Ribbon microphones utilize a thin aluminum ribbon as the primary element for capturing sound. The ribbon is suspended within a magnetic field and acts as a diaphragm that vibrates in response to sound waves. As the ribbon moves, it generates an electrical signal proportional to the sound pressure. Ribbon microphones capture audio with warmth and accuracy, producing detailed and nuanced recordings especially valued for capturing vocals and instruments in studio recordings. As a result, ribbon microphones dominated the recording industry from the 1930s to the 1950s. With advancements of technology and the introduction of new, less delicate microphone types, ribbon microphones declined in popularity during the second half of the twentieth century. However, in recent years, there has been a resurgence of interest in ribbon microphones, driven by their distinct sound qualities and vintage appeal.

5

What is the main idea of the text?

A. Ribbon microphones are ideally suited for the recording of human voices because they capture audio with warmth and accuracy.
B. Some microphones use the vibrations of a metal ribbon to capture sound.
C. Ribbon microphones, which use a thin ribbon to capture sound, were widely used in studio recordings from the 1930s to 1950s and are becoming popular again today.
D. Although ribbon microphones were extremely popular during the mid-twentieth century, they fell out of favor because they were too delicate.

Reading: Information, Ideas, and Structure

The following text is from Sinclair Lewis's 1920 novel *Main Street*. Carol is a senior in college considering her future.

Carol was determined to earn her living. But how she was to earn it, how she was to conquer the world—almost entirely for the world's own good—she did not see. Most of the girls who were not betrothed meant to be teachers. Of these there were two sorts: careless young women who admitted that they intended to leave the "beastly classroom and grubby children" the minute they had a chance to marry; and studious, sometimes bulbous-browed and pop-eyed maidens who at class prayer-meetings requested God to "guide their feet along the paths of greatest usefulness." Neither sort tempted Carol.

6

Which of the following best characterizes Carol's position toward the two types of students who were preparing to be teachers?

A. She found them unattractive.
B. She was intimidated by their religious convictions.
C. She admired the honesty they displayed about their intentions.
D. She did not wish to join either of the two types.

Penicillin is a widely-used antibiotic obtained from *Penicillium* molds. In the early stages of penicillin's development, researchers found that oxygen posed a major problem. When exposed to oxygen, the *Penicillium* mold would divert its metabolic resources away from penicillin production and instead focus on other metabolic pathways. This resulted in lower penicillin yields and made it difficult to efficiently produce the antibiotic on a large scale. Howard Florey and Norman Heatley overcame this obstacle by developing a method to cultivate the *Penicillium* mold in deep fermentation tanks where oxygen levels could be controlled.

7

Based on the text, which of the following was a major effect of the method developed by Florey and Heatley?

A. It allowed for penicillin to be obtained from substances other than *Penicillium* molds.
B. It made penicillin a more powerful antibiotic.
C. It protected the *Penicillium* culture from potential contaminants.
D. It helped make large-scale production of penicillin more efficient.

Certain animals have evolved specialized visual systems that are particularly adept at perceiving and tracking moving objects. This adaptation is especially useful for animals that rely on hunting or evading predators. For example, the dragonfly is known for its remarkable ability to track and catch flying prey in mid-air. Dragonflies possess large compound eyes that consist of thousands of independent visual units called ommatidia, each containing its own photoreceptor cells. Their specialized neural circuitry quickly processes and combines inputs from various ommatidia, allowing dragonflies to accurately track the movement of prey and swiftly maneuver towards it.

8

According to the text, what is true about dragonflies?

A. Their visual processing capabilities are specialized for detecting and following fast-moving objects such as other flying insects.
B. They are the only type of insect to possess compound eyes consisting of thousands of ommatidia.
C. They are unable to see objects that do not move.
D. They have no need to avoid predators.

Practice Set 2: Medium-Hard

The following text is from Jane Austen's 1817 novel *Persuasion*.

Frederick was, at that time, a remarkably fine young man, with a great deal of intelligence, spirit, and brilliancy; and Anne an extremely pretty girl, with gentleness, modesty, taste, and feeling. Half the sum of attraction, on either side, might have been enough, for he had nothing to do, and she had hardly anybody to love. They were gradually acquainted, and when acquainted, rapidly and deeply in love.

1

Based on the text, which choice best characterizes the motivations for the relationship between Anne and Frederick?

A. mutual convenience
B. mitigated boredom
C. fearful obedience
D. carefree relief

Influential Austrian architect Otto Wagner was a proponent of functionalism, a design philosophy that highlights the practical aspects of a building's design. Wagner believed that architecture should serve the needs of its users and adapt to the demands of modern life. He emphasized the integration of form and function, eliminating unnecessary ornamentation and focusing instead on user experience. His designs aimed to optimize the functionality of buildings, enhance usability, and promote a harmonious relationship between architecture, technology, and society.

2

What is the main idea of the text?

A. Functionalist architecture integrates form and function to optimize the user experience.
B. Otto Wagner's architecture prioritized practicality, usability, and adaptability.
C. Many architects have followed in the footsteps of functionalist Otto Wagner.
D. Otto Wagner, an architect from Austria, aimed to promote harmony between individuals and the buildings they live in.

The following text is from "When You Are Old," an 1893 poem by William Butler Yeats.

When you are old and grey and full of sleep,
And nodding by the fire, take down this
   book,
And slowly read, and dream of the soft look
Your eyes had once, and of their shadows
   deep;

How many loved your moments of glad
   grace,
And loved your beauty with love false or
   true,
But one man loved the pilgrim soul in you,
And loved the sorrows of your changing face;

And bending down beside the glowing bars,
Murmur, a little sadly, how Love fled
And paced upon the mountains overhead
And hid his face amid a crowd of stars.

3

In the first stanza, the phrase "full of sleep" most directly indicates which of the following about the subject?

A. She is drowsy due to illness.
B. She has lost her youthful beauty.
C. She lacks energy due to her advanced age.
D. She was once loved by the speaker.

In 1997, Bilbao, Spain became the new Mecca of art and architecture thanks to Frank Gehry's outstanding new Guggenheim museum. The entire north of Spain, from Santander in the west to the rugged Pyrenees in the east, soon flourished with an incredible influx of tourists. Although urban planners derided early estimates of 500,000 visitors per year, after the first eight months, nearly 700,000 *turistas* had gaped in awe at Mr. Gehry's work. Aside from bringing immediate and significant revenues into Bilbao, the museum catalyzed the city's urban renewal program. The acrobatic Guggenheim and the graceful infrastructure that arose in its wake teamed up to help Bilbao capture a significant role in the expanding European economy.

4

Based on the text, which of the following is true about Bilbao's urban planners around the time the Guggenheim museum opened?

A. They were surprised by the flood of tourists the museum brought in.
B. They understood what new art museums can do to a city's economy.
C. They initiated a program to make Bilbao the dominant economic power in Europe.
D. They reacted to the Guggenheim's success with outpourings of nationalistic pride.

The field of philosophy can be divided into four main branches: logic, ethics, epistemology (the study of knowledge) and metaphysics (the study of reality and existence). By far the most abstract and theoretical of the four, metaphysics seeks to understand the nature of the world, the universe, and the relationship between mind and matter. What is the ultimate reality of time and space? What is the nature of causation and change? What do we mean by terms like "consciousness" or "identity"? These are some of the central questions of metaphysics, and they have no easy answers.

5

According to the text, what is true about metaphysics?

A. It is the most difficult of the four branches of philosophy.
B. Its practitioners have found answers to theoretical questions concerning reality and existence.
C. It serves as the foundation for all philosophical studies.
D. It is more abstract than epistemology.

During the 2016 US presidential election, three Washington state electors, despite having pledged to vote for the candidate who won the statewide popular vote, instead cast their votes for another candidate. Under state law, these "faithless electors" were subject to penalty or replacement due to their actions. But were such laws enforceable? In the resulting case *Chiafolo v. Washington*, the US Supreme Court unanimously held that they were. As a result of this historic holding, the power of states in the Electoral College system was preserved, and the stability of the presidential election process was maintained.

6

Which choice best states the main idea of the text?

A. A group of electors in the 2016 US presidential election inappropriately violated their pledge.
B. The unanimity of the holding in *Chiafolo v. Washington* was a victory for election stability.
C. The central question before the US Supreme Court in *Chiafolo v. Washington* was whether states can enforce "faithless elector" laws.
D. The landmark US Supreme Court case *Chiafolo v. Washington* held that states may penalize or replace faithless electors.

The public health services in Canada and the United Kingdom (UK) differ in several ways. Canada has a decentralized system where healthcare is managed by each province and territory, with federal funding and standards. The UK has a centralized system known as the National Health Service (NHS), which provides healthcare services across the country. Funding in Canada comes from general tax revenues and provincial/territorial insurance plans, while the UK funds the NHS through taxation and national insurance contributions. Coverage and access vary, with both countries aiming for universal access to necessary services. Service delivery involves a mix of public and private providers in Canada, while the UK relies primarily on NHS-employed healthcare professionals.

7 According to the text, what is one key difference between the public health services in Canada and the UK?

A. The funding for Canada's system is decentralized, while the UK's is federally funded.
B. In the UK, most healthcare professionals are employed directly by the government, while in Canada, all healthcare professionals are privately employed.
C. In Canada, unlike in the UK, the goal of the system is to provide universal access to medically necessary services.
D. Delivery of healthcare services falls under the jurisdiction of local authorities in Canada, while in the UK, the system is managed at the national level.

In the 16th century, the invention of the printing press significantly increased the speed and efficiency of book production compared to the previous method of hand-copying texts. The process began with the creation of individual metal letters, called type, which were used to compose the text. The typesetter arranged the individual metal types in a composing stick (a handheld tray with an adjustable frame) to form words, sentences, and paragraphs. Once the text was set, the typesetter transferred the arranged type from the composing stick to a larger frame called a "chase" to hold the type in place. An oil-based ink was applied to the raised surfaces of the type. Next, the press operator would activate the press, bringing a heavy flat plate down onto the inked type and paper. Because each page had to be printed individually, it could take anywhere from two weeks to several months to produce a book from start to finish.

8 Based on the text, what can be inferred about book production in the 16th century?

A. Using the method of hand-copying texts would require more than two weeks to produce a book from start to finish.
B. Producing a book using a printing press required exactly two individuals: a typesetter and a press operator.
C. Errors were more common when texts were hand-copied than when they were produced on a printing press.
D. Oil-based inks were only used in books produced on a printing press, not in books that were produced by other means.

Reading: Information, Ideas, and Structure

Structure and Purpose

Preview Quiz

Fill in your answer:

1) How are these questions different from the Central Ideas and Details questions?

2) Will you be asked for the purpose of the entire text or for the purpose of a specific piece of it?

Choose the best answer:

3) During photosynthesis, carbon dioxide undergoes a series of reactions to form a nongas molecule, usually one with three carbon atoms. In some of the most important food crops on earth, however, a four-carbon molecule is formed. This "C4" photosynthesis minimizes water loss and maximizes carbon dioxide uptake, which is particularly beneficial in hot and arid environments. Because C4 plants can produce higher yields in regions where water is limited, C4 plants such as cassava and sweet potato are staple foods for millions of people in those regions.

Which choice best describes the function of the first sentence in the text as a whole?

A) It introduces a feature of photosynthesis that is explored in greater detail in the next sentence.
B) It explains how ordinary (non-C4) photosynthesis fails to minimize water loss.
C) It suggests that the nongas molecule formed during photosynthesis can only contain either 3 or 4 carbon atoms.
D) It provides background information that sets up the distinction made later in the text.

These questions ask you about an author's **reason** for including a specific detail or for using a certain word or phrase, or about how the author has **organized** the passage to accomplish a particular goal. The context of the surrounding sentences will point you toward the author's intent.

Watch out for **wrong answer choices** that

- are true statements but don't express the author's intent
- are overly broad or too extreme
- mischaracterize one part of the passage or present the ideas out of sequence

Some of these questions will ask for the purpose of the entire passage as a whole, a variation on the "what is the main idea" questions we've already seen. But most of the time, a purpose question will ask for the function of a particular section of the text, usually a sentence or part of a sentence.

To attack these, first read the text as a whole and summarize the main idea for yourself. Then, re-read the part they're asking about and consider how that section fits into the big picture. Can you predict a description of its role?

As usual, we'll walk through the process with an example.

Example: *During photosynthesis, carbon dioxide undergoes a series of reactions to form a nongas molecule, usually one with three carbon atoms. In some of the most important food crops on earth, however, a four-carbon molecule is formed. This "C4" photosynthesis minimizes water loss and maximizes carbon dioxide uptake, which is particularly beneficial in hot and arid environments. Because C4 plants can produce higher yields in regions where water is limited, C4 plants such as cassava and sweet potato are staple foods for millions of people in those regions.*

Which choice best describes the function of the first sentence in the text as a whole?

> *TIP:*
> As with the other Reading & Writing questions, the best strategy is to read the **question** before you read the **passage**.

Let's see if we can come up with a prediction before we look at any answer choices. First, read the whole text from start to finish, and try to briefly summarize it in your head. For this one, our summary might be something like this: "C4 plants use a special kind of photosynthesis, which is really important in dry places." Now re-read the first sentence, since that's what the question asked us about. What is it doing there? A good prediction might be "setting the scene" or "explaining the context," or something along those lines.

Reading: Information, Ideas, and Structure

Now we're ready to read the answer choices.

A) *It introduces a feature of photosynthesis that is explored in greater detail in the next sentence.*
B) *It explains how ordinary (non-C4) photosynthesis fails to minimize water loss.*
C) *It suggests that the nongas molecule formed during photosynthesis can only contain either 3 or 4 carbon atoms.*
D) *It provides background information that sets up the distinction made later in the text.*

Choice A is half right, half wrong. While this sentence does introduce a feature of photosynthesis (the creation of a nongas molecule), the next sentence does not explore that feature in detail. If it did, the second sentence here would be providing specific information about how the nongas molecule is created. Instead, the second sentence of this text is merely pointing out that some plants do this differently. That's a related point, but it's not exploring the first point in detail. Choice A is out.

Choice B is misusing other parts of the text. The passage does tell us that C4 photosynthesis minimizes water loss, so it's not a crazy step for us to infer that non-C4 photosynthesis *doesn't* minimize water loss. But that's not the purpose of this first sentence! The first sentence doesn't tell us anything about water loss, so this is much too big a leap. (It's also relevant to note that when we predicted an answer, we didn't mention water loss at all.)

Choice C is too extreme. This sentence tells us that the nongas molecule can contain 3 carbon atoms, and a later sentence tells us that it can also contain 4. But nothing in the text establishes that these are the *only* two possibilities. And again, this doesn't match our prediction.

Choice D is the best match. This sentence gives us the background (how photosynthesis generally works) to help us understand the distinction the author is about to make (that in some plants, the nongas molecule contains 4 rather than 3 carbon atoms). Choice **D** is the winner.

Structure and Purpose

Try It

1) Composting is a natural process that converts organic waste into nutrient-rich compost. Organic waste materials, such as kitchen scraps and yard trimmings, are collected and layered in a compost bin or pile. The carbon-to-nitrogen ratio is balanced by alternating between carbon-rich "browns" and nitrogen-rich "greens." Microorganisms break down the organic materials through decomposition, generating heat and transforming the pile into compost. Adequate moisture, aeration, and periodic turning of the pile are essential. After maturation and curing, the resulting compost can be used to enrich soil, providing nutrients and improving its overall health.

Which choice best describes the function of the reference to "kitchen scraps and yard trimmings" in the overall structure of the text?

Predict: _____

A) to introduce a feature of the composting process that is explained in greater detail later in the text
B) to suggest a weakness of the practice of composting
C) to explain how organic waste can be converted into nutrient-rich compost
D) to provide some examples of organic waste materials

TIP:

Some "purpose" questions will ask for the function of a particular section of the text, while others will ask for the overall purpose of the text as a whole. Be sure to read the question carefully so you fully understand your task.

Reading: Information, Ideas, and Structure

A few questions may ask about the overall **organization** of the passage; for these, you'll need to understand the purpose of multiple parts of the text instead of just one part. Prediction is less important for these questions. Instead, use a process of elimination approach, looking to tie each abstract term in an answer choice to something specific in the passage. For example, if the choice says the author "draws an analogy in order to dispute a common view," ask yourself, *What's the analogy? Was it drawn to dispute something? What's the view it's disputing? Is that view common?* If there's anything that doesn't match, eliminate that answer.

Example: The use of drones, or unmanned aerial vehicles (UAVs), has become increasingly widespread in a variety of fields, including agriculture, conservation, and military operations. While UAVs offer many potential benefits, such as the ability to access difficult or remote areas and to gather data more efficiently and safely, they also raise a number of ethical and legal concerns. For example, the use of UAVs for surveillance or to collect data on individuals raises privacy issues, and the potential for UAVs to be used for malicious purposes or to cause accidents or injuries raises concerns about safety. As a result, there is ongoing debate about the appropriate regulations and guidelines that should be put in place to ensure the responsible and ethical use of UAVs.

Which choice best describes the overall structure of the text?

A) *It describes both the benefits and the drawbacks of the use of UAVs, then describes the current state of the issue.*
B) *It argues on behalf of the use of UAVs, then explores the counterargument.*
C) *It presents a similarity between multiple uses of UAVs, then supports that claim with examples.*
D) *It illustrates the potential harm of UAVs, then suggests that they should be banned.*

Start with choice A. Does the text describe the benefits of UAVs? Yes: the ability to access difficult or remote areas and to gather data efficiently and safely. Does it describe the drawbacks? Yes, in the next sentence. Does it describe the current state of the issue? Yes, there is ongoing debate. Everything matches up, so choice A is looking good.

Now choice B. Does the text argue on behalf of the use of UAVs? No—this text maintained a neutral tone, exploring both sides of the issue without ever making an argument. Eliminate choice B.

As for choice C, the text does mention multiple uses of UAVs, but it doesn't present any particular similarity between them. And choice D is much too strong: the text never suggests that UAVs should be banned. The best answer is **A**.

Try It 2) The US Postal Service relies on several types of automated sorting machines to efficiently process mail. Optical character recognition machines use optical sensors to scan the addresses on letters and packages and translate them into a digital format that can be interpreted and processed by the sorting machine. Additionally, advanced video coding systems are employed for the sorting of irregularly shaped or oversized mailpieces. These machines use cameras and image recognition software to capture images of the mail and analyze their characteristics. The system can identify the type, shape, and dimensions of the mailpiece, enabling accurate sorting based on predetermined criteria.

Which choice best describes the overall structure of the text?

Predict: _____

A) It presents a claim about the postal service, then offers several examples to illustrate the claim.
B) It describes the advantages of postal sorting technology, then notes some disadvantages.
C) It explains how the postal service sorts irregularly shaped packages, then provides additional detail.
D) It explores the current state of postal machine technology, then advocates for a change.

Reading: Information, Ideas, and Structure

Chapter Answer Key

| ***Try It*** | 1) D |
| | 2) A |

Practice Set 1: Easy-Medium

The following text is from O. Henry's 1902 short story "The Duplicity of Hargraves."

When Major Pendleton Talbot, of Mobile, Alabama, and his daughter, Miss Lydia Talbot, came to Washington to reside, they selected for a boarding place a house that stood fifty yards back from one of the quietest avenues. It was an old-fashioned brick building, with a portico upheld by tall white pillars. The yard was shaded by stately locusts and elms, and a catalpa tree in season rained its pink and white blossoms upon the grass. Rows of high box bushes lined the fence and walks. It was the Southern style and aspect of the place that pleased the eyes of the Talbots.

1

Which choice best states the main purpose of the text?

A. To explore the character and background of Major Talbot
B. To explain in detail how the Talbots came to reside in the Washington boarding house
C. To describe the boarding house physically and suggest what the Talbots liked about it
D. To hint at Major Talbot's interest in architectural detail

Scholars of Greek and Roman maritime history have traditionally believed that the range of ancient trading vessels was sharply limited by the shipmasters' fears of the open sea. Unlike war ships, which had better navigational capacities and were free of the heavy cargo that increased the risk of capsizing, nonmilitary vessels were thought to follow a coast-hugging route whenever possible. Archaeologist Brendan Foley argues that the recently discovered wrecks of ancient Greek trading ships at the bottom of the eastern Mediterranean, many miles away from shore, call this belief into question. On the other hand, nautical expert Jeffrey Royal asserts that these wrecks might have occurred during a period of turbulent weather, when mariners might have chosen to head for deeper water to avoid being pushed onto rocks by the storm.

2

Which choice best describes the function of Royal's assertions in the overall structure of the text?

A. They summarize the disagreement between Foley's argument and the traditional view.
B. They reinforce Foley's theory that trading ships usually avoided the open sea.
C. They disprove Foley's statements about the wrecks found in the eastern Mediterranean.
D. They provide a possible alternative explanation for the evidence that Foley cites.

Reading: Information, Ideas, and Structure

The CRISPR-Cas9 gene editing system, first developed in 2012 by Jennifer Doudna and Emmanuelle Charpentier, is a revolutionary tool for genetic engineering that allows researchers to make precise edits to the DNA of living cells. The system consists of two components: a guide RNA molecule that recognizes and binds to a specific target sequence in the DNA, and a Cas9 protein that acts as molecular scissors to cut the DNA at the target site. By introducing synthetic guide RNA molecules that are programmed to recognize specific genes, researchers can use the Cas9 protein to make precise cuts in the DNA and introduce desired changes, such as deleting or inserting specific genes.

3

Which choice best describes the function of the first sentence in the overall structure of the text?

A. It explains how RNA molecules can be used to bind to specific DNA targets.
B. It describes the background of the invention of the CRISPR-Cas9 system.
C. It presents the rationale for experiments that involve deleting or inserting specific genes.
D. It introduces the CRISPR-Cas9 system and summarizes its function.

In David Armitage's view, the sweeping rights language of the Declaration of Independence is far less important than the way it sought to establish America's political sovereignty. As support, Armitage points to <u>18th century letters by Richard Henry Lee</u>, who argued that America would never be recognized by other European powers until it officially declared itself separate from Great Britain. In 1776, America's most pressing need was not a recitation of fundamental principles, but a formal announcement of a new political entity that could as a result contract alliances, conduct war, and conclude peace.

4

Which choice best describes the function of the letters by Richard Henry Lee in David Armitage's argument?

A. They provide corroborating evidence.
B. They represent a contradictory example.
C. They invoke authoritative sources.
D. They compare specific viewpoints.

In May of 1989, over 100,000 protesters converged on the city of Beijing in the People's Republic of China to protest the policies of the Communist Party of China. The protestors marched. They went on hunger strikes. They demanded political reform. They were met with rigid opposition and violence from the Chinese government. At the same time, forces of liberalization were sweeping Europe. The citizens of countries across Communist East Europe petitioned their governments for changes. The fall of the Berlin wall that year provided a strong symbol of the fall of Communist U.S.S.R.

5

Which choice best states the main purpose of the text?

A. To provide a history of Chinese politics
B. To analyze the collapse of communism
C. To describe a sequence of events
D. To detail various methods of protest

In 2013, researchers collected leaf samples from multiple populations of flowering dogwood trees across the southeastern United States and analyzed the genetic markers of the samples. The study revealed significant genetic diversity within flowering dogwood populations, indicating the presence of diverse genetic variants and alleles within the species. Furthermore, the researchers identified distinct genetic clusters or groups within the populations, suggesting the existence of population structure. This indicates that certain populations of flowering dogwood may have unique genetic characteristics and adaptations based on their geographical locations.

6

Which choice best describes the function of the last sentence in the overall structure of the text?

A. to summarize the study's chief finding
B. to present an example that illustrates a challenge faced by the researchers
C. to describe part of the methodology used in the study
D. to explain the significance of one of the study's findings

While ancient Greece is often associated with a high regard for learning and intellectual pursuits, it is estimated that the overall literacy rates were relatively low by modern standards. However, this varied by time period and region. During the 5th and 4th centuries BCE, known as the Classical period, the city-state of Athens had a notable focus on education and intellectual pursuits. Athenian citizens, particularly the upper class, received an education that included reading, writing, and arithmetic. The Athenian playwright Aristophanes, in his comedies, often made references to a literate audience. Additionally, inscriptions and graffiti found in Athens and other urban centers suggest a relatively higher literacy rate among the general population compared to other regions of ancient Greece.

7

Which choice best describes the function of the reference to Aristophanes's comedies in the overall structure of the text?

A. It supports the text's central claim about literacy rates in Athens.
B. It introduces a potential counterargument to the point made in the preceding sentence.
C. It suggests that the audience for comedies might not be representative of Athens as a whole.
D. It indicates that Athens is less like other urban centers than its graffiti might suggest.

Reading: Information, Ideas, and Structure

Practice Set 2: Medium-Hard

The following is the full text of writer and civil rights activist James Weldon Johnson's 1917 poem "To America," which addresses America directly in order to pose a series of questions about the African American experience.

> How would you have us, <u>as we are?</u>
> Or sinking 'neath the load we bear?
> Our eyes fixed forward on a star?
> Or gazing empty at despair?
>
> Rising or falling? Men or things?
> With dragging pace or footsteps fleet?
> Strong, willing sinews in your wings?
> Or tightening chains about your feet?

1

Which choice best describes the function of the underlined portion in the text as a whole?

A. It implies that African Americans are heavily burdened.
B. Together with the next line, it offers America a dichotomy of choices.
C. It questions whether African Americans should continue to pursue progress.
D. It challenges America to confront its history of injustice.

The following text is adapted from Frank Norris's 1903 novel *The Pit*.

> Suddenly the meaning and significance of it all dawned upon Laura. The Great Grey City, brooking no rival, imposed its dominion upon a reach of country larger than many a kingdom of the Old World. For, thousands of miles beyond its confines was its influence felt. Out, far out, far away in the snow and shadow of Northern Wisconsin forests, axes and saws bit the bark of century-old trees, stimulated by this city's energy. <u>Her force turned the wheels of harvester and seeder a thousand miles distant in Iowa and Kansas.</u> Her force spun the screws and propellers of innumerable squadrons of lake steamers crowding the Sault Sainte Marie. For her and because of her all the Central States, all the Great Northwest roared with traffic and industry; sawmills screamed; factories, their smoke blackening the sky, clashed and flamed; wheels turned, pistons leaped in their cylinders; cog gripped cog; beltings clasped the drums of mammoth wheels; and converters of forges belched into the clouded air their tempest breath of molten steel.

2

Which choice best describes the function of the underlined portion in the text as a whole?

A. It sets up a more detailed example indicating the true purpose of Laura's force.
B. It highlights important information about Laura's personal background.
C. It serves as part of a series of examples that demonstrate the breadth of the city's influence.
D. It illustrates the evils of industry due to its dependence on human labor.

In accepting her 1993 Nobel prize, Toni Morrison examined in parable form the perils faced by generations coming of age in the late twentieth century. She told the story of a wise elderly woman being confronted by clever and mischievous youths. "Is there no context for our lives," they ask, ". . . no song, no literature, <u>no poem full of vitamins</u>?" Through a deep, meditative dialogue, the youths find the poetry in their despair. Morrison's sage then affirms the youths' character and ability to navigate the world, saying, "I trust you now."

3

Which choice best describes the function of the underlined portion in the text as a whole?

A. It underscores the point that the written word is nourishing.
B. It mocks the old woman's health.
C. It illustrates the cruelty of human beings.
D. It exposes an implicit political argument.

The traditional economic models assume that people take all available information and make consistent and informed decisions that are in their best interest. But a new group of economists, known as behavioral economists, argue that the traditional method leaves out something important: state of mind. For example, one can think differently about money if one is feeling vengeful, optimistic, or sorrowful. And what's more, actions under these conditions are indeed predictable, if the underlying environment is better understood. So, behavioral economics seeks to enrich the understanding of decision-making by integrating the insights of psychology into economics.

4

Which choice best describes the overall structure of the text?

A. A theory is put forward, a controversial definition is discussed, and a debate is begun.
B. A school of thought is introduced and a clarifying example is discussed.
C. A revolutionary viewpoint is distinguished from the more traditional theory and endorsed by the author.
D. A methodology is referenced and a question is posed.

In a 2021 article published in the *Journal of High Energy Physics*, authors Stefano Giusto and Raffaele Savelli used a holographic approach to investigate the dynamics of a three-dimensional gravitational theory. The holographic principle, a key concept in string theory, suggests that the information about a volume of space can be encoded on its boundary. The authors used this principle to relate the gravitational theory in the bulk of space to a quantum field theory on the boundary. They then used this relationship to study the dynamics of the gravitational theory and investigate its properties.

5

Which choice best describes the function of the second sentence in the overall structure of the text?

A. It presents the central finding reported by Giusto and Savelli.
B. It defines a term that helps explain the structure of the article written by Giusto and Savelli.
C. It provides context that clarifies the question that Giusto and Savelli sought to answer.
D. It states a generalization challenged by Giusto and Savelli.

In the 2020 New Zealand general election, prime minister Jacinda Ardern secured a resounding victory that far exceeded the expectations of many polls. Several factors may have contributed to the divergence between the polls and the actual outcome. First, Ardern's handling of various crises, including the response to the Christchurch mosque shootings and the COVID-19 pandemic, generated significant public support and a surge in popularity; some polls may have underestimated the extent of the "Jacinda Effect" on voter preferences. Second, in the weeks leading up to the election, some voters were swayed by the growing momentum and success of Ardern's leadership, resulting in a last-minute shift in support that the polls did not fully capture. Third, the 2020 New Zealand election witnessed a significant increase in youth voter turnout compared to previous elections; young voters are typically underrepresented in polls.

6 Which choice best describes the function of the second sentence in the overall structure of the text?

A. It provides a transition between the election outcome discussed in the first sentence and the possible causes analyzed in the rest of the passage.
B. It explains why the polling for the 2020 New Zealand general election was inaccurate.
C. It emphasizes the unexpected nature of Jacinda Ardern's victory by providing an example.
D. It reveals the significance of the role played by young voters in the 2020 New Zealand general election.

The J-curve hypothesis is a conceptual framework used to understand the dynamics of social movements. The theory suggests that after a period of gradual progress and resistance at the beginning of a movement, there comes a tipping point where the movement experiences a sudden surge in momentum and significant progress. In the context of the US civil rights movement, the J-curve theory suggests that while progress may have been slow and incremental initially, the cumulative impact of grassroots mobilization, nonviolent protests, legal challenges, and public advocacy ultimately led to a transformative phase in the mid-twentieth century. This era saw landmark events and legislation that moved the trajectory of the civil rights movement sharply upward, <u>resembling the shape of a "J" on a graph</u>.

7 Which choice best describes the function of the underlined portion in the text as a whole?

A. It suggests a potential problem with the traditional interpretation of the civil rights movement.
B. It clarifies the history and theoretical background of the term "J-curve."
C. It explains why the civil rights movement was able to make such significant progress in the mid-twentieth century.
D. It helps illustrate the meaning of the term "J-curve."

Compare and Contrast

Preview Quiz

1) The best approach to a Compare and Contrast question consists of several distinct steps. Put the steps below in the right order.

   1st: _____   Read Text 1.
   2nd: _____   Read Text 2.
   3rd: _____   Read the question.
   4th: _____   Summarize.
   5th: _____   Predict an answer.
   6th: _____   Evaluate the choices.

Choose the best answer.

2) **Text 1**

   The human brain is wired to seek comfort in the familiar, and habits provide a sense of predictability and security. As a result, habits play an important role in purchase decisions. Understanding and leveraging the power of habits can be a valuable marketing strategy for businesses to attract and retain customers.

   Text 2

   While habits can influence purchase decisions, they are not the sole determining factor. Consumers are increasingly becoming more conscious and intentional about their purchases, considering factors such as sustainability, ethics, and social responsibility. In addition, the rise of e-commerce and online shopping has provided consumers with more options and opportunities to explore new products and brands.

   Based on the texts, how would the author of Text 2 most likely respond to the claims of the author of Text 1?

   A) By disputing the idea that habits provide a sense of security.
   B) By agreeing that businesses should focus their marketing strategies on leveraging the power of habits.
   C) By denying the importance of the rise of e-commerce and online shopping.
   D) By arguing that habits may be a less powerful influence on purchase decisions than Text 1 claims them to be.

Reading: Information, Ideas, and Structure

These questions ask you to compare or contrast two different passages on a related theme. Remember, no matter how these questions are phrased, *the answers are in the text.* You don't have to guess how the author of Text 2 would probably respond to the author of Text 1; instead, find the place in Text 2 where the author addresses the point.

Common **wrong answer choices** will

- confuse one passage's point of view for the other's
- include a statement that an author would probably agree with but that the passage never directly addressed
- be phrased in a way that's too broad, too narrow, or too extreme

As usual, our process begins with the **question**. Read carefully! You may be asked about the overall relationship between the two passages, but sometimes the question is more specific: for example, you may be asked how the authors of Text 2 would respond to a specific sentence or claim from Text 1 rather than the text as a whole.

Next, read the entire first text. Stop and summarize the big idea that the question is focused on (whatever Text 2 is being asked to respond to). **Write it down**.

Then, read the entire second text and consider its relationship to what you wrote. Does Text 2 agree with that position overall? Does it disagree? Is there a specific objection made? Are the claims quite similar, but with one important difference? Whatever you notice, that's your prediction. Move on to the answer choices and look for the best match.

> **TIP:**
> Always read *all* of Text 1, even if the question is only asking you to respond to a single underlined claim. The context matters.

> **TIP:**
> You don't have to answer the questions in the order they appear on the test. Feel free to skip the more time-consuming question types (like Compare and Contrast questions) at first and return to them at the end of the section. If you'd like to flag a question to remind yourself to come back to it, click the ⃞ symbol next to the question number.

Let's take a look at an example.

Example: **Text 1**

The human brain is wired to seek comfort in the familiar, and habits provide a sense of predictability and security. As a result, habits play an important role in purchase decisions. Understanding and leveraging the power of habits can be a valuable marketing strategy for businesses to attract and retain customers.

Text 2

While habits can influence purchase decisions, they are not the sole determining factor. Consumers are increasingly becoming more conscious and intentional about their purchases, considering factors such as sustainability, ethics, and social responsibility. In addition, the rise of e-commerce and online shopping has provided consumers with more options and opportunities to explore new products and brands.

Based on the texts, how would the author of Text 2 most likely respond to the claims of the author of Text 1?

A) *By disputing the idea that habits provide a sense of security.*
B) *By agreeing that businesses should focus their marketing strategies on leveraging the power of habits.*
C) *By denying the importance of the rise of e-commerce and online shopping.*
D) *By arguing that habits may be a less powerful influence on purchase decisions than Text 1 claims them to be.*

On the next page, we'll rearrange this wall of words so we can approach it in the right order.

TIP:

There's no need for panic if you encounter an unfamiliar vocab word in the passage. Often, you'll be able to figure it out from the context anyway. At other times, it will be a word that doesn't end up mattering, because you can answer the questions without needing it. If you do happen to get a question that asks about the word, just use your knowledge of the general tone and big themes of the passage as a whole and that section in particular to see if you can knock out answer choices, and then go with your gut.

Reading: Information, Ideas, and Structure

We need the question first.

> *Based on the texts, how would the author of Text 2 most likely respond to the claims of the author of Text 1?*

Now we know our task: in this case, we're going to be focusing on how Text 2 would respond to Text 1 as a whole. So next, we'll read Text 1 and summarize its claims.

> **Text 1**
>
> *The human brain is wired to seek comfort in the familiar, and habits provide a sense of predictability and security. As a result, habits play an important role in purchase decisions. Understanding and leveraging the power of habits can be a valuable marketing strategy for businesses to attract and retain customers.*

What's the big idea here, in a few words? Keep it simple: maybe something like "habits are a big deal and businesses should make use of them."

> **Text 2**
>
> *While habits can influence purchase decisions, they are not the sole determining factor. Consumers are increasingly becoming more conscious and intentional about their purchases, considering factors such as sustainability, ethics, and social responsibility. In addition, the rise of e-commerce and online shopping has provided consumers with more options and opportunities to explore new products and brands.*

This author takes a more nuanced view of habits: "Sure, they play a role, but they're not the only thing that matters." That's our prediction. Now we evaluate the choices.

> A) By disputing the idea that habits provide a sense of security.
> B) By agreeing that businesses should focus their marketing strategies on leveraging the power of habits.
> C) By denying the importance of the rise of e-commerce and online shopping.
> D) By arguing that habits may be a less powerful influence on purchase decisions than Text 1 claims them to be.

TIP: Remember to consider language strength. A choice may have the right general idea but be written too strongly to be correct.

Choice A is wrong: Text 2 did dispute some of Text 1's ideas, but not that specific one.

Choice B is wrong too: this puts Text 2 too much in agreement with Text 1. And anyway, Text 2 never took a position on how businesses should focus their marketing strategies.

Choice C is just backwards: Text 2 is the one arguing for the importance of these things, not denying their importance.

That leaves Choice **D**, which is the right answer.

Try It   Based on the texts, how would the author of Text 2 most likely respond to Text 1's claims about the potential health benefits of red wine?

1) Analyze the question. What are we being asked to respond to from Text 1?

_____

Text 1

Numerous studies have suggested that moderate red wine consumption can have positive effects on heart health due to the presence of antioxidants, particularly resveratrol. Resveratrol has been linked to improved cardiovascular function, reduced inflammation, and increased levels of HDL cholesterol, known as the "good" cholesterol. Additionally, red wine has shown potential in protecting against age-related cognitive decline and certain types of cancer.

2) Summarize the relevant claims of Text 1.

_____
_____

Text 2

The health benefits attributed to red wine can often be obtained through other means, such as a healthy diet and regular exercise. Excessive consumption of alcohol, even in the form of red wine, can have detrimental effects on health, including liver damage, increased risk of addiction, and various negative impacts on physical and mental well-being. Moreover, the potential benefits of red wine must be weighed against the associated risks, such as an increased risk of certain cancers, adverse interactions with medications, and potential harm to pregnant women or individuals with specific health conditions.

3) Predict. How would Text 2 respond to what you wrote in #2 above?

_____

4) Choose the best answer:
   A) By denying that red wine consumption can have positive effects on heart health.
   B) By suggesting that the risks associated with red wine may outweigh its potential benefits.
   C) By disputing the idea that resveratrol increases levels of HDL cholesterol.
   D) By arguing that it is too risky for healthy individuals to consume even moderate amounts of red wine.

Reading: Information, Ideas, and Structure

Chapter Answer Key

Try It

1) Any claims about the potential health benefits of red wine.

2) Red wine is good for heart health due to antioxidants like resveratrol. Red wine may also protect against some cancers and against age-related cognitive decline.

3) Moderate consumption may have benefits, but you can get those benefits in other ways. Red wine also has risks.

4) B

Practice Set 1: Easy-Medium

Text 1
Carbon markets—trading systems in which polluting companies can buy or sell carbon emissions credits—are an essential tool for combating climate change. By putting a price on emissions, carbon markets incentivize companies to reduce their carbon footprint. This market-based approach allows for emissions reductions to be achieved in a cost-effective and efficient manner. Moreover, carbon markets have the potential to drive innovation and investment in low-carbon technologies, ultimately leading to a more sustainable future.

Text 2
Carbon markets merely perpetuate environmental injustices. They allow companies in wealthy nations to continue polluting while buying credits from developing countries, which can hinder their development. Worse, carbon markets do not address the root causes of climate change, such as the reliance on fossil fuels and the overconsumption of resources.

1. Based on the texts, how would the author of Text 2 most likely respond to the claims of the author of Text 1?

A. By arguing that carbon markets are not as beneficial to businesses as they might appear.
B. By disputing the need for countries to work together to combat climate change.
C. By contending that carbon markets are a poorly conceived idea that may lead to unjust outcomes.
D. By agreeing that investment in low-carbon technologies is an important and necessary step.

Text 1
The controversy surrounding the use of genetically modified organisms (GMOs) in agriculture is largely based on misconceptions and misinformation. <u>GMOs have been extensively tested and have been shown to be safe for human consumption and the environment.</u> Furthermore, GMOs have the potential to increase crop yields and reduce the need for harmful pesticides and herbicides.

Text 2
While evidence of GMO safety in the short term certainly exists, the long-term effects of their use are still unknown. In addition, the use of GMOs often involves the patenting of living organisms, which can have negative impacts on farmers' livelihoods and which concentrates power in the hands of a few large corporations.

2. Based on the texts, how would the author of Text 2 most likely characterize the underlined claim in Text 1?

A. It is completely baseless and factually incorrect.
B. It is at least partially true, but it fails to address an important issue.
C. It is likely biased and intended to curry favor with large corporations.
D. It is a compelling argument but ultimately irrelevant to the point at issue.

Reading: Information, Ideas, and Structure

Text 1

<u>Did the Ancient Greeks see the color blue?</u> According to linguist Guy Deutcher, this has been a topic of some controversy for well over a century. British politician and classicist William Gladstone noticed that Homer's epics, the *Iliad* and the *Odyssey*, contain no reference to the color blue. Famously, Homer refers to the sea as being "wine dark" instead.

Text 2

Retinal cones take information from the various wavelengths of visible light and convert it into a chemical signal. While humans have only three types of cones, the mantis shrimp has 16 and can detect wavelengths from ultraviolet to infrared. But even though these significant discoveries tell us something about how different the experience of color can be among different species, they do not shed any great psychological light on whether or not two humans can share anything as simple as our perception of the color red.

3

How would the author of Text 2 most likely respond to the question posed in the first sentence of Text 1?

A. The Greeks didn't see blue because all humans have the same types of retinal cones.
B. The Greeks saw blue because seeing is physiological and not linguistic or psychological.
C. The Greeks didn't see blue, because they weren't aware of how brains worked.
D. We don't know whether the Greeks saw blue as we do.

Text 1

In F. Scott Fitzgerald's *The Great Gatsby,* the character of Jay Gatsby represents the American dream and its ultimate failure. Through Gatsby's tragic downfall, Fitzgerald critiques the American dream and its emphasis on materialism and the pursuit of wealth. Gatsby's character serves as a cautionary tale against the dangers of blindly pursuing success without considering the cost to oneself and others.

Text 2

Gatsby's pursuit of wealth and status is driven not just by materialism, but also by his desire to win back the love of his life, Daisy. This is a manifestation of his desire for a deeper connection and a sense of belonging, which are also important aspects of the American dream. Gatsby's tragic downfall can also be attributed to the corrupt society in which he lives, which values wealth and social status above all else.

4

Based on the texts, how would the author of Text 2 most likely respond to Text 1's claim regarding the theme of the American Dream in *The Great Gatsby*?

A. By agreeing that Jay Gatsby is driven in part by the American dream but arguing that this drive consists of more than a mere desire for wealth.
B. By conceding that Jay Gatsby's failure to achieve financial success is tragic and suggesting that Daisy is to blame.
C. By challenging the idea that materialism is a concern for Jay Gatsby and arguing that his real interest is social status.
D. By taking offense to the notion that F. Scott Fitzgerald intended a large-scale critique of the American way of life.

Text 1

Food irradiation involves the application of ionizing radiation to food products in order to target microorganisms, including bacteria, viruses, and parasites. Supporters of the process claim it enhances food safety. However, food irradiation may lead to the formation of harmful byproducts, such as free radicals, which can have negative health implications. <u>Additionally, many critics have expressed concern about the potential loss of essential nutrients and the impact of irradiation on the overall quality and taste of the food.</u> Alternative methods of food safety, such as improved hygiene practices throughout the food production and handling chain, provide the same benefits without the potential drawbacks.

Text 2

Food irradiation is a valuable tool that significantly reduces the risk of foodborne illnesses by effectively eliminating or reducing harmful pathogens and pests present in food products. The process has been extensively studied and proven to be effective in reducing microbial contamination without causing significant changes to the nutritional value, taste, or texture of the food. It provides an additional layer of protection against foodborne pathogens, ensuring that consumers can enjoy safer and healthier food options.

5

Based on the texts, how would the author of Text 2 most likely respond to the claims expressed by the critics in the underlined sentence of Text 1?

A. Taste and nutrient loss are less important issues than protection against food-borne illnesses.
B. Extensive research has proven the critics' concerns to be unfounded.
C. Improved hygiene practices are not sufficient to mitigate the risks posed by harmful pathogens.
D. The critics have not considered the negative impact of free radicals.

Practice Set 2: Medium-Hard

Text 1

The suprachiasmatic nuclei (SCNs) are a cluster of cells in the hypothalamus that act as the primary circadian pacemaker in humans and other animals. These nuclei are responsible for controlling the body's internal clock, which regulates a wide range of biological processes, including sleep-wake cycles, hormone secretion, and body temperature. Research has shown that SCNs receive input from light-sensitive cells in the retina, which helps to synchronize the body's circadian rhythms with the 24-hour day-night cycle. Additionally, disruptions to the SCNs, such as damage to the hypothalamus or exposure to prolonged periods of darkness, can result in sleep disorders, mood disturbances, and other negative health outcomes.

Text 2

While SCNs undoubtedly play an important role in controlling human circadian rhythms, other factors may also contribute to this complex biological process. Some research has suggested that environmental factors, such as social cues or meal timing, may have a stronger influence on circadian rhythms than previously thought. Furthermore, certain genetic mutations have been found to affect circadian rhythms in humans, suggesting that there may be other molecular pathways involved in circadian regulation.

1

Based on the texts, how would the author of Text 2 most likely respond to the claim made in the first sentence of Text 1?

A. By arguing that Text 1's own statements about the effect of exposure to prolonged darkness act to undermine the claim.
B. By agreeing that SCNs may play a significant role in circadian regulation but adding that other factors may also be involved.
C. By distinguishing between the function of SCNs in humans with genetic mutations and the function of SCNs in non-human animals without such mutations.
D. By conceding that disruptions to SCNs can result in sleep disorders but suggesting that other evidence is needed before any conclusion about the role of SCNs can be drawn.

Text 1

Traditional physics theory holds that high temperatures and pressures are required to initiate nuclear fusion reactions. But this view is far too limited. The evidence that "cold fusion" is possible has existed for decades. In 1989, Martin Fleischmann and Stanley Pons conducted a simple electrolysis experiment using heavy water and palladium electrodes. Despite the standard air pressure and room temperature, evidence of nuclear reaction products was recorded.

Text 2

There is no theoretical basis for the concept of cold fusion. While it's certainly a tempting idea—if valid, it could have significant implications for the future of clean energy production—it simply flies in the face of our understanding of nuclear physics. The so-called evidence is in fact inconclusive, as many of the results cited can be explained by more conventional processes. In addition, numerous scientists have tried and failed to replicate the results reported by experimenters in the 1980s, suggesting that their results may have been due to experimental error.

2 Based on the texts, how would the author of Text 2 most likely respond to the "traditional physics theory" discussed in Text 1?

A. By arguing that it fails to recognize the other factors that are capable of initiating nuclear fusion reactions.
B. By asserting that no convincing evidence exists to challenge its claim about the requirements of nuclear fusion.
C. By disputing the relevance of the Fleischmann-Pons experiment, since it was conducted at standard air pressure and room temperature.
D. By advocating an alternative theory that could lead to better progress in the production of clean energy.

Text 1

According to 17th century alchemist Johann Joachim Becher, a key component of any combustion reaction is a substance called "phlogiston." Becher argued that when a combustible material burns, it releases phlogiston into the air, leaving behind the "ash" or "residue" of the original material. Many scientists of his era, noting that <u>a piece of wood becomes less heavy when it burns</u> (perhaps due to the release of some substance) found the theory extremely compelling.

Text 2

While the phlogiston theory enjoyed a period of popularity, it was ultimately replaced by the combustion theory put forward by Antoine Lavoisier in 1777. Lavoisier showed that when a substance burns, it combines with oxygen from the air, forming new compounds (some of which have lower mass than that of the original material) and releasing heat and light.

3 Based on the texts, how would the author of Text 2 most likely respond to the piece of evidence for the phlogiston theory noted in the underlined portion of Text 1?

A. By disputing the idea that a piece of wood becomes less heavy when it burns.
B. By positing that such observations do not account for the mass of the phlogiston released during combustion.
C. By arguing that the mass change of wood during combustion occurs because the products of the reaction weigh less than the original material.
D. By suggesting that phlogiston release may explain mass changes for only some materials and not others.

Text 1

The 21st century is witnessing the birth, or at least the rebirth, of American culture. To be sure, America has always produced great ideas and entertainment: jazz, Constitutionalism, alien movies, cheeseburgers, rock and roll. But in the large, these triumphs have been attributed to our distant heroes—a genius entrepreneur here or a revolutionary statesman there. Perhaps it's the stripping away of our national identity as a nation of consumers, but Americans are feeding, nourishing, and entertaining ourselves in ways that are more meaningfully profound and authentically American than those of generations past.

Text 2

Not long ago, cultural trends took months or years to travel across the United States. In our frenzied era of smart phones, we think this unacceptable, as though waiting two weeks for a hot new item to hit stores were some kind of federal emergency. But this seeming inconvenience allowed trends to settle in and absorb a modicum of local character. Our demand for plentiful and immediate content destroys the meaningful context of cultural trends. The breakneck pace of American life will be the end of culture.

4

Based on the texts, how would the author of Text 2 most likely characterize the argument presented in Text 1?

A. As questionable, because it offers too many different theories for the source of the rebirth of American culture.

B. As wrongheaded, because it ignores the cultural context lost by the speed of communications in the modern era.

C. As overly optimistic, because there is not yet enough evidence to determine whether the new cultural trends are here to stay.

D. As potentially correct, but lacking a clear explanatory context.

Text 1

The tuatara, an ancient reptile species endemic to New Zealand, can live to be over 100 years old. Its long lifespan can be attributed to its slow metabolic rate and negligible senescence, meaning the animals show little or no signs of aging as they grow older. The tuatara's slow metabolism minimizes cellular damage and reduces the accumulation of age-related issues. Furthermore, the phenomenon of negligible senescence allows tuataras to maintain their reproductive capabilities and physiological functions over extended periods without significant decline. These factors, coupled with efficient DNA repair mechanisms and low reproductive rates, support the idea that their longevity is a result of their unique biological adaptations.

Text 2

While metabolic rate and negligible senescence may contribute to tuataras' extended lifespan, other factors cannot be ignored. One such factor is their isolated and predator-free environment in the islands of New Zealand, which reduces external threats and allows them to live longer. Additionally, their low reproductive rates may enable better resource allocation for individual survival rather than reproduction.

5

Based on the texts, how would the author of Text 2 most likely respond to the claims made by the author of Text 1?

A. By agreeing that low reproductive rates are the most important reason why tuataras are able to live such long lives.
B. By disputing the notion that tuataras' lifespans are unusually long.
C. By contending that tuataras' metabolic rates are irrelevant to the length of their lifespans.
D. By arguing that the causal factors leading to tuataras' long lifespans may not be limited to their biological adaptations.

Reading: Evidence and Logical Reasoning

For these questions, the author will be making some kind of argument—it might be an interpretation of a work of art, a scientific hypothesis, a theory about a historical event, or any other kind of claim. You'll be asked to demonstrate your understanding of the author's reasoning.

Strategy in Brief

Read the question.	Evaluate exactly what your task is for this question. Are you looking to strengthen an argument here? Are you supposed to take the next logical step? Something else?
Isolate the claim.	Read the text carefully. What is the author's overall point? Make sure you can identify the individual sentence (or part of a sentence) in which the author makes this clear. If the question asked about a specific claim that was not the overall point of the passage, find that claim and highlight it in the text.
Consider the evidence.	In most of these arguments, the text will already provide at least partial support. How convinced are you? What else is needed?
Predict.	Read the question carefully and form a prediction in your mind of the kind of answer you're looking for. What does the right answer need to accomplish?
Evaluate the choices.	Analyze the answers carefully, keeping your overall task in mind. Remember, you're not being asked to decide *whether this answer choice is true*—for purposes of this test, you have to assume that it is. The question is simply this: if the choice *is* true, what does that do to the argument?

Command of Evidence – Illustrate the Claim

Preview Quiz

Fill in your answer:

1) What is the difference between "illustrate the claim" questions and "strengthen/weaken" questions?

2) In answering these questions, it generally (is / is not) helpful to already be familiar with the topic or work of literature that the question discusses.

Choose the best answer:

3) "We Wear the Mask" is an 1896 poem by Paul Laurence Dunbar that explores the ways in which individuals mask their true selves in order to conform to societal expectations. The poem presents the mask as a kind of living entity that conceals the true identity of the wearer: _____

   Which quotation from the poem most effectively illustrates the claim?

   A) "We wear the mask that grins and lies, / It hides our cheeks and shades our eyes,"

   B) "This debt we pay to human guile; / With torn and bleeding hearts we smile,"

   C) "Why should the world be over-wise, / In counting all our tears and sighs? / Nay, let them only see us while / we wear the mask."

   D) "We sing, but oh the clay is vile / Beneath our feet, and long the mile; / But let the world dream otherwise, / We wear the mask!"

The "command of evidence" questions are designed to test your understanding of how authors can support their claims. For some of these questions, the evidence is **quantitative** data presented in a chart or graph, as we'll see in the chapter beginning on p. 95. For now, we'll be focusing on the questions that use **textual** evidence.

In the "illustrate the claim" variety of these questions, there will be no doubt what claim the author is making. Your job is to consider what research findings, quotations, or other textual evidence would give the best example of the author's position.

Many of these questions involve literary analysis of an excerpt of poetry or prose. You are not expected to already know the work you're analyzing! The text will provide all the background information you need. Read through the text and then **highlight the claim** that you're being asked to illustrate. Then carefully review the choices to **find the best match**.

> ***TIP:***
> To highlight in the Bluebook app, select some text and click "Annotate" on the upper right corner of the screen.

Common **wrong answer types** include

- quotations that are relevant to the work as a whole but not to the specific claim
- quotations that are famous or impressive but have the wrong focus
- choices that are half right, half wrong

> ***TIP:***
> You won't need to know any advanced literary terms for these questions, nor will you be expected to already be familiar with the poem or prose. Everything you need to know is right there in the text and the question.

Here's an example question to demonstrate the process.

Example: *"We Wear the Mask" is an 1896 poem by Paul Laurence Dunbar that explores the ways in which individuals mask their true selves in order to conform to societal expectations. The poem presents the mask as a kind of living entity that conceals the true identity of the wearer: _____*

Which quotation from the poem most effectively illustrates the claim?

The text has given us a title, author, and date, as well as a brief description of some of the poem's themes. But the actual claim we need to focus on is in the last sentence. Notice we have two requirements for the right answer: it should present the mask as a *living entity*; and it should present the mask as something that *conceals the true identity* of the wearer.

Now, let's take a look at the answer choices.

A) "We wear the mask that grins and lies, / It hides our cheeks and shades our eyes"
B) "This debt we pay to human guile; / With torn and bleeding hearts we smile"
C) "Why should the world be over-wise, / In counting all our tears and sighs? / Nay, let them only see us while / we wear the mask."
D) "We sing, but oh the clay is vile / Beneath our feet, and long the mile; / But let the world dream otherwise, / We wear the mask!"

Several of these choices (A, C, and D) suggest a mask that conceals the true identity of the wearer. But only choice A presents it as a living entity (something that can "grin" and "lie"). Though the other choices may be relevant to the background information that the text supplied about the poem, only choice A fulfills the specific task that has been set for us. Choice **A** is the answer.

> ***TIP:***
>
> It's essential to focus on the specific claim that the question is asking about. Illustrating *that claim* is our only concern.

Reading: Evidence and Logical Reasoning

Try It   Use the passage below to practice the steps discussed above.

In Kate Chopin's 1899 novel *The Awakening*, the open water serves as a powerful symbol of freedom, liberation, and self-discovery for the protagonist. The novel references the ocean to emphasize the profound connection between the natural world and the human spirit: _____

1) List the elements that the right answer must illustrate:
   - Element #1:
   - Element #2:

2) Evaluate the answer choices below by considering how well it satisfies each of the elements you listed.

		Element #1	Element #2
A)	"The voice of the sea speaks to the soul."	_____	_____
B)	"The bird that would soar above the level plain of tradition and prejudice must have strong wings."	_____	_____
C)	"There are some people who leave impressions not so lasting as the imprint of an oar upon the water."	_____	_____
D)	"There were strange, rare odors abroad—a tangle of sea smell and of weeds and damp, new-plowed earth, mingled with the heavy perfumes of white blossoms somewhere near, but the night sat lightly upon the sea and the land."	_____	_____

3) What is the best answer?

Chapter Answer Key

Try It

1) Element #1: the quote must reference the ocean
Element #2: the quote must emphasize the connection between the natural world and the human spirit

2)
	Element #1	Element #2
A)	Y	Y
B)	N	Y
C)	N	N
D)	Y	N

3) A

FROM THE BLOG

Brains need to be calm to be "reason-able." During a stress response, the amygdala (which initiates the freeze, fight, or flight response) is activated, and the prefrontal cortex (responsible for planning, organizing, problem-solving, motivation, and impulse control) is effectively shut down. Arm yourself with the things that help keep the prefrontal cortex in charge: regular exercise, mediation, and plenty of sleep.

Reading: Evidence and Logical Reasoning

Practice Set 1: Easy-Medium

"Nie Zheng, Man of Valor" is a story from *Records of the Grand Historian*, a history of China written in 91 BCE by Sima Quan. In the story, Yan Zhongzi comes to Nie Zheng's home to offer him a gift of gold, but Zheng turns it down out of pride. Later, Nie Zheng comes to regret refusing the gift, saying, _____

1

Which quotation from "Nie Zheng, Man of Valor" most effectively illustrates the claim?

A. "I have been content to humble my will and shame my body, living as a butcher here by the marketplace and well, only because I am fortunate enough to have my old mother to take care of."

B. "Though our family is poor and I am living in a strange land and earning my way as a common butcher, I am still able to find some sweet or tasty morsel with which to nourish my mother."

C. "Ah! I am a man of the marketplace and well, swinging a knife and working as a butcher, while Yan Zhongzi is chief minister to one of the feudal lords."

D. "Yan Zhongzi did not consider it too far to come a thousand miles, venturing far out of his way just to befriend me. I treated him very shabbily indeed!"

In Jane Austen's 1811 novel *Sense and Sensibility*, a widowed mother and her three daughters must adjust to life in a new home. Mrs. Jennings, their busybody neighbor, wears on their patience with her endless attempts to find suitable husbands for the teenaged girls. She means no harm in these efforts. For Mrs. Jennings, matchmaking is a source of amusement necessary to fill her days, as the novel makes clear: _____

2

Which quotation from *Sense and Sensibility* most effectively illustrates the claim?

A. "Mrs. Jennings was a good-humored, merry, fat, elderly woman, who talked a great deal and seemed very happy and rather vulgar."

B. "She was full of jokes and laughter, and before dinner was over had said many witty things on the subject of lovers and husbands."

C. "A widow with an ample fortune, Mrs. Jennings had only two daughters, both of whom she had lived to see respectably married, and she had now therefore nothing to do but to marry off all the rest of the world."

D. "She was remarkably quick in the discovery of attachments, and had enjoyed the advantage of raising the blushes and the vanity of many a young lady by insinuations of her power over such a young man."

US Congresswoman Tammy Baldwin, one of the first openly gay individuals elected to Congress, is a longtime activist for LGBTQ rights. When she addressed the crowd at the Millennium March for Equality on April 30, 2000 on the National Mall, she made clear that her previous marches and other activism inspire her in her legislative work, including legislation not specifically related to LGBTQ rights: _____

3

Which quotation from Baldwin's speech most effectively illustrates the claim?

A. "If I close my eyes, I can remember being here in 1987 [for another LGBTQ rights march]. I marched to replace my fear with courage, my isolation with belonging, my anger with hope."

B. "If I close my eyes again, I can remember coming to this city, this historic place, these steps in January, 1999. Only this time, I climbed these steps to take the oath of office."

C. "And as I climbed those steps, I remembered all those who had marched and mobilized—those who helped pave the way for my election and the election of those who will come after me."

D. "The lessons learned from you, from my participation in this civil rights movement, and from organizing against AIDS are now being applied, empowering me as I fight every day the battle for health care for all, increasing educational opportunities, and fighting for many others who lack a voice in our democracy."

"Love Song," a 1917 poem by William Carlos Williams, uses contrasting imagery to describe love as an uplifting force with a profound effect: _____

4

Which quotation from the poem most effectively illustrates the claim?

A. "The stain of love / Is upon the world, / Yellow, yellow, yellow, / It eats into the leaves,"

B. "There is no light— / Only a honey-thick stain / That drips from leaf to leaf / And limb to limb, / Spoiling the colors / Of the whole world."

C. "I am alone. / The weight of love / Has buoyed me up / Till my head / Knocks against the sky."

D. "See me! / My hair is dripping with nectar— / Starlings carry it / On their black wings."

Margaret Fuller was an influential writer, feminist, and social reformer who played a significant role in the transcendentalist movement of 19th century America. Fuller emphasized the importance of sharing knowledge and empowering others when she wrote, _____

5

Which quotation from Margaret Fuller most effectively illustrates the claim?

A. "We have waited here long in the dust; we are tired and hungry; but the triumphal procession must appear at last."
B. "If you have knowledge, let others light their candles in it."
C. "Let every woman, who has once begun to think, examine herself."
D. "There are noble books but one wants the breath of life sometimes."

Charlotte Brontë's 1853 novel *Villette* explores themes of isolation, love, and the role of women in society. In the novel, Brontë suggests that reality rarely aligns with our preconceived notions and desires: _____

6

Which quotation from the novel most effectively illustrates the claim?

A. "Life is so constructed, that the event does not, cannot, will not, match the expectation."
B. "I believe in some blending of hope and sunshine sweetening the worst lots. I believe that this life is not all; neither the beginning nor the end."
C. "No mockery in this world ever sounds to me so hollow as that of being told to cultivate happiness. What does such advice mean?"
D. "To see and know the worst is to take from Fear her main advantage."

Paul Verlaine's 1866 Poem "Il Pleure Dans Mon Coeur" ("It Rains in My Heart") juxtaposes the external and internal world to underscore the speaker's melancholy: _____

7

Which quotation from a translation of the poem most effectively illustrates the claim?

A. "It rains in my heart / As it rains on the town, / What languor so dark / That it soaks to my heart?"
B. "Oh sweet sound of the rain / On the earth and the roofs!"
C. "It rains for no reason / In this heart that lacks heart. / What? And no treason? / It's grief without reason."
D. "By far the worst pain, / Without hatred, or love, / Yet no way to explain / Why my heart feels such pain!"

Practice Set 2: Medium-Hard

"A Valediction: of Weeping" is a 1633 poem by John Donne. The speaker, about to depart from his lover for a distant journey, uses a financial metaphor to suggest that her presence makes his sadness worthwhile: _____

1

Which quotation from the poem most effectively illustrates the claim?

A. "Let me pour forth / My tears before thy face, whilst I stay here, / For thy face coins them, and thy stamp they bear, / And by this mintage they are something worth"
B. "For thus they be / Pregnant of thee; / Fruits of much grief they are, emblems of more, / When a tear falls, that thou falls which it bore, / So thou and I are nothing then, when on a diverse shore"
C. "On a round ball / A workman that hath copies by, can lay / An Europe, Afric, and an Asia, / And quickly make that, which was nothing, all; / So doth each tear / Which thee doth wear"
D. "A globe, yea world, by that impression grow, / Till thy tears mix'd with mine do overflow / This world; by waters sent from thee, my heaven dissolved so"

"Song of Myself" is an 1892 poem by Walt Whitman. The poem uses joyful language to assert that every individual is worthy of praise, while also emphasizing humanity's interconnectedness: _____

2

Which quotation from the poem most effectively illustrates the claim?

A. "A child said *What is the grass?* Fetching it to me with full hands; / How could I answer the child? I do not know what it is any more than he."
B. "I celebrate myself, and sing myself, / And what I assume you shall assume, / For every atom belonging to me as good belongs to you."
C. "I think I could turn and live with animals, they're so placid and self-contained, / I stand and look at them long. / They do not sweat and whine about their condition. / They do not lie awake in the dark and weep for their sins."
D. "I am not an earth nor an adjunct of an earth, / I am the mate and companion of people, all just as immortal and fathomless as myself, / (They do not know how immortal, but I know.)"

In Henry James's 1903 novel *The Ambassadors,* an American character embarks on a voyage of self-discovery during a trip to Europe. The novel uses figurative language to describe Paris as a vibrant and alluring city that captivates the protagonist with its sophistication: _____

3

The quotations from the novel given below are all from a scene that takes place in Paris. Which quotation most effectively illustrates the claim?

A. "He came down the Rue de la Paix in the sun and, passing across the river, indulged more than once in a sudden pause before the bookstalls of the opposite quay."
B. "The prompt Paris morning struck its cheerful notes."
C. "He watched little brisk figures whose movement was as the tick of the great Paris clock."
D. "The air had a taste as of something mixed with art, something that presented nature as a white-capped master chef."

Man and Superman is a 1905 play by George Bernard Shaw. The play skewers societal norms and conventional morality with sharp and witty dialogue: _____

4

Which quotation from the poem most effectively illustrates the claim?

A. "Self-sacrifice enables us to sacrifice other people without blushing."
B. "You don't get tired of muffins. But you don't find inspiration in them."
C. "We live in an atmosphere of shame. We are ashamed of everything that is real about us; ashamed of ourselves, of our relatives, of our incomes, of our accents, of our opinions, of our experience, just as we are ashamed of our naked skins."
D. "We shall never be able to keep the secret unless everybody knows what it is."

In his 1925 poem "in Just-," e.e. cummings explores themes of childhood and whimsy on a carefree Spring day. In its description of the season, the poem displays an attitude of gleeful celebration: _____

5

Which quotation from the poem most effectively illustrates the claim?

A. "the little / lame balloonman / whistles far and wee"
B. "and eddieandbill come / running from marbles and / piracies and it's / spring"
C. "when the world is puddle-wonderful"
D. "and bettyandisbel come dancing / from hop-scotch and jump-rope"

The 17th century thinker Gottfried Wilhelm Leibniz emphasized the close connection between mathematics and other disciplines. He argued that a universal language of symbols and ratios underlies all knowledge and understanding, even when we are not aware of it. For example, he said, _____

6 Which quotation from Gottfried Wilhelm Leibniz most effectively illustrates the text's claim?

A. "Perceptions which are at present insensible may grow some day: nothing is useless, and eternity provides great scope for change."
B. "Imaginary numbers are a fine and wonderful resource of the divine intellect, almost an amphibian between being and non-being."
C. "Music is the hidden arithmetical exercise of a mind unconscious that it is calculating."
D. "There is nothing in the intellect which has not come from the senses, except the intellect itself."

William Makepeace Thackeray's 1848 satirical novel *Vanity Fair* explores the moral corruption and social climbing of its characters. The novel suggests that human beings are inherently subjective, perceiving their world through a self-centered lens that ultimately shapes their experiences: _____

7 Which quotation from the novel most effectively illustrates the text's claim?

A. "The moral world has no particular objection to vice, but an insuperable repugnance to hearing vice called by its proper name."
B. "Long brooding over lost pleasures exaggerates their charm and sweetness."
C. "Are not there little chapters in everybody's life, that seem to be nothing, and yet affect all the rest of history?"
D. "The world is a looking-glass, and gives back to every man the reflection of his own face."

Command of Evidence – Strengthen/Weaken

Preview Quiz

1) What should you read first, the passage or the question?

2) For these questions, an answer choice that uses weak language is generally (more / less) likely to be right than an answer choice that uses strong language.

3) To help decide on the right answer, it is a (good / bad) idea to rely on your own knowledge of the subject from outside the passage.

Choose the best answer.

4) The Mississippi kite, a bird of prey native to the prairies of North America, has adapted to living in areas of human settlement. When humans arrive in a previously uninhabited area, many other wild animals face steep declines in their populations, but the Mississippi kite flourishes. While some scholars point to the lower number of natural predators as the likely explanation, researcher Julie Savidge hypothesizes that nesting opportunities in urban areas were a key reason for the kites' success.

   Which finding, if true, would most directly support Julie Savidge's hypothesis?

   A) Grasshoppers, a major food source for Mississippi kites, thrive in urban and suburban areas due to the abundant grasses available on landscaped lawns.
   B) Mississippi kites prefer to nest in trees, which are more plentiful in towns and urban areas than in the open prairie.
   C) Owls, hawks, and falcons frequently prey on Mississippi kites in the prairie but are seldom seen in areas of human settlement.
   D) The Mississippi kite is known for its aerobatic flight displays, which are performed during courtship and for territorial defense.

As always, our first step is to **read the question** carefully. It's crucial to identify **which claim** you are supposed to support. Usually, this will be the overall point of the text, but some questions are more subtle: there may be multiple points of view in the same text, and your job is to support just one of them. Next, read the text, **find the claim**, and either highlight it on the screen or jot it down on your scratch paper.

Now, consider the argument that you've just read. What **evidence** has the arguer provided for their claim? Do you see a **weakness** in their argument that you could help patch up with the right answer choice? Or is there just not enough evidence one way or the other? **Predict** your answer, to the extent that it's possible to do so. This may mean you know exactly what you're looking for, but maybe not. It's still helpful to have an idea of a general type of information that would be useful.

> **TIP:**
> To highlight in the Bluebook app, select some text and click "Annotate" on the upper right corner of the screen.

Now it's time to **attack the answer choices**. As you read each one, remember that you are *not* trying to decide whether or not the answer choice is true. Assume it is! The question to ask yourself is this: **does this make the claim more likely to be true**?

Common **wrong answer types** include choices that

- are irrelevant to the specific claim that the question asked about
- weaken the author's claim instead of strengthening it
- strengthen the author's position *slightly* but don't go far enough

> **TIP:**
> The language strength of the choice can be a good tiebreaker. For the Central Ideas & Details questions, a choice using weaker language was more likely to be right, because it was easier to support. For these questions, the opposite is true! **A choice with *stronger* language is more likely to be right**, because it's more likely to have a real impact on the author's argument.

Try It   A group of researchers conducted long-term field observations and data collection on a population of woolly monkeys in Yasuní National Park, Ecuador. They studied various aspects of their ecology and behavior, including population density, group size, home range, diet, and ranging patterns. The monkeys were observed to consume a wide variety of fruits as they ranged through large tracts of forest habitat. The researchers concluded that woolly monkeys play a crucial role in seed dispersal.

1) What is the researchers' conclusion?

2) What evidence do we have so far?

3) What kind of evidence might help?

Mbabaram is an extinct Aboriginal language that was spoken by the Mbabaram people in north Queensland, Australia. Although Mbabaram is completely unrelated to English, the two languages both happened to develop the word "dog" to refer to the same type of animal. This is an example of a "false cognate," a linguistic phenomenon in which a pair of words share similar sounds and meaning but different etymologies. However, although the Aragonese word "nueit" sounds similar to the English word "night," which has the same meaning, these terms should not be considered false cognates.

4) What is the central claim of the text?

5) Summarize the steps of the argument.

6) What kind of evidence might strengthen this text's claim?

Let's practice the whole process: analyzing an argument, predicting an answer, and then examining the answer choices.

Example: *The Mississippi kite, a bird of prey native to the prairies of North America, has adapted to living in areas of human settlement. When humans arrive in a previously uninhabited area, many other wild animals face steep declines in their populations, but the Mississippi kite flourishes. While some scholars point to the lower number of natural predators as the likely explanation, researcher Julie Savidge hypothesizes that nesting opportunities in urban areas were a key reason for the kites' success.*

Which finding, if true, would most directly support Julie Savidge's hypothesis?

Before we even see the answer choices, let's put some of the earlier steps into practice. First, what is the claim we need to support? Find Julie Savidge in the text and underline or highlight her hypothesis.

Now, what's the context? There's a bird that does well when humans arrive, and people wonder why. Julie Savidge's take is that they succeed because of nesting opportunities in urban areas.

Great, that's what we're looking for: something to support the idea that <u>nesting opportunities</u>, specifically, are the reason for the kites' success. Now we're ready to look at some answer choices.

> A) *Grasshoppers, a major food source for Mississippi kites, thrive in urban and suburban areas due to the abundant grasses available on landscaped lawns.*
> B) *Mississippi kites prefer to nest in trees, which are more plentiful in towns and urban areas than in the open prairie.*
> C) *Owls, hawks, and falcons frequently prey on Mississippi kites in the prairie but are seldom seen in areas of human settlement.*
> D) *The Mississippi kite is known for its aerobatic flight displays, which are performed during courtship and for territorial defense.*

> **TIP:**
> Always be sure to read *all* the choices. You won't know which one best supports the claim until you've considered them all.

Choice A doesn't tell us anything about nesting opportunities. If anything, this choice might actually *weaken* the argument, because it gives us another possible reason for the kites' success: towns provide them with lots of food.

Choice B is about nesting! If this is true, this definitely helps support the argument: this tells us why *nesting* might be the reason that kites do well where people are. Hold on to this one.

Choice C is the opposite of what we want! This supports the other viewpoint in the passage (the "some scholars"), not Julie Savidge's viewpoint. Remember, we're not just looking to support the idea that kites do well in towns; we want to support the idea that *nesting opportunities are the reason why*.

Reading: Evidence and Logical Reasoning

Choice D is interesting but irrelevant. Oh well! It sounds like these birds put on a good show.

Of these answers, only one helps out our argument the way we need. Choice **B** is the clear winner.

Now let's return to the arguments you analyzed earlier. Consider all your previous work as you evaluate the answer choices.

Try It

7) A group of researchers conducted long-term field observations and data collection on a population of woolly monkeys in Yasuní National Park, Ecuador. They studied various aspects of their ecology and behavior, including population density, group size, home range, diet, and ranging patterns. The monkeys were observed to consume a wide variety of fruits as they ranged through large tracts of forest habitat. The researchers concluded that woolly monkeys play a crucial role in seed dispersal.

Which of the following, if true, would most directly support the researchers' conclusion?

Mark each answer choice with an "S" (if it strengthens the argument), a "W" (if it weakens the argument) or an "I" (if it is irrelevant).

____ A) Many plants have adaptations that allow their seeds to be carried away by the wind.
____ B) Woolly monkeys live in small groups consisting of several adult females, one dominant male, and their offspring.
____ C) An analysis of spatial distribution of tree species found greater tree diversity and more seedlings in areas where the woolly monkeys ranged than in areas where woolly monkeys were absent.
____ D) Human-caused disturbances, including hunting and habitat fragmentation, pose a significant threat to woolly monkey populations.

Which choice is the best answer? _____

Try It

8) Mbabaram is an extinct Aboriginal language that was spoken by the Mbabaram people in north Queensland, Australia. Although Mbabaram is completely unrelated to English, the two languages both happened to develop the word "dog" to refer to the same type of animal. This is an example of a "false cognate," a linguistic phenomenon in which a pair of words share similar sounds and meaning but different etymologies. However, although the Aragonese word "nueit" sounds similar to the English word "night," which has the same meaning, these terms should not be considered false cognates.

Which of the following, if true, would most directly support the claim?

Mark each answer choice with an "S" (if it strengthens the argument), a "W" (if it weakens the argument) or an "I" (if it is irrelevant).

____ A) Both "nueit" and "night" developed from the same Indo-European root word.

____ B) Aragonese is not an extinct language.

____ C) There is no linguistic relationship between Aragonese and the Mbabaram language.

____ D) In Aragonese, the words "nit" and "nuet" can also mean "night."

Which choice is the best answer? _____

CHALLENGE:

A variation of this question type asks you to **weaken** the text's claim instead of strengthening it. The process for these questions is almost exactly the same. Read the question, read the text, isolate the claim, consider what evidence has been supplied for it so far, and then look for any potential weaknesses. Only the final step is different: when forming your prediction, look for ways to make the conclusion *less* likely to be true rather than *more* likely to be true.

For both types of question, the best answer choices are strongly worded to have a significant impact on the argument. The wrong answers will either not go far enough, or they'll go in the wrong direction (strengthening rather than weakening), or they'll simply be irrelevant (neither strengthening nor weakening at all).

Chapter Answer Key

Try It

1) Woolly monkeys play a crucial role in seed dispersal.

2) Woolly monkeys consume a wide variety of fruits and travel through a wide range of habitat.

3) Something showing that the actions of the woolly monkey actually result in dispersal of seeds.

4) The words "nueit" and "night" should not be considered false cognates.

5) False cognates occur when two words share similar sounds and meaning but different etymologies. The words "nueit" and "night" sound similar and have the same meaning.

6) Something showing that the two words have related etymologies.

7) A. W
   B. I
   C. S
   D. I

   Best answer: C

8) A. S
   B. I
   C. I
   D. I

   Best answer: A

Command of Evidence – Strengthen/Weaken

Practice Set 1: Easy-Medium

In the frigid waters of the Arctic Ocean, the Arctic cod (*Boreogadus saida*) is a critical source of food for marine mammals, birds, and other fish. This species is known for its unique adaptations to the harsh environment, including the ability to survive in water temperatures below 0°C. Scientists hypothesize that a specialized molecule in the Arctic cod's bloodstream may act as an antifreeze, allowing the fish to maintain fluidity in its body tissues even in subzero temperatures.

1 Which finding, if true, would most directly support the scientists' hypothesis?

A. A glycoprotein found in Arctic cod blood prevents freezing by binding to ice crystals and preventing them from growing.
B. The *nototheniidae*, a family of ray-finned fishes native to the waters near Antarctica, are believed to possess a similar antifreeze molecule.
C. The primary food source for Arctic cod is plankton and krill, both of which are found in abundance in the Arctic Ocean.
D. Arctic cod females lay their eggs under the sea ice in the spring; the eggs hatch and develop in the relative safety of the ice-covered water.

Teotihuacan was an ancient city in central Mexico that collapsed between the 6th and 8th centuries CE for mysterious reasons. Some historians believe that the collapse was caused by internal conflict, as the city was torn apart by social factors such as inequality and political instability. Others argue that Teotihuacan was invaded and conquered by a neighboring group, such as the Toltecs or the Chichimecs. However, archaeologist Michael E. Smith claims that the chief cause of the collapse was widespread famine due to uncontrollable environmental factors.

2 Which finding, if true, would most directly support Smith's claim?

A. Archaeological evidence shows significant changes in the material culture of the region during the 7th century CE, which could be indicative of a change in the ruling order.
B. The distribution of housing and other structures in the ruins of Teotihuacan suggest that by the 6th century CE, the city's ruling elite had become increasingly isolated from the rest of society.
C. Studies of sediment cores in the Valley of Mexico have revealed evidence of volcanic eruptions, though the dates of the eruptions remain uncertain.
D. An analysis of tree-ring data from the nearby Sierra Madre Mountains shows evidence of several severe droughts during the 5th and 6th centuries CE, which likely impacted the agricultural productivity of the region.

Dolley Madison, who held the title of First Lady of the United States from 1809 to 1817, was a woman of great intelligence, grace, and charm. Her popularity with the public played a key role in helping President Madison win office in the first place, which became clear early in the campaign when members of the opposing party attacked her viciously in the press. <u>Somehow, though, she never seemed bothered by the remarks: no matter what was printed, she would laugh it off and hold her head high.</u>

3

Which quotation from the 1800s would most directly support the underlined claim?

A. After losing to Madison, Charles Pinckney remarked, "I might have had a better chance had I faced Mr. Madison alone. I was beaten by Mr. and Mrs. Madison."
B. According to Margaret Bayard Smith, "It would be absolutely impossible for anyone to behave with more perfect propriety than she did."
C. On one occasion, when asked for her reaction to a nasty article, Dolley simply smiled and said, "It was as good as a play."
D. President Martin Van Buren later called Dolley "the most brilliant hostess this country has ever known."

A student is studying the ancient medical technique of "leeching," which involves the application of leeches to the skin for the purpose of bloodletting. The leeches would draw a significant amount of blood from the patient, which was believed to help remove toxins from the body and balance the humors. The physician would apply the leeches to specific areas of the body, usually the arms or the legs. The student argues that these locations were chosen in order to maximize the amount of blood drawn by the leeches.

4

Which finding, if true, would most directly support the student's claim?

A. In the period during which leeching was popular, the body was believed to be governed by a careful balance of four basic fluids, or "humors": blood, phlegm, yellow bile, and black bile.
B. The arms and legs feature a rich network of veins located close to the surface of the skin, which makes it easier for leeches to access the blood.
C. Leeching has fallen out of favor because the resulting blood loss increases the risk of infection and because of a lack of scientific evidence to support its effectiveness.
D. The use of leeches on other parts of the body, such as the face or torso, was considered more dangerous and potentially harmful to the patient.

Theory of Mind (ToM) refers to the ability to understand and attribute mental states to oneself and others, including beliefs, desires, intentions, and emotions. It plays a crucial role in children's social interactions and communication. In a 2011 study, researchers assessed a sample of 3- to 5-year-old children and collected information about their TV viewing habits, including the amount of educational TV programming they watched. They also evaluated the children's ToM skills using age-appropriate measures, such as understanding false beliefs and recognizing different perspectives. Children who watched more educational TV shows exhibited higher levels of ToM understanding compared to those who had lower exposure to educational content. The researchers concluded that exposure to educational TV programming could aid in ToM development in preschoolers.

5

Which finding, if true, would most directly support the researchers' conclusion?

A. Educational TV programs can enhance children's cognitive skills, such as attention, memory, and problem-solving abilities.
B. High-quality educational TV programs use engaging storytelling and visuals to effectively teach children literacy, mathematics, and science.
C. By presenting characters and scenarios that require understanding others' perspectives and emotions, educational TV programs help children develop empathy and perspective-taking skills.
D. Exposure to rich and diverse language through various media can contribute to language acquisition and communication abilities.

In a 2008 study, Anna Nowak-Wegrzyn and colleagues investigated the effects of extensively heated egg protein on egg-allergic children. The study involved a double-blind, placebo-controlled food challenge where participants consumed muffins containing baked egg. The researchers found that a significant number of participants with egg allergy demonstrated tolerance to the baked egg products, experiencing no allergic reactions. Nowak-Wegrzyn concluded that the heating process alters the allergenic properties of egg proteins, making them less likely to trigger an allergic response.

6

Which finding, if true, would most directly support Nowak-Wegrzyn's conclusion?

A. Not all individuals with egg allergies can tolerate baked egg products, and the level of tolerance can vary among individuals.
B. Heat denatures egg proteins, altering their shape and making them less likely to bind to the antibodies responsible for initiating allergic reactions.
C. When children with egg allergies are gradually introduced to small amounts of baked egg, the immune system can build a tolerance to egg proteins over time.
D. During baking, eggs undergo coagulation, a process by which proteins form a network of interconnected structures resulting in solidification and firmness.

Reading: Evidence and Logical Reasoning

Practice Set 2: Medium-Hard

A recent study of college students found that over 50% of students self-reported their GPAs as significantly higher than their official academic records indicated. Biometric evaluation indicated a lack of any of the physical markers of an attempt to deceive. Moreover, many of these same students later increased their GPAs the exact amount of the discrepancy in reporting. Researchers concluded that the students' inaccurate reporting represented not a desire to mislead but an optimistic expression of future academic intent.

1. Which finding, if true, would most directly support the researchers' conclusion?

A. Many of the students reported GPAs more than five-tenths of a point higher than their actual GPAs.
B. When the students reported false information about their disciplinary records, many displayed increased heart rates and other indicia of physical distress.
C. Some of the students who reported their GPAs accurately seemed uncomfortable with the interviewing process.
D. Several students lied about not only their GPAs, but their country of origin, age, and socioeconomic status.

In 1974, the US House of Representatives held hearings to determine whether then-president Richard Nixon's actions during the Watergate scandal merited his impeachment, the first step in a process that could ultimately result in his removal from office. The opening statement at the impeachment hearings, delivered by Congresswoman Barbara Jordan, denounced Nixon's behavior in forceful terms and made a powerful argument in favor of impeachment. <u>However, Jordan stopped short of calling for an end to Nixon's presidency; she did not state a conclusion as to whether Nixon should be removed from office, suggesting only that Congress needed to begin the process of exploring the evidence of his alleged offenses.</u>

2. Which quotation from Jordan's speech would most directly support the underlined claim?

A. "Impeachment must proceed within the confines of the constitutional term 'high crimes and misdemeanors.' Common sense would be revolted if we engaged upon this process for petty reasons."
B. "The President has engaged in a series of public statements and actions designed to thwart the lawful investigation by government prosecutors. Moreover, the President has made public announcements and assertions which the evidence will show he knew to be false."
C. "If the impeachment provision in the Constitution of the United States will not reach the offenses charged here, then perhaps that 18th-century Constitution should be abandoned to a 20th-century paper shredder!"
D. "Has the President committed offenses, and planned, and directed, and acquiesced in a course of conduct which the Constitution will not tolerate? That's the question. We know that. We know the question. We should now forthwith proceed to answer the question."

A physician hypothesized that practicing yoga several times a week could significantly improve patients' cardiovascular health. Two groups of patients were studied, none of whom had regularly practiced yoga prior to the start of the experiment. For one year, Group A attended yoga sessions every Monday, Wednesday, and Friday morning, while Group B did not. At the end of the year, Group B's health had not changed, but most members of Group A had lower blood pressure and a decreased resting heart rate, both of which are indications of improved cardiac function.

3 Which finding, if true, would most directly weaken the physician's hypothesis?

A. During the experiment, many members of Group A engaged in other activities known to improve cardiovascular health, while the members of Group B did not.
B. At the start of the experiment, the average blood pressure and resting heart rates for Group A were lower than those of Group B.
C. Both groups were provided with information about healthy eating practices and advised to exercise regularly.
D. None of the members of Group B expressed an interest in practicing yoga after the experiment was concluded.

Fever has long been regarded as a symptom of disease, a byproduct of the inflammation brought on by infection. A team of researchers at the University of Alberta hypothesized that fever in fact regulates and controls infection, speeding recovery from illness. To test their hypothesis, the scientists infected two groups of teleost fish with *Aeromonas veronii* bacteria, then administered antifever medication to one group while allowing fever to develop unimpeded in the other. A control group of uninfected fish was also observed.

4 Which finding from the study, if true, would most directly support the researchers' hypothesis?

A. The infected fish that did not receive antifever medication exhibited symptoms of fatigue and muscle weakness.
B. The infected fish that received antifever medication cleared their infection in about 14 days, while the infected fish that did not receive antifever medication cleared their infection in about 7 days.
C. The infected fish that did not receive antifever medication showed a higher capacity to heal *A. veronii*-associated wounds than did the infected fish that received antifever medication.
D. The uninfected fish did not exhibit any symptoms of illness and showed no change in their wound healing capacity.

The Aurignacians, a group of early modern humans who lived in Europe during the Upper Paleolithic period, created intricate cave paintings considered to be some of the earliest known examples of human art. While some scholars believe the paintings were chiefly practical in nature, perhaps intended to communicate information about hunting techniques or to identify important resources in the area, others argue that the paintings served a primarily spiritual or religious purpose. The paintings were clearly created with great care and attention, featuring detailed depictions of animals that were likely important to the Aurignacian culture and may have held significant symbolic meaning. Additionally, the cave environment may have been considered a sacred space, and the act of creating the paintings may have been seen as a way to communicate with the spiritual realm or to honor and pay tribute to the animals depicted.

5

Which finding, if true, would most directly weaken the claim made by the scholars who favor the view expressed in the underlined portion of the text?

A. Many of the paintings feature strange, otherworldly creatures that are not found in the natural world, such as half-human, half-animal figures or creatures with exaggerated features.
B. The paintings have generally been found deep within caves, often in areas that would have been difficult for the Aurignacians to access.
C. Some of the paintings show animals with arrows or spears sticking out of their bodies, or with bright arrow-shaped lines tracing a path to the heart.
D. The paintings have been found in several locations in Europe, including in the Chauvet-Pont-d'Arc Cave and the Lascaux Cave, both in France, and the Altamira Cave, in northern Spain.

The human body burns calories all the time, not just when we're engaging in cardiovascular activity. The rate at which the body uses energy to maintain vital bodily functions when at rest is called the resting metabolic rate (RMR). In a study at the University of Alabama at Birmingham, a group of researchers claimed to have demonstrated that strength training can increase the RMR. Before and after a group of ten women underwent a 16-week strength training program, researchers measured the amount of oxygen consumed and carbon dioxide produced by each participant when at rest, a technique known as indirect calorimetry. Because the rates of oxygen consumption and carbon dioxide production reflect the body's energy expenditure, this technique is a useful way to measure RMR.

6

Which finding, if true, would most directly support the researchers' claim?

A. By the end of the study, most of the participants in the study had lost a moderate amount of weight.
B. The average rate at which participants consumed oxygen during strength training was greater at the end of the 16-week program.
C. Muscles are metabolically active tissue, meaning they require energy to function even at rest.
D. The average rate at which participants produced carbon dioxide while at rest was greater at the end of the 16-week program.

Command of Evidence – Quantitative

Preview Quiz

1) The quantitative Command of Evidence questions (do / do not) test your math skills.

2) A background in science (is / is not) necessary to do well on these questions.

Choose the best answer.

3) The common bumblebee goes through several distinct life stages. A bumblebee larva is 0 to 14 days old and 0 to 15 millimeters (mm) in length. After a brief pupal stage in a cocoon, the bumblebee emerges as an adult. Adult bumblebees are more than 21 days old, and their size depends on their sex and their role in the colony: the queen is 17 to 22 mm in length, a worker is 10 to 14 mm in length, and a male is 13 to 16 mm in length. A student recorded information about four bumblebees and asserted that three are workers and one is a queen.

Bee	Age (days)	Length (mm)	Mass (milligrams)
A	27	13.2	140
B	32	12.9	113
C	75	19.4	681
D	39	13.9	174

Which choice best describes data from the table that support the student's assertion?

A) The ages of the bees range from 27 to 75 days, and D's length is 174 mm.

B) None of the bees are more than 22 mm in length, and B is 32 days old.

C) Each of the bees has a mass between 113 and 681 milligrams, and only A is less than 30 days old.

D) All the bees are more than 21 days old, and all except C have lengths ranging from 10 to 14 mm.

Reading: Evidence and Logical Reasoning

These questions are similar to the last two sets, in that your overall task is to use evidence to support the author's argument. The difference lies in what kind of evidence you'll be using: this time, the answers will come from tables, graphs, or other visual representations of data.

Don't panic—this isn't as hard as it seems. Although many of these texts are science-based, **you don't need to understand the science**. As always, no outside knowledge of the passage's topic is necessary; in fact, relying on that outside knowledge can be a quick trip to the wrong answer. Our task here is to use the information we've been given to support the specific claim that they've asked us about, and that's it.

Typical **wrong answer choices** will:

- get the numbers wrong
- accurately report the numbers but misinterpret their meaning
- accurately report the numbers and their meaning, but don't support the claim

It's that last bullet point that's usually the tough one. Just like for the other "command of evidence" questions, a crucial first step here is to **identify the claim** that the text is making. What are we trying to show? **Predict an answer** on that basis. What kind of evidence are we looking for? For instance, if the overall point is that two things are similar, we can probably eliminate answer choices that focus on a difference between them instead of a similarity.

For the remaining answer choices, first make sure they're accurately stating the data, and then consider what impact that information has on the specific claim you've been asked about. Does it support the claim? Does it undermine it? Or does it not necessarily do anything at all?

> **TIP:**
> The data provided in the chart or graph will include some irrelevant information. Focus on what matters, mentally crossing out the rest. What's relevant to the specific claim referenced in the question?

Example: The common bumblebee goes through several distinct life stages. A bumblebee larva is 0 to 14 days old and 0 to 15 millimeters (mm) in length. After a brief pupal stage in a cocoon, the bumblebee emerges as an adult. Adult bumblebees are more than 21 days old, and their size depends on their sex and their role in the colony: the queen is 17 to 22 mm in length, a worker is 10 to 14 mm in length, and a male is 13 to 16 mm in length. A student recorded information about four bumblebees and asserted that three are workers and one is a queen.

Bee	Age (days)	Length (mm)	Mass (milligrams)
A	27	13.2	140
B	32	12.9	113
C	75	19.4	681
D	39	13.9	174

Which choice best describes data from the table that support the student's assertion?

Let's see what we can do before we examine the answer choices. First, what's the student's assertion here? It's right there at the end of the passage: the student is saying that three of these four are "worker" bumblebees and one is a "queen." Given what the rest of the text told us about these categories, we can conclude that the lengths of three of these bees (the workers) should be 10-14 mm, while the length of the remaining one (the queen) should be 17-22 mm. Moreover, since both workers and queens are adults, we also know that all four bees should be more than 21 days old.

Right off the bat, what do you notice about the data? There's a whole column that we don't need! You can mentally cross off the entire "mass" column, since there was nothing about mass in the passage. This also means that <u>any answer choices that even *mention* mass would have to be wrong.</u>

TIP:

Some wrong choices will get the data wrong—but not all. It's not enough that the choice accurately reports the data. It also has to be relevant! Keep your focus on *the task set for you in the question* above all else.

Now let's take a look at our choices.

- A) The ages of the bees range from 27 to 75 days, and D's length is 174 mm.
- B) None of the bees are more than 22 mm in length, and B is 32 days old.
- C) Each of the bees has a mass between 113 and 681 milligrams, and only A is less than 30 days old.
- D) All the bees are more than 21 days old, and all except C have lengths ranging from 10 to 14 mm.

We can already eliminate choice C, since it mentions mass. Eliminate choice A for getting the data wrong: 174 is D's mass in milligrams, not its length in millimeters.

Choices B and D both accurately report the data. But how relevant is B? The fact that the lengths are all under 22 mm doesn't help us distinguish between worker bees and queen bees, which is the point we're really trying to make. Choice D is the one that points out that exactly three of the four bees have lengths in the "worker" category, and its information about age supports the idea that they're all adults. Choice **D** is the winner.

> **TIP:**
> The right answer doesn't have to completely *prove* the claim we've been asked to support. It just has to make that claim *more likely to be true*.

Try It

Ice Cream Butterfat Contents and Price Ranges

Ice cream type	Butterfat content	Price range (per pint)
Regular	10-16%	$2.99-$4.99
Premium	14-18%	$4.99-$6.99
Low-fat	3-8%	$2.99-$4.99
Non-dairy	varies	$4.99-$6.99

Ice creams can vary widely in their butterfat content, which refers to the amount of fat derived from milk or cream used in the ice cream formulation. A higher butterfat content contributes to a richer, denser, and more indulgent ice cream, but customers pay for the privilege: _____

Which choice most effectively uses data from the table to complete the text?

1) What is the claim we're trying to strengthen?

2) Which rows and/or columns from the table are the most relevant?

3) Predict an answer:

4) For each answer choice, consider two questions. First, does it accurately report the data? And second, what effect does it have on the claim (does it Strengthen it, does it Weaken it, or is it Irrelevant)?

Is it accurate? (Y/N)   What effect? (S/W/I)

____ ____ A) premium ice cream contains more butterfat than regular or low-fat ice cream, and it costs more per pint.

____ ____ B) non-dairy ice cream can cost as much as premium ice cream but its butterfat content varies.

____ ____ C) low-fat ice cream contains less butterfat than other ice cream types yet costs as much per pint as regular ice cream.

____ ____ D) the non-premium ice creams contain less butterfat than premium and cost less.

Which choice is the best answer? _____

Chapter Answer Key

Try It	1)	Higher butterfat content makes ice cream taste better, but customers pay for the privilege.
	2)	The premium ice cream row
	3)	Premium ice cream has the most butterfat and costs more than other types
	4)	A. Y S B. Y I C. Y W D. N N/A Best answer: A

Practice Set 1: Easy-Medium

INCIDENTS OF INCOMPLETE INACTIVATION BY PATHOGEN IN THE US, 2003-2015

Bacillus anthracis	8
Brucella species	1
Burkholderia pseudomallei	1
Clostridium botulinum	1
Ebola and Marburg viruses	2
Equine encephalitis viruses	3
Francisella tularensis	5
Total	21

In May 2015, the Department of Defense (DOD) discovered that one of its laboratories inadvertently sent live *Bacillus anthracis*, the bacterium that causes anthrax, to almost two hundred laboratories worldwide over the course of twelve years. The laboratory in question incorrectly believed that the samples had been inactivated—that is, that the scientists had destroyed the hazardous effects of the pathogen while retaining characteristics of interest for future use. The accident was hardly unique: between 2003 and 2015, _____

1

Which choice most effectively uses data from the table to complete the text?

A. samples of *Bacillus anthracis* were not completely inactivated in at least 7 other incidents in the US.
B. *Bacillus anthracis* was the pathogen involved in fewer than half of the US cases of incomplete inactivation.
C. scientists failed to completely inactivate Ebola and Marburg viruses at least twice.
D. incomplete inactivation incidents in the US involved fewer than 10 types of pathogens.

Trends in Movie Sales, 2010-2019

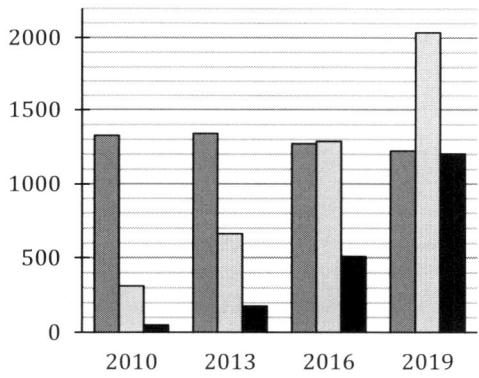

- ■ Movie theater tickets sold (millions)
- □ Movies digitally downloaded (millions)
- ■ Movies streamed at home (millions)

Some media analysts argue that trends in movie sales over time indicate a shift in movie-watching behavior away from movie theaters and towards more convenient and affordable options such as digital downloads and home streaming.

2

Which choice most effectively uses data from the table to support the analysts' argument?

A. From 2010 to 2019, the change in the number of movie theater tickets sold was much smaller than the change in the number of movies streamed at home or downloaded.
B. The greatest number of digital downloads of movies occurred in 2019, while the greatest number of movie theater tickets sold occurred in 2013.
C. From 2010 to 2019, the number of movies downloaded or streamed at home increased, while the number of movie theater tickets sold decreased.
D. In 2016, the number of movies downloaded or streamed was greater than the number of movie tickets sold.

Reading: Evidence and Logical Reasoning

US DROWSY DRIVING FATALITIES

Year	Number of drowsy drivers in fatal crashes	Percent of all drivers in fatal crashes	Fatalities in crashes involving drowsy driving
2018	1,221	2.4%	785
2017	1,319	2.5%	697
2016	1,332	2.5%	803
2015	1,275	2.6%	824
2014	1,306	2.9%	851

Source: National Highway Traffic Safety Administration

Due to the enormous amount of evidence now available, there is a consensus in the scientific community about the hazards of sleep deprivation. Lack of sleep was a factor in some of the most serious accidents in recent memory, including the Exxon Valdez oil spill, the Chernobyl meltdown, and the disaster at Three Mile Island. Moreover, traffic statistics indicate that "drowsy driving"—the act of operating a motor vehicle when feeling fatigued or sleepy—is a significant threat on the roads.

3

Which choice best describes data from the table that support the claim made in the last sentence of the text?

A. The number of fatal crashes caused by drowsy driving increases every year.
B. Hundreds of people die each year in crashes involving drowsy driving.
C. Of all fatal crashes in the US, less than three percent involve drowsy drivers.
D. The number of drowsy driving fatalities was highest in 2014, but the number of drowsy drivers involved in fatal crashes peaked in 2016.

Value of U.S. Agricultural Exports to China

Product	2017 Export Value*	2018 Export Value*	Change in Export Value
Soybeans	$12,400	$3,100	−75%
Pork	$1,100	$550	−50%
Dairy products	$577	$281	−51%
Sorghum	$347	$4	−99%
Wheat	$430	$84	−80%

* in millions of dollars

In recent years, trade tensions between the US and China have resulted in the imposition of tariffs and other trade restrictions on agricultural products, limiting access to the Chinese market. This has had a significant impact on the profitability of U.S. agricultural businesses, particularly those that rely heavily on exports to China. For example, between 2017 and 2018, _____

4

Which choice most effectively uses data from the table to complete the example?

A. the decline in US exports of dairy products to China was very similar to the decline in US exports of pork.
B. the value of US exports of sorghum to China was almost completely wiped out.
C. the value of US exports of wheat to China decreased by more than $400 million.
D. US exports of soybeans to China maintained a value of more than $3 billion.

Carotenoid Mechanisms and Coloration Scores

Type of Animal	Carotenoid Signaling Mechanism	Average Coloration Score* for Males	Average Coloration Score* for Females
Birds	coloration of plumage	5.2	3.8
Fish	coloration of fins and skin	6.9	4.6
Reptiles	coloration of throat and skin	25.6	20.9

* a measure of intensity and brightness of color

In many species, males are more likely to compete for access to females than females are for males. As a result, the males of these species evolved to develop more elaborate and conspicuous traits than the females in order to attract mates. Carotenoids, a type of pigment found in many fruits and vegetables, are believed to indicate an individual's health and nutritional status, with brighter and more saturated colors indicating better health and greater access to high-quality food. Some researchers assert that carotenoids play an important role in mate selection.

5

Which choice best describes data from the table that support the researchers' assertion?

A. In all three animal types, males tend to have higher average coloration scores than females.
B. The average coloration score for male reptiles is approximately five times as high as the average coloration score for male birds.
C. The carotenoid signaling mechanism involves skin coloration for both fish and reptiles, but not for birds.
D. The difference between the average coloration score for males and the average coloration score for females was less than 5 for all three species.

Comparison of Outcomes of Laparoscopic and Open Appendectomies

	Laparoscopic technique	Open technique
Operating time	46.98 ± 2.99 minutes	53.02 ± 2.88 minutes
Length of hospitalization	4.38 ± 1.09 days	4.18 ± 0.77 days
Rate of surgical site infections	7 infections (10.77%)	18 infections (27.69%)

As a general rule, the longer a surgical patient must spend in the operating room, the greater the risk and the slower the recovery. In a 2019 study, 130 appendectomy patients at the Holy Family Hospital in Rawalpindi, Pakistan were randomly assigned either the laparoscopic or the open surgery technique. The findings demonstrated that laparoscopic appendectomy has several advantages over open appendectomy, including _____

6

Which choice most effectively uses data from the table to complete the text?

A. longer operative times and a lower rate of surgical site infections.
B. longer hospital stays and similar operative times.
C. shorter operative times and significantly fewer surgical site infections.
D. hospital stays of similar length and a higher rate of surgical site infections.

Reading: Evidence and Logical Reasoning

Trends in Solid Waste Production
(millions of tons per year)

	2016	2030*	2050*
Middle East/ N. Africa	129	177	255
Sub-Saharan Africa	174	269	516
Latin America/Caribb.	231	290	369
North America	289	342	396
South Asia	334	466	661
Europe & central Asia	392	440	490
East Asia & Pacific	468	602	714

*projected

Rapid population growth, urbanization, industrialization, and changes in consumption patterns have contributed to a global increase in solid waste generation. While solid waste is a global issue, some regions and countries will face particularly dire waste management challenges in the coming years. For example, _____

7

Which choice most effectively uses data from the table to complete the text?

A. by 2050, the East Asia and Pacific region is projected to generate 714 million tons of solid waste per year.
B. in 2016, the amount of solid waste produced by Europe and central Asia was more than double that produced by the middle east and north Africa.
C. by 2030, nearly every region is projected to be generating more than 200 million tons of solid waste per year.
D. between 2016 and 2050, the amount of solid waste produced by North America is projected to increase by more than 100 million tons per year.

Body Temperatures (°C)

		Hours after sleep onset		
Participant	Sex	1	3	5
1	M	36.8	36.6	36.4
2	M	36.9	36.7	36.5
3	M	36.7	36.5	36.3
4	F	36.9	36.7	36.5
5	F	36.8	36.6	36.4
6	F	36.7	36.5	36.3

A study monitored the body temperature of six participants overnight. During sleep, the human body undergoes a natural fluctuation in body temperature. Throughout the night, the body's core temperature continues to decline gradually, reaching its lowest point during the early morning hours. After this thermal nadir, the body temperature gradually begins to rise, marking the transition from sleep to wakefulness.

8

Which choice best describes data in the table that support the claims made in the text?

A. The body temperatures of the male participants first decreased, then increased.
B. The body temperatures of the female participants first increased, then decreased.
C. The body temperatures of all participants gradually decreased during the first five hours of sleep.
D. The body temperatures of the participants varied with no general trend.

Practice Set 2: Medium-Hard

The Mediterranean diet, an eating plan that emphasizes plant-based foods and unsaturated fats, has been associated with numerous health benefits. It may even help stave off dementia. In the UK, a large cohort of participants submitted to genetic testing and completed questionnaires about their eating habits and lifestyles. Researchers used this information to calculate each participant's genetic risk of developing dementia and his or her Mediterranean Diet Adherence Screener (MEDAS) score, where a higher score indicates greater adherence to the diet. After tabulating the number of participants in each group who developed dementia during the 10-year study period, the researchers concluded that a Mediterranean diet may be protective against dementia regardless of an individual's genetic makeup.

1

Which choice best describes data from the graph that strengthen the researchers' conclusion?

A. Greater adherence to the Mediterranean diet was associated with an increased probability of dementia across all categories of genetic risk.
B. Greater adherence to the Mediterranean diet was associated with a decreased probability of dementia across all categories of genetic risk.
C. Greater genetic risk was associated with an increased probability of dementia across both categories of adherence to the Mediterranean diet.
D. Greater genetic risk was associated with a decreased probability of dementia across both categories of adherence to the Mediterranean diet.

Galilean Moons

Moon	Orbital period (Earth days)	Eccentricity* of orbit	Average distance from Jupiter (km)
Io	1.77	0.0041	421,800
Europa	3.55	0.0094	671,000
Ganymede	7.16	0.0013	1,070,000
Callisto	16.69	0.0074	1,883,000

* A measure of how much the orbit deviates from a circular shape.

Io, Europa, Ganymede, and Callisto are four moons of Jupiter known collectively as the Galilean moons. Unlike the other three moons, Io generates a significant amount of electrical activity on its surface. A student asserted that this activity results from strong tidal forces caused by a highly elliptical orbit.

Group	pH	Light intensity (lux)	Average number of ephippia hatched
M	5.0	650	45
N	7.0	650	56
O	9.0	650	65
R	7.0	300	28
S	7.0	650	55
T	7.0	850	68

The *Moina micrura* is a species of microscopic aquatic crustacean. Under certain conditions, *M. micrura* will lay specialized eggs called ephippia that contain dormant embryos. Researchers prepared beakers of water that each contained 120 newly laid ephippia, then divided the beakers equally into six groups. The beakers in the first three groups were exposed to varying pH levels at a constant light intensity and a temperature of 27°C; the beakers in the other three groups were exposed to varying light intensities at a constant pH level and a temperature of 25°C. The results suggest that external environmental factors can significantly affect the hatching of dormant *M. micrura* embryos. For example, while in group R, the average number of ephippia hatched was 28, _____

2

Which choice most effectively uses data from the table to weaken the student's assertion?

A. Of the four, Io's orbit is the closest to Jupiter.
B. The eccentricities of both Europa's and Callisto's orbits are higher than that of Io's.
C. Ganymede's average distance from Jupiter is greater than both Europa's and Io's.
D. Callisto's orbital period is greater than the sum of the other three orbital periods.

3

Which choice most effectively uses data from the table to complete the example?

A. in group M, the average number hatched was 45.
B. in group O, the average number hatched was 65.
C. in group T, the average number hatched was 68.
D. the average number hatched in group N was very similar to the average number hatched in group S.

Depth below surface (cm)	CO_2 content of soil gas (% by volume)		Water content of soil (% by mass)	
	Nov 9	Dec 7	Nov 9	Dec 7
30	0.07	0.09	19.0	17
60	0.14	0.08	15.7	19.5
100	0.20	0.13	11.9	24.2
140	0.42	0.23	10.6	26.3

Carbon dioxide (CO_2) is produced in soil through respiration in plant roots. In a temperate forest in southern Ontario, a scientist hypothesized that the non-growing season would be characterized by temporally variable CO_2 emissions. He also claimed that the amount of moisture in the soil was an important factor controlling CO_2 variability.

Four Asteroids' Rotation Rates and Densities

Asteroid	Rotation period (hours)	Density (g/cm³)
A	5.2	3.5
B	9.1	2.8
C	20.3	1.6
D	30.6	1.3

To determine whether an asteroid is a monolith (a solid, cohesive object) or a rubble pile (a collection of smaller rocks and debris held together by gravity), scientists look to the asteroid's rotation rate and density, among other features. A solid object is more dense and more likely to hold together under the stress of rapid rotation, while a rubble pile is less dense (containing more empty space between the individual rocks and debris) and is more likely to rotate slowly due to its loosely bound nature. If the four asteroids represented in the table above include two monoliths and two rubble piles, then asteroid C is most likely a rubble pile, because _____

4

Which choice best describes data from the table that support the scientist's claims?

A. On November 9, CO_2 content increased as water content decreased; on December 7, CO_2 content increased as water content increased.
B. At each depth, CO_2 content increased between November 9 and December 7, while water content decreased between November 9 and December 7.
C. On both November 9 and December 7, the lowest moisture and lowest CO_2 content were found at the shallowest depth.
D. The range of results for CO_2 contents at the various depths was smaller on December 7 than on November 9, and the average water content was greater on December 7 than on November 9.

5

Which choice most effectively uses data from the table to complete the text?

A. its rotation period is relatively great, indicating less rapid rotation, and its density is relatively low, suggesting more internal empty space.
B. its rotation period is relatively great, indicating more rapid rotation, and its density is relatively low, suggesting less internal empty space.
C. its rotation period is relatively low, indicating less rapid rotation, and its density is relatively high, suggesting more internal empty space.
D. its rotation period is relatively low, indicating more rapid rotation, and its density is relatively high, suggesting less internal empty space.

Crude oil is a naturally occurring mixture of hydrocarbons, which are organic compounds primarily composed of hydrogen (H) and carbon (C) atoms. A study recorded the elemental composition, hydrocarbon (H/C) content, and density, in grams per milliliter (g/mL) of five petroleum crude oil samples.

Sample	C (%)	H (%)	H/C	Density (g/mL)
S1	84.84	13.08	1.84	0.8429
S2	85.24	12.76	1.78	0.8616
S3	83.15	10.30	1.49	1.0030
S4	83.94	13.69	1.94	0.7733
S5	86.18	13.00	1.80	0.8569

As the table indicates, the specific composition of a crude oil sample determines its physical properties. For example, _____

6

Which choice most effectively uses data from the table to complete the text?

A. The sample with the lowest hydrogen content had the greatest density, and the sample with the greatest hydrogen content had the lowest density.

B. The sample with the lowest carbon content had the greatest density, and the sample with the greatest carbon content had the lowest density.

C. The sample with the lowest hydrogen content had the lowest density, and the sample with the greatest hydrogen content had the greatest density.

D. The sample with the lowest carbon content had the lowest density, and the sample with the greatest carbon content had the greatest density.

Cigarette Use and Total Tobacco Use Among U.S. Middle School and High School Students

Year	Cigarette Use (percent)	Total Tobacco Use (percent)
2015	10.8	16.7
2016	8.0	12.2
2017	7.6	12.5
2018	6.1	10.5
2019	5.8	9.6

This table presents data from the National Youth Tobacco Survey, which tracks tobacco use among US middle and high school students. The results suggest that efforts to reduce tobacco use among young people (such as tobacco taxes, restrictions on advertising and sales, and public education campaigns) may be having a positive impact, given that _____

7

Which choice most effectively uses data from the table to complete the text?

A. the percent of young people who report using cigarettes decreased every year over the time period shown.

B. the data show a downward trend in reported tobacco use among young people from 2015 to 2019.

C. among young people who report using tobacco, the fraction who report using cigarettes decreased from 2015 to 2019.

D. the percent of young people who report using tobacco dropped over 4 percentage points in a single year.

Logical Inferences

Preview Quiz

1) For these questions, an answer choice that uses weak language is generally (more / less) likely to be right than an answer choice that uses strong language.

2) To help decide on the right answer, it is a (good / bad) idea to rely on your own knowledge of the subject from outside the passage.

Choose the best answer.

3) A 2014 study involving 176 adult participants aimed to examine how different forms of physical activity affect creative thinking. Participants were asked to complete creativity tasks while walking on a treadmill, while walking outside, or while sitting down. The tasks included the Guilford Alternate Uses Task, in which participants were asked to list as many possible uses for a given object as they could within a certain timeframe; the Compound Remote Associates Test, in which participants were asked to identify a word that was related to three other given words; and the Torrance Test of Creative Thinking, in which participants were asked to complete a series of drawing tasks. Whether the walking took place on a treadmill or outside, those who walked earned higher scores on all three tests than did those who remained seated, suggesting that _____

Which choice most logically completes the text?

A) the increased blood flow to the brain caused by moderate exercise stimulates creative thinking.

B) the meditative and calming effects of walking induce creativity regardless of the setting.

C) any benefits that walking may have on creativity are not limited to the experience of being outside.

D) word-association and drawing tasks are better suited for testing creativity in adult participants than in child participants.

While the previous three question types asked you to evaluate an argument that had already been made, these questions ask you to help create the argument in the first place: you're given the evidence, and your job is to pick the right conclusion. Read through the information in the passage so you have a full understanding of the author's evidence, and **predict** where you think the author is going.

Common **wrong answer types** include the following:

- choices that generally make sense but aren't directly supported by the text
- choices that are related to one aspect of the text but not the part emphasized in the fill-in-the-blank sentence
- answers that go too far

> **TIP:**
> For these questions, a choice that uses *weaker* language is more likely to be right.

Predicting an answer is particularly important for this type of question. Gather the evidence discussed in the text, taking notes if it's helpful to keep your thoughts organized, and decide where this seems to be headed. Then, evaluate those answer choices with a critical eye. The question is this: which of these *has* to be true?

Example: *A 2014 study involving 176 adult participants aimed to examine how different forms of physical activity affect creative thinking. Participants were asked to complete creativity tasks while walking on a treadmill, while walking outside, or while sitting down. The tasks included the Guilford Alternate Uses Task, in which participants were asked to list as many possible uses for a given object as they could within a certain timeframe; the Compound Remote Associates Test, in which participants were asked to identify a word that was related to three other given words; and the Torrance Test of Creative Thinking, in which participants were asked to complete a series of drawing tasks. Whether the walking took place on a treadmill or outside, those who walked earned higher scores on all three tests than did those who remained seated, suggesting that _____*

Which choice most logically completes the text?

There's a lot of extra information in this text that is more detail than we really need. For example, how important is it that we know the exact way in which creativity was measured? For this particular question, not very, because the author isn't trying to cast doubt on the study. The last sentence is focusing on what we can draw overall from the results, so let's keep our eye on the big picture. What were the tests measuring? Creativity. The people who walked earned higher scores than the people who didn't walk, suggesting that the people who walked were *more creative* than the people who didn't. Also, the final sentence emphasizes that this outcome was observed in both groups of walkers, which suggests that it's the walking itself that's having this effect (if anything is), not the setting.

So that's our prediction: walking seems to aid creativity, whether you walk inside or outside.

But be careful not to go too far! We can't say that walking *causes* creativity based on this one study. Keep an eye out for those logical leaps as we examine the answer choices.

> A)   the increased blood flow to the brain caused by moderate exercise stimulates creative thinking.
> B)   the meditative and calming effects of walking induce creativity regardless of the setting.
> C)   any benefits that walking may have on creativity are not limited to the experience of being outside.
> D)   word-association and drawing tasks are better suited for testing creativity in adult participants than in child participants.

Let's start with choice A. If we can't say for sure that walking causes creativity, then we certainly can't say for sure that exercise in general (even "moderate" exercise) causes it. Plus, even if we could say that walking caused creativity, we can't say *how*. This choice is way too specific: we don't know anything about an increased blood flow to the brain.

Choice B gives us another possible way that walking might have an effect: maybe it's not the increased blood flow, but the meditative and calming effects. We still don't know if this is true! It's another possible way that walking *might* influence creativity, if it does. We can't say that this definitely happens, which is what we're looking for. Plus, "regardless of the setting" is too strong. The only settings we can compare are walking on a treadmill versus walking outside. For all we know, various types of outside settings might have very different effects.

Choice C is nice and weak, which is good. This isn't claiming that walking definitely affects creativity; it's just saying that if it does, those effects don't seem to be limited to being outside. That's a lot easier to support than the other choices so far. Hold on to choice C.

Choice D picks up on various details of the text, but not in a way we can justify. Just because this study used these tests for its adult participants, that doesn't necessarily mean that these tests would not be suited for child participants. We just have no way of knowing whether this is true.

Choice C was the best match for our prediction without taking it too far, so it's the winner. The answer is **C**.

> **TIP:**
>
> We're looking for what essentially *has* to be true. Any choices that assume **causation**, make a **prediction**, or describe a **hypothetical** are usually too speculative to be correct.

Reading: Evidence and Logical Reasoning

Try It   In a 2007 study, 1800 rats were divided into several groups and exposed to varying doses of the artificial sweetener aspartame throughout their lifespan. The findings suggested an association between aspartame consumption and the development of two types of cancers, lymphomas and leukemias, in female rats. However, the study faced criticism from the scientific community due to certain methodological limitations, including the rat strain used, the high dose levels tested, and the statistical analysis employed. If these criticisms are valid, _____

1) What would logically complete the text? Predict an answer:

2) Now evaluate each answer choice. For the ones that are wrong, what's wrong with them?

   A) aspartame does not cause cancer in rats.

   B) aspartame might be safer for consumption than the study's findings suggest.

   C) no conclusion can be drawn about human consumption of aspartame because humans were not directly studied.

   D) the study's findings are too dated to be useful.

Chapter Answer Key

> **Try It**
> 1) aspartame may not cause lymphomas or leukemias.
> 2) A is incorrect: the language is too strong.
>   B is correct.
>   C is incorrect: the criticisms of the study did not involve its use of non-human subjects.
>   D is incorrect: the criticisms of the study did not involve its date.

FROM THE BLOG

Here's my test prep advice. First, breathe. Second, breathe some more. Third, a quiz. One question, multiple choice.

Standardized tests are:

- A) a measure of intelligence
- B) a measure of acquired knowledge or skills
- C) a measure of luck
- D) a measure of height

Well, I am inclined to go with D since, on average, older kids (13+) do better on such tests than do younger kids (under 13) and, research shows, that, on average, older kids (13+) are taller than younger kids (under 13). But, I reckon you can recognize that I've conflated correlation with causality.

So, on to answer C. If you believe these are a measure of luck, then my advice about preparation likely won't matter. (Does one get better at the lottery with practice?)

If you believe that these are tests of intelligence, pure and simple, well, then sit back and relax or panic wildly, depending on what you think your IQ is. But, as in C, there's not much to do.

I am sticking with B. Standardized tests, perhaps imperfectly, test reading skills. They test facts and reasoning. They test grammatical rules and conventions. These are tests of acquired knowledge and skills. So build the knowledge and sharpen the skills, and you *can* conquer these tests.

Reading: Evidence and Logical Reasoning

Practice Set 1: Easy-Medium

Recycling conserves natural resources, diverts waste from landfills and incinerators, reduces greenhouse gas emissions, and can generate significant economic benefits for a community. In a recent study of 11,500 people across 28 countries, 82% of respondents indicated that they believe recycling makes a difference, but only 35% actually recycle regularly. The most commonly cited reasons for not recycling included a lack of convenient access and confusion as to what can and cannot be recycled, suggesting that _____.

1

Which choice most logically completes the text?

A. recycling is better as a theory than as a practical solution to the world's problems.
B. a consistent and accessible recycling program with clear rules about recyclables could lead to substantial benefits for a community.
C. many people are aware of only the environmental benefits of recycling and do not consider the economic impact.
D. recycling centers should do a better job educating the community about the benefits of recycling.

In a 2018 study, economists analyzed the impact of minimum wage increases in six different US cities over a five-year period. The researchers found that minimum wage increases led to modest but statistically significant increases in wages for low-wage workers: specifically, a 10% increase in the minimum wage led to a 1.5% increase in wages for workers in the bottom 25% of the wage distribution. Importantly, the study found no significant harm to overall employment levels, suggesting that minimum wage increases _____.

2

Which choice most logically completes the text?

A. can improve the economic well-being of low-wage workers without causing a significant increase in joblessness.
B. are the best way to improve the American economy.
C. may benefit middle-income workers more than minimum wage workers or other low-wage workers.
D. created overall beneficial effects in six US cities but may have detrimental effects in cities outside the US.

Studies on the use of health information technology (HIT) often use different definitions and measurements, making it difficult to compare results across studies. In addition, many studies use small sample sizes, which is particularly problematic when researching complex systems such as healthcare delivery. A large number of the studies also focus on only short-term outcomes rather than following patients over time. These problems indicate that the studies _____.

3

Which choice most logically completes the text?

A. should be repeated with standardized measurements and other controls.
B. are useful for drawing conclusions about short-term outcomes but not long-term impacts.
C. may not provide reliable conclusions that can be generalized beyond the study participants.
D. faced significant challenges that would have been resolved if the research had concerned a less complex field.

Could astronauts really protect us from an asteroid locked into a collision course with Earth? In November 2021, NASA launched its Double Asteroid Redirection Test (DART) mission to find out. The mission's objective was to test the kinetic impactor technique, which involves hitting an asteroid with a spacecraft in order to change its trajectory. The target was a binary asteroid system consisting of a larger body, Didymos, orbited by a moonlet called Dimorphos once every 11 hours 55 minutes. NASA aimed its DART vehicle at Dimorphos with the goal of altering its orbital period by at least 73 seconds. After the impact, researchers announced that Dimorphos's orbit had been shortened to 11 hours 23 minutes, indicating that the kinetic impactor technique _____

4

Which choice most logically completes the text?

A. requires more study to fine-tune the targeting of the asteroid impact.
B. is in need of a re-design, since applying this technique to an asteroid that threatened Earth could actually place the planet in more danger rather than less.
C. may be incapable of inflicting a blow powerful enough to significantly affect the orbit of an asteroid.
D. might serve as a viable option to deflect potentially hazardous asteroids away from Earth.

We experience warmth when molecules of air strike our bodies and transfer their heat. On Earth, where we're surrounded by air, these transfers are happening constantly. But in the exosphere (an atmospheric layer that begins 500 to 1000 km above the Earth's surface), air is incredibly thin: air molecules might be separated by a kilometer or more of empty space. As a result, even though temperatures in the exosphere regularly rise to over 2000°C during the day, _____

5

Which choice most logically completes the text?

A. they can dip down to 0°C overnight.
B. the particle densities are similar to those found in the airless vacuum of space.
C. few gas molecules collide, and some fast-moving particles even escape earth's gravity.
D. if we were suddenly transported to the exosphere, we'd feel cold.

By the 19th century, it was well established in the scientific community that the Earth had once been a molten ball that cooled over time. The prominent physicist Lord Kelvin, assuming that the Earth had cooled uniformly at a constant rate and that there were no other sources of heat for the developing planet, used thermodynamics to estimate that the Earth was between 20 million and 400 million years old. However, later scientists argued that radioactive isotopes can generate heat and affect cooling rates. In the early 20th century, Arthur Holmes measured radioactive decay in rocks to show that the Earth was actually around 4.5 billion years old, an age more than 10 times greater than Kelvin's estimate. This implies that _____

6

Which choice most logically completes the text?

A. radioactive rocks on Earth are older than the Earth itself.
B. Lord Kelvin's estimate was inaccurate because it was based on faulty assumptions.
C. 19th century scientists were incorrect to believe that the Earth had once been a molten ball that cooled over time.
D. radioactive decay affects cooling rates differently on Earth than on other planets.

Reading: Evidence and Logical Reasoning

Practice Set 2: Medium-Hard

In a 2017 experiment, researchers synthesized a nanozyme (a nanoparticle made of cerium oxide) that could both detect and attack pollutants in water. The nanozyme targeted a common pollutant called bisphenol A, known as BPA. Within 30 minutes of exposure to the nanozyme, over 90% of the BPA was degraded; other materials, such as activated carbon and zeolites, were significantly less effective in removing BPA. In addition, the nanozyme was able to detect low concentrations of BPA in water, suggesting that _____

1

Which choice most logically completes the text?

A. nanozymes could be useful not only for the destruction of pollutants but for monitoring water quality as well.
B. BPA is particularly susceptible to short-term cerium oxide exposure.
C. zeolites are more effective at degrading pollutants in water than is activated carbon.
D. activated carbon required more than 30 minutes to detect low BPA concentrations.

Most people expect our national institutions to stand as exemplars for their local corollaries, displaying the acme of aesthetic and scientific achievement. Without the highest levels of funding, however, national institutions will not be able to outperform more localized institutions. Our national zoo, for instance, is continually hampered by real estate and financial constraints and therefore houses many animals in uncomfortably small concrete cages that in no way represent the highest modern zoological standards. It is obvious, then, that _____

2

Which choice most logically completes the text?

A. some of the people who visit the national zoo will be disappointed in the level of care of the habitats.
B. most of the animals in the national zoo are housed in habitats that reflect the current level of zoological habitat standards.
C. the national zoo should raise its standards of habitat development for all of its animals.
D. local zoos enjoy an unfair funding advantage that enables them to outperform the national zoo.

Bacterial species, though unicellular, exist in the natural world as part of a community of other bacterial cells. The individual cells maintain a type of communication with each other by emitting specific chemicals and detecting those emitted by others, a system known as quorum sensing. It is well established that this system affects the production of rhamnolipids, substances that are beneficial for the group as a whole, when the community reaches a certain size: quorum sensing enables the bacteria to determine whether rhamnolipids should be produced (and how many) based on the size of the local bacterial population. Researcher Kerry Boyle and colleagues have found that limiting the amounts of carbon, nitrogen, and iron present in the environment also affects the production of rhamnolipids, suggesting that _____

3

Which choice most logically completes the text?

A. in addition to quorum sensing, an additional system for bacterial communication must exist.
B. bacteria may use quorum sensing to integrate information about resource availability as well as population size.
C. resource availability plays a larger role in rhamnolipid production than does the size of the bacterial population.
D. all three resources are required to be present in sufficient quantities before any production of rhamnolipids can occur.

- 116 -

TM and © 2023 PrepMatters, Inc. All rights reserved.

For centuries, a minority of scholars have argued that William Shakespeare was not the true author of all the works for which he is famous. Due to his relatively humble circumstances, he would have had little direct knowledge with the courtly setting of many of his plays, unlike contemporaries Christopher Marlowe and Francis Bacon. There are stylistic similarities between the work of these writers and the plays attributed to Shakespeare, as well as historical evidence establishing their connections to the theater world. Nonetheless, the fact that Marlowe and Bacon were so widely known may support the theory of Shakespeare's sole authorship: _____

4

Which choice most logically completes the text?

A. a personal familiarity with courtly life is no substitute for a gifted and creative mind.
B. there is no reason to think that Marlowe or Bacon were attempting to copy Shakespeare's style.
C. the similarities could merely be evidence that Shakespeare's writing style was influenced by that of the popular writers of his day.
D. neither one was more qualified than the other to write the Shakespearean sonnets alone.

There has been an undeniable increase in the number of reported cases of autism spectrum disorder (ASD) over the past few decades. In a 2018 study, Santhosh Girirajan and colleagues analyzed the genetic data of over 15,000 individuals with ASD and their family members, as well as a control group of over 10,000 individuals without ASD. The study found that the genetic factors underlying ASD are highly diverse and complex, with multiple mutations and variants contributing to the disorder. The researchers also found that changes in diagnostic criteria have only had a minor effect on the observed increase in ASD cases, and that other factors, such as increased awareness and reporting, are likely more important contributors to the increase. The study did note, however, that changes in diagnostic criteria may have led to an over-representation of individuals with certain genetic mutations in ASD cohorts used in other studies, which suggests that _____

5

Which choice most logically completes the text?

A. these studies may over-estimate the contribution of genetic mutations to ASD.
B. the apparent increase in ASD cases does not necessarily mean that the actual prevalence of the disorder has increased.
C. ASD is caused in greater part by environmental factors than by genetic factors.
D. greater societal awareness of ASD is a more likely explanation for the increase in reported cases than is a change in the way the disorder is defined.

Reading: Evidence and Logical Reasoning

Penguins' ability to survive in some of the coldest climates of the planet is thanks in part to a cluster of arteries and veins pressed against the flipper bone, or humerus. Especially important during long swims in icy waters, the humeral arterial plexus acts both to cool the blood leaving the heart and to warm the blood returning from the flipper tip, helping the penguin to _____

6

Which choice most logically completes the text?

A. maintain a stable body temperature by limiting heat loss through the flippers.
B. avoid the risk of overheating due to exertion.
C. increase its speed through the water.
D. enhance its survival chances during long winter nights on land.

What drove the evolution of bones and teeth? Traditionally, scientists believed that when early vertebrates first evolved their bony scales (a type of external skeleton) about 420 million years ago, they did so purely as a defense mechanism. According to this view, vertebrates did not become predators until the first jawed vertebrates appeared about 20 million years later. But the study of conodonts, a group of extinct marine animals that lived more than 500 million years ago, has altered this picture. Conodont remains show evidence of bony tooth-like structures in the mouth that were likely used to grasp and shred prey, which may have driven other feeding adaptations. This suggests that _____

7

Which choice most logically completes the text?

A. teeth could serve a predatory function in jawed vertebrates.
B. conodonts had no need for protection from either vertebrate or invertebrate predators.
C. the evolution of the vertebrate skeleton may have been driven in part by the need to adapt to different ecological niches.
D. an increase in predatory efficiency may have been one driver in the evolution of bones and/or teeth.

When two neutron stars collide, the result is a rare astronomical event called a kilonova. This causes a huge release of energy in the form of gravitational waves and a burst of electromagnetic radiation, including visible light, X-rays, and gamma rays. After the impact, both the gravitational waves and the electromagnetic radiation begin traveling away from the site at the speed of light, but some of the electromagnetic radiation is absorbed or scattered by dust and gas as it travels, slowing its progress. In August 2017, scientists detected gravitational waves from the collision of two neutron stars 130 million light-years away, and several hours later, a bright burst of light appeared. This suggests that _____

8

Which choice most logically completes the text?

A. any X-rays or gamma rays produced by the collision arrived several hours later than the burst of light.
B. the rate of travel of a gravitational wave is less affected by intervening matter than is the rate of travel of electromagnetic radiation.
C. the burst of electromagnetic radiation was generated several hours later than the gravitational waves.
D. if the collision had occurred less than 130 million light-years away, the burst of light would have preceded or coincided with the gravitational waves.

Writing: Standard English Conventions

These questions are about the mechanics of writing. Think of yourself as an editor reviewing someone else's work: are the commas in the right place? Does the verb agree with the subject? Does the sentence make sense? A mastery of the basic principles of standard English grammar and punctuation will be key here.

Strategy in Brief

Learn the rules.	The trickiest part about these questions is that the correct answers don't always "sound" right because they're not the way most people speak on a daily basis, or even necessarily the way they write in informal situations. Remember that this is a test of formal written English, so the answers must be technically correct according to the grammar books.
Shorter is better.	The SAT loves concise, clean writing. When in doubt, the choice with the fewest words is most likely to be right.
Trust your ear.	As long as the sentence isn't violating a rule of grammar or punctuation, the one that sounds best is most likely to be correct. The test rewards your ability to identify good order, coherence, and unity within passages.
Read carefully.	Read the sentence slowly to look for any errors, and be sure you're reading the sentence exactly as it appears on the screen (some of these sentences are so bad that our eye will "correct" them for us without our even noticing).
Re-read.	Always take the time to reread the sentence in context with your choice plugged in so that you can make sure it works. ***Be careful not to select an answer choice that fixes one error but creates a different one.***

Writing: Standard English Conventions

Sentence Structure

Preview Quiz

Fill in your answer:

1) What is the difference between a "clause" and a "phrase"?

2) What is an "independent clause"?

Correct the sentence fragments below.

3) Many students who use computers.

   _____

4) The doctor from Glasgow eating his breakfast.

   _____

5) Freddie broken a glass.

   _____

Choose the best answer.

6) Taking visual and thematic inspiration from classic film noir, director Ridley Scott—previously best known for the science fiction horror movie "Alien"—repurposed and updated the dark cityscapes of the 1930s genre _____ a grim vision of future Los Angeles perfect for 1982's dystopian "Blade Runner."

   A) in his creating of
   B) was the creator of
   C) to create
   D) created

A **clause** is a string of words that contains both a subject and a verb. Some clauses, known as **independent clauses**, can stand alone as complete sentences:

George walks.
I like fish.

Other clauses (**dependent clauses**) cannot stand alone as complete sentences:

Although I like fish...

While a clause has both a subject and a verb, a **phrase** lacks one or both of those components:

...along with liking fish...

In the punctuation sections coming up, we'll see a lot more about how to connect dependent clauses or phrases to independent clauses, as well as how to link more than one independent clause in the same sentence. But in order for any of that to make sense, you've got to be clear on how to decide whether a particular string of words can stand alone as a sentence or not. So let's jump into sentence structure with a review of some basics.

Writing: Standard English Conventions

Verbs are words that express some kind of action: *talk*, *jump*, *sit*, and *explode* are all examples of verbs. However, not all actions are physical: *think*, *love, own,* and *recognize* are verbs as well. And note that for some verbs, the action expressed is merely that of existing, as in *is, seem,* or *become*.

To identify the **subject** of a verb, consider who or what is doing the action expressed by the verb.

    Example: George walks.
                          subject verb

    Example: The band rocked.
                          subject   verb

Every valid sentence contains a subject and a verb. Some verbs also require an **object**, which is the person/thing *receiving* the action of the verb.

    Example: Everyone likes chocolate.
                          subject   verb   object

We can use other types of words to add bells and whistles to a sentence. **Adjectives**, **adverbs**, and many kinds of **phrases** can modify and describe the various parts of the sentence.

    Example: Everyone in my family really likes Belgian chocolate.
                         subject   verb   object

In this sentence, "in my family" is a prepositional phrase modifying *Everyone,* the word "really" is an adverb modifying *likes,* and "Belgian" is an adjective modifying *chocolate*.

Sentence Structure

If the same subject is performing more than one action, we can connect the verbs with an "and."

Example: Beverly [walked] into the room and [sat] behind her desk.
         subject verb   verb

In a sentence like this, it's important to maintain **parallel structure**: the verbs must match each other. For example, this sentence would be incorrect if we replaced "sat" with "sitting" or "sits."

Try It   Correct each of the following sentences.

1) She enjoys studying vocabulary, solving geometry problems, and to diagram sentences.

   _____
   _____

2) Beverly decided to take a risk and opening her own business.

   _____
   _____

3) Before the start of the July 4th barbecue, the food had been laid out by Javier, the drinks chilled by Sue Ellen, and Barbara lit the grill.

   _____
   _____

Writing: Standard English Conventions

To analyze whether or not a particular answer choice is a valid sentence, start by finding the **main verb**. But be careful! Verbs located inside a modifying phrase, such as a phrase starting with "who," "which," or "that," can never be the main verb of the sentence. These phrases are just the bells and whistles; they're not giving us an actual action. If the only verb you can find is locked into one of those phrases, then we have a **sentence fragment**, not a valid sentence. See how in the examples below, the incorrect versions still seem to be leading up to something?

    Incorrect: `The contribution that she made.`

    Correct: The contribution that she made [was] enormous.
                         subject   verb

-or-

    Correct: Our family greatly [appreciated] the contribution that she made.
                   subject   verb   object

    Incorrect: `Many students who use computers.`

    Correct: Many students [use] computers.
                       subject verb   object

-or-

    Correct: Many students who use computers [shop] at Mike's Electronics.
                            subject   verb

If we find a verb that's not locked into one of those phrases, we next need to check what **form** it's in. The *–ing* form can be tricky, because these words can act as nouns or adjectives as well as verbs.

    Example: Laughing [is] the best exercise.
                   subject verb   object

    Example: The laughing child [ran] down the street.
                   adj.   subj. verb

    Example: The three of us [were laughing] for hours.
                 subject   verb

Notice that when the *–ing* form is acting as a verb, it must be preceded by some version of the verb "to be" (*is laughing, was laughing, has been laughing*, etc).

If the only verb you can find in the answer choice is an *-ing* form alone, you have a sentence fragment. Look to fix it either by

- adding one of the "to be" words (*is*, *was*, etc.) before the *-ing* verb, or
- changing the *-ing* verb to a more active form (e.g., by changing "laughing" to "laughed.")

    Incorrect: `The doctor from Glasgow eating his breakfast.`

    Correct: <u>The doctor</u> from Glasgow [is eating] <u>his breakfast</u>.
                    subject   verb   object

-or-

    Correct: <u>The doctor</u> from Glasgow [eats] <u>his breakfast</u>.
                    subject   verb   object

Try It   Turn the following sentence fragments into complete sentences.

    4) Eduardo making the bed.   _____

    5) The dogs rolling in the mud. _____

    6) Considering my options.   _____

Another verb form that can fool us is the **past participle**, which is the second word in many two-word verb tenses (for example, in the tense "has broken," the past participle is the word "broken"). Like the *-ing* form, a past participle needs an additional word before it in order to act as a verb.

    Incorrect: `Freddie broken a glass.`

    Correct: <u>Freddie</u> [has broken] <u>a glass</u>.
                  subject   verb   object

-or-

    Correct: <u>Freddie</u> [broke] <u>a glass</u>.
                  subject   verb   object

> **TIP:**
> The past participle can also be used with the "to be" words, as in "A glass was broken."

Try It   Turn the following sentence fragments into complete sentences.

    7) We all seen it happen.   _____

    8) The weather been warm. _____

    9) It begun raining.   _____

Of course, the sentences we've seen so far are shorter and simpler than the ones you'll see on the SAT. But the process is still the same. Let's practice taking apart a longer, more complicated sentence to identify the right word for the blank.

> *Taking visual and thematic inspiration from classic film noir, director Ridley Scott—previously best known for the science fiction horror movie "Alien"—repurposed and updated the dark cityscapes of the 1930s genre _____ a grim vision of future Los Angeles perfect for 1982's dystopian "Blade Runner."*

- A) in his creating of
- B) was the creator of
- C) to create
- D) created

To start, we'll try to find the main verb in the original sentence, and then we'll identify its subject. What action words do you see?

> [Taking] both visual and thematic inspiration from classic film noir, director Ridley Scott—previously best [known] for the science fiction horror movie "Alien"—[repurposed] and [updated] the dark cityscapes of the 1930s genre _____ a grim vision of future Los Angeles perfect for 1982's dystopian "Blade Runner."

Well, *taking* is an *–ing* form without one of the "is"-type words before it, so it's not really a verb. The whole opening portion of this sentence (up to the comma) is just an introductory phrase. Similarly, *known* is a past participle without one of the "has"-type words before it, so it's not really a verb either. In this sentence, the entire portion that's set off by dashes is just a phrase modifying *director Ridley Scott*.

Let's try making the sentence simpler by cutting out the two modifying phrases we've identified so far.

> Director Ridley Scott [repurposed] and [updated] the dark cityscapes of the 1930s genre _____ a grim vision of future Los Angeles perfect for 1982's dystopian "Blade Runner."

Now this is starting to make more sense. The words *repurposed* and *updated* are the main verbs. And *Director Ridley Scott* is doing the action of those verbs, so that's the subject.

Next, try plugging the choices in one at a time. Choices B and D would give us another main verb, meaning we'd need an additional "and" to join it with the two verbs we've got so far. Choices A and C turn the whole last section of the sentence into a phrase, one that makes perfect sense in the sentence. But choice A is awkward and much too wordy for what we need, so the correct answer is **C**.

> *TIP:*
>
> Cutting out the modifying phrases is a great way to simplify a sentence to make it easier to analyze the structure.

Try It Turn the following sentence fragments into complete sentences.

10) The two students born in a distant country immigrating to the United States ten years ago.

11) The teacher, who brought 30 years of experience to the classroom, retiring in the spring.

12) Having lived and worked in Los Angeles for many years, unaccustomed to the lifestyle of the countryside.

13) Many critics that would have to admit that they misjudged the artist, having overlooked his important talents.

14) The author, known for his intricate plots, which often involve detailed knowledge of actual historical events.

15) Focusing intently on the details of the experiment right in front of her, the young chemist who didn't notice that anything was wrong with the one set up by her colleague on the other side of the room until the slowly accumulating smoke suddenly set off a blaring fire alarm.

Writing: Standard English Conventions

Chapter Answer Key

Try It

1) She enjoys studying vocabulary, solving geometry problems, and **diagramming** sentences.

2) Beverly decided to take a risk and **open** her own business.

3) Before the start of the July 4th barbecue, the food had been laid out by Javier, the drinks chilled by Sue Ellen, and **the grill lit by Barbara.**

In exercises 4 through 9, more than one valid sentence can be created. Here are some possible answers.

4) Eduardo **makes** the bed   Eduardo **is making** the bed.

5) The dogs **rolled** in the mud.   The dogs **were rolling** in the mud.

6) **I am considering** my options.   I **considered** my options.

7) We all **saw** it happen.   We **have** all **seen** it happen.

8) The weather **has been** warm.   The weather **is** warm.

9) It **began** raining.   It **has begun** raining.

10) The two students born in a distant country **immigrated** to the United States ten years ago.

11) The teacher, who brought 30 years of experience to the classroom, **will be retiring** in the spring.

12) Having lived and worked in Los Angeles for many years, **I was** unaccustomed to the lifestyle of the countryside.

13) Many critics ~~that~~ would have to admit that they misjudged the artist, having overlooked his important talents.

14) The author **is** known for his intricate plots, which often involve detailed knowledge of actual historical events.

15) Focusing intently on the details of the experiment right in front of her, the young chemist ~~who~~ didn't notice that anything was wrong with the one set up by her colleague on the other side of the room until the slowly accumulating smoke suddenly set off a blaring fire alarm.

Sentence Structure

Practice Set 1: Easy-Medium

Each generation seems to have its share of famous kidnappings, from Charles Lindbergh's baby in 1932 to Elizabeth Smart in 2002. However, despite the media attention directed at these high-profile cases, studies _____ the incidence of child abduction in the United States is extremely low.

1

Which choice completes the text so that it conforms to the conventions of Standard English?

A. indicating that
B. that indicate
C. having indicated
D. indicate that

The Venus Flytrap's leaves have modified lobes with sensitive trigger hairs. When an insect touches the hairs, the leaves snap _____ the prey and providing the plant with a unique mechanism for supplementing its nutrient intake.

2

Which choice completes the text so that it conforms to the conventions of Standard English?

A. shut. To trap
B. shut. Thus trapping
C. shut, trapping
D. shut. Trapping

Is video gaming a negative influence on children and on society as a whole? The popularity of this sentiment has led many parents to severely curtail their kids' "screen time," but in doing so, they may have overlooked some potential benefits of the habit. _____ games foster technological literacy and hand-eye coordination, according to their proponents.

3

Which choice completes the text so that it conforms to the conventions of Standard English?

A. Since video
B. While video
C. Because video
D. Video

In 1982, Eastside High School in Paterson, New Jersey was a low-performing school in a high-crime area. Principal Joe _____ an unconventional approach to turn the school around, combining strict disciplinary policies and a no-nonsense attitude with increased academic support for struggling students.

4

Which choice completes the text so that it conforms to the conventions of Standard English?

A. Clark, who used
B. Clark, which used
C. Clark with
D. Clark used

Writing: Standard English Conventions

A community organization in tiny Beetle, California recently garnered a lot of attention for its grassroots effort to oust the deputy mayor after his controversial statements went viral. The group posted a petition online and blanketed social media with their requests for support. However, with fewer than 100 signatures as of today, one week from the _____ unlikely to succeed.

5

Which choice completes the text so that it conforms to the conventions of Standard English?

A. deadline. Making the petition seem
B. deadline; the petition seeming
C. deadline. The petition seems
D. deadline, the petition seems

Compared to Robusta coffee beans, Arabica beans generally have a lower caffeine content and a milder, smoother taste. The cultivation of Arabica _____ specific conditions, including higher altitudes, adequate rainfall, and well-drained soil.

6

Which choice completes the text so that it conforms to the conventions of Standard English?

A. coffee often requiring
B. coffee often requires
C. coffee requiring
D. coffee, which often requires

The Great Pyramids of Egypt were primarily built using limestone blocks, which were quarried and transported from nearby locations. Workers would level the terrain, lay out the foundation, and finally, under the watchful eye of the project overseer, _____ the pyramid's core using large, precisely cut stones. The outer casing stones were then added to create a smooth, polished surface.

7

Which choice completes the text so that it conforms to the conventions of Standard English?

A. they would construct
B. constructing
C. construct
D. constructed

Populations in Brunei, Indonesia, and Malaysia _____ durian, a tropical fruit known for its pungent odor, for hundreds of years. The fruit is rich in nutrients including vitamins B and C, and is believed to have a range of health benefits, such as reducing inflammation, aiding digestion, and promoting healthy skin.

8

Which choice completes the text so that it conforms to the conventions of Standard English?

A. have cultivated
B. to cultivate
C. having cultivated
D. cultivating

Practice Set 2: Medium-Hard

At Northwestern University, Dr. Chad Mirkin has been at the forefront of developing innovative nanoscale materials and technologies with a wide range of applications. Seemingly every day, _____ the science of nanotechnology.

1

Which choice completes the text so that it conforms to the conventions of Standard English?

A. as his team makes a new discovery that further advances
B. his team makes a new discovery that further advances
C. making a new discovery and further advancing
D. making a new discovery to further advance

To convince the town council of the wisdom of permitting the installation of a new parking garage, the businessman described the aesthetic benefits of moving parked cars indoors, _____ that no new taxes would need to be levied in order for the structure to be built.

2

Which choice completes the text so that it conforms to the conventions of Standard English?

A. details how the structure would be paid for, and indicated
B. detailing how the structure would be paid for, and indicating
C. detailed how the structure would be paid for, and indicated
D. he detailed how the structure would be paid for, and indicating

Louisa May _____ years crafting her stories and developing her skills as a writer only to face repeated rejection and discouragement from the male-dominated publishing industry of 19th century America. Despite these obstacles, she eventually succeeded in bringing *Little Women* to print and became one of the most celebrated authors of her era.

3

Which choice completes the text so that it conforms to the conventions of Standard English?

A. Alcott, who spent
B. Alcott, having spent
C. Alcott spent
D. Alcott will be spending

Corvids, the avian family that includes crows, jays, and ravens, have excellent reasoning skills. A study at the University Cambridge comparing corvids' puzzle-solving ability to that of human children demonstrated that corvids can analyze a difficult _____ still displaying a calm demeanor at all times.

4

Which choice completes the text so that it conforms to the conventions of Standard English?

A. problem, devise a unique solution, while
B. problem and devise a unique solution while
C. problem, devising a unique solution, and
D. problem, devise a unique solution, meanwhile

Commas

Preview Quiz

Add commas where necessary. (Some sentences are fine the way they are.)

1) The girl who won the state spelling bee lives next door to me.

2) Louise who studied engineering at MIT designed the city's largest bridge.

3) George described the process as "a miracle of modern science."

4) The truth however is that I never liked snowboarding.

5) The movies that I want to see are Spanish.

6) Noted physicist Albert Einstein sold my uncle this car.

7) Loretta always wanted to be on TV so she was thrilled when she heard about auditions for a new reality show.

8) The heavy ugly coat kept me extremely warm throughout the winter.

9) John looked around him and checked for spiders.

There are really only **three basic functions** that commas can serve in a sentence. Once you've mastered those, comma questions on the SAT become a lot easier.

1. **Setting off unnecessary information**

   Mark off unnecessary ("parenthetical") information with commas. Consider the differences between the two sentences below.

   > The girl <u>who won the state spelling bee</u> lives next door to me.

   > Louise, <u>who studied engineering at MIT</u>, designed the city's largest bridge.

   In the first sentence, the phrase in the middle is **necessary**: we need the information in the phrase to identify which girl we're talking about. In the second sentence, however, we'd know who we were talking about ("Louise") even without the phrase; the phrase gives us extra information, not something crucial to our understanding.

   Unnecessary information can be an entire phrase or a single word, and it can appear anywhere in the sentence:

   > <u>Sleeping soundly in his bed</u>, Justin never heard Santa coming down the chimney.

   > Every time I see that girl, <u>the one with the red hair</u>, she smiles at me.

   > The father addressed the search party, <u>his emotions etched on his face</u>.

   > The truth, <u>however</u>, is that I never liked snowboarding.

TIP:
Remember, when you **DON'T** need the information, you **DO** need the commas.

   In each of these sentences, we could lift out the underlined portion without changing the meaning of the sentence. That's how we know to use commas there.

   CHALLENGE:

   Sometimes the number of items determines whether or not the information is necessary.

   > *My friend Jake told me a great joke the other day.*

   > *My youngest sister, Kate, is attending medical school.*

   In the first sentence, the name "Jake" is necessary information because it identifies *which* of the speaker's friends told a great joke. In the second sentence, however, the name is unnecessary—a person can only have one *youngest* sister, so we don't need the name to figure out who we're talking about.

Writing: Standard English Conventions

Phrases that start with "that" are always necessary to the sentence, while phrases that start with "which" are always unnecessary. So, **"which" phrases always take commas; "that" phrases never take commas.**

Those movies, <u>which are all Spanish</u>, are my brother's favorites.

The movies <u>that I want to see</u> are Spanish.

You can sometimes use this rule even on phrases that don't use a "that" or a "which." If you can insert the word "that" at the beginning of the phrase and the sentence makes sense, don't use a comma.

Dad always said you have to spend money to make money.

In this sentence, there's an unspoken "that." After all, we could have written it as "Dad always said *that* you have to spend money to make money." Therefore, we can treat that whole section of the sentence as a "that" phrase: no commas.

CHALLENGE:

You don't always need a comma before a quotation.

George said, "The process is a miracle of modern science."

"The process is a miracle of modern science," said George.

George described the process as "a miracle of modern science."

When we set off a quote separately from the structure of the sentence with a phrase such as "he said" (as in the first two examples here), we mark that barrier with a comma. However, when the quote is incorporated into the grammar of the sentence (as in the third example), no commas are used.

Try It   Add commas where necessary.

1) The books that I wanted to buy were expensive.
2) My favorite tennis player is Roger Federer who won Wimbledon this year.
3) Although I really like chocolate ice cream vanilla is my favorite.
4) Because Maria enjoyed both writing and photography she decided to join the school's newspaper staff.
5) Joanne an expert in medieval architecture told us that the castle was built in the 1300s.
6) Nobody suspected that the quiet computer salesman was actually an accomplished sword swallower.
7) On the other hand avocados are high in healthful fatty acids.
8) I enjoy the challenge of learning a new language.
9) Dr. Phillips the best-known pediatrician in Chicago received an award from the governor last year.
10) After high school she attended a culinary academy in Paris led by the great chef Victor Richambaud.

TIP:

A clause that can stand alone as a sentence is **never** unnecessary information.

    Incorrect: `Many dog breeds can be mixed, a Chihuahua and an Irish Wolfhound would be a bad combination.`

Neither side of this sentence can be considered unnecessary information, because each side is an independent clause: that is, each side forms a complete sentence on its own. This is called a **comma splice**, and it is always wrong.

To fix it, we could change the punctuation:

    Correct: Many dog breeds can be mixed; a Chihuahua and an Irish Wolfhound would be a bad combination.

Or we could keep the comma but alter one of the clauses so that it can no longer stand on its own:

    Correct: *Although* many dog breeds can be mixed, a Chihuahua and an Irish Wolfhound would be a bad combination.

Or we could simply add one of the FANBOYS after the comma, as we'll see in the next section.

    Correct: Many dog breeds can be mixed, *but* a Chihuahua and an Irish Wolfhound would be a bad combination.

CHALLENGE:

When there are a few words before or after someone's name that tell us that person's occupation and/or place of origin (e.g., "Guatemalan author María Sanchez"), you can think of that entire description as a job title. To punctuate it correctly, there are two simple rules to keep in mind.

If the job title comes before the name, the job title is *never* unnecessary information. So there are really only two possibilities for this kind of sentence: either the *name* is unnecessary information, or nothing is. To check these sentences, lift out the name and see whether you still have a valid sentence.

Correct: The college's new provost, Marcel Ridley, will be arriving on Tuesday.

Try it without the name: "The college's new provost will be arriving on Tuesday." That's a valid sentence, so the name is unnecessary information. Therefore, we set it off with commas.

Correct: Noted physicist Albert Einstein sold my uncle this car.

Take out the name this time and we have this: "Noted physicist sold my uncle this car." That's not a valid sentence, so no commas.

However! The above only applies when the job title comes before the name. **If the name comes first**, then the job title *can* be unnecessary information.

Correct: Albert Einstein, the noted physicist, sold my uncle this car.

Try It — Add commas where necessary.

11) Austrian mathematician Hannah Berg is scheduled to speak next.

12) The evening's top award went to Sally Martinez inventor of the Flybock maneuver.

13) My favorite English teacher Manny Kozlowski just published his first novel.

14) The study was conducted by renowned botanist Frederick Chang.

15) Chad Smith the drummer for the Red Hot Chili Peppers bears a striking resemblance to comedian Will Ferrell.

2. **Comma + FANBOYS = Period**

When a comma is paired with one of the coordinating conjunctions, also known as the "FANBOYS" (*for, and, nor, but, or, yet, so*), it acts just like a period: it separates two clauses that could each stand alone as a sentence.

> *Loretta always wanted to be on TV, so she was thrilled when she heard about auditions for a new reality show.*
>
> *I tried the restaurant that Lauren had recommended, but I wasn't impressed.*

If two independent clauses are separated by a comma alone (without one of the FANBOYS), the comma is wrong.

> Incorrect: `Loretta always wanted to be on TV, she was thrilled when she heard about auditions for a new reality show.`

If two clauses are separated by the comma-plus-FANBOYS combination and either of the clauses *cannot* stand alone as a sentence, the comma is wrong.

> Incorrect: `Loretta always wanted to be on TV, so was thrilled when she heard about auditions for a new reality show.`

Be on the lookout for words that seem very similar to FANBOYS trying to take their place. Common offenders include *however, therefore, also, furthermore,* and *nevertheless.*

> Incorrect: `I tried the restaurant that Lauren had recommended, however I wasn't impressed.`

TIP:

Sometimes, the right answer choice will correct a sentence in a way that you weren't expecting. You may not have the option to either add FANBOYS or change the punctuation. Instead, one of the clauses that can stand on its own as a sentence may just be rewritten so that it can't stand on its own anymore.

> Incorrect: `He faced many obstacles in his early life, the child went on to become president of the United States.`
>
> Correct: Having faced many obstacles in his early life, the child went on to become president of the United States.

- 137 -

TM and © 2023 PrepMatters, Inc. All rights reserved.

Try It Which version(s) of these sentences is/are correct? **Choose <u>all that apply.</u>**

16) Most new businesses fail in the first _____ the chef has high hopes for his new restaurant.
   A. year, but
   B. year, nevertheless

17) Rowing crew is the perfect _____ it works all the major muscle groups and provides a great cardiovascular workout.
   A. exercise,
   B. exercise because

18) Nancy participated in student government throughout high school, _____ was president her senior year.
   A. and she
   B. she

19) Elizabeth couldn't _____ she knew that Mr. Darcy had captured her heart.
   A. refuse, for
   B. refuse because

20) I might make the trip in the _____ might do it tonight.
   A. morning, on the other hand, I
   B. morning, or I

21) I have tried _____ of the items on the menu.
   A. all but one
   B. all, but one

22) _____ some people still prefer vinyl records.
   A. MP3s offer adequate quality of sound, but
   B. Although MP3s offer adequate quality of sound,

23) _____ was sure that it would run correctly.
   A. She had thoroughly bug-tested the program, so
   B. Having thoroughly bug-tested the program, she

24) Everyone I know loves Mr. _____ is by far the best teacher at my school.
   A. Williams, he
   B. Williams, who

3. Lists

Perhaps the most obvious use of commas is to separate items on a list.

I like apples, pears, and kumquats.

The heavy, ugly coat kept me extremely warm throughout the winter.

Just a few things to watch out for here. If the list consists of only two items and they're joined with an "and," don't use a comma.

Incorrect: `The coat was heavy, and ugly.`

Also, make sure you don't use a comma to *introduce* a list.

Incorrect: `I like, apples, pears, and kumquats.`

TIP:

When list items consist of whole actions or phrases, it's easy to confuse a two-item list joined with an "and" (which doesn't take a comma) with a FANBOYS sentence (which does).

Incorrect: `John looked around him, and checked for spiders.`

Correct: John looked around him and checked for spiders.

CHALLENGE:

When a list of two or more adjectives is used before a noun, see whether the sentence would still make sense if you swapped the order of the adjectives. If they would, you need a comma between them.

Try It — Add commas where necessary.

25) The sweet cold lemonade rushed down my throat.

26) The brochure features several colorful photographs.

27) The large Siamese cat purred happily in the corner.

28) Felicia is a happy witty child.

Try It   Which version(s) of these sentences is/are correct? ***Choose <u>all that apply</u>.***

29) She felt _____ hopeful.

    A. happy, and
    B. happy and

30) Chefs _____ of a new dish are as important as its taste.

    A. assert, that the presentation aroma and mouthfeel
    B. assert that, the presentation aroma and mouthfeel
    C. assert that the presentation, aroma, and mouthfeel

31) The best _____ or me.

    A. man will be Jim, Bobby,
    B. man, will be Jim, Bobby

32) Amy picked up a _____ began to read.

    A. magazine, and
    B. magazine and

33) _____ love hockey.

    A. Elliott, Maria, and the children
    B. Elliott, Maria and the children,

34) The garment's most popular _____

    A. colors include, turquoise, burgundy, and aubergine.
    B. colors include turquoise, burgundy, and aubergine.
    C. colors, include turquoise, burgundy, and aubergine.

35) He developed a taste for the finer _____ racked up a substantial amount of debt.

    A. things and soon
    B. things, and he soon
    C. things, and soon

36) The fascinating _____ remained at the Smithsonian for a month.

    A. exhibit, of prehistoric, hunting tools,
    B. exhibit, of prehistoric hunting tools,
    C. exhibit of prehistoric hunting tools,
    D. exhibit of prehistoric hunting tools

Common Comma Errors

Now that we've seen the three reasons to use a comma, let's take a look at some of the reasons *not* to.

- **Separating subject from verb or verb from object**

    You may have learned that a comma indicates a pause in a sentence. That's true! It's just not very helpful. The problem is that we pause for lots of reasons, and not all of them require a comma. If the only purpose the comma is serving is to allow for a breath of air between a lengthy subject and its verb, or between a verb and its object, that is not a good enough reason for the comma to be there.

    Incorrect: `The only thing I could do, was wait.`

    Incorrect: `The necklace I was sure was lost forever, turned up in the bottom of my purse.`

- **Commas before prepositional phrases** (phrases starting with "of," "in," "at," "with," "between," etc.)

    Commas before prepositions are usually incorrect.

    Incorrect: `The dog sat, in the doorway.`

    Incorrect: `We knew that the entire group, of twenty, would be difficult to seat together.`

    TIP:
    Don't start worrying about whether a prepositional phrase is necessary or unnecessary information. Just remember that as a general rule, you don't want a comma before a preposition.

- **Comma splices**

    A comma splice occurs when a comma is used alone (without one of the FANBOYS) to separate two clauses that could each stand alone as sentences.

    Incorrect: `Amy knows me better than anyone, also she'd never betray a friend.`

    Incorrect: `I really like the new app, it makes budgeting much easier.`

Writing: Standard English Conventions

That's it! Those are the only reasons to ever use a comma. So, when trying to decide whether a particular comma belongs in a sentence, ask yourself what purpose it's serving.

- Is it setting off a phrase of unnecessary information?
- Is it separating two clauses that could be sentences (with one of the FANBOYS)?
- Is it separating items on a list?

If the answer to all three questions is no, the comma is **wrong**.

TIP:
A good rule of thumb is that the choice with the fewest commas is most likely to be right.

TIP:
There are a few other functions for commas in English, but they're so easy that they won't be tested—and if they ever were, the answer would be so obvious that you wouldn't have to worry about asking yourself these questions.

Today is Monday, January 24.

I live in Bethesda, Maryland.

That office belongs to George Banks, Ph.D.

Try It — In the blank, write the letter corresponding to the function that the comma or commas are serving in the sentence. If none apply, cross out the comma.

A: Unnecessary information   B: Comma + FANBOYS = period   C: Lists   X: None

37) Sitting in the next room were two students, their parents, and the principal. _____

38) That puppy, which belongs to my neighbor, loves to dig up my mother's azaleas. _____

39) The apparent chaos, is actually a well-ordered system. _____

40) Unfortunately, the weather was cloudy. _____

41) The books were perfectly arranged, in a row. _____

42) We knew a change was coming, and we weren't sure what to expect. _____

43) James no longer needed, my help. _____

44) Gandhi proved, that violence is not a prerequisite for social change. _____

45) My grandmother does not need a cookbook, for she knows all the recipes by heart. _____

46) Having established the crime's timeline, the detective turned his attention to the question of motive. _____

Chapter Answer Key

Try It

1. (no commas)
2. My favorite tennis player is Roger <u>Federer, who</u> won Wimbledon this year.
3. Although I really like chocolate ice <u>cream, vanilla</u> is my favorite.
4. Because Maria enjoyed both writing and <u>photography, she</u> decided to join the school's newspaper staff.
5. <u>Joanne, an</u> expert in medieval <u>architecture, told</u> us that the castle was built in the 1300s.
6. (no commas)
7. On the other <u>hand, avocados</u> are high in healthful fatty acids.
8. (no commas)
9. Dr. <u>Phillips, the</u> best-known pediatrician in <u>Chicago, received</u> an award from the governor last year.
10. After high <u>school, she</u> attended a culinary academy in Paris led by the great chef Victor Richambaud.
11. (no commas)
12. The evening's top award went to Sally <u>Martinez, inventor</u> of the Flybock maneuver.
13. My favorite English <u>teacher, Manny Kozlowski, just</u> published his first novel.
14. (no commas)
15. Chad <u>Smith, the</u> drummer for the Red Hot Chili <u>Peppers, bears</u> a striking resemblance to comedian Will Ferrell.

16. A
17. B
18. A
19. A and B
20. B
21. A
22. A and B
23. B
24. B

25. The <u>sweet, cold</u> lemonade rushed down my throat.
26. (no commas)
27. (no commas)
28. Felicia is a <u>happy, witty</u> child.

29. B
30. C
31. A
32. B
33. A
34. B
35. A and B
36. D
37. C
38. A
39. X
40. A
41. X
42. B
43. X
44. X
45. B
46. A

Writing: Standard English Conventions

Practice Set 1: Easy-Medium

Computer programs can be designed to search for mathematical proofs automatically, without human intervention. This involves encoding mathematical statements and rules into a logical framework that the computer can _____ manipulate. While this approach has limitations, it has been used successfully to solve some challenging mathematical problems.

1

Which choice completes the text so that it conforms to the conventions of Standard English?

A. both understand, and
B. both, understand, and
C. both understand and
D. both understand and,

When dealing with older manuscripts, many publishers routinely update the spelling and punctuation to conform with modern standards. The "corrected" _____ and understand, is thereby made accessible to a wider audience. But professor Ruth Metlow opposes this practice, arguing the archaic spelling and punctuation can provide valuable insights into the historical context of the manuscript.

2

Which choice completes the text so that it conforms to the conventions of Standard English?

A. version, which is easier, to read
B. version, which is easier to read,
C. version which is easier to read,
D. version, which is easier to read

"Groupthink" is a psychological phenomenon that occurs when a group of individuals prioritize group harmony and consensus over critical thinking and independent decision-making. In a groupthink scenario, members of a group may feel pressure to conform to the majority opinion, _____ opinions or alternative ideas may be suppressed or ignored.

3

Which choice completes the text so that it conforms to the conventions of Standard English?

A. also dissenting
B. and dissenting
C. additionally, dissenting
D. dissenting

Garlic, a flavorful ingredient used in many cuisines around the _____ believed to have numerous health benefits. For example, garlic has been found to help lower total and LDL ("bad") cholesterol levels in the blood, which can reduce the risk of heart disease.

4

Which choice completes the text so that it conforms to the conventions of Standard English?

A. world, is
B. world is
C. world and is
D. world, being

TM and © 2023 PrepMatters, Inc. All rights reserved.

Any restaurateur will tell you that surging to the top of the competitive dining scene is no easy task. Despite the name, _____ actually years in the making.

5

Which choice completes the text so that it conforms to the conventions of Standard English?

A. every "overnight success" is
B. every "overnight success," is
C. every, "overnight success" is
D. every, "overnight success" is,

After months of negotiation between four countries in the region, a new trade partnership was announced. The agreement was instantly _____ protests from all sides of the political spectrum.

6

Which choice completes the text so that it conforms to the conventions of Standard English?

A. controversial, sparking
B. controversial, it sparked
C. controversial with it being the spark of
D. controversial, and sparking

In 1957, Wham-O, a toy company in California, began manufacturing plastic hula hoops and launched a marketing campaign to promote them. At the time, there was a growing interest in physical fitness and dance, and the hula hoop appealed to these trends. Its popularity was further fueled by endorsements from celebrities, including Lucille Ball and Jackie Kennedy. Their participation _____ the most popular toy in America.

7

Which choice completes the text so that it conforms to the conventions of Standard English?

A. helped solidify the hula-hoop's status, as
B. helped solidify, the hula-hoop's status as,
C. helped solidify, the hula-hoop's status as
D. helped solidify the hula-hoop's status as

Elementary education does not offer much freedom of choice. Children attend the classes picked out for them, complete the homework they are assigned, and follow many other one-size-fits-all rules. One exception is lunch: in many school _____ from a variety of options.

8

Which choice completes the text so that it conforms to the conventions of Standard English?

A. cafeterias, students are permitted to select their meals
B. cafeterias, students are permitted to select, their meals
C. cafeterias students are permitted to select their meals,
D. cafeterias, students are permitted to select their meals,

Practice Set 2: Medium-Hard

Stationery manufacturers _____ a variety of methods to generate a pure white color in the final result. One common method is to use bleaching agents, such as chlorine or hydrogen peroxide, which remove the natural color from the wood pulp used to make paper. Another method is to add fluorescent dyes or pigments to the paper. These colorants absorb ultraviolet light and emit a visible blue or violet light, which makes the paper appear brighter and whiter to the human eye.

1

Which choice completes the text so that it conforms to the conventions of Standard English?

A. attempting to produce saleable writing paper, may use
B. attempting to produce saleable writing paper may use
C. attempting, to produce saleable writing paper, may use
D. attempting to produce saleable writing paper, may use,

In her _____ innovative routines that blended traditional African styles with contemporary dance forms. Overton Walker was part of a generation of African-American performers who helped to break down racial barriers in the entertainment industry, paving the way for future generations.

2

Which choice completes the text so that it conforms to the conventions of Standard English?

A. performances Aida Overton Walker, a prominent African-American dancer and choreographer, showcased
B. performances, Aida Overton Walker, a prominent African-American dancer and choreographer, showcased
C. performances, Aida Overton Walker, a prominent African-American dancer and choreographer, showcased,
D. performances Aida Overton Walker a prominent African-American dancer and choreographer showcased

---

Over time, medical consensus on the use of hormone replacement therapy (HRT) in menopausal women has _____ between two opposing positions. In the 1990s, HRT was widely prescribed to help manage symptoms of menopause and prevent osteoporosis. However, in the early 2000s, large-scale studies suggested that HRT could increase the risk of breast cancer. This led to a significant shift in medical consensus, and many women stopped taking HRT. More recent studies have suggested that the risks of HRT may be lower than previously thought, leading some experts to argue that the benefits of HRT may outweigh the risks.

3

Which choice completes the text so that it conforms to the conventions of Standard English?

A. shifted back and forth
B. shifted back, and forth
C. shifted, back and forth
D. shifted back and forth,

Under Armour is a sports equipment and apparel company that is headquartered in Baltimore. The _____ comes from Maryland.

4

Which choice completes the text so that it conforms to the conventions of Standard English?

A. founder and executive chairman, Kevin Plank,
B. founder and executive chairman Kevin Plank,
C. founder, and executive chairman, Kevin Plank
D. founder and executive chairman, Kevin Plank

Typhlodromus mites are tiny predators that feed on the eggs, larvae, and adult stages of plant pests. One _____ is that the mites are highly specific in their feeding habits, targeting only certain types of pests and leaving beneficial insects unharmed.

5

Which choice completes the text so that it conforms to the conventions of Standard English?

A. advantage of using the *Typhlodromus* mite as a biological control agent
B. advantage, of using the *Typhlodromus* mite as a biological control agent
C. advantage, of using the *Typhlodromus* mite as a biological control agent,
D. advantage of using the *Typhlodromus* mite as a biological control agent,

Though information is safer when saved to the _____ security threats still exist. Cloud storage providers can be targeted by hackers, resulting in the exposure of sensitive data from thousands of users.

6

Which choice completes the text so that it conforms to the conventions of Standard English?

A. cloud, than it would be sitting in a physical file cabinet
B. cloud, than it would be sitting, in a physical file cabinet,
C. cloud than it would be sitting in a physical file cabinet,
D. cloud, than it would be sitting in a physical file cabinet,

Antilock brakes (ABS) are designed to help prevent skidding during hard braking. When a wheel begins to slow down more rapidly than the _____ that it may be about to lock up, the ABS system momentarily reduces the brake pressure to that wheel. This allows the wheel to continue rotating and maintain traction with the road, which can help the driver maintain control of the vehicle.

7

Which choice completes the text so that it conforms to the conventions of Standard English?

A. others, this indicates
B. others, indicating
C. others and indicating
D. others, the system indicates

Semicolons, Colons, Dashes, and Apostrophes

Preview Quiz

Choose the best punctuation.

1) The weather was terrible (, / ;) it rained all day.

2) I have traveled to Paris (, / ;) France (, / ;) Ireland (, / ;) where my mother was born (, / ;) and Japan.

3) The governor promised not to raise taxes (, / ;) however (, / ;) economists say some increases will be necessary.

4) Professor Westing's midterms are notoriously difficult. I'm not worried (, / ;) however (, / ;) my study group has come up with a solid review process that should put me in a great position to ace the exam.

5) Joe is scared of many things (, / ; / :) including getting attacked by lions, falling into swimming pools, and being buried alive.

6) There's only one thing that scares Joe (, / ; / :) lions.

7) Certain musical genres (; / : / —) classical and electronic, for instance (; / : / —) are often classified as "art music."

Fill in the best answer.

8) What is the difference between *its* and *it's*?

9) What is the difference between *your* and *you're*?

Add apostrophes where necessary. Some sentences may be fine the way they are.

10) Thelmas car was sitting in her sons driveway until the neighbors daughters husband moved it.

11) The girls cars were much cleaner than the boys cars.

12) The womens coalition also fought for childrens rights.

13) I dont think its wise to tell Gerry that he shouldnt play tennis.

14) The Morgans and the Stanleys meet for dinner on Tuesdays.

15) Both girls dresses are beautiful.

Semicolons, Colons, Dashes, and Apostrophes

Semicolons

The semicolon, like the comma-plus-FANBOYS combination, separates two clauses that each could stand on its own as a sentence. So:

Semicolon = period

> Incorrect: The weather was terrible; raining all day.
>
> Correct: The weather was terrible; it rained all day.

TIP:
If you can replace a semicolon in a sentence with a period, the semicolon is correct.

Semicolons do *not* need FANBOYS, so watch out for sentences that insert FANBOYS after a semicolon for no reason.

> Incorrect: The weather was terrible; for it rained all day.

CHALLENGE:

A secondary use for semicolons is to separate items on a complicated list (a list in which some or all of the list items themselves contain commas).

> Incorrect: I have traveled to Paris, France, Ireland, where my mother was born, and Japan.

The commas make it look like this person has traveled to five distinct places: the first is Paris, the second is France, the third is Ireland, the fourth is where their mother was born, and the fifth is Japan. Use semicolons to make it easier to find the divisions between the list items.

> Correct: I have traveled to Paris, France; Ireland, where my mother was born; and Japan.

Try It   Choose the correct punctuation.

1) My favorite team is the Red Sox (, / ;) even though they disappoint me every year.

2) Theodore Roosevelt was the youngest president in U.S. history (, / ;) he was 41 when he took office.

3) Jim's parents completely approved of his decision (, / ;) and this approval allowed him to pursue his goal.

4) Mr. Wilson's tests are (, / ;) according to many students (, / ;) quite challenging (, / ;) they also tend to be extremely time-consuming.

5) I thought that the weather would be cloudy (, / ;) however (, / ;) I was wrong.

- 149 -

Writing: Standard English Conventions

Why do we sometimes surround transitions like "however" with two commas, while at other times we need to use a semicolon and a comma?

The difference lies in **how many sentences you have** when you take the transition word/phrase out. If there's just one, use two commas. If there are two, use a semicolon (or colon, period, etc.) and a comma.

Example 1: The bearded dragon, however, is an expert climber.

Here, without the "however," we just have a single sentence: "The bearded dragon is an expert climber." So we can regard the "however" as unnecessary information and mark it off with a pair of commas.

Example 2: The governor promised not to raise taxes; however, economists say some increases will be necessary.

This time there are two sentences: "The governor promised not to raise taxes" and "Economists say some increases will be necessary." So, we use a semicolon to separate them. The comma after the "however" is there because the "however" is now unnecessary information in the second sentence.

Try It   Choose the correct punctuation.

6) The restaurant's food has been widely praised (, / ;) for example (, / ;) the *Tribune* called its poached salmon dish "a triumph."

7) Woodworking (, / ;) in conclusion (, / ;) is a rewarding hobby for senior citizens and younger people alike.

8) Belinda does well in all her classes (, / ;) however (, / ;) unlike her older brother.

9) Patrick is a talented musician (, / ;) moreover (, / ;) he's a skilled painter as well.

CHALLENGE:

We've already seen that the word "however" might have commas around it, or it might have a semicolon before it and a comma after it. But is it ever the other way around? Can we have a comma before the "however" and a semicolon after it?

Yes. We still need two independent clauses to make the semicolon work. In these sentences, though, the "however" is not contrasting the first half of the sentence from the second half of the sentence; it's contrasting the entire sentence from something that came before it.

Example: *Professor Westing's midterms are notoriously difficult. I'm not worried, however; my study group has come up with a solid review process that should put me in a great position to ace the exam.*

FROM THE BLOG

We love and crave the feeling of success, but the benefits are often distant and unknown, while the costs are near and certain. Many of us, for example, have had to weigh the benefits of eating a donut against making minute progress on our path to physical wellness. This is hardly a fair fight. (A donut!? Please!) We may get a different result, though, if success is reframed as putting on running shoes, drinking a glass of water and ignoring the donut. Instead of feeling daunted by a remote, difficult goal, we open the possibility of an ennobling victory.

It turns out, according to mounting social-science literature, that success is built on just these sorts of small wins. To get where you want to be on the SAT, the first step may be to commit to studying three punctuation rules a day, reviewing one Reading question type, or completing a single probability question. Once you start, there's a good chance that you'll keep working for 15-30 minutes. Even if you don't, reward yourself anyway. In a small way, you've already won.

Writing: Standard English Conventions

Colons

The function of the colon is to ***introduce***. Most commonly, it introduces a list, but it can also introduce a single item or even a complete sentence.

Correct:	Joe is scared of many things: getting attacked by lions, falling into swimming pools, and being buried alive.
Correct:	There's only one thing that scares Joe: lions.
Correct:	Joe has obviously conquered his fears: he went on an African safari last summer.

A sentence that uses a colon must follow these two basic rules:

- The part *before* the colon must be able to stand on its own as a sentence.

    Incorrect: Joe is scared of many things, including: getting attacked by lions, falling into swimming pools, and being buried alive.

- The part *after* the colon must consist **only** of whatever's being introduced, with nothing else added on.

    Incorrect: Joe is scared of many things: such as getting attacked by lions, falling into swimming pools, and being buried alive.

TIP:

For sentences that use connecting words like "including," choose a comma instead of a colon.

Correct: Joe is scared of many things, including getting attacked by lions, falling into swimming pools, and being buried alive.

The comma is valid because everything after the word "things" in this sentence is unnecessary information.

Try It   Which choice completes the text so that it conforms to the conventions of Standard English?

10) The process of manufacturing a space _____ lengthy, expensive, and fascinating.

   A) suit is:
   B) suit: is
   C) suit is
   D) suit, is

11) There's only one kind of parking space _____ the rare kind.

   A) in Bethesda
   B) in Bethesda:
   C) in Bethesda, just
   D) in Bethesda, it's

12) Beyoncé made clear in her first solo _____ that she was trying to forge a new identity separate from that of Destiny's Child.

   A) album: *Dangerously in Love*
   B) album, *Dangerously in Love,*
   C) album *Dangerously in Love:*
   D) album *Dangerously in Love;*

13) _____ French, Polynesian, and modern American cuisine.

   A) Among the principal influences on the chef's menu were:
   B) The principal influences on the chef's menu were:
   C) There were several principal influences on the chef's menu, which included:
   D) Among the principal influences on the chef's menu were

Writing: Standard English Conventions

Dashes

Dashes can take on many roles in a sentence. They may function as commas, as parentheses, or as colons.

> *Scarlett will wear a bold dress to the party—even if others are appalled.*
>
> *Certain musical genres—classical and electronic, for instance—are often classified as "art music."*
>
> *Some rights are inalienable—life, liberty, and the pursuit of happiness.*

Be on the lookout for **pairs**. A pair of dashes, like a pair of commas, can set off a phrase of unnecessary information in the middle of a sentence. But you can't have a dash on one end of the phrase and a comma on the other: it's two commas or two dashes, not one of each. Remember to look at the whole sentence, not just the underlined portion, before choosing an answer.

Incorrect: `Paella, a rice-based dish popular in Spain—is my mother's specialty.`

Correct: Paella, a rice-based dish popular in Spain, is my mother's specialty.

-or-

Correct: Paella—a rice-based dish popular in Spain—is my mother's specialty.

> ***TIP:***
>
> To be clear, dashes don't *always* come in pairs. It's just a pattern that appears frequently on the SAT, so it's a good thing to watch out for.

Semicolons, Colons, Dashes, and Apostrophes

Try It — Which choice completes the text so that it conforms to the conventions of Standard English?

14) Many celebrities—particularly _____ overwhelmed by too much exposure.

   A) those in the tabloids are
   B) those in the tabloids, are
   C) those in the tabloids—are
   D) those, in the tabloids, are

15) _____ was a major distribution point during the Gold Rush of the mid-19th century.

   A) Sacramento—the capital of California,
   B) Sacramento the capital of California
   C) Sacramento, the capital of California—
   D) Sacramento, the capital of California,

16) Twenty-six miles later, she glimpsed the finish line, and she felt her heart pound to the beat of a _____ victory.

   A) single, glorious word—
   B) single glorious word;
   C) single, glorious, word,
   D) single glorious word

Writing: Standard English Conventions

Apostrophes

One of the two main uses of an apostrophe is to show **possession**. For singular nouns, this is pretty simple: just add an apostrophe and the letter "s" to the end of the word.

Thelma's car was sitting in her son's driveway until the neighbor's daughter's husband moved it.

Phyllis's first priority was repairing her dress's broken zipper.

For plural nouns, you'll usually just add an apostrophe, without the additional letter "s."

The girls' cars were much cleaner than the boys' cars.

There is one exception: when the plural noun does not already end in "s." For these, add an apostrophe and the letter "s," just as you would for a singular noun.

The women's coalition also fought for children's rights.

> **TIP:**
> The part of the word that comes BEFORE the apostrophe is what we're making possessive.
>
> the <u>student</u>'s plans = one student with multiple plans
>
> the <u>students</u>' plan = multiple students who share one plan

---

Try It — Assuming the sentences below are correctly punctuated, evaluate whether the word in question is singular or plural.

		How many...	one	more than one
17)	The girl's dresses are over there.	girls?	___	___
18)	The men's pants are striped.	men?	___	___
19)	Max is the class's best student.	classes?	___	___
20)	The mice's cheese was hidden.	mice?	___	___
21)	I believed my sisters' story.	sisters?	___	___

The other function of the apostrophe is to form **contractions**. The apostrophe replaces the letters or numbers removed when the contraction is formed.

I don't think it's wise to tell Gerry that he shouldn't play tennis.

Wendy's unsure why the books she'd like to read haven't been available at the library.

The Berlin Wall fell in '89.

Semicolons, Colons, Dashes, and Apostrophes

Common apostrophe errors

Don't use an apostrophe to make a pronoun possessive.

We make nouns possessive by attaching an apostrophe. But pronouns (*he*, *she*, *it*, *they*) don't work that way—when we want to make them possessive, we use an entirely different word instead. For example, we don't say, "This is *he's* book." We say, "This is *his* book." Words like *its* and *your* work the same way as *his*—they're just a bit tougher to remember because they each look or sound like a word that uses an apostrophe.

We can use apostrophes with pronouns only when we're making contractions. For example, "it's" is a contraction that stands in for the phrase "it is" (or "it has"). So when faced with an "it's" on the SAT, the easiest way to test it is to try replacing the "it's" with the complete phrase. You can use similar tests for "you're," "they're," and "who's."

> **TIP:**
> The **only** reason to attach an apostrophe to a pronoun is to make a contraction.

Try It   Use the stated rule to choose the correct word.

If "it is" makes sense, use "it's." Otherwise, use "its."

22) Our basketball team beat (its/it's) biggest rival in overtime.

23) The forecasters say (its/it's) going to rain tomorrow.

If "you are" makes sense, use "you're." Otherwise, use "your."

24) (Your/You're) going to love the new jacket I bought.

25) Is this (your/you're) backpack?

If "they are" makes sense, use "they're." Otherwise, use "their."

26) The students were curious about (their/they're) new classmates.

27) I think (their/they're) going to enjoy the field trip.

If "who is" makes sense, use "who's." Otherwise, use "whose."

28) (Whose/Who's) going to be the captain next year?

29) Everyone is wondering (whose/who's) gym bag that is.

> **TIP:**
> The following are ***always wrong***:
>
> its'   their's
>
> your's   her's

Writing: Standard English Conventions

Don't use an apostrophe to pluralize.

An apostrophe cannot make something plural. Unless you're making a contraction or showing possession, there's no need to involve an apostrophe.

Incorrect: `The Morgan's and the Stanley's meet for dinner on Tuesday's.`

Correct: The Morgans and the Stanleys meet for dinner on Tuesdays.

CHALLENGE:

The toughest apostrophe questions will have two words in a row that both contain apostrophes. The testmakers are trying to confuse you by throwing so much at you at once, so don't let them succeed. Focus on one word at a time. For that first word, first ask yourself this: *does this need an apostrophe at all?* If your answer to that question is yes, then move on to the second question: *where should the apostrophe go?* Use that information to eliminate as many answer choices as you can, and then start the process over with the second word.

Example: Which of these sentences is correct?

A) Both girl's dresses' are beautiful.
B) Both girls dresses are beautiful.
C) Both girls' dresses' are beautiful.
D) Both girls' dresses are beautiful.

First, does the word "girls" need an apostrophe? Yes: it indicates that these dresses belong to the girls. Cross out choice B. Second, where should that apostrophe go? The word "both" at the beginning of the sentence tells us that we're talking about multiple girls here, so we can cross out choice A.

Now, does the word "dresses" need an apostrophe? No: there's nothing owned by the dresses, and there's no contraction here. That lets us cross out choice C, so the correct answer must be **D**.

Semicolons, Colons, Dashes, and Apostrophes

Try It — Add apostrophes where necessary. (Some sentences are fine the way they are.)

30) Felicia claims that the phone is hers.
31) Is this Mr. Smith's book?
32) The suitcase and its contents were destroyed.
33) The problem is theirs, not mine.
34) Oak trees' roots go deep beneath the soil.
35) The Smiths are friends of my parents.
36) It's beginning to look a lot like Christmas.
37) That old tree's going to die soon.
38) I'm not sure who's coming to the party.

FROM THE BLOG

It's a myth that the SAT is not "prep-able." Apart from playing the lottery, can you think of anything you don't get better at by practicing?

Writing: Standard English Conventions

Chapter Answer Key

Try It			
	1) ,	17)	one
	2) ;	18)	more than one
	3) ,	19)	one
	4) , , ;	20)	more than one
	5) ; ,	21)	more than one
	6) ; ,	22)	its
	7) , ,	23)	it's
	8) , ,	24)	You're
	9) ; ,	25)	your
	10) C	26)	their
	11) B	27)	they're
	12) B	28)	Who's
	13) D	29)	whose
	14) C	30)	(no apostrophes)
	15) D	31)	Is this Mr. <u>Smith's</u> book?
	16) A	32)	(no apostrophes)
		33)	(no apostrophes)
		34)	Oak <u>trees'</u> roots go deep beneath the soil.
		35)	(no apostrophes)
		36)	<u>It's</u> beginning to look a lot like Christmas.
		37)	That old <u>tree's</u> going to die soon.
		38)	<u>I'm</u> not sure <u>who's</u> coming to the party.

Practice Set 1: Easy-Medium

Nadia _____ when she became the first gymnast ever to be awarded a perfect score of 10.0 at the Olympic Games. Decades later, she is still considered one of the greatest gymnasts of all time.

1

Which choice completes the text so that it conforms to the conventions of Standard English?

A. Comăneci was 14 years old;
B. Comăneci was 14 years old,
C. Comăneci, was 14 years old
D. Comăneci was 14 years old

Karen Horn, a German economist and philosopher, has written extensively on the moral obligations of the modern employer. She argues that a business has a responsibility to provide _____ employees with a workplace culture that fosters dignity and respect.

2

Which choice completes the text so that it conforms to the conventions of Standard English?

A. its'
B. it's
C. its
D. they're

In wave-exposed rocky headlands, *Pisaster ochraceus* serves as a keystone _____ as one of the few predators capable of withstanding the harsh conditions, it controls the populations of the dominant prey species and thereby regulates the entire ecosystem. However, in the more complex intertidal communities found in wave-sheltered habitats, the impact of *P. ochraceus* is far less pronounced.

3

Which choice completes the text so that it conforms to the conventions of Standard English?

A. predator:
B. predator,
C. predator
D. predator, meaning:

The _____ in a criminal investigation is limited by one crucial factor: inadmissibility. Because polygraph results can be influenced by unrelated emotional factors as well as mental or physical disabilities, most jurisdictions do not allow them to be admitted into evidence.

4

Which choice completes the text so that it conforms to the conventions of Standard English?

A. usefulness of a polygraph ("lie detector") test,
B. usefulness, of a polygraph, or "lie detector" test
C. usefulness of a polygraph; or "lie detector" test
D. usefulness of a polygraph ("lie detector") test

Writing: Standard English Conventions

In 1883, at the age of 19, Anandi Gopal Joshi traveled from India to the United States to attend the Women's Medical College of Pennsylvania. A few years later, having become the first Indian woman ever to receive a medical degree, she returned home to Kolhapur to set up a clinic for women and children. Joshi was a pioneer for women's education and empowerment in _____ her legacy continues to inspire generations of women.

5

Which choice completes the text so that it conforms to the conventions of Standard English?

A. India with
B. India, and
C. India and;
D. India: and

It is now well established that children who are overscheduled may experience a range of negative impacts to their physical, emotional, and social well-being. Nonetheless, parents say that their kids' sports _____ more demanding than ever.

6

Which choice completes the text so that it conforms to the conventions of Standard English?

A. teams' schedules are
B. team's schedules are
C. team's schedule's is
D. teams' schedules' is

In 2018, the Amsterdam-based dealer Jan _____ the art world when he announced that a painting called "Portrait of a Young Gentleman" was in fact an authentic Rembrandt. The painting had been previously attributed to a follower of Rembrandt, but new research using X-ray and infrared technology confirmed that it had been created by the master himself.

7

Which choice completes the text so that it conforms to the conventions of Standard English?

A. Six's surprise announcement for
B. Sixs' surprised
C. Six's surprisingly announced to
D. Six surprised

To clean up an oceanic oil spill, several methods are available. One option is mechanical removal. Booms, skimmers, _____ and then separate it from the surface of the water.

8

Which choice completes the text so that it conforms to the conventions of Standard English?

A. sorbents and vacuums, are employed to contain the oil in one region,
B. sorbents, and vacuums are employed to contain the oil in one region
C. sorbents and vacuums are employed to contain the oil in one region;
D. sorbents, and vacuums, are employed to contain the oil in one region;

Semicolons, Colons, Dashes, and Apostrophes

In 2008, a team led by Jakob Vinther of Yale University published the first analysis of fossilized dinosaur _____ possible full-color reconstructions of creatures that lived over 100 million years ago.

9

Which choice completes the text so that it conforms to the conventions of Standard English?

A. pigments; making
B. pigments; an achievement that made
C. pigments, this made
D. pigments, making

Musical instruments are often classified into families based on how they produce sound. For example, string instruments (such as guitars and violins) produce sound through the vibration of _____ by contrast, woodwinds (such as flutes and saxophones) produce sound through the vibration of a column of air.

10

Which choice completes the text so that it conforms to the conventions of Standard English?

A. strings,
B. strings; for
C. strings;
D. strings

Thermophotovoltaic (TPV) generators are a type of energy conversion device that convert thermal radiation into electricity. Although TPV technology is still in the research and development phase, it has been used successfully _____ military power systems, remote oil and gas exploration, and wireless monitoring of the structural health of bridges and other buildings.

11

Which choice completes the text so that it conforms to the conventions of Standard English?

A. in, at least, three contexts:
B. in at least three contexts:
C. in, at least, three contexts;
D. in at least three contexts,

Much of the lumber that is used commercially has been treated with chemicals to prevent decay and insect damage. This can significantly increase the life of a construction _____ that project is a playground, it is not without risks. Over time, chemicals such as arsenic, chromium, and copper can leach out of the wood and be absorbed by children who come into contact with the playground equipment or the soil around it.

12

Which choice completes the text so that it conforms to the conventions of Standard English?

A. project, but when
B. project when
C. project; although when
D. project but when,

Writing: Standard English Conventions

Practice Set 2: Medium-Hard

Most biologists agree that the evolution of the bacterial flagellum, a complex structure that enables bacteria to swim, occurred through a gradual process of natural selection. Dr. Howard Berg has a different _____ he suggests that the flagellum evolved through a series of modifications to a pre-existing structure known as the bacterial rotary motor.

1

Which choice completes the text so that it conforms to the conventions of Standard English?

A. view; however,
B. view: however,
C. view, however,
D. view, however;

Although the game of chess is known to be over one thousand years old _____ exact origins are unclear. The game is believed to have originated in northern India or central Asia, then spread over time to other parts of the world.

2

Which choice completes the text so that it conforms to the conventions of Standard English?

A. old; however, its
B. old, however, its
C. old, its
D. old; its

Famous for their incredible strength—at widths 10,000 times thinner than that of a human _____ carbon nanotubes offer a wide array of intriguing possibilities for the future of technology.

3

Which choice completes the text so that it conforms to the conventions of Standard English?

A. hair, they are stronger than steel—
B. hair, they are stronger than steel
C. hair—they are stronger than steel—
D. hair, they are stronger than steel,

Driving South Africa's Garden Route when _____ best, from February to April, is a truly spectacular experience. The scenic stretch of coastline is characterized by sandy beaches, picturesque villages, and a number of nature reserves.

4

Which choice completes the text so that it conforms to the conventions of Standard English?

A. its at its
B. its at it's
C. it's at its
D. it's at it's

A number of private companies now offer individuals the chance to fly beyond the Earth's atmosphere and experience space firsthand. However, the price tag for such "space tourism" puts it firmly out of reach for most would-be travelers: _____ $250,000 for the experience.

5

Which choice completes the text so that it conforms to the conventions of Standard English?

A. which is at a minimum
B. because it costs, at a minimum,
C. one must pay, at a minimum,
D. at a minimum,

When a company considers switching to a new computer system, the matter cannot be considered lightly. Although a wide variety of factors can impact the decision—price, memory capacity, ease of use, and many _____ the recommendation of a trusted information technology consultant is of primary importance.

6

Which choice completes the text so that it conforms to the conventions of Standard English?

A. others,
B. others—
C. others;
D. others

A funny movie can have a lasting cultural impact, perhaps to a surprising extent. According to Dr. _____ comedy that saves us: laughter transforms our mood, builds social connections, and helps us lead happier, more satisfying lives.

7

Which choice completes the text so that it conforms to the conventions of Standard English?

A. Mishkin, its
B. Mishkin, it's
C. Mishkin: it's
D. Mishkin its

The Tawahka people are an indigenous group who primarily live in the rainforests of the eastern Honduran region of La Mosquitia. Within the community, young people and old people _____ spiritual connection to their natural world, and their traditional practices and beliefs center around maintaining a harmonious relationship with the environment.

8

Which choice completes the text so that it conforms to the conventions of Standard English?

A. alike maintain a strong
B. alike, maintain a strong,
C. alike: maintain a strong
D. alike maintain: a strong,

As the _____ at LaRoche University, Elissa Scalise Powell has seen her share of family dramas. The institute aims to promote high-quality genealogical research and help genealogists of all levels improve their skills and understanding of family history.

9

Which choice completes the text so that it conforms to the conventions of Standard English?

A. director, of the Genealogical Research Institute of Pittsburgh (GRIP)
B. director—of the Genealogical Research Institute of Pittsburgh, (GRIP),
C. director of the Genealogical Research Institute of Pittsburgh (GRIP)—
D. director of the Genealogical Research Institute of Pittsburgh (GRIP)

The diffusionist theory, which posited that cultural similarities between different civilizations could be explained by the diffusion or spread of ideas and technologies from a single (usually European) source or culture, has been widely discredited by anthropologists. However, it is not hard to understand how it became so dominant. With their _____ diffusionists were unable to adequately comprehend the complex and multi-faceted nature of cultural interaction and change.

10

Which choice completes the text so that it conforms to the conventions of Standard English?

A. worldviews constrained by the Eurocentric societies in which they lived,
B. worldviews, constrained by the Eurocentric societies in which they lived,
C. worldviews (constrained by the Eurocentric societies in which they lived)
D. worldviews—constrained by the Eurocentric societies in which they lived—

The southern white rhino is a subspecies of white rhinoceros found in southern Africa. In 2021, thousands of southern white rhinos roamed the savannahs of Namibia, Zimbabwe, and neighboring countries. _____ their species had been nearly hunted to extinction a hundred years earlier: conservation efforts such as protected areas and anti-poaching measures helped their population rebound.

11

Which choice completes the text so that it conforms to the conventions of Standard English?

A. They did not—and still do not know—that
B. They did not know—and still do not, that
C. What they did not know—and still do not:
D. They did not—and still do not—know that

Some avian experts specialize in nest analysis. Based on _____ location and the materials from which it is constructed, they can determine what species of bird was responsible for its construction.

12

Which choice completes the text so that it conforms to the conventions of Standard English?

A. the nests
B. the nests'
C. a nests'
D. a nest's

A 1985 study evaluated methods for masking tinnitus, the phenomenon commonly referred to as a "ringing in the ears." Subjects were first subjected to continuous white noise at 20, 40, and 60 _____ followed, at 2, 4, 10, and 20 pulses per second. Because participants found the interrupted sounds to be more annoying than the continuous noise, the researchers concluded that interrupted noise is not suitable as a tinnitus masker.

13

Which choice completes the text so that it conforms to the conventions of Standard English?

A. decibels, interrupting sounds
B. decibels, interrupting the sounds'
C. decibels. Interrupted sounds
D. decibels' interrupted sounds

Verbs

Preview Quiz:

Choose the correct form of the verb.

1) Mammals, particularly those with thick fur, (is/are) well protected from the cold.

2) Angel is well suited to his new job in customer service, having an even temper and thick skin that (allows/allow) him to remain calm, cool and collected at all times.

3) The studies by the prominent professor (concludes/conclude) that change is inevitable.

4) The trauma team (was/were) the first to arrive.

5) Each of my siblings (works/work) after school.

6) Neither of the two chickens (has/have) been very well trained.

7) Although many people enjoy fly fishing, very few (studied/have studied) its unusual history.

would have bought	will buy	would buy

Match each of the sentences to the verb tense from the box above that best completes it.

8) If I win the game, I _____ a new shirt.

9) If I won the lottery, I _____ a house.

10) If I had won the bet, I _____ that new car.

Writing: Standard English Conventions

Agreement

The subject of a sentence must ***agree*** with the verb: that is, if the subject of a sentence is singular, the verb must be singular, and if the subject is plural, the verb must be plural.

If you're not sure what the subject is, ask yourself who or what is doing the action of the verb. Don't be too limited in your answer—the subject could be a single word or a long, complicated phrase. To make it easier to "hear" which verb is right, say that subject immediately before the verb. If you're still not sure, try replacing that word with "it" (if the subject is singular) or "they" (if the subject is plural).

Example: *Mammals, particularly those with thick fur, (is/are) well protected from the cold.*

The subject here is "mammals." That's plural: the mammals **are** well protected from the cold.

Example: *Angel is well suited to his new job in customer service, having an even temper and thick skin that (allows/allow) him to remain calm, cool and collected at all times.*

This one's trickier. First, what's the subject of this verb? That is, who or what is doing the action of allowing Angel to remain calm, cool, and collected? Well, two things: his "even temper and thick skin." They **allow** him to remain calm, cool, and collected. Note that "Angel" is not the subject that we care about here! Angel is the subject of the sentence, but he's not the subject of this particular verb.

To make it easier to identify the subject, ***cross out any prepositional phrases***.

Example: *The studies by the prominent professor (concludes/conclude) that change is inevitable.*

The <u>studies</u> ~~by the prominent professor~~ **conclude** that change is inevitable.

Example: *The point of the lectures (was/were) difficult to grasp.*

The <u>point</u> ~~of the lectures~~ **was** difficult to grasp.

> **TIP:**
>
> **Don't** trust your ear on agreement questions. It's too easy for the test to hide the subject and trick you.

A noun indicating a group (such as *class, family*, or *herd*) is singular even though the group consists of more than one person/thing.

Example: *The trauma team (was/were) the first to arrive.*

There's just one team: it **was** the first to arrive.

Example: *The cast (was/were) nominated for an ensemble acting award.*

Again, just one cast. It **was** nominated.

These words are ***always singular***:

every	everyone	anyone	someone	no one
each	everybody	anybody	somebody	nobody
	everything	anything	something	nothing

Example: *Each of my siblings (works/work) after school.*

Cross out the prepositional phrase "of my siblings," and the subject we're left with is "each." That's singular. So change it to "it" or "he" to make it easier to hear the right verb: he **works** after school.

Example: *No one in either of the classes (know/knows) how to diagram a sentence.*

<u>No one</u> ~~in either of the classes~~ (know/knows) how to diagram a sentence.

He **knows** how to diagram a sentence.

If you're not sure whether a subject is singular, try inserting the word "one" after it. Does it still make sense?

Example: *Neither of the two chickens (has/have) been very well trained.*

"Neither one of the two chickens" makes sense. So, "neither" must be singular here. Change it to an "it" to make it easier to hear the right verb: It **has** been very well trained.

Example: *Many of the reasons for attending the event (remains/remain) difficult to understand.*

"Many one of the reasons" doesn't make sense. Therefore, "many" must be plural: They **remain** difficult to understand.

Try It Choose the correct form of the verb.

1) The time and place for the meeting (has/have) yet to be determined.
2) The party is shaping up to be a good one; George will be attending with Susanna, and Felicia (is/are) going to perform with her band.
3) The entire herd (is/are) scheduled to be sheared tomorrow.
4) The Appalachian mountain chain, which is far older and flatter than the Rocky Mountains, (is/are) a popular destination for long range hikers.
5) Members of the school board, who meet monthly to discuss the policies of the school district, (is/are) now investigating the open campus policy for the high school seniors.
6) Several of the reporters (object/objects) to the coronation.
7) Who among the students (is/are) the tallest?
8) A fascinating and ingenious watercolor from Picasso's blue period and a laughably banal attempt at pseudo-cubism painted by one of his contemporaries (has/have) been displayed in the great hall.
9) Anna May Wong, whose varied career spanned film, television, stage and radio, (was/were) the first Chinese-American movie star.
10) A concise summary of both books (was/were) written by George.
11) The Scarlet Macaw, with its vibrant red, blue and yellow feathers, (eat/eats) the sodium-rich material available at so-called "clay licks."
12) Juju, a Nigerian musical style that draws on several percussion traditions, (was/were) created by Tunde King.
13) The entire group of students (is/are) to be suspended.

Tense

Make sure that any verbs in the sentence are conjugated correctly. For most questions, this just means "listening" for what sounds right or wrong in a sentence. Below are a few of the key things to watch out for.

The verb must **match** the rest of the sentence and the text as a whole. If there are other verbs nearby that are in the present tense, then the verb in the question should probably also be in the present tense. But the most important thing is to pay attention to the **context** and **meaning** of the sentence. The text will tell you what tense it needs to be in.

> *Example:* *I went to the grocery store and (select/selected) my favorite brand of toothpaste.*
>
> The verb *went* is in past tense, and there's no indication in the sentence that the timeframe is changing. Therefore, we'll want the past tense again: I **selected** my favorite brand.
>
> *Example:* *After Ann finishes her homework, she (will go / goes) to the movies.*
>
> This time, the word *after* tells us that the two verbs should not match. Although *finishes* is in present tense, going to the movies is what's going to happen after that, in the future. "She **will go** to the movies" is correct.

> **TIP:**
>
> ***Do*** trust your ear on verb tense questions. You know what sounds right!

Simpler is better. Don't use a complicated tense (e.g., *had walked, has walked, will have been walking*) when a simple tense will do (e.g. *walks, walked*).

> *Example:* *Jimmy stopped by the house because he (forgets/forgot/has forgotten) his wallet.*
>
> Keep it simple! He **forgot** his wallet.

> **TIP:**
>
> A good rule of thumb for the "Standard English Conventions" questions is that the choice with the fewest words is most likely to be right.

So when are the multi-word tenses correct? Use these when there's a complicated timeline: for example, two past actions, where one of them happened further in the past than the other.

Example: *The teacher (discussed/had been discussing) mitosis when the fight broke out.*

The fight *broke* out, past tense. We want to position the mitosis discussion as a background action that was already going on when the fight started, so **had been discussing** is correct. If we used *discussed* instead, we'd be putting both events in the same timeframe: as if, in response to a fight breaking out, the teacher discussed mitosis.

The multi-word tenses can also be useful for actions that started in the past but continue to the present day.

Example: *Although many people enjoy fly fishing, very few (studied/have studied) its unusual history.*

In this sentence, we're not trying to describe a specific time in the past when few people studied the history of fly fishing. Instead, we're saying that in general, few people studied it in the past *and* few people study it today. That makes **have studied** the right choice.

CHALLENGE:

Sometimes, the conjugation of a verb can tell us something about the attitude of the speaker. We call this the verb's **mood**.

The **subjunctive** most often shows up in dependent clauses that describe a wish, request, or command, or that use an "if" to talk about something that is not actually true. Notice the difference here:

Indicative:	Subjunctive:
The senator <u>listens</u> to us.	*We demand that the senator <u>listen</u> to us.*
I <u>am</u> not a tree.	*If I <u>were</u> a tree, I would be a maple.*
You <u>are</u> patient.	*Management asks that you <u>be</u> patient.*
Her mother says that she always <u>finishes</u> her vegetables.	*It is important that she <u>finish</u> her vegetables.*

The **conditional** tells us that whatever we're describing is in some way dependent on some condition. The kind of conjugation we choose tells us how likely or unlikely we think it is that the condition will be met.

Possible:	*If I win the game, I <u>will buy</u> a new shirt.*
Improbable:	*If I won the lottery, I <u>would buy</u> a house.*
Impossible:	*If I had won the bet, I <u>would have bought</u> that new car.*

TIP:

Notice that the "would" is never in the *if* part of the sentence. For example, it's never "If I would have won the game..."

TIP:

The constructions "would of" and "could of" are **always wrong.** It's would *have* and could *have*.

Writing: Standard English Conventions

> ***Try It*** Choose the correct form of the verb.
>
> 14) The moving crate (bursted/burst) before I could duct tape it.
>
> 15) She devours the ice cream and then (drank/drinks) the soda.
>
> 16) The Everest climbers could (of/have) (froze/frozen) to death.
>
> 17) Cookie Monster (drank/has drank) too much milk and ate too many cookies.
>
> 18) The chess players who lost the game have (brought/brung) shame on their country.
>
> 19) I (felt/have felt) very ill after I ate the entire bag of cotton candy.
>
> 20) If I hadn't gotten in, I (would have/have) heard by now.

Chapter Answer Key

Try It

1)	have	11)	eats
2)	is	12)	was
3)	is	13)	is
4)	is	14)	burst
5)	are	15)	drinks
6)	object	16)	have frozen
7)	is	17)	drank
8)	have	18)	brought
9)	was	19)	felt
10)	was	20)	would have

Writing: Standard English Conventions

Practice Set 1: Easy-Medium

Educators have long used details about the personal lives of our political leaders to enrich the story and enhance learning. For example, legends about William Henry Harrison, who died from complications of pneumonia just a month into his presidency, _____ history books.

1

Which choice completes the text so that it conforms to the conventions of Standard English?

A. is often told in high school
B. is told often in high schools'
C. are often told in high school
D. which are often told in a high school's

Antimatter, a substance consisting of particles with charges opposite to those of regular matter, _____ for the first time by scientists at CERN in 2010. The experiment, which was led by Canadian physicist Jeffrey Hangst, managed to store 38 antihydrogen atoms for about 170 milliseconds.

2

Which choice completes the text so that it conforms to the conventions of Standard English?

A. were successfully stored
B. have been stored successfully
C. has successfully stored
D. was successfully stored

Human activity can have both positive and negative effects on the natural world. In the 19th century, human-caused pollution eradicated two plant diseases in English cities. The pollution from coal burning in the industrial cities _____ toxic to the fungi that caused the diseases.

3

Which choice completes the text so that it conforms to the conventions of Standard English?

A. was
B. were
C. being
D. it was

The *da capo* aria is a vocal form that emerged during the Baroque period in the early 18th century. George Frideric Handel, the renowned composer, created immensely popular *da capo* arias characterized by complex vocal lines that showcase the virtuosity of the singer. However, Handel's body of work, including his *da capo* arias, _____ as overly repetitive, with limited opportunity for improvisation or variation.

4

Which choice completes the text so that it conforms to the conventions of Standard English?

A. have been criticized by some musicians
B. have been criticized, by some musicians,
C. has been criticized by some musicians
D. has not made the criticism of some musicians

While some countries are experiencing declining populations due to factors such as low fertility rates and aging populations, the population of our planet as a whole is still rapidly increasing. If current trends continue, the global population, estimated at around 7.9 billion in 2021, _____ 9.7 billion by 2050.

5 Which choice completes the text so that it conforms to the conventions of Standard English?

A. has reached
B. had reached
C. is reaching
D. will reach

For some crops, hybrid strains—strains created by cross-breeding two or more different varieties of a crop species—are consistently able to outperform non-hybrid strains. For example, hybrid corn strains such as Pioneer P1368AM _____ widely adopted by farmers due to their higher yields and improved resistance to disease and environmental stressors.

6 Which choice completes the text so that it conforms to the conventions of Standard English?

A. was
B. has been
C. is
D. have been

Under section 35 of the Canadian Constitution, Indigenous peoples in Canada have the right to practice their own customs, traditions, and ways of life, including their own systems of land tenure and resource management. As a result, the concept of collective ownership of land and resources _____ and may be protected under Canadian law.

7 Which choice completes the text so that it conforms to the conventions of Standard English?

A. is recognized
B. are recognized
C. recognize
D. recognized

In 1978, Richard F. Haines coined the term "indicator species" to describe a plant or animal whose presence or absence _____ important information about its local environment. In North America, the common loon (*Gavia immer*) is considered an indicator species because of its high degree of sensitivity to changes in water quality and habitat degradation.

8 Which choice completes the text so that it conforms to the conventions of Standard English?

A. have revealed
B. were revealing
C. reveals
D. reveal

Writing: Standard English Conventions

Practice Set 2: Medium-Hard

The Union victory at Gettysburg in July of 1863 is generally considered to be the turning point of the US Civil War. According to one historian, if the south _____ the battle, the resulting boost in the Confederate Army's morale and momentum would have led to the capture of key Union cities, possibly including Washington, D.C.

1

Which choice completes the text so that it conforms to the conventions of Standard English?

A. would of won
B. would have won
C. won
D. had won

Supply chain problems, an unusually volatile crude oil market, and rampant market speculation have led to high rate of fluctuation in local gasoline prices. For the last six months, each of the gas stations in one town _____ price signs three times a day.

2

Which choice completes the text so that it conforms to the conventions of Standard English?

A. have been changing their
B. has been changing its
C. is going to change their
D. have changed their

Scientists are consistently puzzled as to why the polar bear, like many other animals, _____

3

Which choice completes the text so that it conforms to the conventions of Standard English?

A. eat their young.
B. eats its young.
C. will eat their young.
D. their young are eaten.

In 2016, the US implemented a near-total ban on the commercial trade of African elephant ivory, with limited exceptions for certain antiques and other items. The ban was aimed at curbing the illegal trade in ivory and protecting African elephant populations, which _____ by poaching and habitat loss.

4

Which choice completes the text so that it conforms to the conventions of Standard English?

A. have been threatened by
B. will have been threatened by
C. are threatening
D. is threatened by

A key step in embryonic development is the establishment of polarity: the embryo must define the orientation or axis along which different body parts and a significant amount of tissue _____ This will determine the position and orientation of specific structures and organs in the developing embryo.

5

Which choice completes the text so that it conforms to the conventions of Standard English?

A. have been formed.
B. is to be formed.
C. are to be formed.
D. is forming.

Pronouns

Preview Quiz

Choose the correct form of the pronoun.

1) The company is rightfully proud of (its/their) hardworking employees.

2) The success of new electronic devices is dependent on the strength of (its/their) marketing campaign.

3) The email was sent to Kenneth, Lydia, and (I/me).

4) I don't know the gentleman next to (who/whom) I am sitting.

What is wrong with these sentences?

5) The best teammates are those who fit in as a member of the family.

6) Everyone said that Betty had inherited her mother's good looks, but she privately believed that there was only one true beauty in the family.

7) When my husband looks at our daughter, he sees a younger version of myself.

Writing: Standard English Conventions

Agreement

Look carefully at the sentence to identify which word the pronoun is standing in for. If you had to swap out the pronoun for one noun from elsewhere in the sentence, which one would make the most sense? That word is the pronoun's **antecedent**. If the antecedent is singular, the pronoun must be singular (e.g. *she, him, I*). If the antecedent is plural, the pronoun must be plural (*we, they, us*).

Example: The company is rightfully proud of (its/their) hardworking employees.

Try swapping out the pronoun: The company is rightfully proud of the company's hardworking employees. So "the company" is the antecedent. Since that's a singular word, we need the singular ***its***, not the plural *their*.

Example: The success of new electronic devices is dependent on the strength of (its/their) marketing campaign.

Whose marketing campaign? The devices' marketing campaign. The word "devices" is plural, so ***their*** is correct.

Try It   Underline the antecedent and then choose the correct pronoun.

1) The Oglethorpe Bookstore buys thousands of books each year, most of (it/them) paperback novels.

2) Unlike (its/their) predecessors, which suffered from confusing interfaces and frequent crashes, the smartphone introduced by Boggle Corp. is easy to use and reliable.

3) Each of the most successful movies of the last twenty years, including *Avatar*, *Titanic*, and *The Lord of The Rings*, faced only middling reviews when (they/it) opened.

4) When the Supremes released the single "Baby Love" in 1964, (it/they) instantly established themselves as pop superstars.

5) As a student, (you/we) are responsible for planning (your/our) own schedule.

Agreement problems don't have to be limited to the subject-verb or pronoun-antecedent varieties. Any time you see a sentence involving a comparison, take a moment to check whether something singular is being compared to something plural.

    Incorrect: `The best teammates are those who fit in as a member of the family.`

    Correct: The best teammates are those who fit in as <u>members</u> of the family.

-or-

    Correct: The best <u>teammate is one who fits</u> in as a member of the family.

    Incorrect: `All the girls in the class want to be a ballerina.`

    Correct: All the girls in the class want to be <u>ballerinas</u>.

-or-

    Correct: <u>Each of</u> the girls in the class <u>wants</u> to be a ballerina.

Case

When a pronoun is standing in for a subject or an object, it takes one of these forms:

Subject	
Singular	**Plural**
I	we
you	you
he/she/it	they
who	who

Object	
Singular	**Plural**
me	us
you	you
him/her/it	them
whom	whom

For most pronoun questions, you can just trust your ear. For example, the sentence "Him hates asparagus" just sounds wrong, and indeed, it is.

When the pronoun is buried in a list, cross out everything on the list except for the pronoun to make it easier to "hear" what sounds right.

    Example: *The email was sent to Kenneth, Lydia, and (I/me).*

        Get rid of Kenneth and Lydia and it's much easier to hear it: "The email was sent to **me**."

TIP:

Do trust your ear for pronoun case questions.

- 181 -

To choose between *who* and *whom*, trusting your ear doesn't really help: we rarely use *whom* in day-to-day life, and so we don't have much of a sense for when it sounds right. However, there is a trick that can help. Try replacing the who/whom with *he* and then with *him*. Which one sounds right? If *he* sounds right, then "who" is correct. If *him* sounds right, then "whom" is correct. (To remember which is which, think about matching the m's: whoM goes with hiM).

> *TIP:*
> For plural subjects, you can plug in *they* instead of *he*, and *them* instead of *him*. Matching the m's still works.

Example: *The salesman (who/whom) sold me this computer must have made a hefty commission.*

Here, "he sold me this computer" sounds better than "him sold me this computer," so **who** is correct.

Example: *I don't know the gentleman next to (who/whom) I am seated.*

In this one, "next to him" sounds better than "next to he," so **whom** is correct.

TIP:

When a pronoun immediately follows a preposition, you always use the object case (e.g. *her, them, us*), instead of the subject case (e.g. *she, they, we*).

Example: *The proposal that was written by (he/him) and his partner failed to win the grant.*

Since "by" is a preposition, the correct word is **him**.

Example: *According to Cindy, there exists an easy friendship between Marcia and (her/she).*

Because it follows the preposition "between," **her** is the right choice.

Pronouns

You can use the *–self* **pronouns** (*myself, himself, herself*, etc.) only when the subject and the object are the same: that is, when the pronoun is referring back to the person doing the action of the sentence.

Correct: When I look at my daughter, I see a younger version of myself.

Incorrect: `When my husband looks at our daughter, he sees a younger version of myself.`

Try It   Choose the correct pronoun.

6) Did you give the marbles to Carlos and (he/him)?

7) At his wife's suggestion, Dr. Rodriguez made a note to remind (him/he/himself) to mail the letter on his way home.

8) (Who/Whom) lies buried in Grant's tomb?

9) You can contact Jeffries, Mitchelson or (I/me/myself) for more information.

10) The book that made the bestseller list, a book co-authored by Steven Wilson and (I/me), is a work of which both of (we/us) can be proud.

11) (Whose/Who's/Whom is) afraid of the big, bad wolf?

Writing: Standard English Conventions

Ambiguity

If a pronoun has no clear antecedent (for example, if the sentence uses the word "he" when more than one man has been mentioned), it is incorrect. In these sentences, the error is not that the wrong pronoun was used; it's that a pronoun was used at all.

Incorrect: `Everyone said that Betty had inherited her mother's good looks, but she privately believed that there was only one true beauty in the family.`

When we say that Betty inherited "her mother's good looks," that's fine—at this point in the sentence, the word "her" could only be referring to Betty. But who exactly believed that there was only one true beauty in the family? The "she" could be referring to Betty, or it could be referring to Betty's mother. Since we have no way of knowing which one is right, the pronoun should not be used.

Incorrect: `In an effort to blend in with the locals, Carrie tried to avoid mispronouncing the complicated place names, but it failed.`

This time, the problem is not that the "it" could be referring to more than one noun. The problem is that it's not referring to anything! There's no specific noun in this sentence that this "it" could be pointing back to, so the "it" is incorrect.

Try It   Circle any ambiguous pronouns.

12) Governor McAllister's son told us that he had decided not to run for reelection because he wanted to spend more time with his family.

13) Neither Jorge nor Edward believed that he would win the lottery.

14) We have been dependent on fossil fuels for decades, but now that the environmental impact has become clear, activists are urging citizens to change it.

Chapter Answer Key

Try It

1) <u>thousands of books</u>   them
2) <u>smartphone</u>   its
3) <u>Each</u>   it
4) <u>the Supremes</u>   they
5) <u>student</u>   you… your
6) him
7) himself
8) Who
9) me
10) me … us
11) Who's
12) Governor McAllister's son told us that <u>he</u> had decided not to run for reelection because <u>he</u> wanted to spend more time with <u>his</u> family.
13) (no changes)
14) We have been dependent on fossil fuels for decades, but now that the environmental impact has become clear, activists are urging citizens to change <u>it</u>.

Writing: Standard English Conventions

Practice Set 1: Easy-Medium

Trinidadian guppies are small, colorful fish found in rivers and streams in the Caribbean nation of Trinidad and Tobago. Among males, intense competition for mating opportunities has resulted in the evolution of elaborate courtship displays and ornament. When a male guppy has a larger tail and brighter coloration, _____ more successful in attracting mates and fathering offspring.

1

Which choice completes the text so that it conforms to the conventions of Standard English?

A. him being
B. they are
C. he is
D. it will be having

The health benefits of bicycling are undeniable, though many people just taking up the sport have something of a rough beginning. Experts agree that it's common for _____ when first learning to ride.

2

Which choice completes the text so that it conforms to the conventions of Standard English?

A. new cyclists to fall and hurt them
B. a new cyclist to fall and hurt themselves
C. new cyclists to fall and hurt themselves
D. a new cyclist to fall and hurt him

At the University of Bath, a multidisciplinary research center focuses on a range of social policy issues that includes the field of terrorism studies. The field _____ today has only existed for a short time. Initially, terrorism was studied primarily as a security or criminal justice issue, with a focus on understanding the motivations and tactics of terrorist groups and developing strategies to counter their activities. However, in recent years, scholars in the field have increasingly emphasized the need to examine the social and political contexts in which terrorism arises, as well as the broader social and psychological factors that may contribute to radicalization and violence.

3

Which choice completes the text so that it conforms to the conventions of Standard English?

A. as we know it
B. as it is known to we
C. as we know them
D. that those of us know

Jalāl ad-Dīn Muḥammad Balkhī Rumi, known in the Western world simply as Rumi, was a Persian jurist, _____ works have been translated into many languages and read by people all over the world.

4

Which choice completes the text so that it conforms to the conventions of Standard English?

A. mystic, and poet, his
B. mystic, and poet whose
C. mystic, and he was a
D. mystic and a poet his

Practice Set 2: Medium-Hard

A 1990 study at the Massachusetts Institute of Technology found that adult schizophrenia was linked to a region on human chromosome number six. Some scientists even explored the possibility of using a patient's genetic information to aid in diagnosis. However, doctors soon found that all their sophisticated DNA information was meaningless if _____ with clinical examination and symptom analysis.

1

Which choice completes the text so that it conforms to the conventions of Standard English?

A. he or she didn't combine it
B. they didn't combine it
C. it wasn't combined by him or her
D. he or she wasn't to combine it

Type A lipid profile, also known as the "atherogenic" lipid profile, is characterized by high levels of low-density lipoprotein (LDL) cholesterol, and low levels of high-density lipoprotein (HDL) cholesterol. Both high LDL levels and low HDL levels can increase the risk of heart disease. Type B lipid profile, on the other hand, is characterized by an elevated level of another type of fat found in the blood called a triglyceride; _____ also associated with an increased risk of heart disease.

2

Which choice completes the text so that it conforms to the conventions of Standard English?

A. it is
B. they are
C. which is
D. high triglyceride levels are

The four papers that Einstein published in 1905 were so revolutionary that experts view _____ as watershed moments in the history of science.

3

Which choice completes the text so that it conforms to the conventions of Standard English?

A. this
B. them
C. him
D. it

The Russian journalist Sergei Shereshevsky had an extraordinary memory. Shereshevsky suffered from synesthesia, a condition in which sensory experiences are blended together. In his case, he saw every sound and every letter as having its own unique color and texture. This helped him to remember information in a very vivid and detailed way. In one experiment, Shereshevsky was recorded reciting a lengthy poem after listening to it only once. When researchers compared his recitation to the version he had listened to, they discovered that everything, including the word order, the emphases, and the pauses for breath, _____

4

Which choice completes the text so that it conforms to the conventions of Standard English?

A. was exactly as he remembered them.
B. were exactly as he remembered them.
C. was exactly as he remembered it.
D. being exactly as he remembered them.

Writing: Standard English Conventions

Misplaced Modifiers

Preview Quiz

Consider the following sentence:

While riding his bicycle, Sam's dog barked at him.

1) What is wrong with the sentence above?

   _____

   _____

2) Write a corrected version of the sentence.

   _____

   _____

Consider the following sentence:

The ball was kicked by John.

3) The sentence above is written in "passive voice." What does that mean?

   _____

   _____

4) Rewrite the sentence in active voice.

   _____

   _____

Sometimes, poor construction of a sentence will cause a phrase that is intended to modify one thing to either modify something else or modify nothing at all. That may sound a little dry, but this particular error actually has the side benefit of often creating some unintentional humor. When the SAT gives you a chance to laugh, you should grab it.

> Incorrect: `While riding his bicycle, Sam's dog barked at him.`

TIP:
The overall rule here is that *grammar has a short memory*. You want to get the thing being described as close as possible to the thing describing it.

The problem here, of course, is that Sam's dog isn't riding the bicycle (we hope). *Sam* is. When a sentence begins with a phrase containing a –ing or –ed verb, like this one does, the phrase must modify the **very first noun that follows the comma**. So one easy way to fix a misplaced modifier is to change the wording in the independent clause so that the noun you want to modify comes first.

> Correct: While riding his bicycle, <u>Sam was barked at by his dog</u>.

The other major way to fix this kind of problem is to change the introductory phrase, usually by adding the subject to it.

> Correct: <u>While Sam was riding his bicycle,</u> his dog barked at him.

The hardest part about these questions is usually spotting the problem in the first place.

Try It — Each of the following is a common situation in which you should be on the lookout for misplaced modifiers, followed by an example. Write a corrected version of each sentence.

- **An introductory phrase using verbs in –ing or –ed form.**

  1) `Having slept through my alarm, the school bus arrived before I was fully dressed.`

  _____

- **Passive voice** ("The ball was kicked by John" rather than "John kicked the ball") **in either the sentence or the answer choices.**

  2) `Finding no evidence of guilt, the suspect was acquitted by the jury.`

  _____

- **Multiple prepositional phrases.** These are often easiest to fix by just changing the order of the phrases.

  3) `I found a dress in a thrift store that I'd been looking for to wear to a party.`

  _____

TIP:
In **passive voice**, the subject of the sentence is not the one doing the action. Since this affects the word order, a misplaced modifier can often be fixed (or caused!) by switching from passive to active voice.

Chapter Answer Key

Try It — More than one valid sentence can be created in each of these exercises. Here are some possible answers.

1) **Because I** slept through my alarm, the school bus arrived before I was fully dressed.

   Having slept through my alarm, **I wasn't fully dressed when the school bus arrived**.

2) Finding no evidence of guilt, the **jury acquitted the suspect**.

   Because the jury found no evidence of guilt, the suspect was acquitted.

3) **In a thrift store,** I found a dress that I'd been looking for to wear to a party.

FROM THE BLOG

The more you feel in control, the more confident you will be and the better you will do! As you go about your day and week and find yourself thinking about the SAT, try to imagine every scenario and every question and visualize HOW you will handle it. Don't imagine an easy test but rather some of the hard questions and weird things you have seen and what you would do: Plug in numbers? Speak up if the proctor makes an error. Move past a question that isn't clicking. Read purposefully S-L-O-W-L-Y to have a chance to figure things out.

Also, please do all you can to be excited for the test. Nerves are normal. We actually need some pressure to be at our best. Turning butterflies to a sense of nervous excitement harnesses that energy and puts it to work in a productive way.

Misplaced Modifiers

Practice Set 1: Easy-Medium

At Yoko Ono's 1966 exhibit at the Indica Gallery in London, a visitor noticed a painting on the ceiling on which something tiny was printed on an otherwise white canvas. After making his way up a ladder and picking up a provided magnifying glass, _____

1

Which choice completes the text so that it conforms to the conventions of Standard English?

A. the word "YES" surprised him.
B. it was the word "YES" that surprised him.
C. he was surprised to read the word "YES."
D. the word "YES" was a surprise to him.

The first new play from the acclaimed writer since he'd gone into seclusion over a decade earlier, _____

2

Which choice completes the text so that it conforms to the conventions of Standard English?

A. every performance of *The Cosmonaut*'s four-week run was sold out.
B. all four weeks of *The Cosmonaut*'s performances were sold out.
C. *The Cosmonaut*'s four-week run was completely sold out.
D. *The Cosmonaut* sold out every performance of its four-week run.

Professional gamer Nathan Kim is a proponent of mechanical keyboards, a type of computer keyboard that uses individual mechanical switches for each key rather than the rubber dome switches or membrane switches that are found on many standard keyboards. Arguing that that their durability and distinctive feel outweigh all other considerations, _____ that mechanical keyboards are worth their somewhat higher price.

3

Which choice completes the text so that it conforms to the conventions of Standard English?

A. Kim contends
B. Kim's contention is
C. it is contended by Kim
D. the contention of Kim is

Adobe, a building material made from a mixture of clay, sand, straw, and water, has been used for thousands of years in the construction of homes and other structures in arid regions of the world. _____ in the 13th century, the Great Mosque of Djenné in Mali, West Africa is the largest adobe building in the world.

4

Which choice completes the text so that it conforms to the conventions of Standard English?

A. Constructing it with their hands
B. A construction by hand
C. Constructed by hand
D. Due to constructing it by hand

Writing: Standard English Conventions

Practice Set 2: Medium-Hard

Since _____ in 2009, Adele's music has had ever-increasing commercial success. While her debut album "19" sold millions of copies, her second studio album, "21," became the best-selling album of the twenty-first century.

1

Which choice completes the text so that it conforms to the conventions of Standard English?

A. winning the Grammy for Best New Artist
B. her having won the Grammy for Best New Artist
C. she won the Grammy for Best New Artist
D. the Grammy for Best New Artist was won by her

Some scientists believe that the best approach to controlling cancer is to manipulate the body's own immune system rather than to try to attack the cancer cells directly. New medicines containing beta-glucan appear to work along these lines. Using this indirect approach, _____

2

Which choice completes the text so that it conforms to the conventions of Standard English?

A. cancerous growths are detected and destroyed by immune cells activated by the medicines.
B. the medicines activate immune cells to detect and destroy cancerous growths.
C. the detection and destruction of cancerous growths is caused by the medicines' activation of immune cells.
D. immune cells activated by the medicines detect and destroy cancerous growths.

_____ snake venom, researchers are hoping to build better medications for human snakebite victims by analyzing compounds in opossum blood.

3

Which choice completes the text so that it conforms to the conventions of Standard English?

A. Immune to
B. Since they are immune to
C. Because opossums are immune to
D. Being immune to

Julia Child was a beloved cookbook author and television personality known for hosting "The French Chef" on PBS. Her warm humor and distinctive physical presence endeared her to millions who didn't care about cooking, but she was also an accomplished chef. _____ at the famous Le Cordon Bleu cooking school in Paris, her detailed knowledge of French cuisine impressed even the most advanced culinary experts.

4

Which choice completes the text so that it conforms to the conventions of Standard English?

A. Trained
B. Having trained
C. She had trained
D. Thanks to her training

Writing: Expression of Ideas

Transitions

Preview Quiz

Choose the most logical transition.

1) Smith's movies often receive glowing reviews. (For instance / Therefore / Similarly), I bought a ticket for his newest film as soon as I heard about it.

2) Smith's movies often receive glowing reviews. (Similarly / For instance / However), the *New York Times* called his newest film "an instant classic."

3) Smith's movies often receive glowing reviews. (For instance / However / In fact), it often seems that no filmmaker is more universally beloved.

4) Smith's movies often receive glowing reviews. (Therefore / Similarly / In fact), his paintings are widely respected by critics.

Write in your answer.

5) What is the difference between the words *subsequently* and *consequently*?

6) What is the difference between the words *accordingly* and *similarly*?

Writing: Expression of Ideas

A well-written text should flow well from one topic to the next. Sometimes, this means making effective use of **transition** words and phrases such as *also, however, therefore, while, conversely, on the other hand,* and *in addition.*

Transitions can drastically change the meaning of a passage even when they don't create grammatical problems. Consider the difference in meaning in the examples below:

> *My sister, who just announced that she'd like to visit me this summer, is allergic to cats and dogs. <u>Unfortunately</u>, I bought a cat for my apartment last week.*

> *My sister, who just announced that she'd like to visit me this summer, is allergic to cats and dogs. <u>Therefore</u>, I bought a cat for my apartment last week.*

As these examples illustrate, the most important thing to consider when attacking transition questions is the *context*. When you work through transition questions on the test, be sure to ask yourself not just what is correct grammatically, but what makes the most sense in the context of the sentence and the paragraph. Consider the relationship between the ideas connected by the transition and ask yourself this: Is this a **continuation** in the same direction? Is it a **contrast**? Or is it something else?

Most transition words and phrases can be organized into the three broad categories shown on the next page: continuation words, contrast words, and sequence words.

Transitions

CONTINUATION

Addition or Similarity	Cause & Effect	Emphasis	Examples	Summary or Conclusion
<ul><li>moreover</li><li>similarly</li><li>likewise</li><li>furthermore</li><li>additionally</li><li>in addition</li><li>also</li><li>further</li><li>what's more</li><li>by the same token</li></ul>	To introduce the **cause**:<ul><li>For</li><li>Because</li><li>since</li></ul>To introduce the **effect** or **result**:<ul><li>therefore</li><li>thus</li><li>consequently</li><li>hence</li><li>as a result</li><li>accordingly</li><li>to these ends</li></ul>	<ul><li>in fact</li><li>indeed</li></ul>	<ul><li>for instance</li><li>for example</li><li>specifically</li><li>that is</li></ul>	<ul><li>in other words</li><li>in sum</li><li>to conclude</li><li>in conclusion</li><li>in brief</li><li>therefore</li><li>thus</li></ul>

CONTRAST

- though
- although
- nevertheless
- nonetheless
- still
- instead
- meanwhile
- however
- regardless
- by/in comparison
- by/in contrast
- alternatively
- but
- whereas
- on the other hand
- on the contrary
- conversely
- after all
- despite
- yet

TIME OR SEQUENCE

- first
- second
- third
- next
- later
- last
- finally
- previously
- currently
- subsequently
- afterward

TIP:
This list is not exhaustive! The English language offers a wide variety of ways to connect sentences and ideas. This is just a glimpse of some of the transitions that are most commonly seen on the SAT.

Writing: Expression of Ideas

The best way to handle a transition question is to follow a multi-part strategy.

Read.	Carefully read the first sentence or sentences (the part of the text that comes before the blank). Then, skip the blank—do NOT look at the answer choices yet—and read the second part of the text.
Summarize.	What was the big point of the first section? Try to summarize it in just a few words. Then, repeat: what was the big point of the second section?
Analyze and predict.	Consider what kind of relationship exists between those two big ideas. Is the second part continuing in the same direction? Is it a contrast? Or is it something else? Decide what transition word *you* might write into that blank if you didn't have answer choices.
Review the choices.	Go to the answer choices and find the best match for your prediction.
Re-read.	As a final step, read the whole text again with your answer choice plugged into the blank. Does it still make sense?

> **TIP:**
> These questions are generally ***not about the grammar***. In most cases, all four answer choices will be grammatically correct.

Let's explore that "analyze and predict" step a bit further. The first task here is to decide whether we need a **continuation** word, a **contrast** word, or something else. The tough part often is choosing between the options within those categories, especially in the continuation category. Look closely at the relationship between the ideas. In some cases, the second part of the text is taking the claim made in the first part a step farther, perhaps by implying a **cause-and-effect** relationship. In that case, try "therefore," "thus," "consequently," "hence," "accordingly," or "as a result."

Example: *Smith's movies often receive glowing reviews. <u>Therefore,</u> I bought a ticket for his newest film as soon as I heard about it.*

In other cases, we're simply moving from a general claim to a specific **illustration** of that claim. For these sentences, "for example" or "for instance" might work.

Example: *Smith's movies often receive glowing reviews. <u>For instance,</u> the New York Times called his newest film "an instant classic."*

If we want to use the second part of the text to **emphasize** the point made in the first part, try "indeed" or "in fact."

Example: *Smith's movies often receive glowing reviews. <u>In fact,</u> it often seems that no filmmaker is more universally beloved.*

Another possibility might be that the second part of the text isn't extending the first point at all, but rather switching to a new topic that is similar to the first one. In these situations, some good options include "similarly," "likewise," "additionally," "also," "moreover," and "by the same token."

Example: *Smith's movies often receive glowing reviews. <u>Similarly,</u> his paintings are widely respected by critics.*

The flow chart on the next page gives one example of a process for identifying the exact relationship between the sentences so you can choose the right transition word.

> **TIP:**
> Yes, there is some overlap in some of these categories. Some transition words can work in more than one way. Don't worry: in an SAT question, there will only be one choice that logically fits the sentence.

Writing: Expression of Ideas

Transitions Flow Chart

Is this a continuation, a contrast, or part of a sequence?

- **continuation** → **Are we introducing a new point or developing the same point?**
  - **new** → moreover, similarly, likewise, furthermore, additionally, also, and, by the same token
  - **same** → **Is there a cause & effect relationship?**
    - **yes** → **Does the transition introduce the cause or the effect/result?**
      - **cause** → for, because, since
      - **effect** → therefore, thus, consequently, hence, accordingly, as a result, to these ends
    - **no** → **Is it providing emphasis, examples, or a summary?**
      - **emphasis** → in fact, indeed
      - **examples** → for instance, for example, specifically
      - **summary** → in other words, in sum, to conclude, in conclusion, in brief, overall
- **contrast** → though, although, nevertheless, nonetheless, still, instead, meanwhile, however, regardless, by contrast, by comparison, alternatively, but, whereas, on the other hand, conversely, despite, yet
- **sequence** → first, second, third, next, later, last, finally, previously, currently, subsequently, afterward

---

TIP:

Although there can be many subtle differences that indicate a continuation in the same direction, the contrast keywords are extremely similar in meaning. Generally speaking, if you can use the word "however," you can probably use the word "nevertheless" as well. So in a transition question, if you see both of those words among your answer choices, neither one is likely to be the right answer.

Try It — Which choice completes the text with the most logical transition? **Choose A, B, _or both_**.

1) The umpire made one bad call after another. _____ the game was completely unfair.

   Prediction: _____

   A. Next,
   B. As a result,

2) The intern had very little experience; _____ he had never worked in an office before.

   Prediction: _____

   A. Indeed,
   B. Subsequently,

3) We drove for three straight days. _____ on Friday, we arrived at our destination.

   Prediction: _____

   A. Finally,
   B. At last,

4) My English teacher tells a lot of jokes during class. _____ my history teacher is quiet and withdrawn.

   Prediction: _____

   A. Similarly,
   B. In contrast,

Writing: Expression of Ideas

> **CHALLENGE:**
>
> The words "similarly" and "accordingly" are closely related but not exactly the same. Both indicate a continuation rather than a contrast. The difference lies in whether you're introducing a new example or just continuing/extending the same one you started with.
>
> To introduce a new example that's like the one already mentioned, use "similarly":
>
> *Example: Wearing a helmet should be a regular habit for everyone who rollerblades. <u>Similarly,</u> skaters should wear pads on their knees and elbows.*
>
> Use "accordingly" to continue / expand on the same example rather than introduce a new one.
>
> *Example: Wearing a helmet should be a regular habit for everyone who rollerblades. <u>Accordingly,</u> I bought a helmet on the same day I bought my skates.*

Chapter Answer Key

Try It	1)	B
	2)	A
	3)	A and B
	4)	B

Practice Set 1: Easy-Medium

When a beam of light passes through a medium containing small particles, such as dust, smoke, or mist, the light interacts with the particles and scatters in many directions. _____ the medium becomes visible, a phenomenon known as the Tyndall effect.

1

Which choice completes the text with the most logical transition?

A. Overall,
B. By the same token,
C. As a result,
D. Regardless,

Long-distance runners use two kinds of cognitive strategies to cope with the physical and mental challenges of their sport. "Associative" strategies involve focusing their attention on the internal sensations of running (such as breathing rate and muscle fatigue) in order to maintain a sense of control over their physical state and stay motivated. _____ "dissociative" strategies involve focusing on external stimuli (such as the scenery or other runners around them) to distract themselves from the physical discomfort and maintain a positive mental attitude.

2

Which choice completes the text with the most logical transition?

A. Similarly,
B. In contrast,
C. In other words,
D. Still,

Art scholars use semiotics, the study of signs and symbols, to analyze how visual elements are used to convey meaning and how cultural contexts can shape interpretation. _____ the use of certain colors or shapes might be associated with specific cultural or historical ideas, while the arrangement of elements within a painting might create a certain mood or convey a particular message.

3

Which choice completes the text with the most logical transition?

A. Meanwhile,
B. Additionally,
C. Therefore,
D. For example,

Although the word "heart" implies a complicated multi-chambered organ such as that found in the human chest, the word actually covers a wide variety of structures. The heart of the lancelet, a tiny sea creature found in shallow coastal waters, is nothing more than a single muscular tube that contracts rhythmically to circulate blood. Unlike in larger chordates, there is no complex network of blood vessels; lancelets rely instead on the movement of fluids within their body cavity to distribute nutrients and oxygen. _____ despite its simplicity, the lancelet must be said to possess a circulatory system due to its possession of a beating heart.

4

Which choice completes the text with the most logical transition?

A. Still,
B. Besides,
C. Consequently,
D. In sum,

Writing: Expression of Ideas

A recent study investigated the impact of aging on the flavor and tenderness of beef strip loins. The researchers found that aging the beef for a period of 14 to 21 days can significantly improve its tenderness, with the collagen in the meat breaking down over time. _____ the study also noted that prolonged aging beyond 21 days can lead to a decline in tenderness and a decrease in desirable flavor compounds.

5

Which choice completes the text with the most logical transition?

A. Moreover,
B. In conclusion,
C. However,
D. In fact,

The death of Nero in 68 CE left a power vacuum in the Roman empire, as there was no clear successor to the throne. _____ the ensuing chapter of Roman history was rife with political instability and conflict, marked by the rapid succession of four different emperors over the course of a single year.

6

Which choice completes the text with the most logical transition?

A. Despite this,
B. As a result,
C. Alternatively,
D. In other words,

Although the 1913 Bohr model of the atom was a significant advancement in atomic theory, it is now known to be inaccurate in several ways. First, the model suggests that electrons move in circular orbits, when in fact they orbit in complex patterns described by quantum mechanics. _____ the Bohr model assumes that electrons have a definite position and momentum, which is incompatible with the Heisenberg uncertainty principle. Despite these inaccuracies, however, the Bohr model provides a useful conceptual framework for understanding atomic structure and behavior, and as a result, it is still taught in introductory science courses today.

7

Which choice completes the text with the most logical transition?

A. Second,
B. For instance,
C. Thus,
D. Regardless,

In 2016, singer-songwriter Bob Dylan was awarded the Nobel Prize for Literature "for having created new poetic expressions within the great American song tradition." _____ some protested the idea of such a prestigious award going to a rock musician, for many others, it was a long-overdue recognition of the enduring influence of a true American original.

8

Which choice completes the text with the most logical transition?

A. Because
B. Although
C. Due to the fact that
D. Given that

Practice Set 2: Medium-Hard

Bipedalism (the ability to walk on two feet) has played a key role in the evolution of our species. Compared to other forms of locomotion, such as quadrupedalism or swimming, bipedalism is less stable and requires a more complex series of muscular and skeletal movements to maintain balance and motion. _____ bipedalism also offers unique advantages such as greater efficiency of energy expenditure and the ability to free up the hands for carrying objects or manipulating tools.

1

Which choice completes the text with the most logical transition?

A. Indeed,
B. However,
C. Moreover,
D. By comparison,

Purple loosestrife (*Lythrum salicaria*) is an invasive plant species that has had a significant impact on North American wetlands since its introduction from Europe in the early 19th century. The plant is highly adaptable, outcompetes native plants, alters the natural balance of the ecosystem, and impedes water flow. _____ it reduces biodiversity, impacting ecosystem functions and ultimately altering the physical structure of wetlands. This has been detrimental to the health of North American wetlands, causing long-term damage that is difficult to reverse.

2

Which choice completes the text with the most logical transition?

A. For example,
B. Nonetheless,
C. Finally,
D. Accordingly,

The use of limestone as a soil additive is a long-established practice that dates back centuries, with evidence of its use found in ancient Roman and Egyptian civilizations. However, while limestone has traditionally been employed by conventional large-scale farms to address issues such as soil acidity and erosion, evidence suggests a shift in usage. _____ small-scale farmers are turning to limestone as a natural and sustainable means of improving soil quality, while many organic farmers are using limestone to enhance soil structure and promote plant growth. As a result, the use of limestone is becoming more widespread and diverse, reflecting a growing awareness of the importance of soil health in modern agriculture.

3

Which choice completes the text with the most logical transition?

A. Similarly,
B. Increasingly,
C. In other words,
D. Furthermore,

Writing: Expression of Ideas

Andy Warhol was a prominent American artist and a leading figure in the Pop Art movement of the 1960s. His work, which often featured images of celebrities and everyday objects, sought to challenge traditional notions of art and to blur the lines between high and low culture. While Warhol's work was highly influential and his contributions to the art world are widely recognized, some critics contend that his popularity and commercial success may have overshadowed his artistic merit. _____ Warhol's impact on the art world and on popular culture more broadly remains undeniable, and his work continues to be celebrated and studied by art enthusiasts around the world.

4

Which choice completes the text with the most logical transition?

A. Nevertheless,
B. Accordingly,
C. Furthermore,
D. In other words,

The mandates of journalistic ethics require reporters to maintain impartiality and objectivity in their reporting, regardless of their personal beliefs or biases. Journalists must also strive to ensure that their reporting does not infringe on the privacy of individuals, particularly those who may be vulnerable or marginalized. In the digital age, the risks posed by rapidly-spreading misinformation only underscore the importance of accuracy and reliability in reporting. _____ journalists must remain vigilant in upholding ethical standards and commit to providing the public with truthful, unbiased information.

5

Which choice completes the text with the most logical transition?

A. Similarly,
B. In other words,
C. To this end,
D. Conversely,

Early sunscreens contained UV-B absorbers such as para-aminobenzoic acid, which was effective in preventing sunburn but did not provide protection against UV-A radiation. At the time, UV-B radiation was seen as the primary cause of sun-related skin damage, but later research established that UV-A radiation can also harm skin cells and increase the risk of skin cancer. _____ the development of sunscreens with broad-spectrum protection against both UV-B and UV-A radiation became a priority in the field of dermatology in the 1980s and 1990s. This led to the introduction of new sunscreen ingredients such as avobenzone, which blocks both types of radiation and thus significantly enhances the efficacy of modern-day sunscreens.

6

Which choice completes the text with the most logical transition?

A. Consequently,
B. In fact,
C. Instead,
D. Moreover,

- 204 -

TM and © 2023 PrepMatters, Inc. All rights reserved.

While both Neanderthals and Cro-Magnons are classified as members of the *Homo* genus, some researchers argue that they are separate species due to differences in physical characteristics and genetics. Neanderthals are known for their robust builds, large brow ridges, and prominent nasal cavities, while Cro-Magnons are characterized by their more gracile features and higher cranial capacity. _____ genetic analysis has shown that Neanderthals and Cro-Magnons interbred to some degree, suggesting that they may have been distinct but related groups rather than entirely separate species.

7

Which choice completes the text with the most logical transition?

A. Hence,
B. However,
C. By the same token,
D. In addition,

Avogadro's number, which is approximately 6.022×10^{23}, represents the number of particles in one mole of a substance. The number is significant because it provides a way to relate macroscopic properties of a substance, such as its mass, volume, and density, to the microscopic properties of its constituent particles. _____ knowing the molar mass of a substance allows us to calculate the number of particles present in a given mass of the substance, or the mass of a given number of particles.

8

Which choice completes the text with the most logical transition?

A. Besides,
B. Nevertheless,
C. For example,
D. Still,

For 160 million years, dinosaurs ruled the earth. Their success was due in part to evolutionary adaptations that allowed them to thrive in a variety of environments, and in part to the distinct geographic arrangement of the continents at the time, which allowed the animals to occupy a wide range of habitats, find new food sources, and avoid competition with other predators. These factors made the creatures ideally suited for the conditions around them, allowing them to outcompete countless other life forms. _____ were it not for the catastrophic environmental disruption that struck their world 65 million years ago, dinosaurs might have remained the dominant species on Earth to this day.

9

Which choice completes the text with the most logical transition?

A. Indeed,
B. Specifically,
C. Nonetheless,
D. On the other hand,

Rhetorical Synthesis

Preview Quiz:

1) When evaluating an answer choice for a rhetorical synthesis question, how important are the following considerations?

	very important	somewhat important	unimportant
Using proper grammar and punctuation	_____	_____	_____
Using sophisticated vocabulary words	_____	_____	_____
Satisfying the task set out in the question	_____	_____	_____

Choose the best answer.

2) While researching a topic, a student has taken the following notes:

- Burkina Faso is a country in western Africa.
- Its capital city is Ouagadougou.
- Ouagadougou is home to several important sculptures that reflect the region's cultural heritage.
- The Naba Koom statue is one the city's most famous sculptures.
- The statue is 6 meters tall and is located in front of the railway station.
- It depicts a woman holding a calabash full of water.
- A calabash is a type of gourd native to western Africa.
- The water is extended towards the rail station as a welcome for visitors to the city.

The student wants to emphasize the significance of the calabash in the Naba Koom statue. Which choice most effectively uses relevant information from the notes to accomplish this goal?

A) The Naba Koom statue is a 6-meter-tall sculpture in Ouagadougou, the capital of Burkina Faso.
B) In her hands, the Naba Koom statue holds a calabash—a type of gourd native to western Africa—which is filled with water.
C) The Naba Koom statue extends her calabash full of water towards the rail station as a welcome for visitors to Ouagadougou.
D) Several important sculptures in Ouagadougou reflect the region's cultural heritage, and the Naba Koom statue is one of the most famous of these.

Rhetorical Synthesis

All the other Writing question types ask you to evaluate someone else's work, but this one turns the tables on you: it's now your job to help create the writing yourself. You'll be placed in the position of a student writing a research paper, where the research has already been completed for you. Based on a list of bullet points that the research has yielded, you'll be asked to select the sentence that best satisfies a specific goal.

Read the question carefully. Your task is *not* just to pick the sentence that you think is the best written; in fact, the correct answer may be no more polished than any of the others. Instead, you must pick the sentence that does the best job of emphasizing some specific point, or making a comparison, or introducing an author to a new audience, or something else entirely—whatever goal was specified in the question.

You don't necessarily need to use all the bullet points. There may be some information provided that is irrelevant to the task set for you in the question. The longest answer is not necessarily the right one.

You don't necessarily need to use *any* of the bullet points. While the information in one or more of the bullet points will certainly be included in the right answer, it's not always essential to read them first. If you're pressed for time in this section, consider skipping the bullet points entirely and just picking the answer choice that best serves the goal laid out for you in the question. In many cases, there will only be one.

FROM THE BLOG

People can, effectively, be stressed out of their minds.
When brains are stressed, thinking is not clear, leaving us far from an optimal learning mood. Addressing your stress level – with breaks, with rest, with whatever you need – is a key part of preparing for the SAT.

Writing: Expression of Ideas

Time to take a detailed look at an example.

Example: *While researching a topic, a student has taken the following notes:*

- *Burkina Faso is a country in western Africa.*
- *Its capital city is Ouagadougou.*
- *Ouagadougou is home to several important sculptures that reflect the region's cultural heritage.*
- *The Naba Koom statue is one the city's most famous sculptures.*
- *The statue is 6 meters tall and is located in front of the railway station.*
- *It depicts a woman holding a calabash full of water.*
- *A calabash is a type of gourd native to western Africa.*
- *The water is extended towards the rail station as a welcome for visitors to the city.*

The student wants to emphasize the significance of the calabash in the Naba Koom statue. Which choice most effectively uses relevant information from the notes to accomplish this goal?

A) *The Naba Koom statue is a 6-meter-tall sculpture in Ouagadougou, the capital of Burkina Faso.*
B) *In her hands, the Naba Koom statue holds a calabash—a type of gourd native to western Africa—which is filled with water.*
C) *The Naba Koom statue extends her calabash full of water towards the rail station as a welcome for visitors to Ouagadougou.*
D) *Several important sculptures in Ouagadougou reflect the region's cultural heritage, and the Naba Koom statue is one of the most famous of these.*

The question asks us to emphasize the significance of the calabash in the Naba Koom statue, so that's our main focus. Choices A and D can be quickly eliminated, as they don't mention the calabash at all. Choice B tells us what the calabash is, but not *why* it's present in the sculpture. Only choice C emphasizes the significance of the calabash: it's a gesture of welcome for visitors to the city. The right answer is **C**.

TIP:

For many of the Writing questions, a major consideration when evaluating an answer choice is how well-written its version of the sentence is. That is **not** a consideration for Rhetorical Synthesis questions. All we care about here is the task set for us in the question. The right answer is the one that does the best job of accomplishing *that specific task*; it won't necessarily be any better written than any of the other options.

Notice that we really didn't need to have read the bullet points about the Naba Koom statute in order to pick the right answer.

> **Try It** It's often possible to pick the right answer choice *without reading the bullet points at all*. Use the question below to practice: try picking the right answer when you have no bullet points at all to read.
>
> The student wants to explain, to an audience already familiar with DNA testing methods, why forensic scientists prefer STR analysis over RFLP.
>
> 1) List the elements that the right answer must contain:
>
>   Element #1:
>
>   Element #2:
>
> 2) Evaluate the answer choices below by considering how well it satisfies each of the elements you listed.
>
> | | Element #1 | Element #2 |
> |---|---|---|
> | A) Short Tandem Repeat (STR) analysis is a widely used technique in forensic DNA testing that has come to replace older methods such as Restriction Fragment Length Polymorphism (RFLP). | _____ | _____ |
> | B) STR analysis offers a high degree of discrimination or resolving power, meaning it can differentiate between individuals with great accuracy. | _____ | _____ |
> | C) RFLP analysis requires a larger amount of DNA for testing compared to STR, but it is still suitable for analysis if a large enough sample is available. | _____ | _____ |
> | D) The advantages of STR analysis over RFLP include its higher sensitivity, its faster processing time, and its potential for automation. | _____ | _____ |
>
> 3) What is the best answer?

Writing: Expression of Ideas

Chapter Answer Key

Try It

1) Element #1: the sentence should be tailored for an audience that is already familiar with DNA testing methods
Element #2: the sentence should compare STR analysis to RFLP and explain why STR is preferred.

2)
	Element #1	Element #2
A)	N	N
B)	Y	N
C)	Y	N
D)	Y	Y

3) D

Practice Set 1: Easy-Medium

While researching a topic, a student has taken the following notes:

- Hyperion is a coast redwood (*Sequoia sempervirens*) tree located in Redwood National Park in California.
- It measures 115.7 meters tall.
- Centurion is a mountain ash (*Eucalyptus regnans*) tree located in Tasmania, Australia.
- It measures 100.5 meters tall.
- Hyperion and Centurion are the two tallest known trees in the world.

1

The student wants to compare the heights of the two trees. Which choice most effectively uses relevant information from the notes to accomplish this goal?

A. Hyperion, which measures 115.7 meters tall, is a coast redwood tree located in Redwood National Park in California.
B. Some trees, including a *Sequoia sempervirens* tree in California and a *Eucalyptus regnans* tree in Australia, are more than 100 meters tall.
C. Hyperion, a coast redwood tree located in California, and Centurion, a mountain ash tree located in Australia, are the two tallest known trees in the world.
D. Hyperion measures 115.7 meters tall, while the slightly shorter Centurion measures 100.5 meters tall.

While researching a topic, a student has taken the following notes:

- Olafur Eliasson is a Danish-Icelandic artist.
- He created *The Weather Project* in 2003.
- *The Weather Project* is a large-scale installation consisting of a giant artificial sun, a misty atmosphere, and a reflective ceiling.
- These elements combined to create an illusion of a seemingly endless horizon.

2

The student wants to describe *The Weather Project* to an audience unfamiliar with Olafur Eliasson's work. Which choice most effectively uses relevant information from the notes to accomplish this goal?

A. Eliasson's 2003 installation *The Weather Project*, which created an illusion of a seemingly endless horizon, included such features as a giant artificial sun, a misty atmosphere, and a reflective ceiling.
B. Danish-Icelandic artist Olafur Eliasson created *The Weather Project* in 2003.
C. The components of *The Weather Project* jointly created an illusion of a seemingly endless horizon.
D. *The Weather Project*, a large-scale installation created by Danish-Icelandic artist Olafur Eliasson in 2003, used a giant artificial sun, a misty atmosphere, and a reflective ceiling to create an illusion of a seemingly endless horizon.

Writing: Expression of Ideas

While researching a topic, a student has taken the following notes:

- The viperfish is a marine animal in the genus *Chauliodus*.
- Viperfish are found in tropical and temperate waters, often at depths of 5,000 feet or more.
- The viperfish has a large mouth with hinged lower jaws and long, needle-like teeth.
- Extending from the viperfish's spine is a light-producing organ.
- Viperfish use the glowing organ to attract prey.

3

The student wants to explain the viperfish's predation habits while emphasizing prominent aspects of its appearance. Which choice most effectively uses relevant information from the notes to accomplish this goal?

A. The viperfish uses its long, needle-like teeth to trap prey lured by a light-producing organ extending from its spine.
B. Viperfish, of the genus *Chauliodus*, are equipped with long, needle-like teeth and hinged lower jaws.
C. Because viperfish dwell at depths of 5,000 feet or more, they need to use a light-producing organ to attract prey.
D. The viperfish is found in tropical and temperate waters, roughly 5,000 feet below the ocean surface.

While researching a topic, a student has taken the following notes:

- Claudio Monteverdi (1567-1643) was a prolific Italian composer of both secular and sacred music.
- He is credited with helping to develop the operatic form.
- He wrote the opera *L'Orfeo* in 1607.
- A madrigal is a type of secular vocal music.
- Monteverdi wrote the dramatic madrigal "Il Combattimento di Tancredi e Clorinda" in 1624.

4

The student wants to emphasize a difference between the two works. Which choice most effectively uses relevant information from the notes to accomplish this goal?

A. The musical works *L'Orfeo* and "Il Combattimento di Tancredi e Clorinda" were both completed by Claudio Monteverdi in the 1600s.
B. Monteverdi helped to develop the operatic form and composed a significant number of musical works, including *L'Orfeo* and "Il Combattimento di Tancredi e Clorinda."
C. While both works were composed by Monteverdi, *L'Orfeo* is an opera, while "Il Combattimento di Tancredi e Clorinda" is a madrigal.
D. "Il Combattimento di Tancredi e Clorinda" was a dramatic madrigal, a type of secular vocal music, written by Monteverdi in 1624.

While researching a topic, a student has taken the following notes:

- Historians use a variety of methods to construct historical narratives.
- Traditional methods include archival research and textual analysis.
- These methods do not always capture the stories of marginalized groups.
- Historians can also use digital history, which involves analysis with digital tools and technologies.
- This technique better represents the perspectives of marginalized groups.

5

The student wants to explain an advantage of the use of digital history. Which choice most effectively uses relevant information from the notes to accomplish this goal?

A. For historians aiming to capture the stories of marginalized groups, traditional methods are not always sufficient.
B. The use of digital history better positions historians to explore the perspectives of marginalized groups, whose stories may not have been fully represented in traditional historical narratives.
C. Historians can use digital tools and technologies, a method known as digital history.
D. As techniques for constructing a historical narrative, traditional methods and digital history vary in the degree to which they are able to represent the perspectives of marginalized groups.

While researching a topic, a student has taken the following notes:

- In 2015, the UK-based company Moggyblog.com coined the term "pawternity leave."
- The term is a combination of the terms "paternity leave" and "paw."
- "Pawternity leave" refers to time off work given to employees who have recently adopted a new pet.
- In India, the publisher Harper Collins offers its employees one week of paid leave following adoption of a pet.
- Mparticle, a data platform provider, offers two weeks of paid leave to employees who adopt a rescue dog.

6

The student wants to provide an explanation and example of the term "pawternity leave." Which choice most effectively uses relevant information from the notes to accomplish this goal?

A. The term "pawternity leave," coined by Moggyblog.com in 2015, is a combination of the terms "paternity leave" and "paw."
B. Harper Collins and Mparticle both offer forms of "pawternity leave," a term coined by the UK-based company Moggyblog.com.
C. "Pawternity leave" refers to time off work given to employees who have recently adopted a new pet; for instance, the data platform provider Mparticle offers two weeks of paid leave to employees who adopt a rescue dog.
D. In 2015, Moggyblog.com coined the term "pawternity leave" to refer to time off work given to employees who have recently adopted a new pet.

Writing: Expression of Ideas

While researching a topic, a student has taken the following notes:

- Numerical modeling is a key tool for the understanding of glacier dynamics.
- Numerical models are computer-based simulations that represent the physical processes occurring within and around glaciers.
- These models are based on mathematical equations that describe the physics of ice flow.
- A 2014 study used numerical modeling to simulate the behavior of the Jakobshavn Isbrae glacier in Greenland.
- Researchers inputted data and ran simulations with different scenarios.
- They found that water infiltrates the ice during the summer melt season.
- This reduces the friction between the ice and the bedrock.
- As a result, the glacier accelerates and flows more rapidly during this period.

7

The student wants to explain the findings of the 2014 study and mention the source of the information. Which choice most effectively uses relevant information from the notes to accomplish this goal?

A. The Jakobshavn Isbrae glacier flows more rapidly during the summer melt season, according to computer simulations performed as part of a 2014 study.
B. In 2014, researchers used mathematical equations to simulate the behavior of the Jakobshavn Isbrae glacier.
C. During the summer melt season, water infiltrates glacier ice, reducing the friction between the ice and the bedrock.
D. Glacier dynamics can be modeled with computer-based simulations, as researchers proved in a 2014 study of the Jakobshavn Isbrae glacier.

While researching a topic, a student has taken the following notes:

- The *mulieres Salernitanae* were a group of female physicians and authors in medieval Salerno, Italy.
- They were associated with *Schola Medica Salernitana*, which was one of the leading medical schools during the 11th to 13th centuries.
- One prominent figure associated with the group was Trotula.
- Trotula's works have had a significant impact on the field of medicine.
- One of her most famous treatises is *Trotula Major*.
- The work addressed various topics related to women's health and gynecology.

8

The student wants to introduce Trotula and her impact on the field of medicine to an audience already familiar with the *mulieres Salernitanae*. Which choice most effectively uses relevant information from the notes to accomplish this goal?

A. Trotula was a medieval medical practitioner associated with the renowned medical school *Schola Medica Salernitana*.
B. The *mulieres Salernitanae* of Salerno were female medical practitioners during the medieval period, known for their contributions to medical practice and the authorship of medical treatises.
C. Trotula, a medical practitioner who was associated with the famed *mulieres Salernitanae,* was a physician and author who wrote several influential works on women's health.
D. *Schola Medica Salernitana* flourished during the 11th to 13th centuries and was one of the leading centers of medical education at the time; one famous figure associated with the school was Trotula.

Practice Set 2: Medium-Hard

While researching a topic, a student has taken the following notes:

- The term "language loss" refers to the phenomenon of languages dying out due to a lack of living speakers.
- More than 6,900 languages exist on Earth.
- The number of speakers per language varies widely.
- The 20 languages with the most speakers account for 50% of the global population.
- The 100 languages with the most speakers account for 80% of the global population.
- A language is considered "critically endangered" if it is spoken by so few people that it is likely to be lost within a few years.
- More than 3,000 languages are critically endangered.

1

The student wants to emphasize the scope of the language loss problem. Which choice most effectively uses relevant information from the notes to accomplish this goal?

A. The term "language loss" refers to the phenomenon of languages dying out due to a lack of living speakers.
B. Although 6,900 languages exist on Earth, thousands of these languages are spoken by so few people that they are likely to be lost forever within the next few years.
C. 6,900 languages are spoken on Earth, but the number of speakers varies widely; the 20 languages with the most speakers account for 50% of the global population.
D. Many languages are considered "critically endangered," meaning that they are spoken by so few people that they are likely to be lost within a few years.

While researching a topic, a student has taken the following notes:

- A "quantum computer" is a type of computer that uses the principles of quantum mechanics to perform calculations.
- Classical computers use bits that can take one of two values (either 0 or 1).
- Quantum computers use quantum bits (or "qubits"), which can exist in multiple states at the same time.
- In 2019, researchers conducted an experiment with a quantum computer called Sycamore in an effort to demonstrate the ability of a quantum computer to perform a task that is beyond the reach of classical computers.
- Sycamore was given a calculation task that would have taken a classical supercomputer thousands of years to complete.
- Sycamore completed the task in 200 seconds.

2

The student wants to emphasize the significance of the experiment involving Sycamore. Which choice most effectively uses relevant information from the notes to accomplish this goal?

A. The computer involved in the 2019 experiment used quantum bits, each of which could exist in multiple states at the same time.
B. Sycamore is a quantum computer—a computer that performs calculations using the principles of quantum mechanics—that was involved in a 2019 experiment.
C. By completing in only 200 seconds a task that a classical supercomputer would have taken thousands of years to complete, Sycamore demonstrated the ability of a quantum computer to perform a task that is beyond the reach of classical computers.
D. If the task given to Sycamore in the 2019 experiment had been given to a computer using bits that can take one of two values (0 or 1), that computer would have required thousands of years to complete the task.

Writing: Expression of Ideas

While researching a topic, a student has taken the following notes:

- The relationship between blood pressure and cognitive decline in older adults has been the subject of considerable research.
- Research on this topic has been primarily conducted on white populations.
- A 2017 study investigated whether the conclusions of previous research would hold true for black populations.
- The researchers analyzed data from a large, ongoing cohort study.
- They found that high blood pressure was associated with cognitive decline in both black and white individuals.
- They also found that black individuals were at greater risk for both conditions.

3

The student wants to emphasize the aim of the study. Which choice most effectively uses relevant information from the notes to accomplish this goal?

A. Researchers wanted to determine whether previous conclusions about the relationship between blood pressure and cognitive decline, which were based on research primarily conducted on white populations, would also hold true for black populations.
B. After analyzing data from a large, ongoing cohort study, researchers determined that high blood pressure was associated with cognitive decline in both black and white individuals.
C. Researchers concluded that black individuals are at greater risk than white individuals for both high blood pressure and cognitive decline.
D. Researchers analyzed data from a large, ongoing cohort study of both black and white individuals.

While researching a topic, a student has taken the following notes:

- Tardigrades are exceptionally hardy creatures known for their ability to survive in extreme environments.
- In 2015, a study exposed tardigrades and several other small invertebrates to extreme temperatures and radiation.
- Most of the species tested were not able to survive.
- Tardigrades survived exposure to temperatures as low as −272°C (one degree above absolute zero) and as high as 151°C.
- The tardigrades also survived ionizing radiation doses of up to 5700 gray (Gy).
- A dose of 10-20 Gy usually lethal for humans.

4

The student wants to emphasize how hardy the tardigrade is relative to other small invertebrates. Which choice most effectively uses relevant information from the notes to accomplish this goal?

A. A 2015 study determined that tardigrades can survive temperatures ranging from −272°C to 151°C and ionizing radiation doses of up to 5700 Gy.
B. Most of the species tested in the 2015 study were not able to survive the extreme temperatures and radiation to which they were exposed.
C. While most small invertebrates are not able to survive exposure to ionizing radiation doses of 5700 Gy, tardigrades were shown to survive these conditions in a 2015 study.
D. Compared to other small invertebrates, tardigrades are exceptionally hardy: they can survive temperatures ranging from −272°C to 151°C and ionizing radiation doses of up to 5700 Gy.

While researching a topic, a student has taken the following notes:

- Teatro Campesino was a Chicano theater group founded in 1965 in Delano, California by Luis Valdez.
- Its primary goal was to use theater as a tool for political activism.
- Performances incorporated elements of traditional Mexican culture.
- The plays focused on issues of importance to the Chicano community, such as the exploitation of farmworkers and the importance of union organizing.
- Performances often took place in the fields where farmworkers were laboring.
- The plays energized farmworkers and drew attention to their plight.
- Luis Valdez was closely connected to labor leader César Chávez and his United Farm Workers union.

5

The student wants to explain how the Teatro Campesino used theater as a tool for political activism. Which choice most effectively uses relevant information from the notes to accomplish this goal?

A. Teatro Campesino's performances, which often took place in fields where Chicano farmworkers were laboring, focused on issues such as the exploitation of farmworkers and the importance of union organizing.
B. Luis Valdez, who was closely connected to labor leader César Chávez and his United Farm Workers union, founded Teatro Campesino in 1965.
C. Founded in 1965 in Delano, California, Teatro Campesino performed plays that incorporated elements of traditional Mexican culture.
D. The performance settings, cultural influences, and subject matter of Teatro Campesino's plays energized Chicano farmworkers and drew attention to their plight.

While researching a topic, a student has taken the following notes:

- An ant foraging for food leaves behind a trail of pheromones.
- Other ants detect the pheromones and follow the same path.
- Ants can adjust the strength and direction of the trail based on changing conditions.
- Ants are one of many species that solve problems by working in parallel.
- This strategy involves a large number of creatures performing simple actions whose collective impact can solve a complex problem.

6

The student wants to make and support a generalization about animal behavior. Which choice most effectively uses relevant information from the notes to accomplish this goal?

A. Many species are capable of working in parallel: a large number of creatures performs simple actions whose collective impact can solve a complex problem.
B. Large groups of animals can work in parallel to solve a complex problem: ants can collectively establish a trail to a food source and adjust the trail based on changing conditions.
C. Ants can adjust the strength and direction of a food trail based on changing conditions; thus, though the individual ants are performing simple actions, their collective impact can solve a complex problem.
D. An ant foraging for food leaves behind a trail of pheromones; other ants detect the pheromones and follow the same path.

Writing: Expression of Ideas

While researching a topic, a student has taken the following notes:

- The parathyroid glands are small endocrine glands located in the neck.
- They produce and release parathyroid hormone (PTH).
- PTH helps maintain the balance of calcium in the blood, bones, and other tissues.
- It acts on the bones, kidneys, and intestines to increase calcium absorption, reabsorption, and mobilization.
- PTH also acts on the kidneys to reduce the reabsorption of phosphorus.
- This helps maintain the balance of phosphorus in the body by preventing excessive buildup.

7

The student wants to explain what parathyroid glands are and describe their effect on the body. Which choice most effectively uses relevant information from the notes to accomplish this goal?

A. Parathyroid glands, which produce and release parathyroid hormone, are located in the neck.
B. By reducing the reabsorption of phosphorus, parathyroid hormone prevents excessive phosphorus buildup.
C. The parathyroid glands are small endocrine glands that produce parathyroid hormone to regulate calcium and phosphorus levels in the body.
D. Parathyroid hormone acts to increase calcium absorption, reabsorption, and mobilization.

While researching a topic, a student has taken the following notes:

- Workers renovating houses with lead-based paint should always wear personal protective equipment (PPE).
- PPE includes disposable coveralls, gloves, shoe covers, and face masks.
- This equipment protects workers from lead dust.
- Lead is a toxic metal that can affect various organs and systems.
- When lead dust is inhaled, it can enter the bloodstream and accumulate over time, leading to lead poisoning.
- In children, lead exposure can result in learning disabilities, reduced IQ, and behavioral issues.
- In adults, lead exposure can cause cognitive impairment and mood disorders.
- Prolonged exposure to lead dust can contribute to the development of respiratory conditions, including bronchitis and pneumonia.
- Lead can cause increased blood pressure and an increased risk of heart attacks and strokes.

8

The student wants to explain why workers should wear protective equipment when working in homes with lead-based paint. Which choice most effectively uses relevant information from the notes to accomplish this goal?

A. Protective equipment prevents workers from inhaling lead, a toxic chemical that can lead to harmful neurological, respiratory, and cardiovasculatory effects.
B. The acronym PPE refers to personal protective equipment, which can include disposable coveralls, gloves, shoe covers, and face masks.
C. Exposure to lead dust can lead to lead poisoning, which can cause cognitive impairment and respiratory conditions over time.
D. Lead buildup in the bloodstream is associated with an increased risk of cardiovascular problems such as high blood pressure, heart attacks, and strokes.

Math Section Overview

There are four general categories of math topics covered on the test.

- *Algebra*

    These questions focus on interpreting, manipulating, and solving linear equations. Make sure your algebra skills are strong and that you understand what each piece of a linear equation represents.

- *Advanced Math*

    Sort of next-level algebra, these problems will ask you to work with quadratic and other non-linear equations such as exponential functions and higher-order polynomials. You may be asked to characterize parts of these equations as well as to work with and solve them.

- *Problem Solving and Data Analysis*

    This category covers topics such as ratios, percentages, unit conversions, and working with charts/tables of data.

- *Geometry and Trigonometry*

    Problems in this category involve finding area or volume; using your knowledge of SOH-CAH-TOA; and working with similar triangles and other polygons.

Section Breakdown

Algebra
13-15 per section
≈ 35%

Advanced Math
13-15 per section
≈ 35%

Problem-Solving and Data Analysis
5-7 per section
≈ 15%

Geometry and Trigonometry
5-7 per section
≈ 15%

Strategy in Brief

Because the SAT is very different from most tests you take in school, the best method for solving SAT Math problems is often not the way you were taught in the classroom. The strategies we present in this introductory section are tailored to standardized testing and can be helpful in raising your score.

It is often helpful to ask yourself a series of questions when confronted with a difficult math problem.

- What specifically am I being asked to solve? Can I simplify the problem?

- Can I approximate? Is there a shortcut that will eliminate some complicated calculations?

- Do I know a formula?

Many find going through this checklist takes some of the mental burden off answering math questions, since the first moments are spent reacting instead of thinking. If you know a formula that's relevant to the question, be sure to get it down on your scratch paper. Simply writing out a formula will often help clarify what a question is asking for.

If you don't know how to get to the answer, start by writing down what you *do* know. Perhaps the question is asking for the measure of angle A, and all you can see how to figure out is the measure of angle B. Go ahead and fill that in. Once it's on the page, you may find that angle B actually helps you determine angle C, and the sum of angles B and C is supplementary to angle A, and so on… and before you know it, you've solved the problem. The key is to get your pencil moving—it's sitting and staring at the problem that's the enemy.

Back-solving and Substitution

Preview Quiz

Solve each of the following.

1) If the product of three consecutive odd integers is 1,287, what is the middle integer?

    A) 11
    B) 13
    C) 15
    D) 17

2) During a certain leap year, the number of non-rainy days is 30 more than half the number of rainy days. How many of this year's days are rainy? (Note: A leap year has 366 days.)

    A) 168
    B) 198
    C) 213
    D) 224

3) If $8^b + 8^b + 8^b + 8^b = a$, then which of the following expresses a in terms of b?

    A) 2^{6b}
    B) 2^{3b+2}
    C) 32^b
    D) 8^{4b}

4) The base of a triangle is decreased by 20%, while the height of the triangle is increased by 50%. What is the ratio of the triangle's new area to its old area?

    A) 6:5
    B) 3:10
    C) 10:3
    D) 25:3

Math: Strategy

Back-solving means trying the given answers until you find the one that works. This strategy takes advantage of the fact that most math problems on the SAT are multiple-choice.

Start in the middle.	Focus on either choice B or choice C. Substitute this value for the number that answers the question.
Plug in.	Use this number to evaluate all other unknowns in the question. If you've gone back through the entire question and everything works, select this answer and move on. You're done!
Cross it out.	If the number doesn't work, cross out the choice and consider whether the one you tried was too large or too small. Eliminate the other choice or choices that will have the same problem.
Continue.	If there's only one choice left, select it and move on. If there are two, try one of the remaining choices to see which one is your answer.

Let's walk through the process with a few examples.

Example: If the product of three consecutive odd integers is 1,287, what is the middle integer?

A) 11
B) 13
C) 15
D) 17

This problem tells us that there is a set of three consecutive odd numbers (three odds in a row, such as *3, 5, 7* or *5, 7, 9*) that multiply together to result in the number 1,287. We could set up some algebra to solve this, but it's difficult and time-consuming. Instead, we'll work backwards from the answer choices.

Let's start with choice B. If 13 is the middle number, then our set of three odd numbers would have to be *11, 13, 15*. So, turn to the calculator. Does it work?

$$11 * 13 * 15 = 2145$$

We didn't get 1287, so this is the wrong answer. Eliminate choice B.

And there's more. More specifically, choice B was wrong because it was too *big*. Choices C and D are even bigger, so they must be wrong as well. We're already done: choice **A** must be the right answer. You can double-check it to be sure:

$$9 * 11 * 13 = 1287$$

Let's try another.

Example: During a certain leap year, the number of non-rainy days is 30 more than half the number of rainy days. How many of this year's days are rainy? (Note: A leap year has 366 days.)

    A) 168
    B) 198
    C) 213
    D) 224

Start with choice B again. If 198 is the number of rainy days, then "half the number of rainy days" is 198/2 = 99. The number of non-rainy days must be 30 more than that amount, so 99 + 30 = 129. Okay: now we know that if there are 198 rainy days, then there are 129 non-rainy days. That gives us a total of 198 + 129 = 327 days in the year. But the problem told us that the total number of days should be 366, not 327. Therefore, this answer is too small. Eliminate choice B and choice A (which is even smaller).

Now we go to choice C. If 213 is the number of rainy days, then "half the number of rainy days" is 213/2 = 106.5. Uh-oh—this isn't going to work! We need a whole number of days in both categories.

The answer must be **D**, but let's double-check it to be sure:

$$\text{rainy} = 224$$
$$\text{non-rainy} = 224/2 + 30 = 142$$
$$\text{Total} = 224 + 142 = 366$$

Try It   Solve each of the following.

1) If $0 < x - \dfrac{1}{x} < 1$, which of the following could be x?

    A) $\dfrac{7}{8}$
    B) $\dfrac{11}{8}$
    C) $\dfrac{17}{8}$
    D) $\dfrac{19}{8}$

2) Marta owns 3 more than half the number of rare coins that Brigitta owns. If Brigitta owns 18 more rare coins than Marta, how many does Marta own?

    A) 24
    B) 33
    C) 36
    D) 42

TIP:

When you back-solve, as soon as you get an answer that works, you can stop. There's no need to check all the remaining choices.

Math: Strategy

Many math problems contain variables or other unknown quantities. **Substitution** is the practice of replacing these unknowns with numbers, so that you can solve the problems using arithmetic instead of algebra.

Choose a number or numbers.	Substitute on the side where there's more "action"—e.g., for the equation $x = 3y$, substitute a simple number for y. If there are multiple equations, start with the variable that the equations have in common. Pick easy numbers like 2 or 3 (or 100 for percentage problems, 60 for mph problems, etc). Avoid using 0 or 1.
Write it down.	Don't skip this step! It's easy to lose track of what you started with when you're several steps in.
Solve.	Use your number(s) to work through the problem on your scratch paper. When you reach an answer, circle it on the page.
Check.	Plug your original number(s) into **every** choice, crossing out all choices that do not match your circled answer.
Repeat as needed.	If more than one answer choice remains, pick a different number and try again with only the remaining choices.

FROM THE BLOG

You don't want to end up with a mistake on your admission ticket that you only discover on the day of the test. So take your time when registering. Don't register when you are in a rush. Don't register late at night when you are tired. Don't register on a smartphone. And above all else, double-check to make sure everything is accurate before the morning of the SAT.

Again, we'll walk through a few examples to see how it works.

Example: If $8^b + 8^b + 8^b + 8^b = a$, then which of the following expresses a in terms of b?

A) 2^{6b}
B) 2^{3b+2}
C) 32^b
D) 8^{4b}

This ugly-looking exponents problem becomes a lot easier if we can get rid of some of the abstraction by using actual numbers in place of the letters. To begin, pick a number you'd like to use for b. It should be a nice, small number that's easy to work with, but not zero or one. How about two? Write it down:

$$b = 2$$

Next, plug that value into the original equation to get a value for a.

$$8^2 + 8^2 + 8^2 + 8^2 = a$$
$$64 + 64 + 64 + 64 = a$$
$$256 = a$$

Okay, so if $b = 2$, then $a = 256$. Now, what was the question asking us? We want to identify the choice that "expresses a in terms of b." The phrase "in terms of b" doesn't mean anything! All that tells us is what the choices will look like: they'll each have a b in them. For our purposes, we can mentally cross that part of the question out. All we really need to do is find the answer choice that equals a.

Well, we already know that if $b = 2$, then a must equal 256. So next, plug 2 in for b in each answer choice. The one that comes out to 256 is our winner.

A) $2^{6b} = 2^{6(2)} = 2^{12} = 4096$

Nope, too big. Eliminate choice A.

B) $2^{3b+2} = 2^{3(2)+2} = 2^8 = 256$

Hey, that works! But wait: we're not done. It's still possible that another answer choice will also equal 256, so we have to check the remaining options.

C) $32^b = 32^2 = 1024$
D) $8^{4b} = 8^{4(2)} = 8^8 = 16777216$

Only choice **B** works, so that's the right answer.

TIP:

When you use the substitution strategy, always be sure to check **all** the choices in case there's more than one that works.

That first problem featured **variables in the answer choices**, which is one of the big tip-offs that a problem might be a good candidate for the substitution strategy. But in general, this is a good approach for any problem that is all about the **relationships** between numbers instead of the numbers themselves: for example, a problem that asks for an average or a ratio of two values. Let's look at another example.

Example: The base of a triangle is decreased by 20%, while the height of the triangle is increased by 50%. What is the ratio of the triangle's new area to its old area?

A) 6:5
B) 3:10
C) 10:3
D) 25:3

Draw a triangle and assign it a base and height. You can use any numbers you want, but you can make life easier by picking values that work well with the problem. Since we're dealing with percent here, let's use 10.

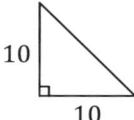

Now, 20% of 10 is $0.20(10) = 2$. The base should be decreased by that much, so the new base is $10 - 2 = 8$. And what about the height? 50% of 10 is $0.50(10) = 5$. The height should be *increased* by that much, so the new height is $10 + 5 = 15$.

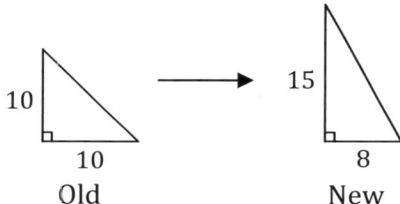

Old   New

The question was about the areas of these triangles, so we next need to calculate the area for each.

$$\text{Area of a triangle} = \frac{1}{2}bh$$

$$\text{Old area} = \frac{1}{2}(10)(10) = 50$$

$$\text{New area} = \frac{1}{2}(8)(15) = 60$$

Therefore, the ratio of the new area to the old area is 60/50, which simplifies to 6/5. The answer is **A**.

TIP:

A ratio is just a fraction. The ratio 60:50 is equivalent to the fraction 60/50, which simplifies to 6/5, which is equivalent to the ratio 6:5.

Try It Solve each of the following.

3) In a certain class, there are b boys and twice as many girls as boys. If four girls leave this class, then, in terms of b, how many girls remain in the class?

   A) $\dfrac{b-4}{2}$

   B) $\dfrac{b}{4} - 2$

   C) $2b + 4$

   D) $2b - 4$

4) If the average of x and y is 10 and the average of y and z is 6, what is the average of x and z in terms of y?

   A) $\dfrac{2y+8}{3}$

   B) $\dfrac{y+8}{2}$

   C) $16 - y$

   D) $8 - y$

Math: Strategy

Each strategy you just learned is specific to certain math problems on the SAT. One of the keys to mastering them is knowing which technique to use for which problems. Here are some tips that will help you to make this important distinction:

You should use **back-solving** for:

- questions with only numbers (no variables) in the answer choices
- tricky word problems that would be difficult to set up with algebra
- "could be" questions

You should use **substitution** for:

- questions with variables in the answer choices
- problems focused on ratios, percentages, or other *relationships* between unknown quantities
- "must be" questions

You should **NOT** use back-solving for:

- answer choices with unknown variables
- indirect questions (e.g., "Which of the following is NOT...?")

You should **NOT** use substitution for:

- problems with all fixed numerical values in the choices

For each of the problems in the practice sets that follow, first decide which of the two strategies is more suitable, and then use that method to solve the problem.

Chapter Answer Key

Try It	1) B
	2) A
	3) D
	4) C

Practice Set 1: Easy-Medium

1

If $(x-1)(x-2) = (x+4)(x+8)$, what is the value of x?

A. -2
B. -1
C. 0
D. 1

2

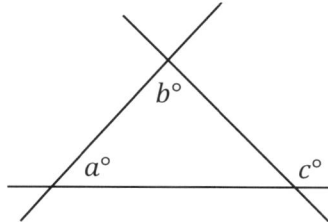

Three lines intersect to form a triangle as shown above. Which of the following expresses the value of c?

A. $a + b$
B. $180 - a$
C. $180 - b$
D. $90 - b$

3

Within a certain calling region, a telephone company charges 15 cents per minute for the first hour and 10 cents per minute beyond the first hour. If a telephone call within this region cost $23.00, how long was the conversation?

A. 1 hour, 8 minutes
B. 2 hours, 33 minutes
C. 3 hours, 20 minutes
D. 3 hours, 50 minutes

4

If $0 < c < d < 1$, then which of the following has the greatest value?

A. d^2
B. cd
C. c
D. d

5

Each side of a square has length s. When all side lengths are doubled, the area of the square increases by 108 square centimeters. What is the value of s in centimeters?

A. 4
B. 5
C. 6
D. 8

6

What number is 3 greater than twice the square root of itself?

A. 1
B. 3
C. 4
D. 9

7

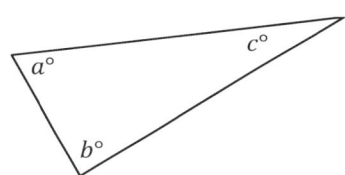

Note: Figure not drawn to scale

In the figure above, if $a + b = c$, then what is the value of c?

A. 10
B. 30
C. 60
D. 90

8

A certain store sold 40% more books on Saturday than it sold on Friday. If the store sold 35 books on Saturday, how many books did the store sell on Friday?

A. 14
B. 21
C. 25
D. 49

Math: Strategy

Practice Set 2: Medium-Hard

1 If the ratio of Gena's age to Sally's age is 2:3, and the ratio of Tim's age to Sally's age is 3:4, what is the ratio of Tim's age to Gena's age?

A. 8:9
B. 9:8
C. 1:2
D. 2:1

2 Which of the following is a solution set for $9z + 5 = 2z^2$?

A. $\left\{-\frac{1}{2}, \frac{1}{2}\right\}$
B. $\left\{-5, \frac{1}{2}\right\}$
C. $\left\{-\frac{1}{2}, 5\right\}$
D. $\left\{\frac{1}{2}, 5\right\}$

3 Let a and b be nonzero numbers such that a is $\frac{2}{3}$ of b. What is the ratio of b^2 to a^2?

A. 16 to 9
B. 9 to 4
C. 3 to 4
D. 2 to 3

4 If $2p = 3q = 4r$, what is the average of $p, q,$ and r in terms of r?

A. $\frac{3r}{2}$
B. $\frac{13r}{18}$
C. $\frac{13r}{9}$
D. $\frac{4r}{9}$

5 On a certain 25-question test, students receive 1 point for each correct answer and lose $\frac{1}{3}$ point for each incorrect answer. If Tyrrell answered every question on this test and earned a total of 17 points, how many questions did Tyrrell answer correctly?

A. 17
B. 18
C. 19
D. 21

6 If 20% of m is equal to n, what is 20% of $4m$ in terms of n?

A. $8n$
B. $4n$
C. $2n$
D. $\frac{n}{4}$

7 Penny needs to buy two hundred 6-inch nails for a construction project. If the pre-tax price of n 6-inch nails is p dollars, which of the following represents the total pre-tax price of Penny's order in terms of n and p?

A. $\frac{200n}{p}$
B. $\frac{n}{200p}$
C. $\frac{200p}{n}$
D. $\frac{p}{200n}$

8

Michael is five years older than James will be in three years. James is now j years old. In terms of j, how old will Michael be in three years?

A. $j + 3$
B. $j + 5$
C. $j + 8$
D. $j + 11$

9

If $x = 4y^2$ and $z = 2y - 6$, which of the following expresses x in terms of z?

A. $2z^2 + 9$
B. $(z + 8)^2$
C. $(z + 6)^2$
D. $2z^2 + 3z + 9$

10

A certain brand of tea is sold for d dollars per ounce. If z ounces are needed to make a single cup of tea, which of the following expresses how many dollars it would cost to make s cups of tea?

A. sdz
B. $\dfrac{dz}{s}$
C. $\dfrac{sz}{d}$
D. $\dfrac{d}{sz}$

11

Fred originally had $2 more than two-thirds the amount of money that Barney had. After Barney gave $5 to Fred, they both had the same amount of money. How much money did Barney originally have?

A. $36
B. $30
C. $26
D. $24

12

A passenger train departs for a 450-mile journey and travels at a rate of 75 miles per hour. A second train departs the same station x hours later for the same destination and arrives at the same time as the first train. What was the average speed, in terms of x, of the second train?

A. $150(6 - x)$
B. $150x$
C. $\dfrac{450}{x}$
D. $\dfrac{450}{6 - x}$

13

If $a = 2x^{-2}$ and $b = 2x^{\frac{1}{2}}$, then which of the following is equivalent to $a^2 b^2$?

A. $\dfrac{1}{8x^3}$
B. $\dfrac{16}{x^3}$
C. $4x^2$
D. $16x^2$

14

A biologist will use the partially completed table below to provide information about a sample of 62 moths.

	Male	Female	Total
Spotted		18	
Non-spotted	11		
Total	?		62

Which of the following could be the total number of male moths in the collection?

A. 43
B. 48
C. 55
D. 62

Math: Strategy

Mastering the Calculator

Preview Quiz

Choose the best answer(s).

1) What is the calculator policy on the SAT? <u>Choose all that apply.</u>

   A) You can use an on-screen calculator that's built into the testing software.
   B) You can use your own calculator.
   C) You can use a calculator on some math problems but not all.
   D) You can use a calculator on all problems in the math section.
   E) You are not permitted to use a calculator.

Solve.

2) Which of the following (x, y) points is a solution to $3x - y \leq 4$ and $x > 2$?

   A) $(-1, 0)$
   B) $(0, -5)$
   C) $(3, 7)$
   D) $(4, 1)$

3) If $-1 < a < 0$, which of the following values is the greatest?

   A) a^2

   B) $0.5a$

   C) $\dfrac{2}{a}$

   D) $\left|\dfrac{1}{a+1}\right|$

The SAT permits you to use a calculator on as many math problems as you choose. You can use your own calculator that you bring from home, or you can use the on-screen graphing calculator that's built into the testing software. Trust us on this: no matter how much you like your trusty TI-84, **the built-in calculator is better**.

If you've ever used the Desmos calculator in a math class before, congratulations: you already know how to use this. If you haven't, don't worry, because it's very easy to learn.

When you click on the calculator icon, you'll see a screen like this.

Type whatever expression you want into the window on the left, and the answer will display automatically.

There are many intuitive keyboard shortcuts. For example, to find the square root of something, type `sqrt`, and those letters will automatically convert to a radical. To enter π, type `pi`. To apply an exponent, use the ^ symbol on your keyboard (press shift, 6). To calculate absolute value, type `abs(`. And here's how you find the average (the arithmetic mean) of the numbers 5, 8, 12, and 13:

Percentages are maybe the easiest of all. Let's say a problem asks you to find 35% of 17. Type in 35%, and the calculator will automatically supply the word "of." Then just type in the 17.

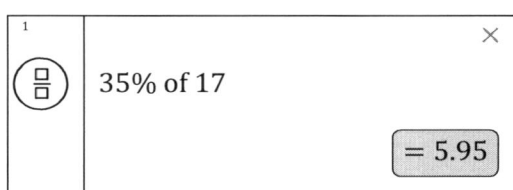

Click that symbol to the left of the problem and the calculator will convert the answer into a fraction:

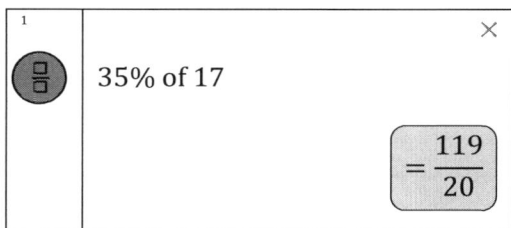

You can also click the ⌨▲ icon on the bottom left of the screen to access these and other functions by clicking buttons on a traditional calculator screen.

Try It   3, 10, 1, −4, 6, 2

1) What is the positive difference between the mean and the median of the given data set?

2) A circle has a radius of 3.5 inches. Which of the following is closest to the area of the circle, in square inches? (Note: the area of a circle with radius r is given by $A = \pi r^2$.)

   A) 7.0
   B) 12.3
   C) 22.0
   D) 38.5

3) The expression $\sqrt{27} + \sqrt{12}$ is equivalent to which of the following?

   A) $5\sqrt{3}$
   B) $4\sqrt{6}$
   C) $6\sqrt{3}$
   D) $9\sqrt{2}$

Math: Strategy

To **graph** an equation, type it into that box on the left. If you want to graph more than one equation at a time, press ENTER and type in the next equation in the box below it. The equations can be in any format: you do not have to isolate y in the equation to solve.

Calculator

1. $y = 2x + 1$
2. $3x + 2y = 11$

Hover over or click on the lines and the calculator will automatically display the coordinates of helpful points, such as an x-intercept, a y-intercept, or the point of intersection. In addition, although you can't see it in this image, the lines are color-coded to make it easier to tell which graph matches which equation.

The controls on the upper right of the screen help you control how much of the graph you see. Use the + and − buttons to zoom in and out, or click on the wrench icon to zoom to a specific interval by setting the minimum and maximum values for the x-axis and/or the y-axis.

There's more. See that little ⚙ symbol above the equations? Click on that to get an automatic table of points.

Calculator		
$y = 2x + 1$		

x	$2x + 1$
-2	-3
-1	-1
0	1
1	3
2	5

$3x + 2y = 11$

The graph will automatically highlight those points, and you can type in whatever additional x values you want to see the corresponding y values. And, see that little ⊕ icon to the left of the table? Clicking on that will automatically zoom the window in or out so that you have the best view of the important features of the graph.

Math: Strategy

You can use these features to solve a wide variety of problems.

Example: Which of the following (x, y) points is a solution to $3x - y \leq 4$ and $x > 2$?

A) $(-1, 0)$
B) $(0, -6)$
C) $(3, 7)$
D) $(4, 1)$

Let's walk through the steps of solving this one using the calculator. First, click the ✲ symbol above the equations and click "Delete All" to clear our previous entries. Then enter the two given inequalities (for the ≤ symbol, type < followed by =). Next, enter all four answer choices; the calculator will plot those points. You can even label the points as A, B, C, and D.

Calculator

1. $3x - y \leq 4$
2. $x > 2$
3. $(-1, 0)$ ☑ Label: A
4. $(0, -6)$ ☑ Label: B
5. $(3, 7)$ ☑ Label: C
6. $(4, 1)$ ☑ Label: D

Choice C is the only point in the overlapping portion of the shaded regions, so the answer is **C**.

Try It Solve the problems below by graphing them on the built-in calculator.

$$3x + 2y = 8$$
$$x - y = 4$$

4) What is the solution (x, y) to the system of equations above?

5) On the xy-plane, what are the x-intercepts of the graph of $f(x) = 2x^2 + x - 15$?

6) What is the diameter of the circle given by $(x - 3)^2 + y^2 = 9$, in coordinate units?

The calculator is also helpful for **back-solving** and **substitution**.

Example: If $-1 < a < 0$, which of the following values is the greatest?

A) a^2

B) $0.5a$

C) $\dfrac{2}{a}$

D) $\left|\dfrac{1}{a+1}\right|$

To solve this, first pick a number for a that falls within the boundaries set for us by the problem. Let's use $a = -0.2$ for our example. Enter that into the calculator, and then enter each answer choice exactly as it appears. The calculator will automatically plug in -0.2 for a in each answer choice and calculate the result.

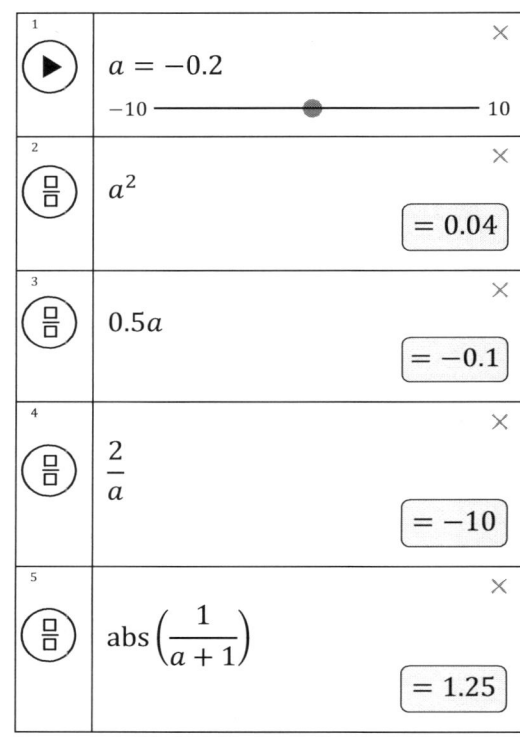

TIP:

You don't have to use "a" as your constant: almost any letter will work the same way. However, there are a few exceptions: the letters x, y, t, e, and i all have other mathematical meanings, so the calculator won't interpret them in this way.

Of these options, 1.25 is the greatest, so the answer is **D**.

We can also use this approach to try a range of different values. Take another look at that first entry again, the one where we set the value of a. See the long horizontal line with a circle in the middle of it? That's called a **slider**, and it will let us change the value of a to whatever we want. Try dragging that slider to the left and right and watch the results of all the other entries change.

If you only want to test whole number values for a, click in that top row and change the "Step:" value to 1. If you like, you can fill in a minimum and maximum value for a as well.

You can also let the calculator show you the results of changing the value. Click the ⊙ button on the left side of that top row and the calculator will automatically cycle through different values for a.

TIP:

The built-in calculator is a powerful aid for this test, but it can't do everything. It's still in your interest to learn the algebraic way to solve these problems so that you have *both* methods at your disposal and can choose the best one to solve a particular problem. **Let the calculator be a tool, not a crutch.**

Chapter Answer Key

Try It	1) 0.5 or 1/2
	2) D
	3) A
	4) $(3.2, -0.8)$
	5) $(-3, 0)$ and $(2.5, 0)$
	6) 6

Math: Strategy

Practice Set 1: Easy-Medium

1

$$f(x) = 2x^2 + 13x - 7$$

The quadratic function f is defined above. Which of the following is an x-intercept of the graph of $y = f(x)$ in the xy-plane?

A. $(-7, 0)$
B. $(-1, 0)$
C. $(1, 0)$
D. $(7, 0)$

2

At the Robinson School, 24% of fifth-graders ride the bus to school. If there are 75 fifth-graders at the Robinson School, how many of them ride the bus to school?

3

$$12, 10, 5, 39, 8$$

What is the median of the list of data shown above?

A. 5
B. 10
C. 11
D. 14.8

4

What is the solution (x, y) to the system of equations below?

$$6x - y = 1$$
$$4y - x = 19$$

A. $(-9, -55)$
B. $(0, 4.75)$
C. $(1, 5)$
D. $(21, 10)$

5

$$f(x) = -2(x - 1)(x + 3)$$

Which table gives three values of x and their corresponding values of $f(x)$ for the given function?

A.
x	1	2	3
$f(x)$	-16	-20	-28

B.
x	1	2	3
$f(x)$	0	-10	-24

C.
x	1	2	3
$f(x)$	0	10	24

D.
x	1	2	3
$f(x)$	6	0	-10

6

The graph of $2x + y < -4$ includes NO points in which of the following quadrants of the xy-plane?

A. Quadrant I
B. Quadrant II
C. Quadrant III
D. Quadrant IV

7

$$y = x^2 + 2x$$
$$y = x^2 - 2x + 2$$

In the xy-plane, the graphs of the equations shown intersect at $(m, 1.25)$. What is the value of m?

Practice Set 2: Medium-Hard

1

In the equation $2x^2 + bx + 8 = 0$, b is a constant. For which of the following values of b does the equation have no real solutions?

A. -10
B. 5
C. 8
D. 9

2

$$f(x) = 1500(1.07)^x$$

The exponential function $f(x)$ gives the value of an investment account, in dollars, x years after it was opened. Which of the following is closest to the value of the account 6 years after it was opened?

A. $2000
B. $2104
C. $2127
D. $2251

3

The function f is defined by the equation $f(x) = x^2 + 2x - 3$. The function $g(x)$ is the result of shifting the graph of $f(x)$ up 3 units and right 2 units on the xy-plane. Which of the following could be the equation of $g(x)$?

A. $g(x) = 2(x - 0.5)^2 - 2$
B. $g(x) = (x - 2)^2 - 3$
C. $g(x) = (x - 1)^2 - 1$
D. $g(x) = 3(x + 1)^2 - 4$

4

In the linear function f, $f(0) = 6$ and $f(1) = 9$. Which equation defines f?

A. $f(x) = x + 3$
B. $f(x) = 3x + 6$
C. $f(x) = 6x + 9$
D. $f(x) = 9x + 1$

5

$$x^2 - 6x + y^2 + 8y = -16$$

In the xy-plane, what are the coordinates of the center of the circle given by the equation above?

A. $(3, -7)$
B. $(3, -4)$
C. $(0, -4)$
D. $(2, -1)$

6

$$3x - 5y = 8$$
$$y = x^2 - 1$$

How many solutions exist to the system of equations shown?

A. 0
B. 1
C. 2
D. infinitely many

7

In the xy-plane, the graph of the equation $ax + by = c$ is a vertical line. Which of the following could be the values of a, b, and c?

A. $a = 0, b = 1, c = 1$
B. $a = 0, b = 1, c = 0$
C. $a = 1, b = 0, c = 1$
D. $a = 1, b = 1, c = 0$

8

How many (x, y) pairs of real numbers satisfy the equations $xy = 1$ and $x^2 + y^2 = 9$?

Approximating and Measuring

If you're not sure how to even start a math problem, don't panic! You can often use simple methods to eliminate choices and make an educated guess.

It's okay to round. It's possible to solve all of the problems on the SAT exactly, but you can often save time by approximating. If you're told to square the number 4.9, try thinking of it as a little bit less than 5^2: almost 25.

Trust your eyes. All figures are drawn to scale unless you are told otherwise. Use that to eliminate choices: if an angle looks like less than 90°, it is. (You can double-check by holding up a piece of scratch paper to the screen and measuring the angle against the corner).

Choose something. There is no guessing penalty on the SAT, so there's no reason to ever leave anything blank. Once you've crossed out a few choices using the strategies above, go with your gut and select the choice that makes the most sense to you.

> **TIP:**
> Use the built-in calculator to help you approximate. Many questions about equations become a lot easier if you can take a look at the graph.

FROM THE BLOG

Sleep is crucial to consolidation of learning, test performance, and lowered anxiety. So make sleep a priority. The week before the test, punt on socializing and save that for a well-deserved post-test celebration.

Approximating and Measuring

Practice Set 1: Easy-Medium

1

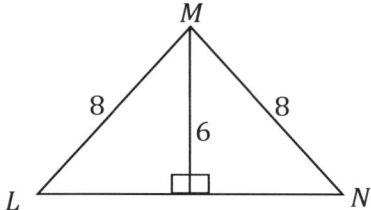

In the figure above, what is the length of $\overline{LN}$?

A. $2\sqrt{7}$
B. 7
C. $4\sqrt{7}$
D. $10\sqrt{2}$

2

A chemist mixed 30 milliliters (mL) of solution A with 40 mL of solution B. The next day, she created another batch of the mixture. If she used 25 mL of solution B in the second batch, how much of solution A did she use?

A. 15 mL
B. 18.75 mL
C. 33.33 mL
D. 35 mL

3

In the xy-plane, the line given by the equation $2x + y = 1$ is perpendicular to the line given by which of the following equations?

A. $-2x + \frac{1}{2}y = 1$
B. $x + 2y = 3$
C. $x - 2y = 1$
D. $2x + y = 3$

4

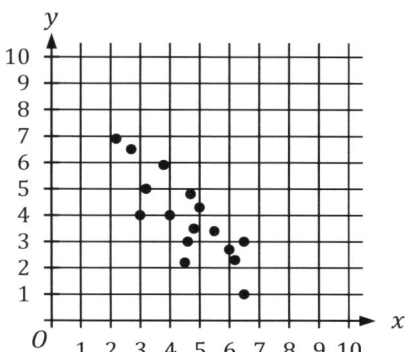

Which of the following equations is the most appropriate linear model for the data shown in the scatterplot above?

A. $y = -8.5x + 1$
B. $y = -x + 8.5$
C. $y = x - 8.5$
D. $y = 8.5x - 1$

5

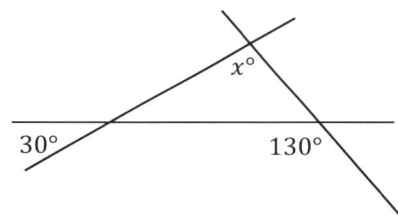

What is the value of x?

A. 30
B. 50
C. 80
D. 100

6

In the xy-plane, which of the following points lies on the line that passes through $(2, 5)$ and $(4, 8)$?

A. $(-3, 3)$
B. $(-2, -1)$
C. $(1, 0)$
D. $(5, 11)$

Practice Set 2: Medium-Hard

1

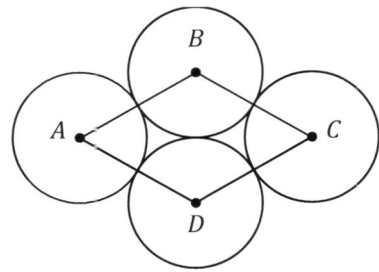

In the figure above, points A, B, C, and D are the centers of four congruent circles, each of which has an area of 9π and is tangent to all adjacent circles. What is the area of rhombus $ABCD$?

A. $9\sqrt{3}$
B. $18\sqrt{3}$
C. $27\sqrt{3}$
D. $9\pi\sqrt{3}$

2

$$f(x) = x^3 + 2x^2 + 5$$

For the function f, defined above, what is a possible value of k such that $f(2k) = 8$?

3

$$g(x) = \frac{x-1}{\sqrt{5-x}}$$

What is the domain of the function $g(x)$, defined above?

A. $x < 1$
B. $x \geq 1$
C. $x < 5$
D. $x \geq 5$

4

The bar graph shows the number of students in each grade at Glen School.

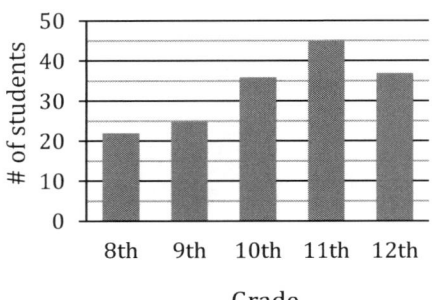

Which of the following is the greatest?

A. The number of 11th and 12th graders
B. The number of 9th and 10th graders
C. The number of 8th and 12th graders
D. The number of 10th and 12th graders

5

School	# of votes	% votes for Site A	% votes for Site B
1	3200	50	50
2	2000	30	70
3	4100	50	50
4	1900	70	30
5	5800	40	60

The table above shows the results of a vote among five high schools as to which site to select for the end of year party. Which high school had the greatest number of votes for the winning site?

A. 1
B. 2
C. 3
D. 5

Algebra

Algebra Essentials

Preview Quiz:

Simplify each of the following:

1) $3(2x + 4) =$

2) $5x + 6 - (2x - 4) =$

3) $\dfrac{8x - 10}{2} =$

4) $3(4x + 2x) - 5x =$

Solve:

5) $x - 10 = 13$

6) $\dfrac{2x}{3} = \dfrac{2x + 4}{5}$

7) $2x + 4 = 12$

8) $2(3x - 5) + 2 = 6x + 1$

9) What is the value of $3(x - y) + xy$ if $x = 2$ and $y = -4$?

10) If $\dfrac{1}{2}x - 3y = 5$, what is x in terms of y?

Math: Algebra

A **term** is a number, a variable, or the product of numbers and variables.

Example: 3xy is a single term.

We can use addition and subtraction to combine **like terms**, which are terms that have the exact same variables with the exact same exponents.

Example: The sum of 3n and 2n is 5n.

If the terms have different variables *or* if the variables have different exponents, they're not like terms and we can't combine them that way.

Example: The sum of $3n$ and $2n^2$ is just $3n + 2n^2$.

Try It   **Simplify** each expression by combining like terms. If the expression is already in simplest terms, write *simplified*.

1) $3x - 2 + x + 5$

2) $x + x^2 + x^3$

3) $x^2 - 0.7x^2$

4) $2x + 3x - 4y - y$

5) $3xy + 2xy - x + 4x$

6) $-3 + y - x + xy$

TIP:

Remember, a variable without a coefficient written in front of it really has a coefficient of 1. You can always write in the "1" to remind yourself that it's there.

Example: $x + x = 1x + 1x =$ **$2x$**

When an expression is placed inside parentheses, we may need to **multiply** the whole expression by something that's outside the parentheses. To do this, make sure to multiply *each individual term* by whatever is outside.

Example: $3(2x + 4)$
$$= 3(2x) + 3(4)$$
$$= \mathbf{6x + 12}$$

Similarly, to **divide** an entire expression by some number, be sure to divide each individual term by the number that's in the bottom of the fraction.

Example: $\dfrac{8x - 10}{2} = \mathbf{4x - 5}$

When **subtracting** an expression in parentheses, it's important to remember to **distribute** that minus sign to each individual term in the expression. You can think of it as multiplying the whole expression by -1.

Example: $5x + 6 - (2x - 4)$
$$= 5x + 6 + (-1)(2x - 4)$$
$$= 5x + 6 + (-1)(2x) + (-1)(-4)$$
$$= 5x + 6 - 2x + 4$$
$$= \mathbf{3x + 10}$$

Use the acronym **PEMDAS** to remember the order of operations: first, simplify any expression in Parentheses; next, apply any Exponents; third, perform any Multiplication or Division; fourth, perform any Addition or Subtraction.

Example: $3(4x + 2x) - 5x$
$= 3(6x) - 5x$ ⟵ first handle the **P**arentheses
$= 18x - 5x$ ⟵ then **M**ultiply
$= \mathbf{13x}$ ⟵ then **S**ubtract

TIP:

To check your work, try plugging in a value for x and evaluating both the original expression and the result in the calculator. If they match, you simplified the expression correctly. For example, if we decide that $x = 2$, then the original expression above is $3\big(4(2) + 2(2)\big) - 5(2) = 26$, and the result is $13(2) = 26$.

For a review of how to use the SAT's built-in calculator to plug in values, see p. 240.

Math: Algebra

> **Try It** **Simplify** each expression by combining like terms. If the expression is already in simplest terms, write *simplified*.
>
> 7) $2x - (3x + 5) + 2$
>
> 9) $\frac{1}{2}(4x + 2) - 3$
>
> 8) $1 + 3(2x - 6)$
>
> 10) $2(3x - 8) + (1 - 4x)$

Some algebra problems will simply ask you to **evaluate** an algebraic expression given certain numeric values for the variables. Plug in carefully, follow PEMDAS, and *write out your steps*, especially where negative numbers are involved. Remember, subtracting a negative number is the same thing as adding a positive number.

Example: If $x = 2$ and $y = -4$, what is the value of $3(x - y) + xy$?

$$3(2 - (-4)) + 2(-4)$$
$$3(2 + 4) - 8$$
$$10$$

TIP:
You can also use the built-in calculator to solve these problems. See pp. 240-241 to learn how.

> **Try It** Find the value of each of the following if $x = -1$ and $y = 3$.
>
> 11) $2(3x - 8) + (1 - 4y)$
>
> 12) $2y - |x + y|$

TIP:
Absolute value bars are like specialized parentheses. To follow PEMDAS, first simplify the expression inside the absolute value bars, then take the absolute value of that result.

Algebra Essentials

An **equation** is an algebra statement that has an equals sign in it. We can solve equations by doing the same thing to both sides (e.g., adding something, subtracting something, multiplying something, etc).

Example: If $x - 10 = 13$, what is the value of x?

$$\begin{array}{rl} x - 10 &= 13 \\ +10 & +10 \end{array} \quad \longleftarrow \text{add 10 to both sides}$$

$$x = 23$$

Some equations require more than one step to solve. To determine what to do first, follow PEMDAS *backwards*—first any addition/subtraction, then the multiplication/division, and so on.

Example: If $2x + 4 = 12$, what is the value of x?

$$\begin{array}{rl} 2x + 4 &= 12 \\ -4 & -4 \end{array} \quad \longleftarrow \text{subtraction first}$$

$$\begin{array}{rl} 2x &= 8 \\ \div 2 & \div 2 \end{array} \quad \longleftarrow \text{then the division}$$

$$x = 4$$

For equations in which two fractions are set equal to each other, there's a shortcut: **cross-multiply** to solve. Multiply the bottom of one fraction by the top of the other one, and vice versa; set the results equal to each other and proceed to combine like terms as usual.

Example: $\dfrac{2x}{3} = \dfrac{2x+4}{5}$

$5(2x) = 3(2x + 4)$

$\begin{array}{rl} 10x &= 6x + 12 \\ -6x & -6x \end{array}$

$\begin{array}{rl} 4x &= 12 \\ \div 4 & \div 4 \end{array}$

$x = 3$

TIP:

If an equation has a lot of fractions in it, try multiplying both sides of the equation by the bottoms of the fractions as a first step. This should eliminate all the fractions and make life easier.

Example: If $\dfrac{3}{4}x + 2 = x - \dfrac{5}{4}$, what is the value of x?

$$4\left(\dfrac{3}{4}x + 2\right) = 4\left(x - \dfrac{5}{4}\right)$$
$$3x + 8 = 4x - 5$$
$$8 = x - 5$$
$$13 = x$$

Math: Algebra

To solve an equation using the built-in calculator, enter it on two separate lines: the left side of the equation on one line, and the right side of the equation on the other. The x-coordinate of the intersection of those two graphs is your solution. Here's that last example again:

$$\text{If } \frac{2x}{3} = \frac{2x+4}{5}, \text{ what is the value of } x?$$

[Calculator screenshot: Line 1 shows $\frac{2x}{3}$, Line 2 shows $\frac{2x+4}{5}$, with the graph showing two lines intersecting at $(3, 2)$.]

The lines intersect where $x = 3$, so the answer is **3**.

TIP:

This approach will only work if the variable is x. If the problem uses a different letter, change it to x when entering it into the calculator.

TM and © 2023 PrepMatters, Inc. All rights reserved.

Try It   Solve for x in each of the following:

13) $4x - 3 = 17$

16) $3x + 2 = 20$

14) $3.4 = 0.2x + 6$

17) $1 - 2x = \dfrac{1}{5}$

15) $\dfrac{x - 3}{2} = 9$

18) $6 = \dfrac{3x}{2} + 8$

TIP:

Whether or not you want to use the graphing approach from the last page, you should certainly be using the calculator to handle messy arithmetic (e.g., dividing by 0.2 in #14 above). There is no reason to do this stuff in your head; it's not what the SAT is trying to test you on, and it's too easy to make a test-day "hasty error" that ends up losing you points on a problem you actually know how to do.

Not all algebra problems ask you to find the value of a variable. Other problems will give you an equation involving two or more different variables and ask you to **solve for one variable**. (These may also be phrased as finding one variable "in terms of" the others). These problems may seem intimidating because they're more abstract, but you already know how to solve them. Use the same algebra skills you used on the last set: do the same thing to both sides of the equation, follow PEMDAS, etc.

Example: If $\frac{1}{2}x - 3y = 5$, what is x in terms of y?

$$\frac{1}{2}x - 3y = 5$$
$$+3y \quad +3y \quad \leftarrow \text{addition first}$$
$$2\left(\frac{1}{2}x\right) = 2(5 + 3y) \leftarrow \text{then multiply}$$
$$x = 10 + 6y$$

TIP:

When multiplying or dividing both sides of the equation by something, make sure you multiply or divide *each individual term* by that number.

Try It   Solve for x in each of the following:

19) $x + 2y = 5$

22) $10x + 20y = 45$

20) $2x - 6 = 8y$

23) $3 - 4x = 12y + 1$

21) $\frac{3x - 9y}{2} = 4$

24) $6x = \frac{y}{4} + 12$

CHALLENGE:

All the equations we've seen so far have had exactly one solution. But occasionally, the SAT will ask us about equations with an infinite number of solutions, or about equations that have no solutions at all.

In both cases, the key is that when you combine the like terms in the equation, you find that *all the variables cancel out*. If what's left at that point is a *true* statement, then the equation had **infinitely many solutions**.

Example: $3x - 4 = 3(x - 2) + 2$
$3x - 4 = 3x - 6 + 2$
$-4 = -4$

This is <u>true</u>, so the equation has **infinitely many solutions**.

If what's left after the variables cancel out is a *false* statement, then the equation had **no solutions**.

Example: $2(3x - 5) + 2 = 6x + 1$
$6x - 10 + 2 = 6x + 1$
$-8 = 1$

This is <u>false</u>, so the equation has **no solutions**.

TIP:

If you use the technique on p. 252 to solve an equation using the built-in calculator, a graph where the lines never intersect means there are **no solutions**, while a graph that shows both equations as the same line has **infinitely many solutions**.

Math: Algebra

Chapter Answer Key

Try It

1) $4x + 3$
2) simplified
3) $0.3x^2$
4) $5x - 5y$
5) $5xy + 3x$
6) simplified
7) $-x - 3$
8) $6x - 17$
9) $2x - 2$
10) $2x - 15$
11) -33
12) 4
13) 5
14) -13
15) 21
16) 6
17) $2/5$ or 0.4
18) $-4/3$ or $-1.\overline{33}$
19) $x = 5 - 2y$
20) $x = 4y + 3$
21) $x = 3y + 8/3$
22) $x = 4.5 - 2y$
23) $x = -3y + 1/2$
24) $x = y/24 + 2$

Practice Set 1: Easy-Medium

1. If $x = 5$ and $y = -3$, what is the value of $x(x + y) - y$?

A. 1
B. 7
C. 13
D. 37

2. Which of the following expressions is equivalent to $3(2a - b) + 4(-5a + b)$?

A. $-14a - 2b$
B. $-14a + b$
C. $a + 7b$
D. $a + b$

3. For what value of x is the equation $3(x - 2) + x = 14$ true?

4. For $x = 6$, what is the value of $|2 - x|$?

A. -8
B. 2
C. 4
D. 8

5. The equation $p = 3n - 16$ can be used to find Max's profit p, in dollars, from selling n cupcakes. How many cupcakes does Max need to sell in order to obtain a profit of $20?

A. 7
B. 8
C. 10
D. 12

6. The real number n is defined such that $-2(n - 3) - 3(4 - n) = 5n + 6$. What is the value of $1 - 2n$?

A. -2
B. 0
C. 4
D. 7

7.
$$\frac{15}{q - 6} = \frac{24}{16}$$

What value of q makes the proportion above true?

A. 10
B. 12
C. 16
D. 32

8. For all real values of x, which of the following expressions is equivalent to $2(4x - 3) + 5(-3x + 6) - 3(4 - 2x)$?

A. $-19x + 30$
B. $-13x + 12$
C. $-x + 12$
D. $6x - 18$

9. If $\dfrac{3 + 2k}{7} = \dfrac{k}{3}$, what is the value of k?

10. If $a = 3, b = 5$, and $c = -2$, what is the value of $(a + b - c)(b + c)$?

A. 18
B. 30
C. 42
D. 54

Math: Algebra

Practice Set 2: Medium-Hard

1

What value of n satisfies the equation below?
$$\frac{9}{2n} = 0.15$$

2

If $a + b = c$ and $c = 10$, what is the value of $a + b + c$?

A. 10
B. 15
C. 20
D. 30

3

If $14n + jn = 22n$ for all nonzero values of n, what is the value of j?

A. 6
B. 8
C. 12
D. 28

4

A beaker currently contains 3 mL of solution A and 5 mL of solution B. After a scientist adds n mL of solution A to the beaker, the mixture will be p percent solution A by volume, where p is defined by the following equation:
$$p = \frac{100(3 + n)}{8 + n}$$

What is n in terms of p?

A. $n = 8p - 300$
B. $n = \dfrac{8p}{300}$
C. $n = \dfrac{300 - 3p}{800}$
D. $n = \dfrac{300 - 8p}{p - 100}$

5

$$5x - 6 + (2 - x) = 2(2x + 7)$$

Which of the following best describes the solution(s) of the equation above?

A. $x = 2$ is the only solution.
B. $x = 0$ is the only solution.
C. The equation has infinitely many solutions.
D. The equation has no solutions.

6

If $2n - m = 14$, then the value of which of the following expressions is -28?

A. $m - 2n$
B. $2m - 4n$
C. $-4n - m$
D. $n + 2m$

7

The equation $d = vt + 0.5at^2$ gives the distance d, in meters, traveled by a machine that accelerates at a constant rate, where v is the machine's initial velocity, in meters per second; a is its acceleration, in meters per second per second; and t is the time, in seconds. If the machine travels 108 meters in 60 seconds, with an initial velocity of 0.3 meters per second, what is its rate of acceleration, in meters per second per second?

8

If $\dfrac{3a + 2}{12} = \dfrac{2x}{9}$, which of the following expressions is equivalent to x?

A. $\dfrac{9a + 6}{8}$
B. $6a - 9$
C. $27a - 12$
D. $18a$

Word Problems

Preview Quiz:

Choose the best answer.

1) The word "product" refers to the result of (adding / multiplying).

2) When you divide one number by another, the result is called the (quotient / difference).

Translate and solve.

3) 27 is three-fourths of the sum of 13 and what number?

4) Early in her life, a baby gained 30 grams per day. If she weighed 3200 grams at birth, how much did she weigh after ten days?

5) George and Sal started their new jobs on the same day. George received a signing bonus of $300, after which he earned $20 per hour. Sal received a signing bonus of $500, after which he earned $18 per hour. After how many hours of work had George and Sal each earned the same amount?

6) A baby weighed 3200 grams when she was born two weeks ago. Since then, she has gained 30 grams each day. Her doctor says that by her first birthday, her weight should be triple her birth weight. To meet this goal, the baby will need to gain an average of x grams per day for the remaining 351 days of the year. What is the value of x, rounded to the nearest gram?

Math: Algebra

One of the goals of the SAT is to highlight practical applications of math reasoning. What that means in practice is lots of word problems. Here's a step-by-step approach.

Read slowly. Read the first sentence slowly. What have they told you, and what does it mean?

Write down values. Clarify your variables (e.g., write "a = number of apples" as well as "$a = 15$"). You can also jot down simple reminders of relationships to help avoid confusion later: for example, "a is bigger than b."

Jump in. Work as you go. If you can put two pieces of information together, do it now. For example, if you're given the rate a car is moving and the time, go ahead and calculate the distance before you even finish reading.

Talk to yourself in sentences. Your brain doesn't necessarily think linearly. If you talk yourself through your process, though (e.g., "now I'm finding how much a crate of melons cost...") you force yourself to be linear and think at a measured, efficient rate.

Track your units. If a question is asking for dollars, but you have a unit that would be gallons per square dollars... something has gone sideways.

Focus on the question. Re-read, if necessary, to make sure you know exactly what the test is asking for.

> *TIP:*
> Thrown off by a long problem with a ton of words? Try breaking the problem into smaller pieces and solving one piece at a time.

Word Problem Translation

Word Problem	Math equivalent
sum	+
product	*
difference	−
quotient	÷
is	=
of	*

Many word problems can be translated directly into algebra using the conversions given above.

Example: *27 is three-fourths of the sum of 13 and what number?*

We have the number 27, followed by the word "is": that's an equals sign. Then we have "three-fourths," so just 3/4. Next is the word "of," which always means multiply. But multiply by what? By "the sum of 13 and" some unknown number. Use x to represent the unknown value; the sum of 13 and that value is $(13 + x)$. Putting it all together, we get this:

27 is three-fourths of the sum of 13 and what number?

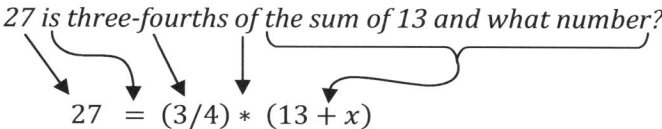

$$27 = (3/4) * (13 + x)$$

Now solve:

$$27 = \frac{3}{4}(13 + x)$$
$$27 = 0.75(13) + 0.75(x)$$
$$27 = 9.75 + 0.75x$$
$$17.25 = 0.75x$$
$$\mathbf{23 = x}$$

Try It — Translate each of these into algebra:

1) The width is 3 inches greater than the height.

2) When n is subtracted from 5, the result is 2.

3) The sum of three consecutive integers is 15.

4) The product of a and b is 4 more than twice the value of c.

Math: Algebra

Rates

Many word problems on the SAT involve *rates*. Look for words like "per" or "each" to identify them: for example, a problem may involve a speed of "35 kilometers per hour," or you may be told that a store sells "1000 books each week."

The simplest of these problems can be solved simply by **multiplying** or **dividing**. Just be sure to write out the equation first so that you know which one to do.

Example: *Early in her life, a baby gained 30 grams each day. How many grams did she gain in the first five days?*

$x = 30(5)$
$x = $ **150 grams**

Example: *If George earns $20 per hour, how long does it take him to earn $60?*

$20(x) = 60$
$x = $ **3 hours**

Try It

5) A group of 5 employees contributed $8 each to buy a joint gift for their coworker. What was the total amount contributed?

6) A market sells 12 eggs for $9.36. What is the price per egg? (No sales taxes apply.)

Often, the problem will give you a *starting value* of some kind. This should typically be either added to or subtracted from the rest of the equation. Again, the first step is to **write out the equation**, plugging in what you know from the problem, so that you can see what steps you need to take to solve it.

Example: Early in her life, a baby gained 30 grams per day. If she weighed 3200 grams at birth, how much did she weigh after ten days?

$x = 3200 + 30(10)$
$x = $ **3500 grams**

Example: When he started at his current job, George received a signing bonus of x dollars. George earns 20 dollars per hour. If he earned a total of 1100 dollars in his first forty hours, what is the value of x?

$1100 = x + 40(20)$
$1100 = x + 800$
$x = $ **300 dollars**

Try It

7) A group of 5 employees decided to pool their money to buy a joint gift for their coworker. Their boss started the pool with a $50 donation. If the employees then contributed $8 each, what was the total amount contributed?

8) At a market, the price of 12 eggs and 1 bottle of soda is $11.61. If the eggs sell for $0.78 each, what is the price of the bottle of soda? (No sales taxes apply.)

Math: Algebra

The next level of difficulty is when you are given **multiple relationships** to deal with in the same problem. For some of these, each relationship might consist of a starting value and a rate, and you'll need to set the two expressions equal to each other to solve.

Example: George and Sal started their new jobs on the same day. George received a signing bonus of $300, after which he earned $20 per hour. Sal received a signing bonus of $500, after which he earned $18 per hour. After how many hours of work had George and Sal each earned the same amount?

$300 + 20x = 500 + 18x$
$300 + 2x = 500$
$2x = 200$
$x = $ **100 hours**

Try It

9) Two departments at a company competed in a charity drive. In the sales department, the manager contributed $50, and five of his employees contributed $8 each. In the accounting department, the manager declined to contribute, but six employees contributed $n each. If the amount raised by the accounting department was the same as the amount raised by the sales department, what is the value of n?

10) At a market, the price of 12 eggs and 7 pints of yogurt is equal to the price of 30 eggs and 1 pint of yogurt. If the eggs sell for $0.78 each, what is the price of 1 pint of yogurt? (No sales taxes apply.)

Other problems may require more than one equation. For these **multi-step** problems, focus on breaking the problem into smaller chunks and doing one thing at a time, writing it all out as you go.

Example: *A baby weighed 3200 grams when she was born two weeks ago. Since then, she has gained 30 grams each day. Her doctor says that by her first birthday, her weight should be triple her birth weight. To meet this goal, the baby will need to gain an average of x grams per day for the remaining 351 days of the year. What is the value of x, rounded to the nearest gram?*

Current weight $= 3200 + 30(14) = 3620$ grams
Goal $= 3(3200) = 9600$ grams
must gain $9600 - 3620 = 5980$ grams
$351(x) = 5980$
$x = 17.04$

Rounded to the nearest gram, the value of x is **17 grams per day**.

> *TIP:*
> If you're having trouble setting up the algebra for a word problem, consider using the back-solving or substitution strategies instead.

Math: Algebra

Chapter Answer Key

Try It
1) $w = h + 3$
2) $5 - n = 2$
3) $x + (x + 1) + (x + 2) = 15$
4) $ab = 2c + 4$
5) $40
6) $0.78
7) $90
8) $2.25
9) $15
10) $2.34

Practice Set 1: Easy-Medium

1. A taxicab company charges passengers $3.50 for the first mile of a trip, then $2.25 for each additional mile. What is the charge for a 10-mile trip?

A. $20.25
B. $23.75
C. $26.00
D. $35.00

2. Mollie operates a juice stand. She charges $1.75 for a cup of carrot juice and $1.25 for a cup of grapefruit juice. Which of the following represents the amount, in dollars, that Mollie will receive if she sells c cups of carrot juice and g cups of grapefruit juice?

A. $1.25c + 1.75g$
B. $1.75c - 1.25g$
C. $1.75c + 1.25g$
D. $0.75(c + g)$

3. The height of one tree is 2 inches less than 3 times the height of a shorter tree. If the height of the taller tree is 64 inches, what is the height, in inches, of the shorter tree?

4. To operate his retail store, Sylvan pays an employee $15.75 per hour. His other costs come to $75 per day. For a day on which the employee works for 8 hours, how much must Sylvan receive from the sale of his products to cover all of his costs, including the employee's pay?

A. $50.75
B. $110.25
C. $143.50
D. $201.00

5. A gym charges a $19.50 monthly membership fee. There is an additional fee of $4.75 to attend a fitness class. If Jessie's fee was $33.75 this month, how many fitness classes did she attend?

A. 1
B. 2
C. 3
D. 4

6. It currently takes Nancy 12 minutes to run 1 mile. Nancy's goal is to run a mile in 8 minutes, and she believes that with practice, she will be able to reduce her 1-mile running time by 30 seconds every week. If Nancy is correct, which of the following represents the number of minutes that it will take Nancy to run 1 mile w weeks from now, where w is an integer less than 8?

A. $8w - 30$
B. $12 - 0.5w$
C. $0.5w + 8$
D. $12 + 8w$

7. For the use of its high-speed internet service, Hotel A charges each guest an initial $4 fee plus $7 an hour. Hotel B charges each guest an initial fee of $14 plus $5 an hour. A guest at Hotel A will have paid the same total amount for internet as a guest at Hotel B after how many hours?

A. 5
B. 6
C. 8
D. 9

Math: Algebra

Practice Set 2: Medium-Hard

1

In a certain bag of marbles, $\frac{1}{4}$ of the marbles are red. Of the marbles that aren't red, $\frac{3}{5}$ are green and the remaining 12 are blue. No marble is more than one color. How many marbles are in the bag?

A. 30
B. 40
C. 54
D. 60

2

A math team earned a total of 155 points by answering e easy questions and h hard questions. The equation $2e + 5h = 155$. Which of the following is the best interpretation of $5h$ in this context?

A. The number of points earned per hard question answered
B. The total number of points earned by answering hard questions
C. The number of points earned per easy question answered
D. The total number of points earned by answering easy questions

3

Michael can text 50 words in 1 minute. Which of the following equations represents the total number of words, w, that Michael can text in h hours?

A. $w = 50(60h)$
B. $w = \dfrac{50}{60h}$
C. $w = 60 + 50h$
D. $w = \left(\dfrac{60}{50}\right)h$

4

At an arcade, Bill starts out with t tokens and loses 4 tokens each time he plays a game. If Bill plays 5 games and has 4 tokens left, what is the value of t?

5

The side lengths of a certain pentagon are consecutive odd integers. If the longest side has length s inches, which of the following gives the perimeter of the pentagon, in inches, in terms of s?

A. $5s - 20$
B. $5s - 10$
C. $5s + 10$
D. $5s + 20$

6

The current population of a certain flamingo colony is 1,258 birds, which is 523 more than half the number of birds in the colony last year. If the number of birds in the colony decreases by the same amount from this year to next year as it did from last year to this year, then the population of the colony next year will be closest to which of the following?

A. 1046
B. 1098
C. 1123
D. 1207

7

Sarah is triple Andy's age, and Andy is double Melissa's age. If Sarah is 30 years old and Melissa is m years old, which of the following equations is true?

A. $\dfrac{m}{6} = 30$
B. $3m = 30$
C. $3m + 2 = 30$
D. $6m = 30$

Coordinate Geometry

Preview Quiz:

1) Label Quadrants I, II, III, and IV:

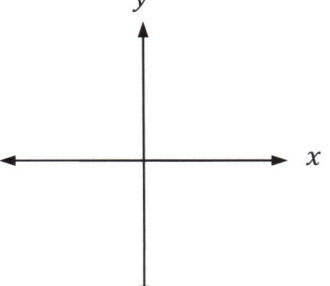

2) What is a *y*-intercept? $(0, y)$

3) What is an *x*-intercept? $(x, 0)$

4) How do you find the slope of the line between two points?

$$m = \frac{y_2 - y_1}{x_2 - x_1}$$

5) What is the most commonly used form of an equation of a line? $y = mx + b$

6) This form is called (standard form / **slope-intercept form** / point-slope form). $y = 4x - 5/2$

What is the relationship between:

7) the slopes of parallel lines? same

8) the slopes of perpendicular lines? reciprocal and opposite sign

9) What is the slope of a horizontal line? _____

10) What is the slope of a vertical line? _____

Solve:

11) On the *xy*-plane, the graph of $y = 4(3)^x$ passes through the point (2, ___)

12) What is the *y*-intercept of $y = -2x^2 + 5x + 17$ on the *xy*-plane?

13) The equation $y = 4x + k$, where k is a constant, represents a line on the *xy*-plane. If the line passes through the point (2, 11), what is the value of k?

14) What is the slope of the line given by $8x - 2y = 5$?
    $-2y = 5 - 8x$
    $-y = \frac{5}{2} - 4x$
    $y = \frac{5}{2} + 4x$
    4

15) On the *xy*-plane, line *t* has a slope of 3 and passes through the point (2, 10). What is the equation of line *t*?

Math: Algebra

Each point on **the *xy*-plane** has both an *x*-coordinate and a *y*-coordinate. The points are written in the order (x, y), where the *x* value is represented horizontally and the *y* value is represented vertically. The center point is $(0, 0)$, also called the **origin**, which is where the ***x*-axis** and the ***y*-axis** intersect. These two lines divide the *xy*-plane into four **quadrants**, as shown below.

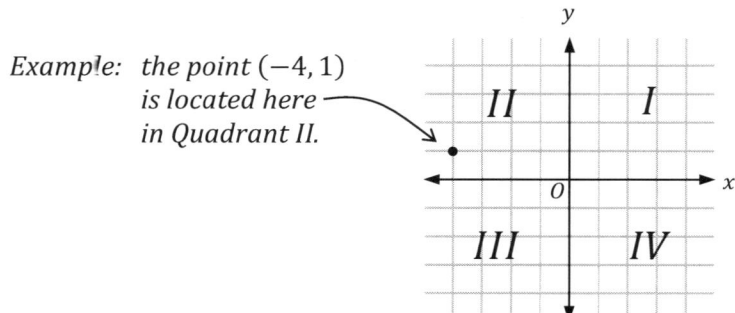

Example: the point $(-4, 1)$ is located here in Quadrant II.

When an equation is **graphed** on the *xy*-plane, the result is a visual representation of the *x* and *y* values that satisfy the equation. For example, in the equation $y = 2x + 3$, when the value of *x* is 1, the value of *y* must be 5, because $2(1) + 3 = 5$. Therefore, the graph of $y = 2x + 3$ must pass through the point $(1, 5)$ on the *xy*-plane.

This works for all kinds of equations, not just linear ones.

Example: On the xy-plane, the graph of $y = 4(3)^x$ passes through a point with an x-coordinate of 2. What is the y-coordinate of this point?

$$y = 4(3)^2 = 4(9) = \mathbf{36}$$

You can use this relationship to identify an equation based on its graph. Just pick one or more (x, y) points on the graph and plug those values into the equations in the answer choices.

Try It

1) The figure shows the graph of which of the following?

A) $y = -\dfrac{3}{2}x + 2$

B) $y = -\dfrac{2}{3}x + 2$

C) $y = \dfrac{2}{3}x + 3$

D) $y = \dfrac{3}{2}x + 3$

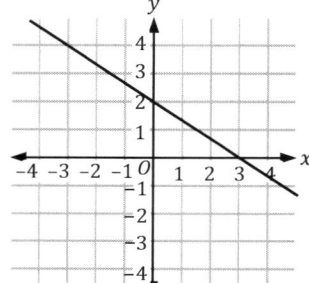

- 270 -

Any point at which the graph of an equation intersects the y-axis is called a **y-intercept**. The x-coordinate of this point will always be zero. Therefore, you can always find the y-intercept of an equation by plugging in zero for x.

Example: What is the y-intercept of $y = -2x^2 + 5x + 17$ on the xy-plane?

$y = -2(0)^2 + 5(0) + 17$
$y = -0 + 0 + 17$
$y = 17$

The y-intercept is the point $(\mathbf{0, 17})$.

TIP:
You can also solve these problems by graphing them on the built-in calculator: see pp. 236-238.

Similarly, any point at which a graph intersects the x-axis is called an **x-intercept**. Because the y-coordinate of this point will always be zero, we can find the x-intercept(s) by plugging in zero for y.

Try It

2) On the xy-plane, what is the x-intercept of the line given by $y = 3x - 6$?

3) On the xy-plane, what is the x-intercept of the horizontal parabola given by $x = 2(y + 1)^2 - 5$?

In all of these equations, x and y are **variables**, meaning they can take on many different values. Some equations on the SAT may also contain a **constant**, which is a letter that represents some specific unknown value. Unlike a variable, a constant cannot take on multiple different values; it has exactly one value no matter what. To find out what that value is, come back to the same rule as before: plug in the coordinates of a point on the graph for x and y.

Example: The equation $y = 4x + k$, where k is a constant, represents a line on the xy-plane. If the line passes through the point $(2, 11)$, what is the value of k?

$11 = 4(2) + k$
$11 = 8 + k$
$\mathbf{3} = k$

- 271 -
TM and © 2023 PrepMatters, Inc. All rights reserved.

Math: Algebra

Try It

4) On the xy-plane, the point $(3, 22)$ lies on the graph of $y = ax^2 + 4$, where a is a constant. What is the value of a?

(OK)

5) The figure below shows the graph of $y = x^3 - 3x^2 + 3x + k$, where k is a constant. What is the value of k?

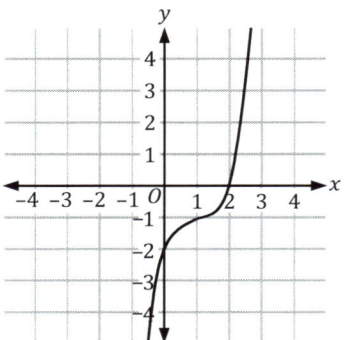

A **linear equation** gives the graph of a straight line on the xy-plane. The equation typically uses the form $y = mx + b$ (known as **slope-intercept form**), where m and b are constants. The constant m gives the **slope**, or rate of change, of the line; the farther the value of m is from zero, the steeper the line. The constant b gives the y-coordinate of the line's y-intercept.

Example: The line $y = 2x - 5$ has a slope of 2 and a y-intercept of $(0, -5)$.

If the test gives you the equation of a line written in some other format (such as $ax + by = c$), use algebra to rearrange the equation into slope-intercept form. It will likely be easier to work with that way.

Example: What is the slope of the line given by $8x - 2y = 5$?

$-2y = -8x + 5$

$y = 4x - \dfrac{5}{2}$

The slope of the line is **4**.

TIP: The slope of a perfectly horizontal line is 0. The slope of a perfectly vertical line is undefined.

To calculate the slope of the line between two known points, use the **slope formula**:

$$m = \frac{y_2 - y_1}{x_2 - x_1}$$

Example: What is the slope of the line between the points $(0, 3)$ and $(-2, 1)$ on the xy-plane?

First, label the points. It doesn't matter which point you call (x_1, y_1) and which (x_2, y_2), as long as you're consistent.

$$\underset{(0\ ,\ 3)}{\overset{x_1\quad y_1}{}} \qquad \underset{(-2,\ 1)}{\overset{x_2\quad y_2}{}}$$

Now plug those values into the formula.

$$m = \frac{1 - 3}{-2 - 0}$$
$$m = \frac{-2}{-2}$$
$$m = \mathbf{1}$$

Try It

6) On the xy-plane, what is the slope of the line that passes through the points $(7, -4)$ and $(3, 2)$?

7) What is the slope of the line shown in the graph below?

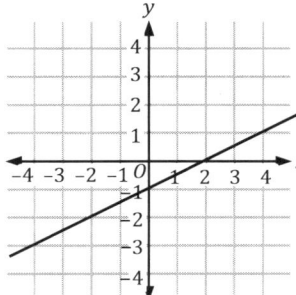

Math: Algebra

If two lines are **parallel**, their slopes are always equal. If two lines are **perpendicular**—that is, they intersect at a 90° angle—their slopes are *opposite reciprocals*. This means you can take the slope of one line, flip that number upside down, and make it the opposite sign: the result is the perpendicular slope. For example, a slope of $\frac{3}{4}$ is perpendicular to a slope of $-\frac{4}{3}$.

Try It

On the xy-plane, line l is represented by $y = 2x + 5$. Line q is parallel to line l, and line p is perpendicular to line l.

8) What is the slope of line q?

9) What is the slope of line p?

If you are given the slope of a line and one point that it passes through, you have enough information to find the equation of the line. Just use the form $y = mx + b$: plug in the slope for m and the coordinates of the point for x and y.

Example: On the xy-plane, line t has a slope of 3 and passes through the point $(2, 10)$. What is the equation of line t?

$y = mx + b$
$y = 3x + b$
$10 = 3(2) + b$
$10 = 6 + b$
$4 = b$

Therefore, the equation of the line is $\boldsymbol{y = 3x + 4}$.

Try It

10) When graphed on the xy-plane, line l passes through the point $(-1, 6)$. If the slope of line l is 2, what is the equation of the line?

11) On the xy-plane, what is the equation of the line that passes through the points $(4, 2)$ and $(0, 6)$?

Chapter Answer Key

Try It	
1)	B
2)	$(2, 0)$
3)	$(-3, 0)$
4)	2
5)	-2
6)	$-3/2$ or -1.5
7)	0.5
8)	2
9)	$-1/2$ or -0.5
10)	$y = 2x + 8$
11)	$y = -x + 6$

FROM THE BLOG

One morning, a student arrived at her test center on a chilly morning of what proved to be a hot day. Dressed in long pants and a wool sweater, she discovered that, unlike her school, this school didn't have AC. As the temperature rose, so did her lethargy. Her performance, however, headed in the other direction.

When it's too warm, students' ability to reason is impaired. In fact, researcher Joshua Graff Zivin found that math performance decreased linearly at temperatures over 70 degrees Fahrenheit, with excessive heat (above 79° F) hurting performance by 1.6 percentile points.

The lesson? Dress in layers for the test. Science proves it's better to keep your cool!

Math: Algebra

Practice Set 1: Easy-Medium

1

Which of the following points in the standard xy-plane lies on the line given by $y = -2x + 5$?

A. $(-1, 3)$
B. $(0, 2)$
C. $(1, -7)$
D. $(2, 1)$

2

In the xy-plane, the point $(-6, 2)$ is translated right 2 units and up 6 units. What are the coordinates of the point after the translation?

A. $(-8, 8)$
B. $(-4, -4)$
C. $(-4, 8)$
D. $(0, 2)$

3

In the xy-plane, the graph of the line given by $y = 2x - 5$ passes through the point $(k, 9)$, where k is a constant. What is the value of k?

4

x	-1	0	1	2
y	-9	-6	-3	0

The table above shows some values of the linear equation y. Which of the following gives the equation?

A. $y = -\dfrac{3}{4}x - 6$
B. $y = \dfrac{1}{3}x + 2$
C. $y = x + 2$
D. $y = 3x - 6$

5

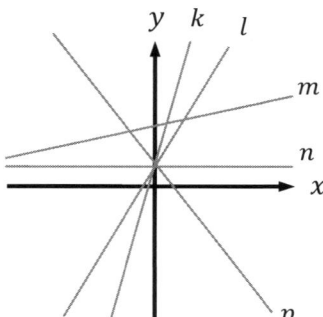

Which line in the figure above has the smallest positive slope? (Assume that line n is perfectly horizontal.)

A. l
B. m
C. n
D. p

6

In the xy-plane, the line that passes through the origin and $(4, -1)$ has a slope that is which of the following?

A. zero.
B. negative.
C. positive.
D. undefined.

7

What is the equation of the line graphed in the xy-plane plane below?

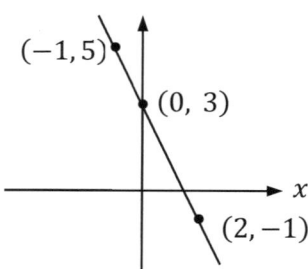

A. $y = -2x + 3$
B. $y = -3x + 2$
C. $y = -x + 3$
D. $y = 2x - 1$

Coordinate Geometry

8

When the equation $y = 8x - 24$ is graphed in the xy-plane, what is the x-coordinate of the line's x-intercept?

9

In the xy-plane, what is the slope of the line that passes through the points $(-1, 5)$ and $(6, 2)$?

A. $-\dfrac{7}{3}$

B. $-\dfrac{3}{7}$

C. $\dfrac{3}{7}$

D. $\dfrac{7}{3}$

10

In the figure below, line l is graphed in the xy-plane. Which of the following gives the equation of line l?

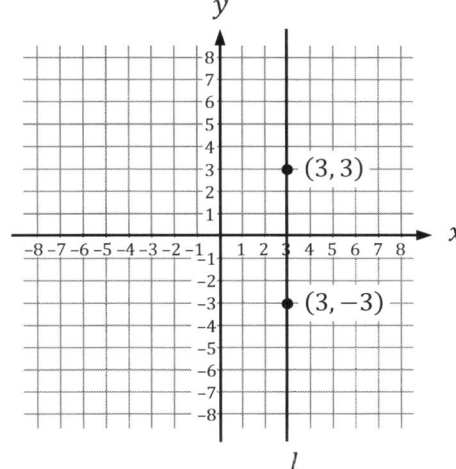

A. $y = x + 3$
B. $y = 3x$
C. $y = 3$
D. $x = 3$

11

In the xy-plane, the line that passes through the points $(1, 1)$ and $(4, -5)$ must also pass through which of the following points?

A. $(0, 3)$
B. $(0, 4)$
C. $(-2, 0)$
D. $(3, 0)$

12

Which of the following is the equation of a line that is perpendicular to the line graphed in the xy-plane below?

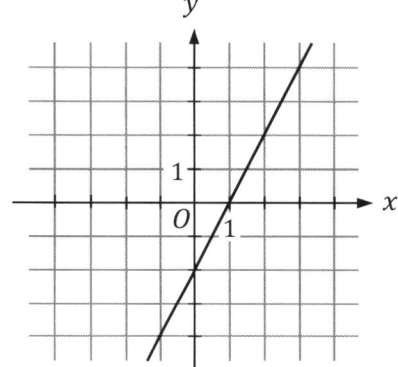

A. $y = 2x - 2$

B. $y = -\dfrac{1}{2}x + 2$

C. $y = \dfrac{1}{2}x - 2$

D. $y = -2x + 2$

13

In the xy-plane, what is the slope of the line given by the equation $3x - 2y = 5$?

Math: Algebra

Practice Set 2: Medium-Hard

1

In the xy-plane, the line given by the equation $5x - 2y = 8$ is perpendicular to the line given by which of the following equations?

A. $2x - 5y = 3$
B. $2x + 5y = 4$
C. $5x - 2y = 6$
D. $-5x + 2y = -1$

2

The shaded region below is bounded by the lines $y = 0$, $x = 0$, and $y = 4 - 2x$. What is the area of the shaded region?

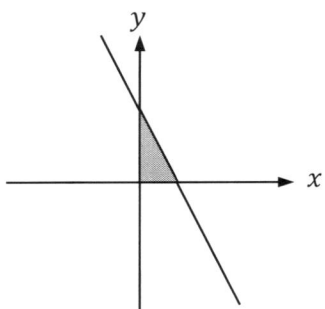

A. 1
B. 2
C. 4
D. 8

3

In the xy-plane, line l is parallel to the line $y = \frac{2}{3}x - 5$ and passes through the point $(6, 7)$. What is the y-coordinate of the y-intercept of line l?

4

In the xy-plane, the equation of line l is $2x - 5y = 7$. Which of the following values is the greatest?

A. the slope of line l
B. the x-coordinate of the x-intercept of line l
C. the y-coordinate of the y-intercept of line l
D. the slope of a line that is perpendicular to line l

5

In the xy-plane, the graph of the equation $y = ax + b$, where a and b are constants, is a horizontal line. Which of the following could be the values of a and b?

A. $a = -1$ and $b = 0$
B. $a = 0$ and $b = 1$
C. $a = 1$ and $b = -1$
D. $a = 2$ and $b = 0$

6

The figure below shows the average revenue per user for a social media company from 2003 to 2019.

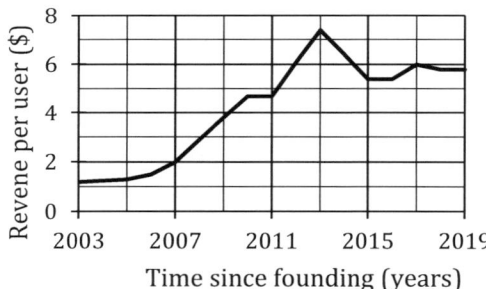

From 2007 to 2010, the company's average revenue per user increased at a rate of $\$m$ per year. Based on the graph, which of the following is the best estimate for the value of m?

A. 0.9
B. 1.5
C. 1.9
D. 2.5

Systems of Equations

Preview Quiz:

Solve each of the following.

1) A small fruit stand sells apples for $1 each and bananas for $0.60 each. If the fruit stand sells a total of 45 apples and bananas for a total of $37.80, how many bananas were sold?

2) If $x - 2y = 5$ and $3x + y = 8$, what is the value of x?

3) The equations $y = 2x - 3$ and $y = -x + 3$ are shown graphed in the xy-plane below. What is the solution to this system of equations?

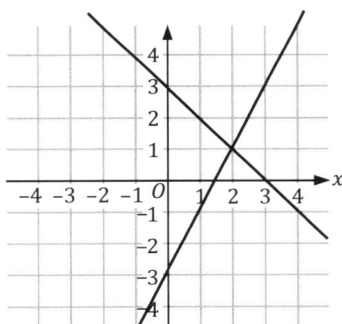

Choose **_all that apply_**.

4) It is possible for a system of two linear equations to have (zero / one / two / three / infinitely many) solutions.

5) The system of equations $y - x = 2$ and $2y - 2x = 4$ has (zero / one / two / three / infinitely many) solutions.

Math: Algebra

Some word problems involve two different properties of the items represented by the variables: for example, perhaps one property is *how many* of the items there are, while the other property is the *dollar value* of the items. In this situation, look to set up a **system** of two equations, one for each property.

Example: A small fruit stand sells apples for $1 each and bananas for $0.60 each. If the fruit stand sells a total of 45 apples and bananas for a total of $37.80, how many bananas were sold?

Number: $a + b = 45$

Price: $(1)a + (0.6)b = 37.80$

TIP: If all the problem is asking you to do is to pick out the correct system of equations from the choices, save yourself some time by looking for the easier equation (e.g., $a + b = 45$) first.

To **solve**, there are two main methods. One is to solve one of the equations for one variable, then plug that into the other equation.

$$a + b = 45$$
$$a = 45 - b$$

$$(1)(45 - b) + (0.6)b = 37.80$$
$$45 - b + 0.6b = 37.80$$
$$-0.4b = -7.2$$
$$b = \mathbf{18}$$

The other (and usually easier) way is to stack the equations and then add or subtract straight down to eliminate one of the variables.

$$\begin{array}{r} a + b = 45 \\ a + 0.6b = 37.80 \\ \hline 0.4b = 7.2 \\ b = \mathbf{18} \end{array}$$

In some cases, you may need to multiply one of the equations by something first to make the coefficients match up.

Example: If $x - 2y = 5$ and $3x + y = 8$, what is the value of x?

$$2(3x + y = 8) \rightarrow 6x + 2y = 16$$
$$x - 2y = 5$$
$$\overline{7x = 21}$$
$$x = \mathbf{3}$$

The elimination method is especially useful if the question is asking for the value of an **expression** instead of the value of an individual variable.

Example: If $x - 2y = 5$ and $3x + y = 8$, what is the value of $4x - y$?

$$\begin{array}{r} x - 2y = 5 \\ 3x + y = 8 \\ \hline 4x - y = \mathbf{13} \end{array}$$

$$3x + 4y = 7$$
$$2x + 4y = 3$$

Try It 1) What value of x satisfies the system of equations above?

$$4p - j = -2$$
$$3p + 2j = 26$$

2) What value of p satisfies the system of equations above?

When a system of linear equations is graphed, the point where the two lines intersect is the solution to the system.

Example: *The solution to the system of equations $y = 2x - 3$ and $y = -x + 3$ is $x = 2, y = 1$.*

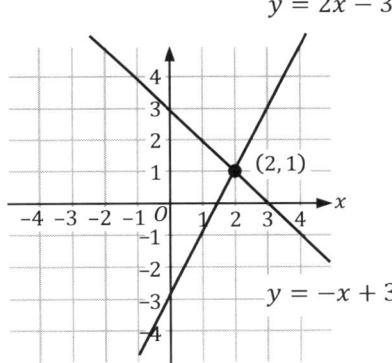

For this reason, the fastest way to solve a system of equations is often simply to graph both lines on the built-in calculator. If you're not sure how, check pp. 236-238 from the Mastering the Calculator section for more information.

Not all graphs of two lines will intersect exactly once. For a system of two linear equations, there are in fact three possible situations: the system can have **one solution** (the lines intersect), **no solutions** (the lines are parallel), or **infinite solutions** (they are both the same line).

The system
$$\begin{cases} y - x = 2 \\ y + x = 0 \end{cases}$$
has one solution:
$x = -1, y = 1$

The system
$$\begin{cases} y - x = 2 \\ y - x = -1 \end{cases}$$
has no solutions.

The system
$$\begin{cases} y - x = 2 \\ 2y - 2x = 4 \end{cases}$$
has infinitely many solutions.

In both of the latter two situations, the slopes of the two lines are the same. This means that in systems with either no solutions or infinitely many solutions, **the coefficients of the variables all match**. If we were to use the elimination method on these systems, the variables would all cancel out. Just as with single-variable equations that have infinite solutions versus no solutions (see p. 255), the distinction between them is what's left after the variables cancel.

If what's left at that point is a *true* statement, then the system had **infinitely many solutions**. If what's left is a *false* statement, then the system had **no solutions**.

Example: $y - x = 2$
$y - x = -1$

What are the solutions to the system of equations above?

$$-\frac{\begin{array}{r} y - x = 2 \\ y - x = -1 \end{array}}{0 = 1}$$

This is <u>false</u>, so the system has **no solutions**.

Example: $y - x = 2$
$2y - 2x = 4$

How many solutions exist to the system of equations above?

$2(y - x = 2) \rightarrow \quad -\frac{\begin{array}{r} 2y - 2x = 4 \\ 2y - 2x = 4 \end{array}}{0 = 0}$

This is <u>true</u>, so the system has **infinitely many solutions**.

$$2a + 4b = 3$$
$$a + 2b = 0$$

Try It   3)   What are the solutions, if any, to the system of equations above?

4)   If $3x + 2y = 10$ and $3x + 2y = 2n$ have infinitely many solutions, where n is a constant, what is the value of n?

FROM THE BLOG

"My parents told me I shouldn't take away time from studying to exercise." That may be the *worst* advice I've heard this year. Why?

- **Faster feet, faster thinking.** New nerve cells are constantly being created in your brain. When you exercise regularly, the neurons created by the hippocampus react more quickly. In essence, they are "smarter."
- **Faster thinking, calmer brains.** You might think that neurons that react quickly would also stress more easily. But studies show that the brains of runners (unforced aerobic exercise) have a greater amount of a specific neurotransmitter that actually "shushes" neurons, thereby calming the brain.
- **Calmer brains, stress resistance, and finding solutions.** Scientists studying brain activation and stress reactions in sedentary and active mice noticed this advantage in the exercisers: "They didn't freeze or cling to dark spaces in unfamiliar situations. They explored. They appeared to be 'stress-resistant.'"

The ideal brain state for learning (and testing!) is relaxed alertness. Physical activity is, well, activating! (Ever fall asleep and run into a tree while out for a jog? Me neither). And, exercise is relaxing, both short-term and long-term.

Mens sano in corpere sana: A sound mind in a sound body.

Math: Algebra

Chapter Answer Key

Try It	1) 4
	2) 2
	3) There are no solutions
	4) 5

Practice Set 1: Easy-Medium

1

What value of x satisfies the system of equations below?

$$x - 2y = 4$$
$$3x + 2y = 6$$

A. $\dfrac{1}{2}$

B. $\dfrac{2}{3}$

C. $\dfrac{5}{2}$

D. 10

2

If $3x + 4 = a$ and $2a = 20$, what is the value of x?

3

In the xy-plane, the graphs of the equations $y = 2x - 5$ and $y = -x + 7$ intersect at which of the following (x, y) points?

A. $(1.5, -2)$
B. $(2, -1)$
C. $(4, 3)$
D. $(4, 6)$

4

What is the solution (x, y) to the system of equations below?

$$2x + 3y = 10$$
$$3y - 7x = -8$$

A. $(0, 2)$
B. $(2, 2)$
C. $(4, 3)$
D. $(1, -9)$

5

$$8x + 6y = 25$$
$$4x - 9y = 17$$

If (x, y) is a solution to the system of equations above, what is the value of $12x - 3y$?

6

Yesterday, a food truck sold a total of 79 hamburgers and hot dogs. Let x represent the number of hamburgers sold and y represent the number of hot dogs sold. Each hamburger costs $7 and each hot dog costs $5. The food truck earned a total of $489 yesterday from its sale of hot dogs and hamburgers. Which of the following systems of equations represents the number of each food item sold?

A. $7y = 5x$
   $35x = 489$

B. $7x + y = 489$
   $x + 5y = 79$

C. $x + y = 489$
   $5x + 7y = 79$

D. $x + y = 79$
   $7x + 5y = 489$

7

Cory has 5 more first cousins than his friend James has. If they have a total of 23 first cousins, how many cousins does Cory have?

A. 9
B. 11
C. 14
D. 18

Math: Algebra

8

Main Street Theater sells two types of tickets: adult tickets and student tickets. For a recent Sunday matinee, Main Street Theater sold a total of 150 tickets. If the theater sold 40 fewer student tickets than adult tickets, how many student tickets were sold?

A. 55
B. 80
C. 95
D. 100

9

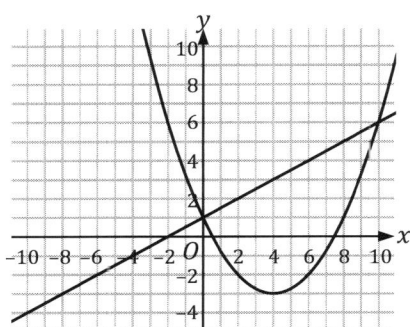

The xy-plane above shows the graphs of the equations $y = \frac{1}{4}x^2 - 2x + 1$ and $y = \frac{1}{2}x + 1$. Which of the following (x, y) points is a solution to this system of equations?

A. $(-2, 0)$
B. $(0.5, 0)$
C. $(6, 4)$
D. $(10, 6)$

10

What are the coordinates of the point of intersection between the lines represented by the equations $y = 3x - 2$ and $x - y = 4$?

A. $(1, 5)$
B. $(5, 1)$
C. $(-1, -5)$
D. $(-5, -1)$

11

If $10x + y = 8$ and $7x - y = 9$, what is the value of $3x + 2y$?

12

$$y = 3x - 4$$
$$y = 3x + 2$$

How many (x, y) solutions exist to the system of equations above?

A. 0
B. 1
C. 2
D. Infinitely many

13

In a math competition, teams earn 2 points for each easy question solved and 5 points for each difficult question solved. There are no other types of questions. If a team solved a total of 25 questions and earned a total of 71 points, how many difficult questions did the team answer?

A. 7
B. 9
C. 13
D. 18

14

$$3y = 6$$
$$x - 4y = 5$$

What is the solution (x, y) to the system of equations above?

A. $(-3, 2)$
B. $(2, -1.75)$
C. $(2, -0.75)$
D. $(13, 2)$

Practice Set 2: Medium-Hard

1

If the sum of two integers is 6 and the sum of twice the first integer and 3 times the second integer is 9, find the sum of the first integer and twice the second integer.

2

A family's change jar contains only nickels, dimes, and quarters. There are twice as many dimes as nickels. If the jar contains 20 coins with a total value of $2.50, how many quarters are in the jar?

A. 5
B. 6
C. 7
D. 8

3

Bob's Party Rentals charges a fixed amount for assembly plus an hourly rate for the rented equipment. If the total pre-tax charge for a five-hour party is $190 and the total pre-tax charge for a two hour party is $100, what is the total pre-tax charge for a three-hour party?

(Note: assume the same quantity of equipment is rented at all three parties).

A. $130
B. $140
C. $150
D. $170

4

If k is a constant, for what value of k will the system of equations below have no real solutions?

$$4x - 3y = 10$$
$$kx - 6y = 12$$

A. -4
B. 0
C. 8
D. 10

5

In triangle ABC, the degree measure of the largest angle is equal to the sum of the degree measures of the other two angles. If the degree measure of the smallest angle is added to the degree measure of the largest angle, the result is twice the degree measure of the remaining angle. What is the degree measure of the smallest angle in the triangle?

A. $15°$
B. $25°$
C. $30°$
D. $60°$

6

$$4x + b = 3x - 11$$
$$4y + c = 3y - 11$$

In the equations above, b and c are constants. If b is c plus $\frac{1}{4}$, which of the following is true?

A. y is x plus $\frac{3}{4}$

B. y is x minus $\frac{1}{4}$

C. y is x plus $\frac{1}{4}$

D. y is x minus $\frac{5}{4}$

Math: Algebra

7. Leslie has a box of c chocolate bars to sell to her neighbors for a school fundraising project. If each of her neighbors buys 2 chocolate bars, there will be 10 bars left in the box. Leslie would need 40 additional chocolate bars if each neighbor were to buy 4 chocolate bars. How many neighbors does Leslie have?

A. 20
B. 25
C. 50
D. 60

8. Abbott owns x hats. Becky owns three more hats than Abbott does. Costello owns two fewer hats than Becky. If the total number of hats owned by these three individuals is twice as great as the number of hats owned by Becky, what is the value of x?

9. In the system of equations below, k is a constant. If the system has infinitely many solutions, what is the value of k?

$$3x + ky = 15$$
$$2x + 5y = 10$$

A. $\dfrac{7}{2}$
B. 5
C. $\dfrac{15}{2}$
D. 9

10. Esther and Frances together have 20 grandchildren, Esther and Gertrude together have 13 grandchildren, and Frances and Gertrude together have 17 grandchildren. How many grandchildren does Frances have?

11. A survey was conducted among 197 families who own *either* one cat *or* one dog (none of the families own both). Each of these families was asked to report whether they live in a house or an apartment. There are three times as many cat-owning families as dog-owning families among apartment residents, and there are four times as many dog-owning families as cat-owning families among house residents. If a total of 129 of the families own dogs and a total of 68 own cats, which of the following is closest to the probability that a dog-owning family selected at random lives in an apartment?

		Type of Pet	
		Dog	Cat
Type of Residence	Apartment		
	House		
	Total	129	68

A. 0.403
B. 0.305
C. 0.282
D. 0.101

Inequalities and Absolute Value

Preview Quiz:

Solve each of the following.

1) $3 - 2x < 9$

2) $0 \leq x + 5 \leq 9$

3) $|4x + 1| = 7$

Sketch the graph for each of the following.

4) $y \geq x + 2$

5) $y = |x|$

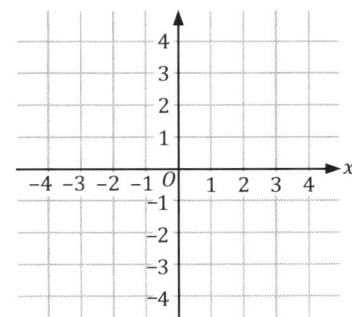

Math: Algebra

Solving an **inequality** such as $3 - 2x < 9$ is just like solving a regular equation with an equals sign, with one extra twist: when you multiply or divide by a negative number, you flip the "greater than" or "less than" sign.

$$3 - 2x < 9$$
$$-3 \quad\quad -3$$
$$-2x < 6$$
$$\div(-2) \quad \div(-2)$$
$$\boldsymbol{x > -3}$$

If the variable is between two inequalities, just make sure that whatever you do to one part of the equation, you do to *all three* parts.

$$0 \leq x + 5 \leq 9$$
$$-5 \quad\quad -5 \quad\quad -5$$
$$\boldsymbol{-5 \leq x \leq 4}$$

Try It

1) Simplify $x + 2 - 3(x + 2) > 4$

2) Simplify $2 < 1 - 2x < 5$

Make sure you know how to translate **inequality word problems** into algebra. A vague statement such as "x is greater than y" translates into an inequality symbol, but a specific statement such as "x is 5 greater than y" does not.

Examples:

p is less than one-half of q. $\quad p < \frac{1}{2}(q)$

x is 7 less than y. $\quad x = y - 7$

a is at least as great as b. $\quad a \geq b$

Try It   Translate each of the following into algebra:

3) The value of x is no greater than 10.

4) The juniors raised $500 more than the seniors did.

5) A container holds a minimum of 5 liters.

6) The rectangle's length is more than 6 inches greater than twice its width.

Graphing an inequality is very similar to graphing regular equations, except that after you draw the lines, you *shade* either above the line (for $y >$) or below it (for $y <$). A solid line means the line itself is included, while a dashed line means it's not.

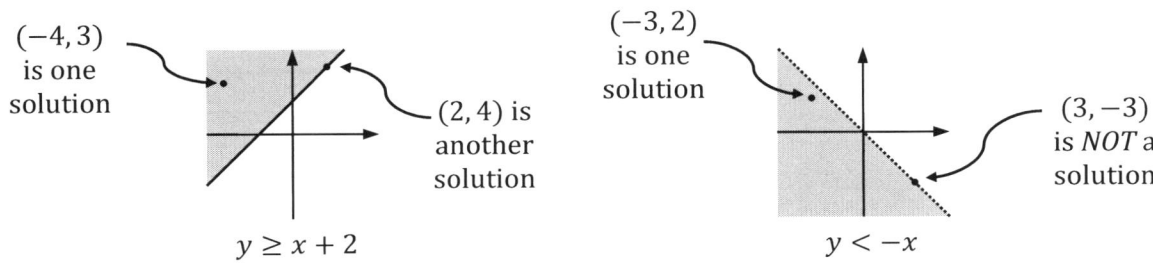

> **TIP:**
> In the built-in calculator, type > = for the $\geq$ symbol.

The **absolute value** of a number is its distance from zero on a number line. Just as you can never have a negative distance, you can never have a negative absolute value.

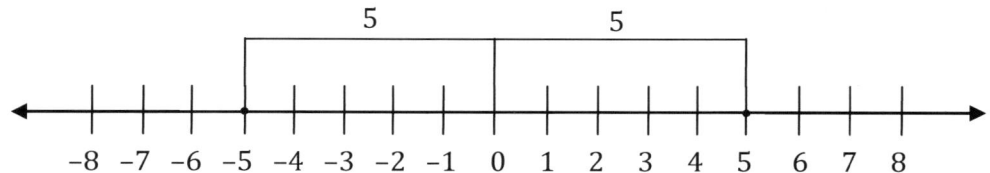

$|5| = 5$ because 5 is five units from zero.

$|-5| = 5$ because -5 is also five units from zero.

Absolute value equations that contain a variable within the absolute value bars are really two equations in one.

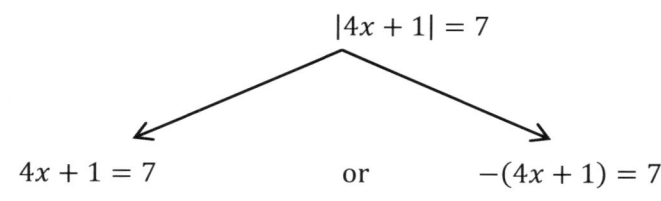

	$4x + 1 = 7$	or	$-(4x + 1) = 7$
Solve both:	$4x = 6$	or	$-4x - 1 = 7$
	$x = \dfrac{6}{4}$	or	$-4x = 8$
	$x = \dfrac{3}{2}$	or	$x = -2$

TIP:

Think of absolute value as "math on sale": it's two for one.

TIP:

Be sure to plug your answers back in to make sure they work.

Try It Solve:

7) $|2x - 5| = 1$

8) $|3x + 8| = -2$

Inequalities and Absolute Value

Now, let's apply all that to **absolute value inequalities**. Remember to flip the inequality if you multiply or divide by a negative number.

Try It   Simplify:

9) $|x - 6| \leq 4$

10) $|x - 6| \geq 4$

Absolute value **graphs** have a distinctive shape because absolute values are always nonnegative.

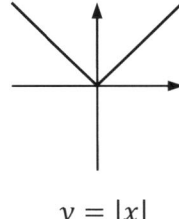

$y = |x|$

> **TIP:**
>
> To graph an absolute value equation on the SAT's built-in calculator, use the command `abs()`.

Chapter Answer Key

Try It
1) $x < -4$
2) $-2 < x < -\dfrac{1}{2}$
3) $x \leq 10$
4) $j = s + 500$
5) $c \geq 5$
6) $l > 2w + 6$
7) $x = 2$ or $x = 3$
8) No solutions
9) $2 \leq x \leq 10$
10) $x \leq 2$ or $x \geq 10$

Practice Set 1: Easy-Medium

1

Which of the following is a solution to the equation $|1 - 2x| = 11$?

A. $x = -4$
B. $x = 3$
C. $x = 5$
D. $x = 6$

2

What is the maximum possible value of q, given that $-2q - 12 \leq -5q$?

3

A scientist tabulating her data finds that all her results fall within the range indicated by the number line below.

Which of the following best represents the scientist's data?

A. $x < 10$ or $x > 20$
B. $10 < x < 20$
C. $10 < x \leq 20$
D. $10 \leq x < 20$

4

Two stores sell the same item for two different prices: one sells the item for x, the other for y. While both prices vary, the positive difference between the two prices is always between $5.00 and $7.50, inclusive. Which of the following must be true?

A. $5 \leq x - y \leq 7.5$
B. $5 \leq |x - y| \leq 7.5$
C. $5 \leq |x + y| \leq 7.5$
D. $5 \leq x \leq 7.5$ or $5 \leq y \leq 7.5$

5

If $y < 0$ and $|x + y| = 6$, then which of the following could be the value of y when $x = 5$?

A. -11
B. -3
C. 3
D. 7

6

Which of the following numbers is a solution to the inequality $3 - 4n > 11$?

A. -3
B. -2
C. -1
D. 1

7

Which of the following could show the graph of $y \leq 2x - 1$ on the xy-plane?

A.

B.

C.

D.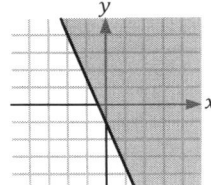

Math: Algebra

Practice Set 2: Medium-Hard

1

On the xy-plane, the graph of $y > -x + 3$ contains NO points in which of the following quadrants?

A. Quadrant I
B. Quadrant II
C. Quadrant III
D. Quadrant IV

2

Which of the following is always equal to $|y - x|$ for all real values of x and y?

A. $|x - y|$
B. $-(y - x)$
C. $x - y$
D. $|x + y|$

3

If $b = 2a$, where a is an integer such that $5a - 6 \leq 9 + 3a$, what is the maximum possible value of b?

A. 2
B. 7
C. 14
D. 15

4

A thermometer indicates that the current outside temperature is a degrees. The actual current outside temperature is b degrees. If the temperature indicated by the thermometer is within 3 degrees of the actual temperature, which of the following best represents this situation?

A. $a + b < 3$
B. $a > b - 3$
C. $-3 < b - a < 3$
D. $b + 3 > a$

5

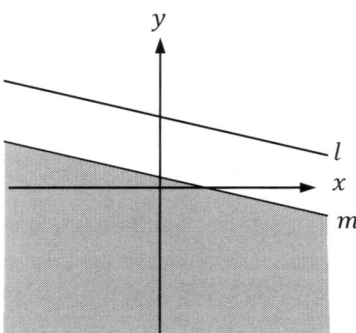

In the xy-plane above, lines l and m are parallel. If line l passes through the points $(-1, 5)$ and $(3, 4)$, which of the following could be the equation of the shaded area (the inequality that includes line m)?

A. $y \leq -\dfrac{1}{4}x + 1$
B. $y \leq 2x + \dfrac{3}{4}$
C. $y \geq \dfrac{3}{4}x + \dfrac{3}{4}$
D. $y \geq -\dfrac{1}{4}x + \dfrac{1}{2}$

6

Nine people weighing a total of 1,400 pounds (lbs) enter an elevator that has a weight limit of 1,500 lbs. One of the nine people is rolling a dolly weighing 15 lbs. On the dolly are b boxes, each weighing 18 lbs. What is the maximum possible value for b that will keep the combined weight of the people, the dolly, and the boxes under the elevator's weight limit?

Advanced Math

Exponents and Roots

Preview Quiz:

Simplify each of the following.

1) $a^b * a^c =$

2) $\dfrac{a^b}{a^c} =$

3) $(a^b)^c =$

4) $a^{-b} =$

5) $a^{1/b} =$

6) $a^c * b^c =$

7) $\dfrac{a^c}{b^c} =$

8) $\sqrt{a} * \sqrt{b} =$

9) $\dfrac{\sqrt{a}}{\sqrt{b}} =$

10) $a^1 =$

11) $a^0 =$

Solve.

12) If $x^2 = 36$, then $x =$ _____

13) If $y = 36$, then $\sqrt{y} =$ _____

Simplify each of the following.

14) $3x(x^4) =$ _____

15) $3^{-2} =$ _____

16) $\sqrt{p^4 q^{12}} =$ _____

17) $\sqrt{9x^8} =$ _____

Solve.

18) If $16^5 * 4^3 = 4^x$, what is the value of x? _____

Math: Advanced Math

As you already know, raising a number to an **exponent** means multiplying the number by itself that number of times.

Example: $2^4 = 2 \times 2 \times 2 \times 2 = \mathbf{16}$

You can simplify many ugly-looking exponent problems by simply rewriting them in this way.

Example: Simplify $x^3 * x^4$.

$\underbrace{x * x * x}_{} * \underbrace{x * x * x * x}_{} = \mathbf{x^7}$

This example illustrates an important rule: when you **multiply** the same base, you **add** the exponents.

Example: $n^5 * n^3 = \mathbf{n^8}$

Something similar happens when you divide.

Example: $\dfrac{x^5}{x^3} = \dfrac{\cancel{x}*\cancel{x}*\cancel{x}*x*x}{\cancel{x}*\cancel{x}*\cancel{x}} = \mathbf{x^2}$

See the relationship? When you **divide** the same base, you **subtract** the exponents.

Example: $n^{12} \div n^2 = \mathbf{n^{10}}$

We can use the same technique to illustrate problems that involve raising an exponent to another exponent.

Example: $(x^3)^2 = (x^3)(x^3) = (x*x*x)(x*x*x) = \mathbf{x^6}$

So when you raise an exponent to another exponent, you **multiply** the exponents.

Example: $(n^5)^3 = \mathbf{n^{15}}$

Try It   Simplify each of the following:

1) $a^4 * a^2 =$

2) $a^9 \div a^3 =$

3) $(a^7)^4 =$

Raising a value to the exponent 1 does nothing to it: the result is the same as the original value. This means whenever you see a variable that has no exponent written, you can always write in a 1 to remind yourself that it's there.

Example: *Simplify* $3x(x^4)$.
$$3 * x^1 * x^4 = \mathbf{3x^5}$$

By definition, when you raise any nonzero value to the exponent zero, the result is one.

Example: $7^0 = \mathbf{1}$

Try It Solve for x:

4) $4^5 * 4^5 * 4^5 * 4^5 = 4^x$

5) $3^6 * 3^4 = 3^x$

6) $\dfrac{3^6}{3^4} = 3^x$

7) $(3^6)^4 = 3^x$

8) Simplify $2x(5x) - 4x^2$.

9) If $a = 2$ and $b = 3$, what is the value of $3(a^0) + 2(b^0)$?

Math: Advanced Math

The key to many tricky exponent problems is to rewrite one or more of the expressions so that the bases match.

Example:
$$16^5 * 4^3 = 4^x$$
$$(4^2)^5 * 4^3 = 4^x$$
$$4^{10} * 4^3 = 4^x$$
$$4^{13} = 4^x$$
$$x = 13$$

Try It   Solve for x:

10) $9^2 = 3^x$

12) $\dfrac{4^5}{2^2 * 2^3} = x$

11) $4^5 * 4^5 * 4^5 * 4^5 = 2^x$

13) $(4^3)^2 = 2^x$

Negative exponents are all about fractions. If the value with a negative exponent is in the numerator, move it to the denominator and make the exponent positive. If the value with a negative exponent is in the denominator, move it to the numerator and make the exponent positive.

Examples: $\dfrac{x^{-5}}{2} = \dfrac{1}{2x^5}$ $\dfrac{5a^{-3}b}{c^2} = \dfrac{5b}{a^3c^2}$

TIP: Be sure to move *only* the value that the exponent is attached to.

You can apply this rule to non-fraction values by simply rewriting them as fractions first.

Example: $3^{-2} = \dfrac{3^{-2}}{1} = \dfrac{1}{3^2} = \dfrac{1}{9}$

Try It   14) What is the value of 2^{-3}?

Roots can be written as fraction exponents: $x^{\frac{1}{2}}$ indicates the square root of x, and $x^{\frac{1}{3}}$ is the cube root of x, and so on. This notation helps illustrate the effect of a root on an expression that contains an exponent: taking the square root means multiplying that exponent by $\frac{1}{2}$.

Example: *Simplify* $\sqrt{a^6}$.
$$(a^6)^{\frac{1}{2}} = a^{6*\frac{1}{2}} = \boldsymbol{a^3}$$

Example: *Simplify* $\sqrt{p^4 q^{12}}$.
$$(p^4 q^{12})^{\frac{1}{2}} = (p^4)^{\frac{1}{2}} * (q^{12})^{\frac{1}{2}} = \boldsymbol{p^2 q^6}$$

Try It 15) Simplify $\sqrt{x^8 y^2}$, where x and y are positive numbers.

Both positive numbers and negative numbers become positive when squared. Therefore, an expression with an even-numbered exponent has two answers: plus and minus.

Example: *If* $x^2 = 36$, *what is the value of* x?
$$\boldsymbol{x = 6 \text{ or } x = -6}$$

However, a square root expression has only one answer.

Example: *If* $y = \sqrt{36}$, *what is the value of* y?
$$\boldsymbol{y = 6 \text{ only}}$$

TIP:
Think of the radical as a function that means "give me the positive root of this number."

Math: Advanced Math

When multiplying or dividing two values that have been raised to the **same exponent**, you can squish them together in parentheses and keep the exponent outside.

Example: $4^5 * x^5 = (4x)^5$

You can also go the other way, eliminating parentheses by distributing the exponents that are attached to them.

Example: $(5n)^2 = 5^2 * n^2 = 25n^2$

These rules apply to roots too.

Example: $\sqrt{9x^8} = \sqrt{9} * \sqrt{x^8} = 3x^4$

To **simplify** a square root, use the rules above to break it up into factors that are perfect squares.

Example: $\sqrt{12} = \sqrt{4*3} = \sqrt{4} * \sqrt{3} = 2\sqrt{3}$

An important note: the rules on this page apply only to problems involving multiplying or dividing. This does *not* work when adding or subtracting!

Example: $(x+3)^2$ is NOT the same thing as $x^2 + 9$.

Try It   Simplify each of the following.

16) $\sqrt{16y^8} =$

17) $\sqrt{45} =$

18) $\sqrt[3]{8n^6} =$

19) $\sqrt[3]{-64} =$

TIP:

To enter a square root on the built-in calculator, just type `sqrt`. For other roots, type `nthroot`. Or, click the keyboard icon on the bottom left of the screen, then click the "functions" button, and then scroll down to the Number Theory category and click the $\sqrt[n]{\square}$ button.

Exponents and Roots

Chapter Answer Key

Try It

1) a^6
2) a^6
3) a^{28}
4) 20
5) 10
6) 2
7) 24
8) $6x^2$
9) 5
10) 4
11) 40
12) 32
13) 12
14) 1/8
15) x^4y
16) $4y^4$
17) $3\sqrt{5}$
18) $2n^2$
19) -4

Math: Advanced Math

Practice Set 1: Easy-Medium

1

$$\frac{8.0 * 10^6}{4.0 * 10^2}$$

The fraction above is equivalent to which of the following?

A. $4.0 * 10^{12}$
B. $2.0 * 10^{12}$
C. $2.0 * 10^4$
D. $4.0 * 10^3$

2

Given that a and b are positive integers, which of the following is equivalent to $\frac{-18a^9b^3}{(-3a^4)(2b)}$?

A. $-3a^5b^2$

B. $-\frac{3a^5}{b^2}$

C. $\frac{3a^5}{b^2}$

D. $3a^5b^2$

3

Which of the following represents the product of $2x^3$ and $3x^2$ for all real values of x?

A. $5x^5$
B. $5x^6$
C. $6x^5$
D. $6x^6$

4

Which of the following is equivalent to the expression $x^{\frac{3}{5}}$?

A. $\sqrt[5]{x^3}$

B. $\sqrt[3]{x^5}$

C. $\frac{x^3}{5}$

D. $\frac{3x}{5}$

5

If $7^{3x+5} = 7^8$, what is the value of x?

6

Given that x is a nonzero number, which of the following is equivalent to the expression $6x^4 - 9x^3 + 3x^2$?

A. $3x^2(2x^2 - 3x + 3)$
B. $6x^4(1 - 3x^2 + 2x)$
C. $x(6x^3 - 9x^2 + 3)$
D. $3x^2(2x^2 - 3x + 1)$

7

On the xy-plane, what is the y-intercept of the graph of $y = 2(4)^x$?

A. $(0, 1)$
B. $(0, 2)$
C. $(0, 4)$
D. $(0, 8)$

8

Let the function f be defined by the equation $f(x) = x^{-\frac{1}{2}}$ for all real values of x. What is the value of $f\left(\frac{9}{4}\right)$?

A. $-\frac{3}{2}$

B. $-\frac{2}{3}$

C. $\frac{3}{2}$

D. $\frac{2}{3}$

Practice Set 2: Medium-Hard

1. If $x > 0$ and $y > 0$, which expression is equivalent to $\sqrt{\dfrac{56x^3y^9}{7(xy)^5}}$?

A. $\dfrac{2y^2\sqrt{2}}{x}$

B. $2xy^2\sqrt{2}$

C. $\dfrac{8y^4}{x^2}$

D. $8x^2y^4$

2. If $x^{-\frac{1}{2}} = \dfrac{1}{4}$, then which of the following could be the value of x?

A. $\dfrac{1}{16}$

B. $\dfrac{1}{4}$

C. 4

D. 16

3. Which expression is equivalent to $(2xy)^3 * 3x^{-2}y$?

A. $6xy^4$

B. $6x^2y$

C. $\dfrac{24y^3}{x}$

D. $24xy^4$

4. Which expression is equivalent to the product of $\sqrt[4]{144a^6}$ and $2\sqrt{3a}$?

A. $12a^2$
B. $24a^2\sqrt{3a}$
C. $24a^4$
D. $12a^4\sqrt{3a}$

5. If $\dfrac{x^2y}{3x} = \dfrac{5}{2}$, where $x \neq 0$, then what is the value of xy?

A. $\dfrac{3}{5}$

B. $\dfrac{5}{6}$

C. $\dfrac{15}{2}$

D. 30

6. Let $x, y,$ and z be positive numbers such that $\sqrt{x} = y$ and $\sqrt{y} = z$. If $z = 4$, what is the value of x?

7. Which of the following is equivalent to $\dfrac{4n^6 - 8n^5}{2n^2 + (2n)^2}$, where $n \neq 0$?

A. $\dfrac{2}{3n^3}$

B. $\dfrac{2n^4 - 4n^3}{3}$

C. $\dfrac{2n^2 - 4n}{3}$

D. $3n^4 - 2n^3$

8. If the cube root of a negative integer is multiplied by the square of a positive integer, the result must be which of the following?

A. zero
B. positive
C. negative
D. imaginary

Math: Advanced Math

Factoring, FOILing, and Fractions

Preview Quiz

Distribute and simplify each of the following:

1) $3x(2 + y) =$

2) $x^3(2x^2 + y) =$

3) $(n + 2)(n - 3) =$

Factor completely:

4) $2ab + 4a =$

5) $x^2 - y^2 =$

6) $x^2 - 2x - 35 =$

7) $a^4 - 36 =$

Solve:

8) $x^2 - 11x + 18 = 0$

9) $\sqrt{x - 2} = x - 4$

When a term is multiplied by a quantity in parentheses, you can **distribute** that term by multiplying it by each item inside the parentheses.

Example: $3x(2 + y) = 3x(2) + 3x(y)$
$$= 6x + 3xy$$

TIP:

Remember, a **term** is a number, a variable, or the product of numbers and variables (e.g., $3xy$). **Like terms** are terms with the same variable and the same exponent. $3x$ and $2x$ are like terms; $3x$ and $2x^2$ are not. See p. 248 for more on this topic.

Try It Simplify each of the following.

1) $2(a + 3b) =$ _____

2) $x(4 - y) =$ _____

3) $3a(b + 2c - d) =$ _____

If the term outside the parentheses and the terms inside the parentheses have any variables in common, use the exponent rules to combine them.

Example: $x^3(2x^2 + y) = x^3(2x^2) + x^3(y)$
$$= 2x^5 + x^3y$$

Try It Simplify each of the following.

4) $3x(2x - 4x^2y) =$

7) $4x(0.5) + 2\left(\dfrac{x}{2}\right) - x$

5) $2n^3p(np^4 - 5n^2 + 3np) =$

8) $2(2x) - 4(3x) =$

6) $3(x - 2) + 5 =$

9) $9x - 3x(2 - y) =$

Math: Advanced Math

Try It Solve for x:

10) $-2(x+5) = 3(-1-x)$

11) $2[4 - (3 + 2x)] = 5$

The previous examples all involved multiplying a quantity in parentheses by a single term. But what if you're multiplying it by another quantity in parentheses?

To multiply two **binomials**, we **FOIL** them: multiply the
  First terms together, then the
  Outer terms, then the
  Inner terms, then the
  Last terms.

Then, add those products together and combine like terms.

TIP: A **binomial** is an expression with exactly two terms, such as $(x + 5)$.

Example: $(n+2)(n-3) = \underbrace{n^2}_{\substack{n \times n \\ \textbf{F}}} \quad \underbrace{-3n}_{\substack{n \times -3 \\ \textbf{O}}} \quad \underbrace{+2n}_{\substack{2 \times n \\ \textbf{I}}} \quad \underbrace{-6}_{\substack{2 \times -3 \\ \textbf{L}}}$

$= n^2 - 3n + 2n - 6$

$= \mathbf{n^2 - n - 6}$

Try It Simplify each of the following.

12) $(x-4)(x+2) =$

13) $(p+5)(q-6) =$

- 308 -

Factoring is just the opposite of distributing. To factor an expression, look to see whether all the terms in the expression can be divided by the same thing. This "thing" could be just a number, like 2, or a more complicated term such as $2x^2y$.

Example: $2ab + 4a$ can be factored as $2a(b + 2)$.

Try It Factor completely:

14) $6x - 3 =$

15) $8n^2 - 4n =$

Factoring a **trinomial** (an expression with three terms) such as $n^2 - n - 6$ is a little more tricky. On the last page, we got to this trinomial by multiplying together two binomials, so that's where we'll end up when we factor it: $(n - 3)(n + 2)$.

Notice that -3 and 2 will *multiply* together to be -6 and *add* together to be -1. That's what we're looking for each time: try to find a pair of numbers that will multiply together to be the last term and add together to be the middle term.

Example: Factor $x^2 - 2x - 35$ completely.

Step One: List the possible pairs of numbers that could multiply together to be the last term.

(1 and -35); (-1 and 35); (5 and -7); (-5 and 7)

Step Two: Check each of those pairs to see which one adds up to the middle term.

$$1 + (-35) = -34$$
$$(-1) + 35 = 34$$
$$\boxed{5 + (-7) = -2}$$
$$(-5) + 7 = 2$$

TIP: Don't forget to consider negative numbers!

Step Three: Plug those numbers into the parentheses.

$(x + 5)(x - 7)$ is the answer.

Try It Factor completely:

16) $x^2 - 3x - 4 =$

17) $x^2 - 10x + 9 =$

Math: Advanced Math

The **difference of squares rule** says that any binomial of the form $a^2 - b^2$ can be factored as $(a+b)(a-b)$. This works whether a and b are variables, numbers, or some combination of both.

Examples:
$$x^2 - y^2 = (x+y)(x-y)$$
$$n^2 - 25 = (n+5)(n-5)$$
$$a^4 - 36 = (a^2+6)(a^2-6)$$
$$= (a^2+6)(a+\sqrt{6})(a-\sqrt{6})$$

Try It   Factor completely:

18) $x^2 - 81 =$ 19) $p^2 - r^6 =$

TIP:

Here are a few other factoring patterns that are handy to know:
$$a^2 + 2ab + b^2 = (a+b)(a+b)$$
$$a^2 - 2ab + b^2 = (a-b)(a-b)$$

When a factorable expression starts out set equal to zero, you can often **solve by factoring**. Factor the expression completely, and then set each factor equal to zero. Then solve both.

Example:
$$x^2 - 11x + 18 = 0$$
$$(x-9)(x-2) = 0$$
$$x - 9 = 0 \text{ or } x - 2 = 0$$
$$x = 9 \text{ or } x = 2$$

TIP:

Take care to check whether the problem is asking for a factor or a solution. A **factor** of this equation is $(x-9)$. A **solution** is positive 9.

Try It   Solve for x:

20) $x^2 - 3x - 4 = 0$ 21) $2x^2 - 6x = 0$

CHALLENGE:

You know how to factor an expression of form $ax^2 + bx + c$ when there is no coefficient on the x^2 term (that is, when $a = 1$). But what about otherwise?

Example: Factor the expression $2x^2 + 13x + 15$.

To start, multiply the first coefficient (a) by the last value (c): in this case, that gives us $2 * 15 = 30$. Our task now is to find a pair of numbers that will multiply together to be 30 and add together to be the middle coefficient (13). In this case, 10 and 3 would work. So now, we rewrite the expression, breaking up the middle term into those two pieces:

$$2x^2 + 10x + 3x + 15$$

Next, **factor by grouping**: factor whatever you can out of the first two terms, and then factor whatever you can out of the last two terms. Here, we can factor $2x$ out of the first two terms, and we can factor a 3 out of the last two. That gives us this:

$$2x(x + 5) + 3(x + 5)$$

We now have two big, ugly terms, and they have something in common: they each have $(x + 5)$ as a factor. So, factor that out of both.

$$(x + 5)(2x + 3)$$

And that's it! The expression is now fully factored.

Try It   22) Solve the equation $2x^2 + 7x - 4 = 0$.

TIP:

You can also solve this problem by graphing it on the built-in calculator. The x-intercepts of the graph are the answers.

Some equations can be solved simply by taking the square root of both sides of the equation. Just remember that even-numbered exponents have *two* solutions: plus and minus.

Example: $(x-4)^2 = 100$

$$x - 4 = 10 \text{ or } x - 4 = -10$$
$$x = 14 \text{ or } x = -6$$

If you can solve an equation by square rooting both sides, you can also solve an equation by *squaring* both sides. However, be careful to square the *entire side.*

Example: $\sqrt{x-2} = x - 4$

Incorrect: ~~$(\sqrt{x-2})^2 = x^2 - 4^2$~~   Correct: $(\sqrt{x-2})^2 = (x-4)^2$
~~$x - 2 = x^2 - 16$~~ $x - 2 = (x-4)(x-4)$

Next, simplify and combine like terms, then solve by factoring if possible. Once you have your solutions, plug them back into the original equation to check that they work.

$$(\sqrt{x-2})^2 = (x-4)^2$$
$$x - 2 = (x-4)(x-4)$$
$$x - 2 = x^2 - 8x + 16$$
$$0 = x^2 - 9x + 18$$
$$0 = (x-3)(x-6)$$
$$x = 3 \text{ or } x = 6$$

Now plug these values back in:

$x = 3$:
$\sqrt{3-2} = 3 - 4$
$\sqrt{1} = -1$
Not true!

$x = 6$:
$\sqrt{6-2} = 6 - 4$
$\sqrt{4} = 2$
True!

In this case, 3 was an **extraneous solution**, meaning it was a value that appeared to satisfy the equation but actually didn't. The only answer to this equation is $x = 6$.

TIP:

You should always check for extraneous solutions if the original equation contained an x either inside a square root or on the bottom of a fraction. That means it's usually quickest to back-solve these problems, if possible. After all, if you do all the algebra, you'll just have to plug those values in at the end anyway to double-check that they're not extraneous. So you may as well skip the extra work and go straight to the plugging-in step.

You can also use the built-in calculator to solve these equations. Enter the left side of the original equation on one line and the right side on another. For the $\sqrt{x-2} = x - 4$ example, we'd get this:

[Calculator screenshot showing line 1: $\sqrt{x-2}$ and line 2: $x - 4$, with their graphs plotted]

There's only one point of intersection: at the point $(6, 2)$. Therefore, the only solution to this equation is $x = 6$.

Try It   Solve:

23) $\sqrt{x + 23} = 3 + x$

Math: Advanced Math

As you know, you can simplify a fraction by canceling out any factor that the numerator and denominator have in common.

Example: Simplify the fraction $\frac{4x}{6}$.

$$\frac{4x}{6} = \frac{\cancel{2}(2x)}{\cancel{2}(3)} = \frac{2x}{3}$$

If either part of the fraction contains a polynomial, the same rule holds. First fully factor both the top and bottom of the fraction, and then cancel out any factor that you find in both.

Example: Simplify the fraction $\frac{x^2-9}{x^2-4x+3}$, where $x > 3$.

$$\frac{x^2-9}{x^2-4x+3} = \frac{(x+3)\cancel{(x-3)}}{(x-1)\cancel{(x-3)}} = \frac{x+3}{x-1}$$

Try It

24) Simplify $\frac{x^2-x-6}{x^2-2x-8}$, where $x > 4$.

TIP:

A common factor is the **only** thing you can cancel out from the top and bottom of a fraction. Other features that the two parts have in common don't count. For example, the expression $\frac{x+3}{x+5}$ **cannot** be simplified as $\frac{3}{5}$.

CHALLENGE:

A **rational expression** is an algebraic expression that takes the shape of a fraction. Remember, to add or subtract fractions, we need a common denominator. Once we have that, we add or subtract straight across the top, leaving the bottom the same.

Example: $\dfrac{1}{3} + \dfrac{5}{6} = \dfrac{2}{2} * \dfrac{1}{3} + \dfrac{5}{6} = \dfrac{2}{6} + \dfrac{5}{6} = \dfrac{7}{6}$

We can do the same thing when the numerator and/or denominator contains variables instead of (or in addition to) numbers.

Example: $\dfrac{1}{x} + \dfrac{5}{6x} = \dfrac{6}{6} * \dfrac{1}{x} + \dfrac{5}{6x} = \dfrac{6}{6x} + \dfrac{5}{6x} = \dfrac{11}{6x}$

Try It   25) Simplify $\dfrac{3}{x} + \dfrac{2}{y}$, where $xy \neq 0$.

If the numerator and/or denominator contain more than one term, no problem—the steps are the same. It's just that in order to find the common denominator (and simplify the result) we'll need to use some of the distributing, factoring, and FOILing skills we've just reviewed.

Example: $\dfrac{1}{x+2} + \dfrac{5}{x-1} = \dfrac{(x-1)(1)}{(x-1)(x+2)} + \dfrac{5(x+2)}{(x-1)(x+2)}$

$= \dfrac{x-1}{(x-1)(x+2)} + \dfrac{5x+10}{(x-1)(x+2)}$

$= \dfrac{x-1+5x+10}{(x-1)(x+2)}$

$= \dfrac{6x+9}{x^2+x-2}$

Try It   26) Simplify $\dfrac{3}{x-4} + \dfrac{2}{x+4}$, where $x^2 \neq 16$.

Two expressions are equivalent if the coefficients of the like terms are equal. So, many abstract-looking problems can be solved by simplifying both sides of the equation and then **matching up the like terms**.

Example: If $2x^3 + 5(3x - 4) + 6 = 2x^3 + px + q$, where p and q are constants, what is the value of $p - q$?

$$2x^3 + 5(3x - 4) + 6 = 2x^3 + px + q$$
$$2x^3 + 15x - 20 + 6 = 2x^3 + px + q$$
$$2x^3 + 15x - 14 = 2x^3 + px + q$$

For these expressions to be equal, $15x$ must be the same thing as px, and -14 must be the same thing as q. Therefore, $p = 15$ and $q = -14$. So:

$$p - q = 15 - (-14) = \mathbf{29}$$

Try It

27) If $(qx - r)(2x + 5) = 8x^2 + 14x - 15$, where q and r are constants, what is the value of $q + r$?

TIP:

For these problems, it's important to be precise about exactly what the coefficient is. If you're told that $2kx + 5 = mx + b$, you might be tempted to think that m is 2. But it's not: it's $2k$.

Chapter Answer Key

Try It

1) $2a + 6b$
2) $4x - xy$
3) $3ab + 6ac - 3ad$
4) $6x^2 - 12x^3y$
5) $2n^4p^5 - 10n^5p + 6n^4p^2$
6) $3x - 1$
7) $2x$
8) $-8x$
9) $3x + 3xy$
10) 7
11) $-3/4$ or -0.75
12) $x^2 - 2x - 8$
13) $pq - 6p + 5q - 30$
14) $3(2x - 1)$
15) $4n(2n - 1)$
16) $(x - 4)(x + 1)$
17) $(x - 1)(x - 9)$
18) $(x + 9)(x - 9)$
19) $(p + r^3)(p - r^3)$
20) $x = -1$ or $x = 4$
21) $x = 0$ or $x = 3$
22) $x = 1/2$ or $x = -4$
23) $x = 2$ only
24) $\dfrac{x - 3}{x - 4}$
25) $\dfrac{3y + 2x}{xy}$
26) $\dfrac{5x + 4}{x^2 - 16}$
27) 7

Math: Advanced Math

Practice Set 1: Easy-Medium

1 Which expression is equivalent to $(2x - 1)(x + 3)$?

A. $2x^2 + 7x - 3$
B. $2x^2 + 7x + 3$
C. $2x^2 + 5x - 3$
D. $2x^2 + 5x + 3$

2 $(4x^3 - 3x^2 + 5) - (6 + 2x^2 - 3x^3)$ is equivalent to which of the following?

A. $x^3 - 5x^2 - 1$
B. $x^3 - x^2 - 11$
C. $7x^3 - 5x^2 - 1$
D. $7x^3 - x^2 - 11$

3 Which of the following is a factor of $x^2 + 2x - 24$?

A. $x - 4$
B. $x + 4$
C. $x - 6$
D. $x - 12$

4 What are the solutions to the quadratic equation $x^2 - 3x - 28 = 0$?

A. -7 and 4
B. -4 and 7
C. 4 and 7
D. -4 and -7

5 The expression $(5p + 6q)(7r - 8s)$ is equivalent to which of the following?

A. $35pr - 48rs$
B. $35pq^2 + 42qr - 48rs^2$
C. $30pr + 35ps - 48qr + 56qs$
D. $35pr - 40ps + 42qr - 48qs$

6 Which of the following is equivalent to $3x^2 - 12$?

A. $3(x - 2)(x + 2)$
B. $3(x - 2)^2$
C. $(3x - 2)^2$
D. $(x - 4)(x + 3)$

7
$$\frac{x^2 + 5x - 14}{x^2 - 4}$$

Where $x > 2$, the expression above is equivalent to which of the following?

A. $\dfrac{x + 7}{x + 2}$

B. $\dfrac{5x - 14}{-4}$

C. $\dfrac{2.5x - 7}{2}$

D. $\dfrac{x + 7}{x - 2}$

8 What is one solution to the equation $x^2 + 5x - 36 = 0$?

9 The expression $(x^2 - 1) - (2x^2 + 1)$ is equivalent to which of the following?

A. $-2x^4 + x^2 + 1$
B. $-x^2 - 2$
C. $-x^2$
D. 1

Practice Set 2: Medium-Hard

1 Which of the following expressions is equivalent to $\dfrac{d^2 + 6d + 9}{d^2 - 9}$, where $d^2 \neq 9$?

A. $-6d$
B. $d + 3$
C. $\dfrac{d-3}{d+3}$
D. $\dfrac{d+3}{d-3}$

2
$$y = (x-5)^2$$
$$y = x+1$$

Which of the following (x, y) points is a solution to the system of equations above?

A. $(-1, 0)$
B. $(5, 0)$
C. $(3, 4)$
D. $(2, 3)$

3 If $(a+b)^2 = (a-b)^2$, which of the following must be true?

A. $a + b = a - b$
B. $a = -b$
C. $ab = 0$
D. $|ab| = 1$

4 If $g + h = 2$ and $gh = -8$, what is the value of $\dfrac{g}{h} + \dfrac{h}{g}$?

5 When a price of d dollars is squared, the result is 4 dollars more than triple the value of d. Which of the following could be the value of d?

A. 1
B. 2
C. 3
D. 4

6 If $r - s = 10$ and $r^2 + s^2 = 20$, what is the value of rs?

7 Which expression is equivalent to $\dfrac{3}{x+1} - \dfrac{1}{x+3}$?

A. $\dfrac{1}{(x+3)(x+1)}$
B. $\dfrac{2x+8}{(x+3)(x+1)}$
C. $\dfrac{2x+10}{(x+3)(x+1)}$
D. $\dfrac{2}{x-2}$

8 If $y = 2\sqrt{x-1}$, for what value of x does $y = 8$?

A. 2
B. 3
C. 16
D. 17

Math: Advanced Math

9

$$\frac{4}{3+x} - \frac{2}{1+x} = 5$$

How many possible real solutions exist for x in the equation above?

A. 0
B. 1
C. 2
D. 3

10

In the figure below, the length of rectangle B is 2 inches greater than the side length of square A, and the width of rectangle B is 5 inches greater than the side length of square A.

A

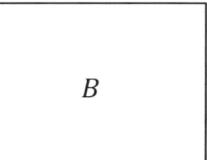
B

If the area of square A is x^2 square inches, which of the following represents the area, in square inches, of rectangle B?

A. $x^2 + 10$
B. $x^2 + 5x + 2$
C. $x^2 + 7x + 10$
D. $x^2 + 10x + 7$

11

If $ax^4y^2 + bx^3y^3 + cx^2y^4$ is equivalent to $(2x^2y - 6xy^2)^2$ for all real values of x and y, what is the value of $a + b + c$?

12

Suppose that the probability of a certain projectile object hitting its target is equal to $\frac{16t^2 - 40t + 125}{100}$, where t is the number of seconds for which the object has traveled. After how many seconds of travel is the object certain to hit its target?

A. 1.25
B. 1.5
C. 2.5
D. 4

13

$$3p(8x^2 - q) = 2x\left(4p^2x + \frac{9}{x}\right)$$

In the equation above, q and p are nonzero constants, x is a variable, and $x \neq 0$. What is the value of q?

14

If $\sqrt{x + 14} = x + 2$, which of the following could be the value of x?

A. -5
B. -2.7
C. 2
D. 3.7

15

$$\frac{6x^2 - 7x + 5}{kx - 3} = 3x + 1 + \frac{8}{kx - 3}$$

In the equation above, k is a constant and $x \neq \frac{3}{k}$. What is the value of k?

A. 1
B. 2
C. 3
D. 4

Function Essentials

Preview Quiz:

If $f(x) = 2x + 3$:

1) What is the value of $f(4)$? _____

2) For what value of x is $f(x) = 7$? _____

The table below gives values of the linear function $f(x)$.

x	−3	−2	−1	0	1	2	3
$f(x)$	−3	−1	1	3	5	7	9

3) What is the value of $f(1)$? _____

4) What is the value of $f(4)$? _____

In the graph of $y = f(x)$ shown below, each of the gridlines represents one coordinate unit.

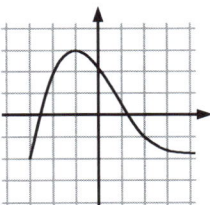

5) What is the value of $f(-1)$? _____

6) How would the graph of $y = f(x + 3) + 2$ look different from the graph of $f(x)$?

_____

If $f(x) = 2x + 4$ and $g(x) = x - 5$:

7) For what value of x is $f(x) = g(x)$? _____

8) What is the value of $f(g(2))$? _____

Math: Advanced Math

The definition of a **function** is that for all values of x, there is a unique value of $f(x)$. You can think of $f(x)$ as the y value: for example, the function notation $f(3) = 9$ tells you that when $x = 3$ on the graph of the function, $y = 9$.

Usually, functions will be defined by a given **equation**. To apply the equation, simply plug in whatever's inside the parentheses for x.

Example: *If $f(x) = 2x + 3$, what is the value of $f(4)$?*

$f(4) = 2(4) + 3$
$= \mathbf{11}$

If the problem gives you the value of $f(x)$ instead of the value of x, that just means you have to plug in your number on the other side of the equals sign.

Example: *If $f(x) = 2x + 3$, then for what value of x is $f(x) = 7$?*

$7 = 2(x) + 3$
$4 = 2x$
$\mathbf{2 = x}$

Try It

1) If $f(x) = 12 - 4x$, what is the value of $f(-2)$?

2) If $f(x) = 3x + 1$, then for what value of x is $f(x) = 19$?

3) Let $f(x) = 2x + k$, where k is a constant. If $f(4) = 1$, what is the value of k?

Functions can also be given as a **table** of values. You can use these values to find the equation, or in some cases, simply follow the pattern to find more values.

Example: The table below gives values of the linear function $f(x)$.

x	-3	-2	-1	0	1	2	3
$f(x)$	-3	-1	1	3	5	7	9

- *What is the value of $f(1)$?*

    In the column where $x = 1$, the value of $f(x)$ is 5. Therefore, $f(1) = \mathbf{5}$.

- *What is the value of $f(4)$?*

    There is no column where $x = 4$. However, we were told this was a *linear* function, so the same pattern that we can see in the table will continue indefinitely. And in the table, when $x = 1, 2,$ and 3, respectively, we can see that $f(x) = 5, 7,$ and 9, respectively. So, continue the pattern: when $x = 4$, $f(x)$ must equal **11**.

A third way that the test may present functions is by showing you the function's **graph**. To answer these, remember that x is the x-coordinate and $f(x)$ is the y-coordinate for all points.

Example: In the graph of $f(x)$ shown below, each of the gridlines represents one coordinate unit.

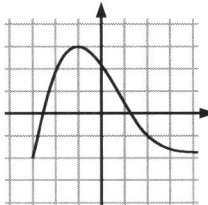

What is the value of $f(-1)$?

The graph passes through the point $(-1, 3)$. Therefore, $f(-1) = \mathbf{3}$.

> **TIP:**
> A point on the graph of a function f can be represented as (x, y) or as $(x, f(x))$. For example, the point in this problem could be written as $(-1, 3)$ or as $(-1, f(-1))$.

Another useful thing about function notation is that it allows us to define several different functions at the same time.

Example: If $f(x) = 2x + 4$ and $g(x) = x - 5$, for what value of x is $f(x) = g(x)$?

$2x + 4 = x - 5$
$x + 4 = -5$
$x = -9$

To find the value of a composite function such as $f(g(x))$, find the innermost value first and then work your way out.

Example: If $f(x) = 2x + 4$ and $g(x) = x - 5$, what is the value of $f(g(2))$?

First, we need the value of $g(2)$. So, start by plugging 2 into the g function:

$$g(2) = 2 - 5 = -3$$

Now that we know that $g(2) = -3$, we can rewrite $f(g(2))$ as just $f(-3)$. So that's all we need now:

$$f(-3) = 2(-3) + 4 = -2$$

The answer is -2.

Try It   If $f(x) = 12 - 4x$ and $g(x) = 2x - 3$, then:

4) What is the value of $f(g(2))$?

5) What is the value of $g(f(2))$?

6) What is the x-coordinate of the point on the xy-plane where the graphs of $y = f(x)$ and $y = g(x)$ intersect?

The limitations of a function are defined by its **domain** (all the possible x values) and **range** (all the possible y values). One way to determine the domain and range of a function is by looking at its graph.

Example: The graph of $f(x) = -x^2 - 4x - 3$ is shown below. What is the domain and what is the range of the function?

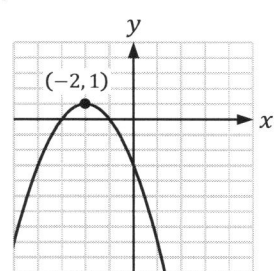

> **TIP:**
>
> **Interval notation** is a way of expressing domain, range, and other sets of numbers. The notation $(2, 5)$ represents all the values from 2 to 5, not including the 2 or the 5: for example, a domain of $2 < x < 5$. By contrast, the notation $[2, 5]$ represents all the values from 2 to 5, *inclusive*: for example, a domain of $2 \leq x \leq 5$.

This graph extends forever to the left and right, so **the domain is all real numbers**: from negative infinity to positive infinity. In interval notation, that's $(-\infty, \infty)$.

However, the range of this function is more limited. Although the graph extends forever downward (so its minimum value is negative infinity), it has a definite maximum point: it will never reach a point higher than the vertex of the parabola. As we can see from the graph, the y-coordinate of that point is 1. Therefore, **the range is $y \leq 1$**: that is, from negative infinity up to and including positive 1. In interval notation, that's $(-\infty, 1]$.

You can also use algebra to test the domain of a function. Any x value that would make the algebra impossible (for example, that would cause you to have to divide by zero, or to take the square root of a negative number) is excluded from the domain, and any y value that would do so is excluded from the range.

Example: Is 3 in the domain of $g(x) = \sqrt{1 - x}$?

No: plugging in 3 for x would require us to take the square root of a negative number.

Example: Is -2 in the range of $h(x) = |x + 4|$?

No: the absolute value of any expression will always be greater than or equal to zero.

You may also be tested on the basic rules of **transformations** and **translations**. Remember, changes *inside* the parentheses affect the graph *horizontally*; changes *outside* the parentheses affect the graph *vertically*.

Vertical transformations:

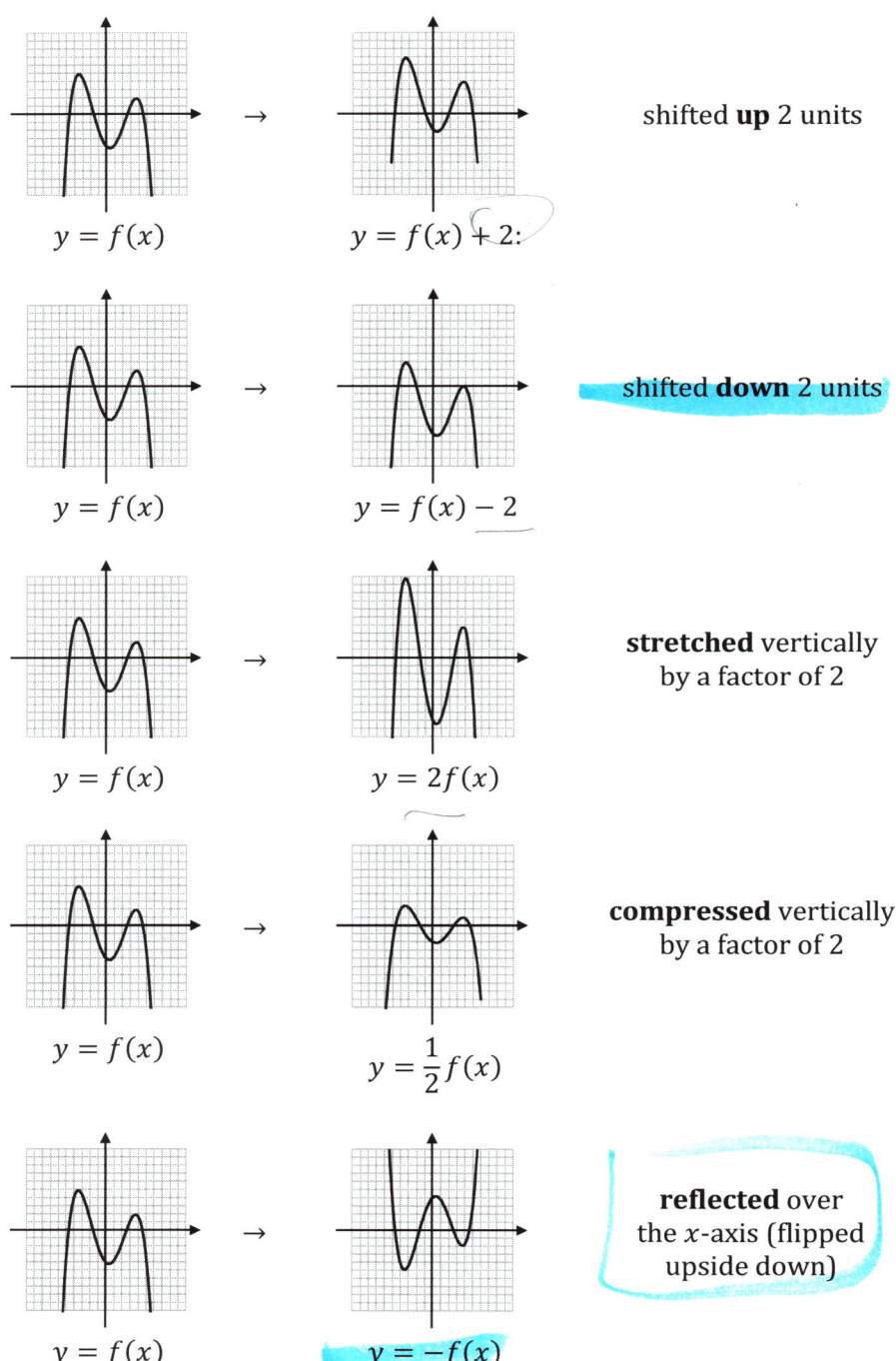

Function Essentials

Horizontal transformations:

TIP:
Inside the parentheses, everything works a bit backwards from what we'd expect. For example, +2 moves the graph *left*, not right.

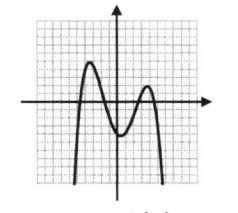
$y = f(x)$ → $y = f(x+2)$ — shifted **left** 2 units

$y = f(x)$ → $y = f(x-2)$ — shifted **right** 2 units

$f(x+3) = Left\ 3$

 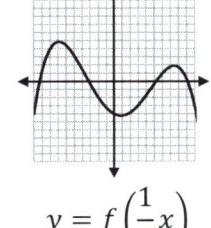
$y = f(x)$ → $y = f\left(\frac{1}{2}x\right)$ — **stretched** horizontally by a factor of 2

 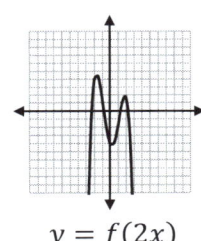
$y = f(x)$ → $y = f(2x)$ — **compressed** horizontally by a factor of 2

 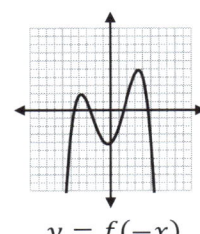
$y = f(x)$ → $y = f(-x)$ — **reflected** over the *y*-axis (flipped horizontally)

Try It

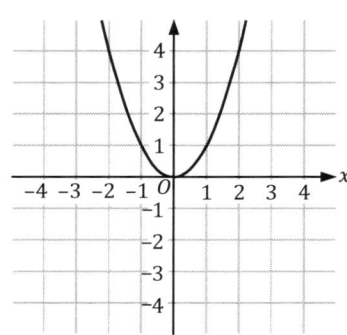

7) If the figure above shows the graph of $y = g(x)$, sketch the graph of $y = -g(x-2) + 1$:

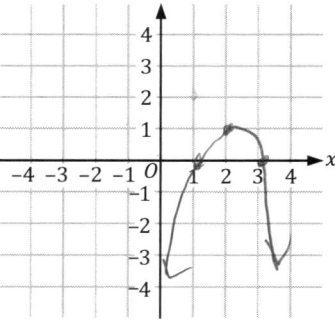

Chapter Answer Key

Try It
1) 20
2) 6
3) −7
4) 8
5) 5
6) 5/2 or 2.5
7)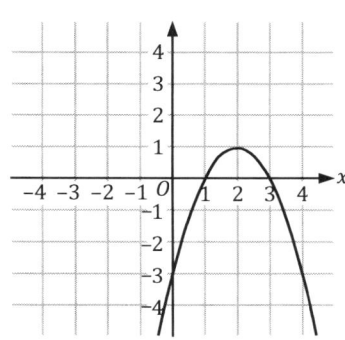

FROM THE BLOG

When reviewing missed questions, there are three big things to consider.

- **Content.** Did you honestly not know the necessary material to answer the question?
- **Process.** Is there a more strategic way you could have approached the problem?
- **Anxiety.** Upon review, does it seem that you really should have gotten that right? Was your mind occupied with other test-takers in the room? Were you concerned that you were "behind" and obsessing over catching up? Were you still stressing out over a previous question that you missed?

These factors can all impact your performance, and they can *all* be addressed. The important thing is to think strategically about how to attack the issues that have the greatest effect on *you*.

Math: Advanced Math

Practice Set 1: Easy-Medium

1

A function f is defined by the equation $f(x) = 2x^2 - 3x + 5$. What is the value of $f(-2)$?

2

If $f(x) = x^2 + 3$ and $g(x) = 2x + 2$, then what is the value of $f(3) - g(2)$?

A. 3
B. 4
C. 6
D. 8

3

The total profit, p, that a manufacturer makes from selling x units of a certain product is equal to $p(x) = 27x - k$, where k is a positive constant. If the manufacturer makes a total profit of $19,850 when it sells 800 units, what is the value of k?

A. 1750
B. 2625
C. 9082
D. 15,225

4

The table below gives values of the function $f(x)$.

x	0	1	2	3
$f(x)$	-4	-3	0	5

If $f(x)$ is a quadratic function, then which of the following could be the equation of $f(x)$?

A. $f(x) = x^2 + 2$
B. $f(x) = x^2 - 4$
C. $f(x) = x - 4$
D. $f(x) = x^2 + x - 2$

5

The quadratic function f is graphed in the xy-plane below. If $f(4) = k$, where k is a constant, then what is the value of $f(k)$?

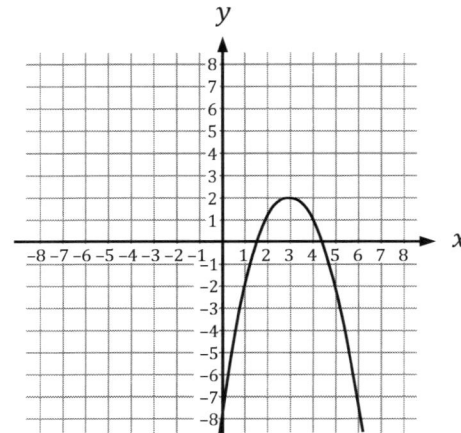

A. -2
B. -1
C. 1
D. 2

6

A ball is thrown straight up in the air from a height of 5 feet. Its height in feet above the ground after t seconds is expressed by $h(t) = 5 + 40t - 16t^2$. In this context, what is the best interpretation of $h(1) = 29$?

A. After 1 second, the ball has traveled 29 horizontal feet from its starting point.
B. After 1 second, the ball is 29 feet above the ground.
C. The ball reaches a height of 1 foot above the ground after 29 seconds.
D. The ball reaches a height of 1 foot above its starting point after 29 seconds.

7

If $f(x) = 1 - x$ and $g(x) = x - 1$, find $f(g(3))$.

Practice Set 2: Medium-Hard

1

Given the tables of values for the functions f and g shown below, what is the value of $g(f(2))$?

x	$f(x)$
0	−3
1	0
2	3
3	6

x	$g(x)$
0	−8
1	−6
2	0
3	10

A. −3
B. 1
C. 6
D. 10

2

Given the function f defined by the equation below, what is $f(1)$?

$$f(x) = \begin{cases} 2x - 1, x \leq 0 \\ x^2 + 1, x > 0 \end{cases}$$

A. 1
B. 2
C. 3
D. 4

3

Let $g(x)$ be defined by the equation $g(x) = |2x| - 6$. Which of the following is an x-intercept of the graph of g in the xy-plane?

A. $(-6, g(-6))$
B. $(-1, g(-1))$
C. $(0, g(0))$
D. $(3, g(3))$

4

The function $g(x)$ is defined by $g(x) = 2x^2$. If $r > 0$ and $g(r) = 36$, what is the value of $g(2r)$?

5

The figure below shows the graphs of the functions $f(x) = -x - 1$ and $g(x) = -x^2 - 6x + 5$ in the xy-plane. For what values of x is $f(x) < g(x)$?

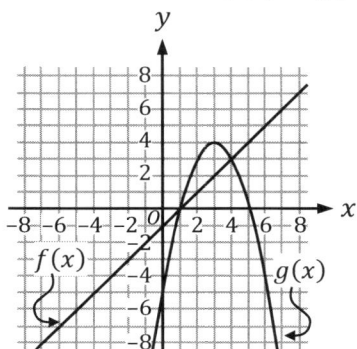

A. $x < 1$ or $x > 4$
B. $1 < x < 4$
C. $0 < x < 3$
D. $x < 0$ or $x > 3$

6

Let the function $g(x)$ be defined by the equation below:

$$g(x) = \frac{x-4}{x-3}$$

Which of the following values is NOT included in the domain of $g(x)$?

A. 0
B. 1
C. 3
D. 4

7

Let $f(x) = 3x^2$ and $g(x) = 2x + 1$. Which of the following expressions represents $f(g(x))$?

A. $12x^2 + 12x + 3$
B. $12x^2 + 6x$
C. $6x^3 + 3x^2$
D. $6x^2 + 1$

Math: Advanced Math

8

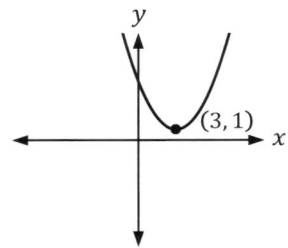

The graph of $y = -f(x - 1)$ is shown in the above. Which of the following could be the graph of $y = f(x)$?

A.

B.

C.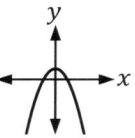

D.

(graph with downward parabola below x-axis)

9

The function $f(x) = 24(1.15)^x$ gives a country's approximate population, in millions, at any time x years after the year 2000. Which of the following is the best interpretation of $f(0) = 24$?

A. The country's population in 2000 was approximately 24,000,000.
B. The country's population in 2024 was zero.
C. The country's population in 2000 was approximately 24.
D. Since 2000 the country's population has increased by 24 million per year.

10

Let $f(x)$ be a linear function such that $f(2) = 7$ and $f(4) = 11$. What is the value of $f(6)$?

11

If $g(x) = 2(x - 1)^2 - x$, then which of the following is equivalent to $g(x + 2)$?

A. $2x^2 + 7x + 6$
B. $2x^2 + 3x + 4$
C. $2x(x + 1)$
D. $x(2x + 3)$

12

$$f(x) = 2x^3 - 5x^2 + 6x - 1$$
$$g(x) = x^3 - 3x^2 - 2x + 8$$
$$h(x) = f(x) - 2g(x)$$

Which of the following defines the polynomial function $h(x)$?

A. $h(x) = 4x^3 - 2x^2 + 4x - 9$
B. $h(x) = 4x^3 - 11x^2 + 2x + 15$
C. $h(x) = x^2 + 10x - 17$
D. $h(x) = x^2 + 8x + 7$

13

x	0	1	2	3	1
y	1	4	5	9	2

Given the table of values above, the relationship between x and y could best be described as which of the following?

A. a linear function
B. an exponential function
C. a polynomial function
D. a relation that is not a function

Linear Functions

Preview Quiz:

The equation $f(x) = -15x + 750$ gives the amount owed, in dollars, on an interest-free loan after x months of payments.

1) What is the best interpretation of the y-intercept of the graph of $y = f(x)$ in the xy-plane?

    _____

2) What is the best interpretation of the slope of the graph of $y = f(x)$ in the xy-plane?

    _____

3) What is the best interpretation of $f(10) = 600$?

    _____

Solve:

4) Paul finds that the relationship between his semester grade point average, $g(s)$, and the number of hours per week he spends studying, s, can be modeled by $g(s) = 0.12s + 1$. Increasing his studying from 18 hours per week to 19 hours per week should raise his semester grade point average by how much?

    _____

Most of the time, the equation of a **line** will have a y term, an x term, and a standalone number: for example, $y = 4x - 1$. These terms may appear in a different order (e.g., $x - y = 3$ is still a line), and it's possible that one or more of these elements may be missing (e.g., $y = 7$, $x = 2$, and $y = x$ are all lines). But the ironclad rule is that the equation can't have any *other* types of terms in it. If an equation has a variable with an exponent (e.g., $y = x^2$) or puts one of the variables on the bottom of a fraction (e.g., $y = 1/x$), etc., the graph cannot be a line.

When equations are defined as functions, the y term is sometimes swapped for a **function notation** such as $f(x)$. All the rules above are the same: for example, $f(x) = 4x - 1$ is a line, as is $g(x) = 7$, while $h(x) = x^2$ is not.

You can also recognize a linear equation by its points. In a linear equation, the rate of change is constant. This means that each time the value of x increases by 1, the value of y must increase or decrease by a specific amount that does not change. That amount is the **slope** of the line.

Example: Given the values below, is $f(x)$ a linear function? Is $g(x)$ a linear function?

x	1	2	3	4
$f(x)$	2	6	10	14

x	1	2	3	4
$g(x)$	2	6	12	36

For the f function, as x increases by 1, y increases by exactly 4 each time. Because this rate of change does not change, $f(x)$ **is a linear function**.

But for the g function, as x increases by 1, y increases by a different amount each time: first by 4, then by 6, then by 12. Because there is no constant rate of change, $g(x)$ **is non-linear.**

Try It

1) If $f(x)$ is a linear function, which one of the following could define $f(x)$?

 A) $f(x) = \sqrt{x + 3}$
 B) $f(x) = 5^x$
 C) $f(x) = -6$
 D) $f(x) = 2x^{-1}$

Do the scenarios below describe linear growth or nonlinear growth?

2) a salary increases by $200 per year _____

3) a salary increases by 2% per year _____

A **linear function** usually takes the form $f(x) = mx + b$, where m and b are constants. As we've already seen in the Coordinate Geometry chapter (see p. 269), when a linear function takes the form $f(x) = mx + b$, the constant m gives the slope of the line, while the constant b gives the y-coordinate of the graph's y-intercept. To interpret these values in the context of a word problem, think of the y-intercept as the **starting point**, while the slope is the **rate of change**.

For example, say a botanist wants to use a linear function to model the height of a plant over the course of a multi-year study. If the plant was 5 centimeters tall at the beginning of the study and it grows at a rate of 3 centimeters per year, then we can use the equation $y = 3x + 5$: the starting point is a height of 5 centimeters, and the rate of change is 3 centimeters per year. In this equation, x represents the time that has passed, in years, and y represents the plant's height at that time. (Note that we could create the same equation in function notation by writing it as $f(x) = 3x + 5$.)

Try It 4) It costs a toy company a total of $250 to manufacture a batch of toys. Create a linear function to model the company's profits from selling x toys at $10 each.

TIP: For this line, should the slope be positive or negative? What about the y-intercept?

The test will often ask you about the meaning of specific numbers or letters in a linear equation. Start by identifying the piece they're asking about: is it the slope, the y-intercept, or something else? Next, write down the appropriate definition, and then fill in the meanings with the context of the problem. For y-intercept questions, the definition to use is this: **y-intercept is the value of y when $x = 0$.**

Example: The equation $f(x) = -15x + 750$ gives the amount owed, in dollars, on an interest-free loan after x months of payments. What is the best interpretation of the y-intercept of the graph of $y = f(x)$ in the xy-plane?

y-intercept = value of y when $x = 0$.

750 = value of amount owed when # of months = 0. That's our answer: $750 is what was owed before any payments had been made. So **$750 is the original amount of the loan.**

Math: Advanced Math

As for slope, the key thing to remember is that slope is the rate of change: every time you increase x by 1, you increase y by the amount of the slope. (For example, in the plant example, every time the number of years increases by 1, the height increases by 3 centimeters.) So the definition to use is this: **slope is the change in y as x increases by 1.**

TIP:
When a problem asks you to interpret the slope, look for answer choices that contain rate words such as "per" or "each."

Example: The equation $f(x) = -15x + 750$ gives the amount owed, in dollars, on an interest-free loan after x months of payments. What is the best interpretation of the slope of the graph of $y = f(x)$ in the xy-plane?

slope = change in y as x increases by 1.

-15 = change in amount owed as # of months increases by 1. So the meaning of the -15 is that with each month that passes, the amount owed on the loan is decreasing by \$15. The most likely interpretation? **The loan payments are \$15 per month.**

Try It

After Sam has driven for x miles, the number of gallons of gasoline remaining in his car's tank is given by $g(x) = 12 - 36x$.

5) What is the best interpretation of the number 12 in the equation?

   Started w/ 12 gallons

6) What is the best interpretation of the number 36 in the equation?

This understanding of slope can help you avoid a lot of unnecessary calculation.

Example: Paul finds that the relationship between his semester grade point average, $g(s)$, and the number of hours per week he spends studying, s, can be modeled by $g(s) = 0.12s + 1$. Increasing his studying from 18 hours per week to 19 hours per week should raise his semester grade point average by how much?

In this equation, $g(s)$ is our y value and s is our x value. Paul has increased the x value by 1. Therefore, the y value must increase by the amount of the slope: **0.12**.

For other problems, you may just need to use the meanings of each of the variables that the problem provided.

Example: The equation $f(x) = -15x + 750$ gives the amount owed, in dollars, on an interest-free loan after x months of payments. In this context, what is the best interpretation of $f(10) = 600$?

When $x = 10$, $f(x) = 600$.

When # of months = 10, amount owed = 600. So the best interpretation is that **after 10 months of payments, the amount still owed will be $600.**

> **TIP:**
> Focus on the **units** to help move quickly through the answer choices. If x is measured in months, you can immediately eliminate any choices that define x as some number of dollars (or any other unit).

Chapter Answer Key

Try It
1) C
2) linear
3) non-linear
4) $f(x) = 10x - 250$
5) The tank held 12 gallons of gasoline when Sam began driving.
6) The car uses an average of 36 gallons of gasoline per mile.

Math: Advanced Math

Practice Set 1: Easy-Medium

1

The total cost C, in dollars, to produce the yearbooks at Greenville High School is modeled by the function $C(n) = 500 + 20n$, where n is the number of yearbooks printed. Which of the following is the best interpretation of the number 500 in this equation?

A. At least 500 yearbooks will be printed.
B. It costs 500 dollars to print 20 yearbooks.
C. The initial cost is 500 dollars regardless of the number of yearbooks printed.
D. After every 20 yearbooks printed, the cost rises by 500 dollars.

2

The profit, in dollars, that Jeremy will make selling cookies in today's bake sale can be modeled by the function $P(x) = 0.25x - 50$, where x represents the number of cookies sold. Which of the following best describes the meaning of the number 0.25 in the equation?

A. Jeremy's total profit will be $0.25.
B. The average selling price of Jeremy's cookies is $0.25 per cookie.
C. The difference between Jeremy's initial costs and total profit is $25.
D. Jeremy will sell a total of 25 cookies.

3

$$C(w) = 17.5 + 4.75w$$

The function above is used to calculate the cost $C(w)$ of shipping a certain package overnight, where w represents the weight of the package in pounds. By how much will the cost change if the weight of the package increases by 6 pounds?

A. The cost will increase by 17.5 dollars.
B. The cost will increase by 22.5 dollars.
C. The cost will increase by 28.5 dollars.
D. The cost will increase by 50.75 dollars.

4

$$f(x) = -0.5x + 2$$

Which table gives three values of x and their corresponding values of $f(x)$ for the given equation?

A.
x	0	1	2
$f(x)$	1.5	1	0.5

B.
x	0	1	2
$f(x)$	2	1.5	1

C.
x	0	1	2
$f(x)$	2	2.5	3

D.
x	0	1	2
$f(x)$	1	1.5	2

5

On Tuesday, Ben was on the second day of a multi-day road trip. The function $d(t) = 58t + 65$ models Ben's distance from home, in miles, after t hours of driving on Tuesday. Based on the model, what was Ben's average driving speed on Tuesday, in miles per hour?

6

Which of the following scenarios could best be modeled by a linear function with a positive slope?

A. Overnight, the outside temperature decreases by 2°F per hour.
B. An investment loses 4% of its value each month.
C. An online newspaper increases its readership by 1000 people per year.
D. A city's population increases steadily for 10 years and then levels off.

7

TAXI CAB RIDE

The graph above displays the total cost C, in dollars, of a taxi cab ride that travels a distance of m miles. What does the C-intercept of the graph represent?

A. The number of taxi cabs used
B. The initial number of miles
C. The increase in cost to ride the taxi for each additional mile
D. The initial cost to travel 0 miles

8

$$p = 750n + 3750$$

Gross domestic product per capita (PPP) is a measure of a country's total output on a per-person basis. An economist uses the model above to estimate the PPP p of a country, in US dollars, in terms of the number of years n that have passed since the country gained independence. Based on the model, what is the estimated increase, in US dollars, of the country's PPP each year?

9

$$f(x) = 150 + 14.75x$$

The linear function f, defined above, models the total cost of installed fencing from a local hardware store, where x represents the number of linear feet of fencing purchased and $f(x)$ represents the cost, in dollars. What is the best interpretation of $f(100) = 1625$ in this context?

A. The total cost for 100 linear feet of installed fencing is $1625.
B. The total cost of 1625 linear feet of installed fencing is $100.
C. The cost of fencing is $1625 per 100 linear feet, before installation.
D. The cost of fencing is $100 per 1625 linear feet, before installation.

10

The table shows four values of x and their corresponding values of $f(x)$. What is the y-intercept of the graph of $f(x)$ on the xy-plane?

x	-1	0	1	2
$f(x)$	0	2	4	6

A. $(-1, 0)$
B. $(0, -1)$
C. $(0, 2)$
D. $(2, 0)$

11

The function $f(t)$ gives the attendance at an annual music festival t years after 1990. During the period from 2002 to 2008, the graph of the function approximates a line with a positive slope. What is the best interpretation of the slope?

A. The rate of increase in attendance per year from 2002 to 2008
B. The festival's attendance in 1990
C. The total attendance from 2002 to 2008
D. The festival's maximum attendance in any year

Math: Advanced Math

Practice Set 2: Medium-Hard

1

Samuel receives a $50 weekly allowance, which he uses to buy equally priced packs of baseball cards (assume no sales tax). The amount of allowance money, A, Samuel has left at the end of the week can be estimated with the function $A(p) = 50 - \left(\frac{25}{4}\right)p$, where p represents the number of packs of baseball cards purchased. What is the meaning of the fraction $\frac{25}{4}$, which is equivalent to the decimal 6.25, in this function?

A. Each pack of baseball cards costs $6.25.
B. Samuel has $25 of allowance money to spend over 4 days.
C. Samuel purchases 6.25 packs of baseball cards.
D. Samuel will buy 25 packs of baseball cards, each costing $4.

2

An area's "water table" is the level below which the ground is saturated with water. A scientist studying a local wetland recorded CO_2 emissions of 10 mol C/m² (moles of carbon per square meter) in areas where the water table was exactly at the surface. She also found that for every 1 centimeter increase in the depth of the water table below the surface, CO_2 emissions increased by 2 mol C/m². Which of the following equations models the amount of CO_2 emissions y, in mol C/m², where x represents the depth of the water table in centimeters below the surface?

A. $y = -2x + 10$
B. $y = -10x + 2$
C. $y = 10x - 2$
D. $y = 2x + 10$

3

The formula to convert temperatures from the Celsius scale to the Fahrenheit scale is $C * \frac{9}{5} + 32 = F$. What is the meaning of the value $\frac{9}{5}$ in this equation?

A. Each degree change in Fahrenheit is equivalent to $\frac{9}{5}$ degrees Celsius.
B. Each degree change in Celsius is equivalent to $\frac{9}{5}$ degrees Fahrenheit.
C. Each Fahrenheit temperature reads $\frac{9}{5}$ degrees higher than its corresponding Celsius temperature.
D. Each Celsius temperature reads $\frac{9}{5}$ degrees higher than its corresponding Fahrenheit temperature.

4

MEDIAN OHIO HOME PRICES, 1940-2000

Year	Median Price
1940	$22,900
1950	$41,000
1960	$57,800
1970	$58,300
1980	$91,200
1990	$96,800
2000	$107,600

The table above represents the median home prices in Ohio between 1940 and 2000. The relationship between time and home price can be modeled by the linear equation $y = 1,600x + 24,000$, where x represents the number of years since 1940 and y represent the median home price. What does the number 1,600 represent in the equation?

A. the average yearly increase in the median home price
B. the average price of one home
C. the decrease in median home price from 1960 to 1970
D. the increase in number of homes sold from one decade to the next

Quadratic Functions

Preview Quiz:

Solve each of the following.

1) $x^2 - 5x - 4 = 0$

2) $x^2 - 7x - 3 = 0$

3) A quadratic has (at least / at most / exactly) ___ roots.

4) A quadratic has (at least / at most / exactly) ___ x-intercepts.

5) What are the coordinates of the x-intercepts of the parabola with equation $y = -4(x-1)(x-3)$?

For the parabolas given by the quadratic functions below, what are the coordinates of the vertex? What is the axis of symmetry?

6) $f(x) = 2(x+3)^2 + 1$

7) $g(x) = x^2 + 2x - 10$

8) Sketch a parabola that has:

2 distinct real roots   1 distinct real root   no real roots

  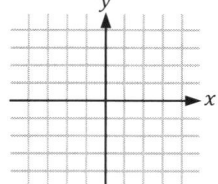

9) What is the product of the roots of $y = 2x^2 + 4x + 6$?

A **quadratic** is an equation of the form $y = ax^2 + bx + c$. On the xy-plane, this produces the graph of a **parabola**. If a is positive, the parabola points up, so that the **vertex** is the lowest point on the graph. If a is negative, the parabola points down, and the vertex is the highest point on the graph. Either way, the value of c is the y-coordinate of the graph's y-intercept.

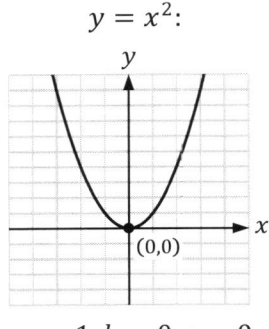
$y = x^2$:
$a = 1, b = 0, c = 0$

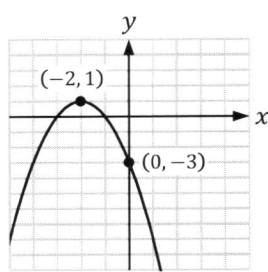
$y = -x^2 - 4x - 3$:
$a = -1, b = -4, c = -3$

The graph of a quadratic may have one, two, or zero x-intercepts. Each of these points represents a distinct real **root** of the equation. Because they are the **solutions** to the equation $ax^2 + bx + c = 0$, they are sometimes also called the **zeros** of the function.

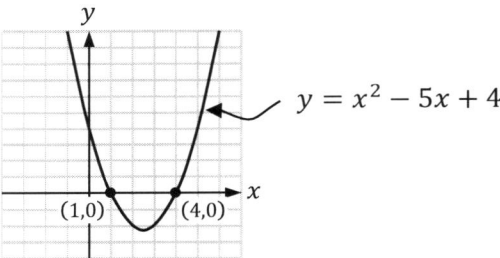

Example: The figure above is the graph of $y = x^2 - 5x + 4$ on the xy-plane. The graph has x-intercepts at $(1, 0)$ and $(4, 0)$ because the solutions to the equation $x^2 - 5x + 4 = 0$ are $x = 1$ and $x = 4$.

TIP:

By definition, every quadratic function has exactly two roots. However, not every parabola has exactly two x-intercepts. Why? Two reasons. First, not every quadratic has exactly two *distinct* roots. For example, the roots of $f(x) = (x - 3)(x - 3)$ are 3 and 3, so the graph has only one x-intercept: at $x = 3$.

And second, not every quadratic has *real* roots. When the roots of a quadratic function are imaginary numbers, the parabola has no x-intercepts at all.

Quadratic Functions

There are several ways to find the solutions to a quadratic equation. If possible, **factor** the quadratic and then set each factor equal to zero.

Example: $x^2 - 5x + 4 = 0$
$(x-1)(x-4) = 0$
$x - 1 = 0$ or $x - 4 = 0$
$x = \mathbf{1}$ or $x = \mathbf{4}$

TIP: For a review of these skills, check the Factoring, FOILing, and Fractions chapter on p. 306.

Not all quadratics can be factored. For the rest, one approach is to use the **quadratic formula**, which says that the solutions to any quadratic of the form $ax^2 + bx + c = 0$ are

$$x = \frac{-b \pm \sqrt{b^2 - 4ac}}{2a}$$

TIP: A quicker way to find the solutions to a quadratic is to graph it. The built-in calculator will automatically highlight the zeros for you.

Example: $x^2 - 7x - 3 = 0$

In this equation, $a = 1, b = -7$, and $c = -3$. So:

$$x = \frac{7 \pm \sqrt{(-7)^2 - 4(1)(-3)}}{2(1)} = \frac{7 \pm \sqrt{49 + 12}}{2} = \frac{7 \pm \sqrt{61}}{2}$$

$$x = \frac{\mathbf{7 + \sqrt{61}}}{\mathbf{2}} \quad \text{or} \quad x = \frac{\mathbf{7 - \sqrt{61}}}{\mathbf{2}}$$

Try It 1) Solve $2x^2 + 3x - 1 = 0$.

TIP:

For any quadratic written in standard $y = ax^2 + bx + c$ form:

- the **sum** of the roots is equal to $-b/a$, and
- the **product** of the roots is equal to c/a.

This is true **whether or not the quadratic is factorable.**

Example: $y = 2x^2 + 4x + 6$
sum of roots is $-4/2 = -2$
product of roots is $6/2 = 3$
actual roots $= -1 + \sqrt{2}i$ and $-1 - \sqrt{2}i$

- 343 -

If you're asked to find the **vertex** of the parabola, the easiest method depends on the form the quadratic is written in. If the equation is given in **vertex form**, $y = a(x - h)^2 + k$, you can just read the vertex directly: it's (h, k).

Example: The parabola given by $f(x) = 2(x + 3)^2 + 1$ has its vertex at the point $(-3, 1)$.

If the equation is in factored form, the x-coordinate of the vertex is just the average of the x-coordinates of the zeros. Once you have that, plug it back into the equation to find the y-coordinate.

Example: What is the vertex of $f(x) = -4(x - 1)(x - 3)$?

The zeros are $x = 1$ and $x = 3$, so the x-coordinate of the vertex is $x = 2$. The y-coordinate is $y = -4(2 - 1)(2 - 3) = 4$. Therefore, the vertex is located at $(2, 4)$.

And if the equation is in standard form, you can use this formula to find the x-coordinate of the vertex:

$$x = \frac{-b}{2a}$$

Example: What is the vertex of $f(x) = x^2 + 2x - 10$?

$$x = \frac{-2}{2(1)} = -1$$

$$y = (-1)^2 + 2(-1) - 10 = -11$$

The vertex is $(-1, -11)$.

TIP: You can also type a quadratic into the built-in calculator in any of these forms. The software will automatically highlight the vertex for you.

Questions about the **minimum value** or **maximum value** of a quadratic function are asking for the y-coordinate of the vertex.

Try It

2) For what value of x does the function $g(x) = -3x^2 + 12x + 2$ reach its maximum value?

3) What is the minimum value of $f(x) = 2x^2 - 4x - 1$?

The **axis of symmetry** of an upward-facing or downward-facing parabola with vertex (h, k) is $x = h$.

Example: *The axis of symmetry for the parabola given by $y = (x - 2)^2 + 1$ is the vertical line $x = 2$.*

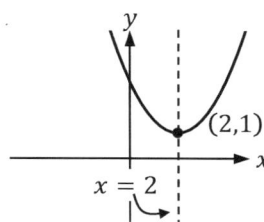

When a quadratic is written in standard $y = ax^2 + bx + c$ form, the expression $b^2 - 4ac$ is called the **discriminant**. Because it is the part of the quadratic formula that is found under the square root, it can be used to determine how many real solutions exist for a particular quadratic. After all, if the value of $b^2 - 4ac$ turns out to be less than zero, then the quadratic formula will require us to take the square root of a negative number, resulting in only imaginary solutions. And because the real solutions are also the x-intercepts of the graph, the graph of such a quadratic will not touch the x-axis at all.

In fact, the discriminant gives us three possible outcomes:

  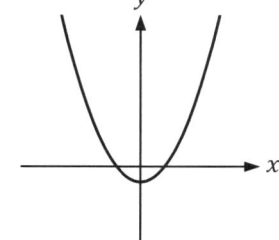

$b^2 - 4ac < 0$: No real roots $b^2 - 4ac = 0$: One real root $b^2 - 4ac > 0$: Two real roots

Try It

4) The equation $x^2 + 2x + 3 = 0$ has how many distinct real solutions?

5) When the equation $y = x^2 + 3x + k$, where k is a constant, is graphed on the xy-plane, the graph has two x-intercepts. If k is an integer, what is the greatest possible value of k?

Math: Advanced Math

CHALLENGE:

The SAT will sometimes ask you to choose an alternate form of a quadratic equation that highlights some specific information by using those values as constants or coefficients. To highlight the y-intercept, choose standard form. To highlight the x-intercepts, choose factored form. To highlight the vertex, choose vertex form.

Example: The figure shows the graph of $y = f(x)$ on the xy-plane. The equation of $f(x)$ is given below in standard form, factored form, and vertex form.

- $f(x) = x^2 - 2x - 15$: shows the y-intercept is $(0, -15)$
- $f(x) = (x + 3)(x - 5)$: shows the x-intercepts are $(-3, 0)$ and $(5, 0)$
- $f(x) = (x - 1)^2 - 16$: shows that the vertex is $(1, -16)$

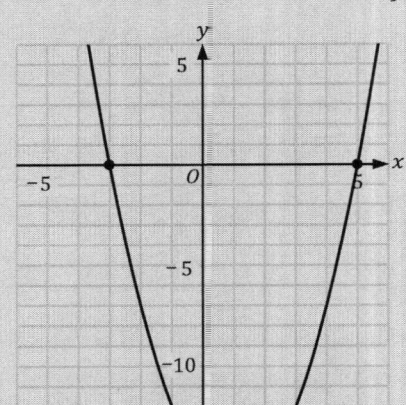

Try It

6) The graph of $f(x) = (2x + 2)(x + 5)$ is shown. In which of the following equivalent forms of the equation does the y-coordinate of the parabola's vertex appear as a constant or coefficient?

A. $f(x) = 2x^2 + 12x + 10$
B. $f(x) = 2(x + 1)(x + 5)$
C. $f(x) = (2x + 10)(x + 1)$
D. $f(x) = 2(x + 3)^2 - 8$

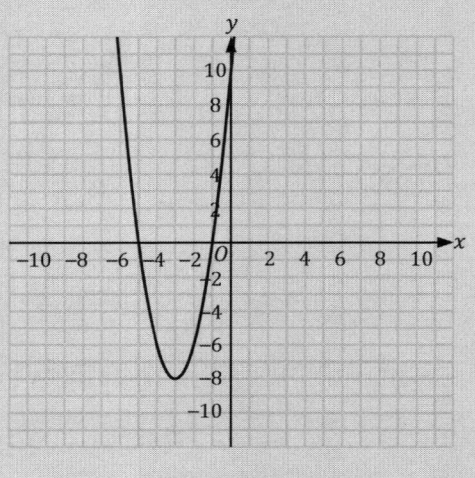

Chapter Answer Key

Try It
1) $x = \dfrac{-3 \pm \sqrt{17}}{4}$
2) 2
3) -3
4) none
5) 2
6) D

Math: Advanced Math

Practice Set 1: Easy-Medium

1

$$f(x) = 2x^2 - x + 5$$

Which table gives three values of x and their corresponding values of $f(x)$ for the given equation?

A.
x	0	1	2
$f(x)$	1	5	11

B.
x	0	1	2
$f(x)$	1	8	19

C.
x	0	1	2
$f(x)$	5	6	11

D.
x	0	1	2
$f(x)$	5	8	19

2

$$f(x) = -2(2x - 2)(x + 3)$$

What is the maximum value of the function defined above?

A. 0
B. 1
C. 8
D. 16

3

The equation $y = 2x^2 - 3x - 7$ has how many distinct real roots and how many imaginary roots?

A. 0 distinct real roots and 2 imaginary roots
B. 1 distinct real root and 0 imaginary roots
C. 2 distinct real roots and 0 imaginary roots
D. 2 distinct real roots and 1 imaginary root

4

$$f(x) = (x - 1)^2 + 3$$

The quadratic function $f(x)$ is defined above. Which of the following gives the axis of symmetry for the graph of $y = f(x)$ on the xy-plane?

A. $x = -1$
B. $x = 1$
C. $y = -1$
D. $y = 1$

5

The figure below gives the graph of the function $f(x) = (x - 3)^2 + 1$ in the xy-plane.

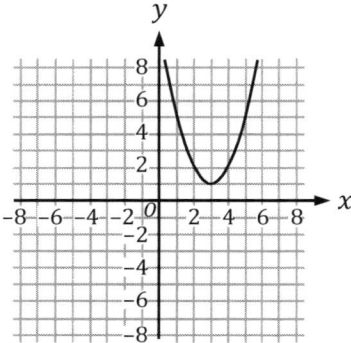

If the parabola is shifted 4 units down, the resulting parabola is the graph of the function $g(x)$. Which of the following defines $g(x)$?

A. $g(x) = (x - 7)^2 + 1$
B. $g(x) = (x + 1)^2 + 1$
C. $g(x) = (x - 3)^2 - 3$
D. $g(x) = -4(x - 3)^2 + 1$

6

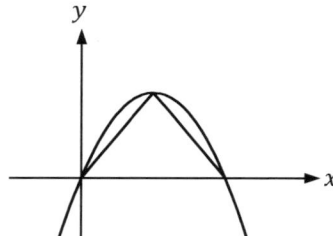

The figure above shows a triangle inscribed in the graph of the quadratic function f whose maximum value is $f(3) = 4$. What is the area of the triangle?

A. 6
B. 10
C. 12
D. 20

Quadratic Functions

Practice Set 2: Medium-Hard

1

If $x = 4$ and $x = -1$ are the roots of the equation $y = x^2 - 3x + k$, where k is a constant, what is the value of k?

4

The equation $y = mx + 3$, where m is a constant, gives the graph of a line on the xy-plane. If the line intersects the graph of $y = x^2 + 3$ at the point $(1, a)$, what is the value of m?

2

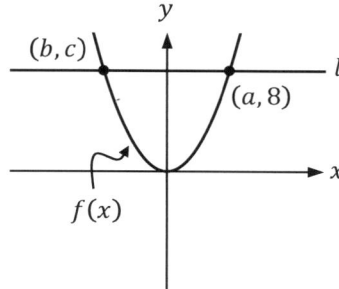

The figure above shows the graph of the equation $f(x) = \frac{1}{2}x^2$. Line l is parallel to the x-axis and intersects the graph of $f(x)$ at the points (b, c) and $(a, 8)$. What is the value of $a + b + c$?

5

Which of the following could be the graph of $f(x) = ax^2 + bx + c$, if $a, b,$ and c are all positive constants?

A.

B.

C.

D.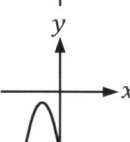

3

For how many distinct values of n is the product of $2n + 3$ and $2n - 5$ equal to -16?

A. None
B. One
C. Two
D. Infinitely many

6

In the xy-plane, the graph of $y = g(x)$ is symmetrical across the y-axis. Which of the following could be the equation that defines $g(x)$?

A. $g(x) = x^2 + 1$
B. $g(x) = (x + 2)^2$
C. $g(x) = x^3 + 3$
D. $g(x) = x^3$

7

$$y = 1$$
$$y = ax^2 + b$$

In the system of equations above, a and b are constants. For which of the following values of a and b does the system of equations have exactly two real solutions?

A. $a = -2, b = -3$
B. $a = -2, b = 4$
C. $a = 1, b = 4$
D. $a = 3, b = 1$

8

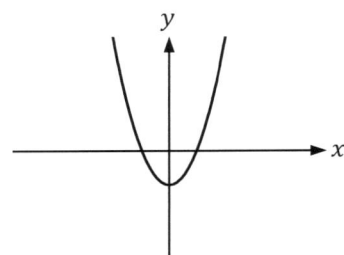

The figure above shows the graph of the equation $f(x) = x^2 - 3$. A square (not shown) is situated so that two consecutive vertices lie at the intersection of $f(x)$ and the x-axis. What is the area of the square?

9

What is the sum of the two solutions to the equation $x^2 - 5x - 24 = 0$?

A. -24
B. 0
C. 1
D. 5

10

The figure below shows the graph of the equation $f(x) = 4x - x^2 - k$, where k is a constant.

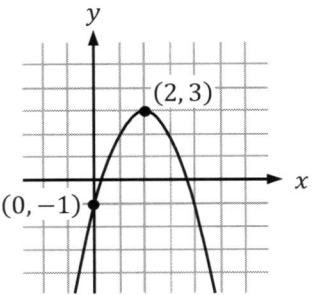

What is the value of k?

A. -1
B. 1
C. 2
D. 3

11

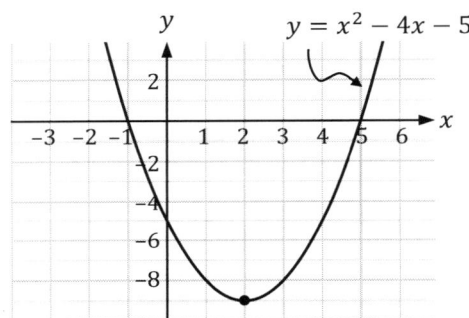

Which of the following is an equivalent form of the equation of the graph shown in the xy-plane above from which the coordinates of vertex A can be identified as constants in the equation?

A. $y = x(x - 4) - 5$
B. $y = (x - 2)^2 - 9$
C. $y = (x + 1)(x - 5)$
D. $y = (x + 5)(x - 3)$

Polynomial, Exponential, Radical, and Rational Equations

Preview Quiz:

Simplify each of the following polynomials:

1) $(3x^3 - 2x + 1) + (2x^2 + 5x - x^3) =$

2) $x(2x^2 - 3x + 4) - 2(3x^2 - x^3 + 1) =$

The polynomial function f is defined by $f(x) = (x + 1)(x + 2)(x - 5)$.

3) What are the x-intercepts of $y = f(x)$? _____

4) What is the y-intercept of $y = f(x)$? _____

Circle the right answer and/or fill in the blanks.

5) The graph of a 4th-degree polynomial function has
   (at least / at most / exactly) _____ x-intercepts.

6) The graph of $f(x) = (x - 3)^2(x + 1)$ has
   (at least / at most / exactly) _____ x-intercepts.

Solve.

7) A town's population is projected to increase by 7% per year for the next twenty years. The current population is 5000 people. If the projection is accurate, what will the town's population be in 15 years? (Round your answer to the nearest whole number.)

[handwritten: $y = a(b)^x$, $5000(1.07)^{15}$, $.07(15)5000 = y$]

8) What is the domain of $f(x) = \sqrt{2x + 10}$?

The rational function g is defined by the equation below:
$$g(x) = \frac{x - 3}{(x - 3)(x - 2)}$$

9) What is the domain of $g(x)$?

10) What are the vertical asymptotes, if any, of the graph of $y = g(x)$ on the xy-plane?

Math: Advanced Math

A **polynomial** function is a function with multiple distinct x terms, such as $f(x) = x^3 - 2x^2 + 5x - 1$. Some polynomial problems will simply ask you to **combine like terms**.

Example: Simplify $(3x^3 - 2x + 1) + (2x^2 + 5x - x^3)$.
$$3x^3 - x^3 + 2x^2 - 2x + 5x + 1$$
$$\mathbf{2x^3 + 2x^2 + 3x + 1}$$

TIP:
Don't assume the terms in both expressions will be presented in the same order.

If the problem requires multiplying a polynomial by a monomial or by another polynomial, use the rules of FOILing and/or the exponent rules to simplify the expression.

Example: Simplify $x(2x^2 - 3x + 4) - 2(3x^2 - x^3 + 1)$.
$$x(2x^2 - 3x + 4) - 2(3x^2 - x^3 + 1)$$
$$(2x^3 - 3x^2 + 4x) - 2(3x^2 - x^3 + 1)$$
$$2x^3 - 3x^2 + 4x - 6x^2 + 2x^3 - 2$$
$$\mathbf{4x^3 - 9x^2 + 4x - 2}$$

Many polynomials can be **factored**. The relationship between the factors of the equation and the x-intercepts of the graph is the same as it is for quadratics.

TIP:
If $x + 1$ is a **factor**, then $x = -1$ is a **zero**.

Example: The graph of $f(x) = (x + 1)(x + 2)(x - 5)$ intersects the x-axis at the points $(-1, 0), (-2, 0),$ and $(5, 0)$.

Factors that appear in the equation an odd number of times indicate points where the graph **crosses** the x-axis. Factors that appear in the equation an even number of times indicate points where the graph simply **touches** the x-axis without crossing it.

Example:

$$f(x) = (x - 1)(x - 4)^2$$

Try It

$$f(x) = -(x+1)(x-2)(x-3)$$
$$g(x) = -(x+1)(x-2)^2(x-3)$$

The polynomial functions f and g are defined by the equations above.

1) What are the x-intercepts of $y = f(x)$?

2) What are the x-intercepts of $y = g(x)$?

3) What is the difference between these two graphs?

The **y-intercept** of a polynomial function, like the y-intercept of any other graph, is just the value of y when $x = 0$.

Example: On the xy-plane, what is the y-intercept of the graph of $f(x) = (x+1)(x+2)(x-5)$?

To solve, find $f(0)$.

$$f(0) = (0+1)(0+2)(0-5)$$
$$= (1)(2)(-5)$$
$$-10$$

The y-intercept is the point $(\mathbf{0, -10})$.

Try It   4) What is the y-intercept of $g(x) = -(x+1)(x-2)^2(x-3)$?

TIP:

Don't forget to consider using the built-in calculator to solve these problems. You can often quickly get an answer just by looking at the graph.

CHALLENGE:

Polynomials: factors, zeros, and remainders

If $(x - 2)$ is a factor of polynomial function $f(x)$, then $x = 2$ is a solution of the equation. Because a solution is the same thing as a zero, this means that $f(2) = 0$. The reverse is also true: if $f(2) = 0$ for polynomial function f, then $(x - 2)$ is a factor of f.

This also means that once you know that $(x - 2)$ is a factor of f, you can plug in 2 for x and set the whole thing equal to zero.

Example: *If $(x - 3)$ is a factor of the function $g(x) = x^3 - 3x^2 - kx + 12$, where k is a constant, then what is the value of k?*

$$g(3) = (3)^3 - 3(3)^2 - k(3) + 12 = 0$$
$$27 - 3(9) - 3k + 12 = 0$$
$$12 = 3k$$
$$\mathbf{4 = k}$$

If $(x - 2)$ is *not* a factor of a polynomial equation, then when we plug in 2 for x we will get a nonzero result. Let's say that in our unknown function f, $(x - 2)$ is not a factor, and specifically, that when we plug it in, the result is 1. In other words, $f(2) = 1$. Another way of saying this is that when the function f is divided by $(x - 2)$, the remainder is 1.

Example: *What is the remainder when $h(x) = 2x^3 - 6x + 1$ is divided by $(x + 1)$?*

$$h(-1) = 2(-1)^3 - 6(-1) + 1$$
$$= 2(-1) + 6 + 1$$
$$= \mathbf{5}$$

This same concept can be expressed through polynomial division.

$$f(x) = x^3 - 3x^2 + 5x - 5$$

All of these statements are true:

- $(x - 2)$ is not a factor of $f(x)$
- 2 is not a solution to $f(x) = 0$
- 2 is not an x-intercept on the graph of $f(x)$
- $f(2) = 1$
- The remainder when $f(x)$ is divided by $(x - 2)$ is 1
- $\dfrac{f(x)}{x - 2} = x^2 - x + 3$ with a remainder of 1
- $\dfrac{f(x)}{x - 2} = x^2 - x + 3 + \dfrac{1}{x - 2}$

$$\begin{array}{r}
x^2 - x + 3 \\
x - 2 \overline{\smash{\big)} x^3 - 3x^2 + 5x - 5} \\
\underline{x^3 - 2x^2} \\
-x^2 + 5x \\
\underline{-x^2 + 2x} \\
3x - 5 \\
\underline{3x - 6} \\
1
\end{array}$$

Polynomial, Exponential, Radical, and Rational Equations

The standard form of an **exponential function** is $f(x) = a(b)^x$, where b is a positive number and $b \neq 1$. These functions model increases or decreases that are not linear: for example, a population that increases at a rate of 15% per year, or a bad investment that loses 5% of its value each month.

In the equation, the constant a gives the y-coordinate of the y-intercept of the graph (the starting population, or the original value of the investment). The constant b is equal to 1 plus the rate of change, represented as a decimal. (For the population example, b would equal $1 + 0.15 = 1.15$. For the investment, b equals $1 + (-0.05) = 0.95$.)

It may be helpful to think of these equations as following this form:

$$A = P(1 + r)^t$$

In this form, A is the final amount, P is the initial amount, r is the rate of change expressed as a decimal, and t is time.

Example: A town's population is projected to increase by 7% per year for the next twenty years. The current population is 5000 people. If the projection is accurate, what will the town's population be in 15 years? (Round your answer to the nearest whole number.)

The starting value of the population is 5000, so that's P. The population is increasing by 7% per year, so the value of r is 0.07. That gives us this:

$$A = 5000(1.07)^t$$

Now rewrite that in function notation:

$$f(x) = 5000(1.07)^x$$

In this equation, x represents the number of years that have passed. So we can solve by finding $f(15)$:

$$f(15) = 5000(1.07)^{15} = 13795.16$$

The population will be approximately **13,795** people.

TIP:

A constant percent increase is *not* a constant rate of growth. If we start with 5000 people and increase by 7% per year, then in the first year, the population will grow by 7% of 5000, which is 350. In the second year, the population must grow by 7% of 5350, which is 374.5. That's more than 350! The amount by which the population is changing is itself increasing every year.

Try It The value of an investment account over time can be modeled by $f(x) = 2000(1.04)^x$, where $f(x)$ represents the value of the account, in dollars, x years after the account was opened.

5) What is the best interpretation of the number 2000 in this equation?

6) What was the value of the account 6 years after it was opened, rounded to the nearest cent?

The graph of an exponential function does not change direction: it either increases forever or it decreases forever.

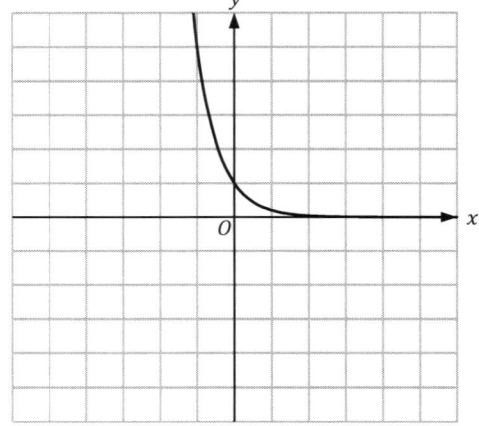

$f(x) = a(b)^x$ where $b > 1$:
exponential **growth**

$f(x) = a(b)^x$ where $0 < b < 1$:
exponential **decay**

TIP:

For an exponential function of form $f = a(b)^x$, the amount by which b differs from 1 is the rate of change.

Try It   For each of the equations below, indicate whether the equation represents exponential growth, exponential decay, or neither. If the equation does represent exponential growth or decay, indicate the rate of change, expressed as a percent.

	growth, decay, or neither?	rate
7) $f(x) = 0.9(1.5)^x$	_____	_____
8) $f(x) = 12(-2.3)^x$	_____	_____
9) $f(x) = 2.7(0.6)^x$	_____	_____

Polynomial, Exponential, Radical, and Rational Equations

CHALLENGE:

For problems involving more than one unit of time—for example, an annual rate that is compounded monthly—we need a more complicated formula:

$$A = P\left(1 + \frac{r}{n}\right)^{nt}$$

The constants A, P, r, and t have the same meaning as in the simpler formula; the constant n is the number of compounding intervals. For example, if an annual rate is compounded quarterly (four times per year), then $n = 4$.

Try It An investment account is opened with an initial investment of $1000. The account earns a 6% annual interest rate that is compounded monthly.

10) Write an exponential equation that models this situation, where $f(x)$ represents the value of the account, in dollars, x years after it was opened.

11) According to the model, what was the value of the account 18 months after it was opened? Round your answer to the nearest cent.

A **radical function** takes the form of a square root: for example, $f(x) = \sqrt{2x + 10}$.

To find the domain of a radical function, take the portion that's under the square root and set it greater than or equal to zero.

Example: What is the domain of $f(x)$, defined above?

$2x + 10 \geq 0$
$2x \geq -10$
$x \geq -5$
The domain is all real numbers greater than or equal to -5. In interval notation, that's $[-5, \infty)$.

A **rational function** takes the form of a fraction: for example, $f(x) = \dfrac{5}{2x - 6}$.

To find the domain of a rational function, take the bottom of the fraction and set it "unequal to" zero.

Example: What is the domain of $f(x)$, defined above?

$2x - 6 \neq 0$
$2x \neq 6$
$x \neq 3$
The domain is all real numbers except 3. In interval notation, that's $(-\infty, 3) \cup (3, \infty)$.

To find the **range** of a function, the easiest technique is usually just to graph the function on your calculator.

Example: What is the range of $p(x) = \sqrt{x - 4}$?

The graph starts abruptly at the x-axis (where $y = 0$) and continues to the right, heading gradually upwards with no apparent upper limit. Therefore, the range is **all real numbers greater than or equal to zero**: $[0, \infty)$.

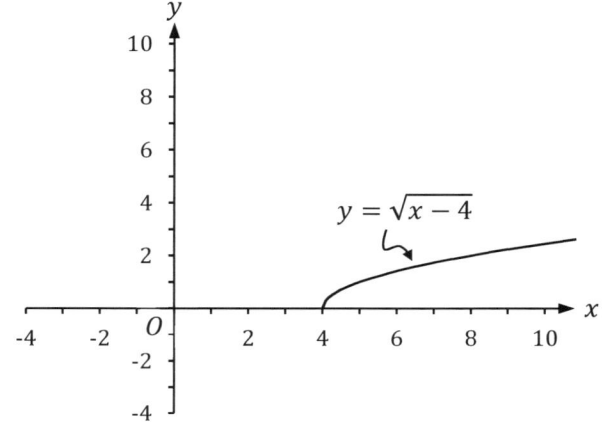

Try It

$$f(x) = 5 - \sqrt{3x+4}$$
$$g(x) = \frac{x+2}{3x+4}$$

The functions f and g are defined by the equations above.

12) What is the domain of $f(x)$?

13) What is the y-intercept of $y = f(x)$, if any?

14) What is the domain of $g(x)$?

15) What is/are the x-intercept(s) of $y = g(x)$, if any?

CHALLENGE:

A value that is not included in the domain of a rational function may show up in the graph as a vertical **asymptote**, which is an imaginary line that the graph approaches but does not reach.

Example:

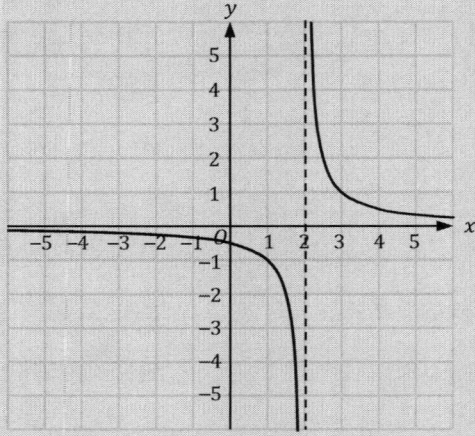

The graph of $f(x) = \dfrac{1}{x-2}$ has a vertical asymptote at $x = 2$.

A factor that appears in both the numerator and the denominator of a rational function appears in the graph as a **hole** rather than an asymptote.

Example:

The graph of $g(x) = \dfrac{x-3}{(x-3)(x-2)}$ has a vertical asymptote at $x = 2$ and a hole at $x = 3$. It is identical to the graph of $f(x) = \dfrac{1}{x-2}$ where $x \neq 3$.

TIP:

A factor that cancels out from the top and bottom is still excluded from the domain.

Polynomial, Exponential, Radical, and Rational Equations

Chapter Answer Key

Try It

1) $(-1, 0), (2, 0),$ and $(3, 0)$
2) $(-1, 0), (2, 0),$ and $(3, 0)$
3) In the graph of $f(x)$, the curve crosses the x-axis at all three x-intercepts. In the graph of $g(x)$, the curve crosses the x-axis at $x = -1$ and $x = 3$ but only touches the x-axis (without crossing it) at $x = 2$.
4) $(0, 12)$
5) The account was opened with an initial investment of $2000.
6) $2530.64
7) growth; rate $= 50\%$
8) neither
9) decay; rate $= 40\%$
10) $f(x) = 1000(1.005)^{12x}$
11) $1093.93
12) $x \geq -4/3$
13) $(0, 3)$
14) $x \neq -4/3$
15) $(-2, 0)$

Math: Advanced Math

Practice Set 1: Easy-Medium

1

In Earth's atmosphere, as altitude decreases, air pressure increases exponentially. The table below gives the approximate average air pressure $p(a)$, in pascals, at several altitudes a, in kilometers, above the Earth's surface.

a	$p(a)$
0	14.7
1	12.8
2	11.2

Which of the following equations best models the data in the table?

A. $p(a) = 12.8(0.998)^a$
B. $p(a) = 12.8(1.15)^a$
C. $p(a) = 14.7(0.873)^a$
D. $p(a) = 14.7(12.8)^a$

2

$$h(t) = -2t^4 + 13t^3 - 28t^2 + 23t + 1.9$$

To become accustomed to weightlessness, astronauts must fly training flights that make repeated ascents and descents in order to simulate the feeling of free-falling. During the first three minutes of one such flight, the motion of the plane could be modeled by the function above, where t represents the time since takeoff, in minutes, and $h(t)$ represents the plane's altitude, in kilometers above sea level. Which of the following is the best interpretation of the number 1.9 in the equation?

A. The flight lasted at least 1.9 minutes.
B. The flight's average rate of ascent was 1.9 kilometers per minute.
C. The plane made a maximum of 1.9 changes of direction during the first three minutes of the flight.
D. The plane took off from an altitude of 1.9 kilometers above sea level.

3

The population of a bacteria colony starts at 1,000. After t hours its population can be expressed by the equation $p(t) = 1,000r^t$. If the population increases by 20% each hour, what is the value of r?

4

In 2000, a census determined that the town of Benderberg had a population of approximately 126,000 people. Ever since, the population has grown at a rate of 7% per year. The equation $y = 126(1.07)^x$ gives Benderberg's approximate population y, in thousands, x years after the census. In 2014, the population of Benderberg was closest to which of the following?

A. 189,000
B. 325,000
C. 514,000
D. 1,887,000

5

$$f(x) = 2x^3 - 5x^2 + 8x - 1$$
$$g(x) = -x^3 + 2x^2 - x + 3$$

For the functions f and g defined above, which of the following gives $f(x) - g(x)$?

A. $x^3 - 7x^2 + 7x - 4$
B. $x^3 - 3x^2 + 7x + 2$
C. $3x^3 - 7x^2 + 9x - 4$
D. $3x^3 - 3x^2 + 9x + 2$

Polynomial, Exponential, Radical, and Rational Equations

6

If $f(x) = 3.2(0.5)^x + 1$, which of the following is the y-intercept of the graph of $y = f(x)$ on the xy-plane?

A. $(0, 1)$
B. $(0, 2)$
C. $(0, 3.2)$
D. $(0, 4.2)$

7

For a toy company that experienced exponential growth, the function $T(x) = 1200(1.15)^x$ gives the number of toys sold per year, $T(x)$, at any time x years after 2015. What is the best interpretation of the number 1200 in this equation?

A. The toy company sold 1200 toys in 2015.
B. The number of toys sold per year increased by 12% per year.
C. The number of toys sold per year increased by 1200 per year.
D. The maximum number of toys sold in any one year was 1200.

8

If $f(x) = \sqrt{x + 30}$ and $g(x) = \dfrac{x}{2} - 9$, for which of the following values of x does $f(x) = g(x)$?

I. $x = 0$
II. $x = 6$
III. $x = 34$

A. I only
B. I and III only
C. II and III only
D. III only

9

The function f is defined as follows:

$$f(x) = \frac{(x+1)(x-3)}{(x-3)(x-1)}$$

For what value or values of x is the function f undefined?

I. -1
II. 1
III. 3

A. I only
B. I and III only
C. II and III only
D. I, II, and III

10

The value of an investment decreases by 11% per year. If the initial value of the investment is \$24,000, which of the following exponential functions models the value of the investment, $A(t)$, in dollars, after t years?

A. $A(t) = 24{,}000(1.11)^t$
B. $A(t) = 24{,}000(0.11)^t$
C. $A(t) = 24{,}000(0.89)^t$
D. $A(t) = 0.89(24{,}000)^t$

11

$$f(x) = -2(x-3)(2x-3)(3x+5)$$

Which of the following is an x-intercept of the graph of the function above on the xy-plane?

A. $(-3, 0)$
B. $\left(\dfrac{2}{3}, 0\right)$
C. $\left(\dfrac{3}{2}, 0\right)$
D. $\left(\dfrac{5}{3}, 0\right)$

Math: Advanced Math

Practice Set 2: Medium-Hard

1

The total amount of money in Kathy's bank account can be calculated by the expression $P\left(1+\frac{r}{n}\right)^{nt}$, where the initial amount P was deposited at an annual rate of r for t years, with interest compounded n times per year. If Kathy noticed that the total amount of money in her bank account was increasing every two months rather than quarterly, the value of which of the following would change?

A. P
B. r
C. n
D. t

2

The graph of which of the following functions must have points in all four quadrants of the xy-plane?

A. a linear function with a nonzero rate of change
B. an exponential function with a nonzero y-intercept
C. a polynomial function with four real zeros
D. a quadratic function with both positive and negative zeros

3

If $g(x) = 2\sqrt{x+1}$ and $g(k) = 50$, where k is a positive constant, what is the value of k?

4

$$f(x) = 3256(1.02)^{4x}$$

Since 2010, the value of a university's endowment has increased at an annual rate of $p\%$, compounded quarterly. The function f models this situation, where $f(x)$ is the value of the endowment x years after 2010. What is the value of p?

A. 8
B. 2
C. 0.08
D. 0.02

5

For the function $h(x) = a\sqrt{x-1} + b$, $h(1) = 2$, $h(5) = 10$, and $h(k) = 18$, where a, b, and k are constants. What is the value of k?

6

If the functions f and g are defined by $f(x) = 80(10)^x$ and $g(x) = f(x-1)$, which of the following gives $g(x)$?

A. $g(x) = 7(10)^x$
B. $g(x) = 8(9)^x$
C. $g(x) = 8(10)^x$
D. $g(x) = 80\left(\frac{1}{10}\right)^x$

7

$$f(x) = px^3 - 3x^2 + 2x + 5$$
$$g(x) = 3x^3 + 5x^2 - qx + 2$$

In the functions $f(x)$ and $g(x)$ defined above, p and q are constants. Given that $f(x) - g(x) = -x^3 - 8x^2 + 6x + 3$, what is the value of $p - q$?

Polynomial, Exponential, Radical, and Rational Equations

8

The half-life decay model can be expressed as $A = A_0 \left(\frac{1}{2}\right)^{\frac{t}{h}}$, where A_0 is the initial amount of a substance at time $t = 0$, A is the amount remaining at time t, and h is the half-life (the amount of time it takes for half of the substance to decay). Based on the equation, which of the following must be true?

A. After three half-lives, $\frac{1}{8}$ of the substance will remain.
B. 50% of the substance will remain when $t = 2$.
C. $A > A_0$ for $0 < t < 2$.
D. As the value of t increases, the value of A_0 decreases exponentially.

9

In the xy-plane, the graphs of linear function $f(x)$ and exponential function $g(x)$ intersect a total of n times. Which of the following is NOT a possible value of n?

A. 0
B. 1
C. 2
D. 3

10

In the xy-plane, the x-intercepts of $y = f(x)$ include 2 and 5. The function has a y-intercept at 4. If f is a third-degree polynomial function, which of the following CANNOT be true of $f(x)$?

A. The graph of $y = f(x)$ has exactly two x-intercepts.
B. $(x + 5)$ is a factor of $f(x)$.
C. The remainder when $f(x)$ is divided by $(x - 2)$ is 5.
D. The function is increasing over the interval $-\infty < x \leq 0$.

11

$$f(x) = 4\sqrt{x}$$
$$g(x) = \frac{x + 2}{x - 9}$$

The functions f and g are defined above, and the function h is defined by $h(x) = g(f(x))$. Which of the following is the best description of the domain of $h(x)$?

A. $x > 0$
B. $x > 0$ and $x \neq 9$
C. $x \geq 0$ and $x \neq \frac{3}{2}$
D. $x \geq 0$ and $x \neq \frac{81}{16}$

12

The data in the scatterplot below could most appropriately be modeled by which of the following exponential functions, where a, b, and c are all positive constants?

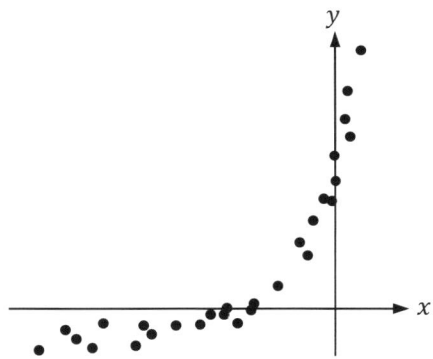

A. $f(x) = a^{(x + b)} + c$
B. $f(x) = a^{(x + b)} - c$
C. $f(x) = a^{(x - b)} + c$
D. $f(x) = a^{(x - b)} - c$

Problem Solving and Data Analysis

Charts and graphs are abundant on the SAT. When answering math questions that accompany a chart or graph, you'll need to put your critical reading skills to work by carefully analyzing the given data and drawing appropriate conclusions.

Focus on what matters.	It's common for the test to present you with a lot more information than you actually need. Always be sure that you're looking at the data that are relevant to the question being asked. (Beware of superfluous data intended solely to distract you!)
Double-check.	If more than one chart or graph is provided, verify that you're consulting the right one before you choose your answer. Check as well that you're not confusing one axis for the other, or one line for another, if multiple lines are graphed in the same figure.
Watch the scale.	The x-axis and the y-axis are not necessarily measured in the same way: for example, there may be a vertical gridline every 5 units and a horizontal gridline every 10. Also, do you need to multiply? Charts will often show you data in "thousands of dollars" instead of simply in dollars.
Extrapolate carefully.	The test may give you a chart that shows the results of a survey of 100 students and then ask you to make a deduction about the student body at large. If so, you'll need to set up a proportion—don't just circle the answer that shows the number of students *in the survey* that fit the category.
Don't go too far.	In some cases, you'll need to decide whether a certain deduction can be drawn from the data in front of you—that is, not whether the deduction is mathematically valid, but whether it can be appropriately drawn at all. Consider issues like **sample size**, **representativeness**, and **potential bias** as you make your decision.

Data Interpretation

Preview Quiz:

1) For a summer academic program in Washington, DC, the fifty participants were chosen from school districts in Maryland (MD), Virginia (VA), West Virginia (WV), or Washington, DC (DC). Based on the circle graph, which school district represents approximately 25% of the participants?

	Red	Green	Blue	Other	Total
Cleo	7	12	5	18	42
Harrison	9	4	13	22	48
Total	16	16	18	40	90

2) The table above shows the number of marbles of various colors owned by Cleo and Harrison. What fraction of Harrison's marbles are green?

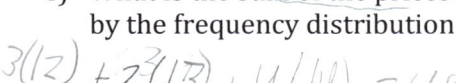

4) What is the sum of the prices represented by the frequency distribution shown?

$3(12) + 2(13) + 4(14) = 118$

5) The scatterplot shows the relationship between two variables, x and y. Which of the following equations is the most appropriate linear model for the data?

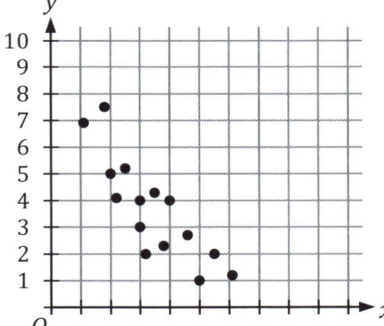

A) $y = -x + 7$
B) $y = x - 7$
C) $y = 7x - 1$
D) $y = 7x + 1$

6) What is the median of the data set represented by the box-and-whisker plot below?

You'll see plenty of **1-variable data distributions** on the SAT, including tables, bar graphs, dot plots, and box-and-whisker plots, as well as **2-variable data distributions**, such as scatterplots and line graphs.

In a **bar graph**, the heights of the bars indicate how many there are in each category. The categories themselves may or may not be numbers.

Example: For a summer academic program in Washington, DC, the fifty participants were chosen from school districts in Maryland (MD), Virginia (VA), West Virginia (WV), or Washington, DC (DC). Based on the bar graph below, how many of the participants come from a home district that is NOT Washington, DC?

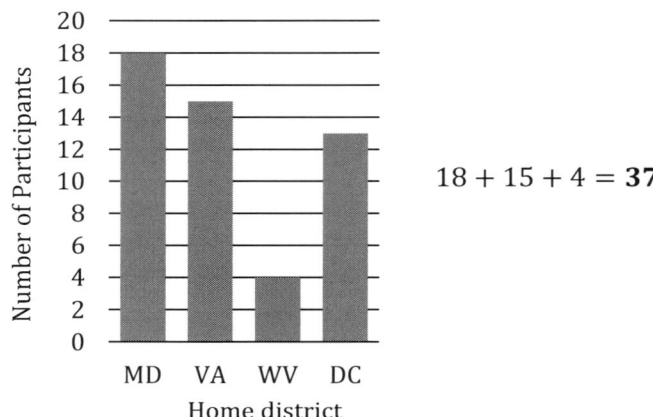

$18 + 15 + 4 = \mathbf{37}$

A **pie chart**, also called a **circle graph**, makes it easy to see what fraction of the whole is represented by each category. For example, this representation of the same summer academic program makes it clear that Washington, DC was the home district for approximately 25% of the participants.

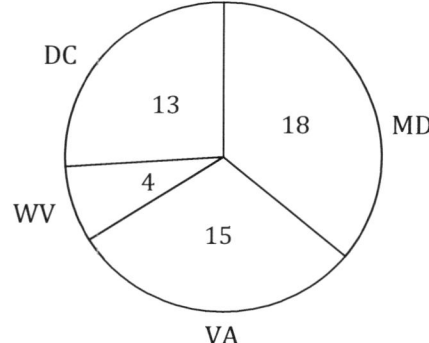

Many questions will be based on a **table** of data. These will often be **part over whole** problems. For these, be very careful to line up which category is the "part" and which is the "whole" (it may not be the total represented by the entire table).

Example:

	Red	Green	Blue	Other	Total
Cleo	7	12	5	18	42
Harrison	9	4	13	22	48
Total	16	16	18	40	90

The table above shows the number of marbles of various colors owned by Cleo and Harrison. What fraction of Harrison's marbles are green?

$$\frac{\text{Harrison's green marbles}}{\text{All of Harrison's marbles}} = \frac{4}{48} = \frac{1}{12}$$

Try It   For the questions below, use the table shown in the example above.

1) Of all the marbles represented in the table, what fraction are blue and owned by Cleo?

    $\frac{5}{90}$

2) What fraction of the blue marbles are owned by Cleo?

    $\frac{5}{18}$

(Hint: these two questions do <u>not</u> have the same answer.)

CHALLENGE:

In a **box-and-whisker plot**, each vertical line displays information about the set. The ends of the "whiskers" are the minimum and maximum values, respectively. The bar in the interior of the box is the median of the set (the center of all the data). To find the edges of the "box," divide the data into two equal sets: the lower half of the data and the upper half of the data. The left side of the box represents the median of the lower half; the right side represents the median of the upper half.

Example: The data set { 2, 4, 5, 5, 10, 11 }:

TIP:

For much more on mean, median, and mode, see p. 368.

A **frequency distribution** is a way of displaying two kinds of information at once: the values themselves and how many there are of each value.

Example: The price list $12, $12, $12, $13, $13, $14, $14, $14, $14 can be represented by any of the following frequency distributions:

Price ($)	Frequency
12	3
13	2
14	4

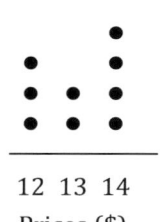

To calculate the sum of the prices, multiply each value by its frequency and add the results.

Example: The sum of the prices is $3(\$12) + 2(\$13) + 4(\$14) = \$118$.

Try It The bar graph below shows all the scores received on the AP European History exam at a local high school last year. Everyone who sat for the exam received a score.

3) How many students sat for the exam?

23

A **scatterplot** is often used to present measurements of related variables. For example, if a scientist wants to measure the growth of an animal population over time, she might use the x-axis to represent the number of years that have passed and the y-axis to represent the population. Each (x, y) point on the scatterplot would then indicate an actual population measurement at a particular time: for instance, the point $(1, 340)$ would show that the population was 340 after 1 year.

Try It   The scatterplot below shows the length, in feet, and the jaw width, in inches, of 15 great white sharks.

4) What is the length, in feet, of the shark with the greatest jaw width?

19 ft

Math: Problem Solving and Data Analysis

Some scatter plots also include a **line of best fit**, which is the line that comes closest to approximating the general trend of the data. Be sure to read carefully—questions about *predicted* values will be based on the line, while questions about actual *recorded* values will be based on the scatterplot points.

Try It   The scatterplot below shows the length, in feet, and the jaw width, in inches, of 15 great white sharks, along with a line of best fit.

5) What is the jaw width, in inches, predicted by the line of best fit for a shark with a length of 15 feet?

15 in

The test will sometimes ask you to select the most appropriate "model" for the data shown in the scatterplot. If the data points appear to be roughly grouped along the path of a line, this just means finding an approximate line of best fit. Use your coordinate geometry skills to estimate the slope and/or y-intercept and start eliminating answer choices that can't be right.

> **TIP:**
> See the Coordinate Geometry chapter on p. 249 for a review of these skills.

Example: The scatterplot shows the relationship between two variables, x and y.

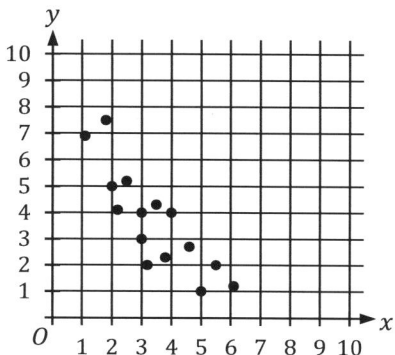

Which of the following equations is the most appropriate linear model for the data?

A) $y = -x + 7$
B) $y = x - 7$
C) $y = 7x - 1$
D) $y = 7x + 1$

Draw a line roughly through the points shown. Where would the line intersect the y-axis? Definitely closer to 7 than to -7, -1, or 1, so choice **A** must be the answer.

TIP:

Everything is drawn to scale on the SAT unless they tell you otherwise, but that doesn't mean they're not out to trick you. Always check the axes to make sure the scatterplot is really showing you what it seems to be showing you. Does the graph start at zero? Are the tick marks on the x-axis the same distance apart from each other as the tick marks on the y-axis? These are just a few of the ways the test will use "gotcha" questions to catch students who are moving too fast.

Another way to represent two-variable data is with a **line graph**. Pay close attention to what's being measured and how it's being measured (the units)—check both the description in the problem and the labels on the axes to be sure.

Try It

Ron recently took a road trip, leaving at noon and arriving at his destination at 6:00 pm. The graph below shows the relationship between time, in hours, and the distance Ron traveled, in miles.

6) At some point during his journey, Ron stopped driving to take a 90-minute break. The break occurred during which of the following time intervals?

A) 12:00 pm – 1:30 pm
B) 1:00 pm – 2:30 pm
C) 2:00 pm – 3:30 pm
D) 3:00 pm – 4:30 pm

Chapter Answer Key

Try It
1) 1/18
2) 5/18
3) 23 students
4) 19 feet
5) 15 inches
6) D

FROM THE BLOG

Go for a walk in the woods. A 2012 University of Michigan study found that memory performance and attention spans improved by 20 percent after people "spent an hour interacting with nature." Our brains can be overwhelmed by the demands placed on them day to day; allowing our minds to wander aimlessly while we are engaged by beautiful surroundings can be hugely restorative.

Math: Problem Solving and Data Analysis

Practice Set 1: Easy-Medium

1

The table below gives the fees at a private shipping company for shipping packages that weigh 5 pounds or less.

Weight (lbs)	Fee ($)
0 – 1	12.50
1.01 – 2	13.20
2.01 – 3	13.60
3.01 – 4	13.85
4.01 – 5	14.10

On Wednesday, Seldon shipped two packages that each weighed 0.5 pounds and one that weighed 4.5 pounds. What was the total of Seldon's fees, in dollars?

$2(12.5) + 1(14.1) = 39.1$

2

2, 2, 2, 3, 3, 3, 3, 4, 4

Which frequency table correctly represents the data listed above?

A.

Number	Frequency
2	4
3	3
4	2

B.

Number	Frequency
2	2
3	3
4	4

C.

Number	Frequency
2	3
3	2
4	4

D.

Number	Frequency
2	3
3	4
4	2

3

The Shannon-Wiener diversity index is a measure of species diversity within a given ecological community. A scientist calculated this index for 14 butterfly communities at various distances from an urban park. A line of best fit is also shown. Based on the figure, which of the following statements is true?

A. As distance from the park increases, the diversity index increases.
B. As distance from the park increases, the diversity index decreases.
C. As distance from the park decreases, the diversity index remains constant.
D. As distance from the park decreases, the diversity index decreases.

4

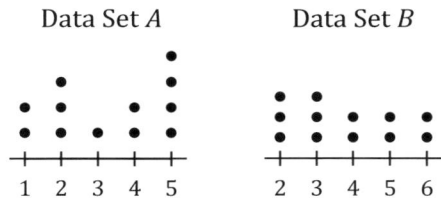

Based on the dot plots above, which of the following statements is true?

A. The least value in Data Set A is greater than the least value in Data Set B.
B. The greatest value in Data Set A is less than the greatest value in Data Set B.
C. The number of values in Data Set A is greater than the number of values in Data Set B.
D. The number of values in Data Set A is less than the number of values in Data Set B.

5

Number of Cups of Coffee and Tea Sold

	Coffee	Tea	Total
Small	127	29	156
Medium	165	42	207
Large	102	38	140
Total	394	109	503

The table above shows the number of small, medium, and large cups of coffee and tea were sold on Monday at a local café. Of all the cups of tea sold, what fraction were size medium?

A. $\dfrac{42}{503}$

B. $\dfrac{42}{109}$

C. $\dfrac{207}{503}$

D. $\dfrac{165}{394}$

6

The bar graph below shows the number of new hybrid, plug-in hybrid, and all-electric vehicles sold in the US between 2015 and 2020.

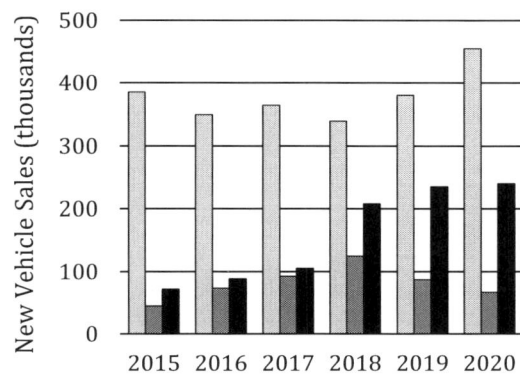

The number of new all-electric vehicles sold in 2019 was approximately twice the number of new plug-in hybrid cars sold in what year?

A. 2015
B. 2016
C. 2018
D. 2019

7

On forty separate days over a six-year period, an economist recorded the price of crude oil and the average retail price of gasoline in her state. The scatterplot below shows these data and a line of best fit.

PRICES OF CRUDE OIL AND GASOLINE

Consider the nine dates on which the crude oil price per barrel was more than $75 and less than $100. On how many of these dates was the actual gasoline price greater than the price predicted by the line of best fit?

Math: Problem Solving and Data Analysis

Practice Set 2: Medium-Hard

1

The table below gives the price per ride, in dollars, for 14 attractions at a local amusement park, as well as the number of rides taken by Lupe on a recent visit. The park also sells a Fun Pass for $43.95 that covers unlimited rides on all the attractions listed except those marked with an asterisk.

Attraction	Price ($)	Rides
Teacups	6.00	0
Carousel	6.00	0
Kiddie copters	6.00	0
Mini-coaster	6.00	0
Bumper boats	8.00	0
Rock wall*	6.00	0
Laser tag*	9.00	0
Mini-golf	8.00	0
Ropes course	8.00	0
Parachuter*	25.00	1
Super slide	6.00	0
Tilt-a-whirl	8.00	0
Roller coaster	8.00	2
Go-karts	8.00	2

* Not included in the Fun Pass

Lupe bought individual tickets for all her rides. If she had bought the Fun Pass (plus individual tickets for any of her rides not included in that pass), how much more money or less money would she have spent?

A. She would have spent $13.05 less.
B. She would have spent $11.95 less.
C. She would have spent $11.95 more.
D. She would have spent $13.05 more.

2

The figure below shows the average US retail price of gasoline in June of each of the years from 1993 to 2021.

During which of the following three-year periods was the average rate of change of the retail price of gasoline the least?

A. 1993-1996
B. 1997-2000
C. 2003-2006
D. 2014-2017

3

The graph below gives the national minimum wage in the US, in dollars per hour, between 1930 and 2000.

Assuming that a similar trend continued, which of the following was most likely the national minimum wage in the US in 2010?

A. $2.90 per hour
B. $5.00 per hour
C. $5.75 per hour
D. $8.00 per hour

4

At a carnival, a game was played in which each player scored a whole number of points between 0 and 50, inclusive. The scores of 22 players are displayed in the bar graph below. Each bar represents a group of players whose scores fell within a ten-point range: for example, the leftmost bar indicates that there were 4 players who each scored 0-10 points.

Which of the following could be the total number of players who scored fewer than 25 points?

A. 4
B. 5
C. 7
D. 11

5

The stem-and-leaf plot below gives the ages of 20 participants in a telephone survey.

Stem	Leaf
2	6 6 7
3	1 5 9 9 9
4	0 3 4 8
5	1 2 5 7
6	0
7	2 3 3

Key: 5 | 1 = 51 years

The oldest participant was how many years older than the youngest participant?

A. 35
B. 46
C. 47
D. 51

6

The scatterplot shows the relationship between two variables, x and y.

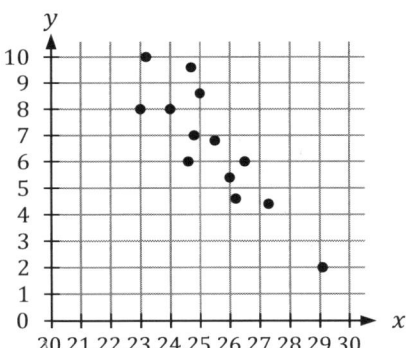

Which of the following equations is the most appropriate linear model for the data shown in the scatterplot?

A. $y = 45 - 1.5x$
B. $y = 18 + 3x$
C. $y = 18 - 3x$
D. $y = 45 + 1.5x$

7

As part of an experiment, a group of five students was asked to estimate each other's heights in feet (ft) and inches (in). For each student, the average (arithmetic mean) of the other students' estimates was recorded in the table below as the student's "estimated height"; the table also gives each student's actual height.

Student	Estimated height	Actual height
A	5 ft, 6 in	5 ft, 7 in
B	6 ft, 1 in	6 ft
C	5 ft, 9 in	5 ft, 10 in
D	5 ft, 4 in	5 ft, 2 in
E	6 ft, 3 in	6 ft, 1 in

The actual height of the tallest student was how many inches greater than the lowest estimated height?

(Note: 12 inches = 1 foot)

Math: Problem Solving and Data Analysis

Ratios, Proportions, and Unit Conversions

Preview Quiz:

Solve each of the following.

1) On a certain map, 2 inches represents 30 miles. How long would a distance of 450 miles appear on this map?

$$\frac{2}{30} = \frac{x}{450} \qquad 30\text{ in}$$

2) Desiree's swimming pool contains 20,800 gallons of water. If one liter is equivalent to approximately 0.26 gallons, how many liters of water are in the pool?

$$\frac{1\text{ li}}{.26\text{ g}} = \frac{?\text{ li}}{20,800} \qquad 80,000 \text{ liters}$$

3) Alicia jogs the same route every morning at an average rate of 5.1 miles per hour. If it takes her 25 minutes to complete her jog, how long is her jogging route, in meters?
(Note: 1 mile equals approximately 1.6 kilometers.)

$$\frac{5.1\text{ miles}}{1} \cdot \frac{1.6\text{ km}}{1\text{ miles}} = 8.16\text{ km per hour} \cdot \frac{1}{60} \cdot 25 = 3.4 \text{ km} = 3,400\text{ m}$$

KM v. CM

4) An area of 1350 square meters is equivalent to an area of how many square kilometers?

$$1,350\text{ m}^2 \cdot \frac{1\text{ km}}{1000\text{ m}} \cdot \frac{1\text{ km}}{1000\text{ m}} = .00135\text{ km}^2$$

5) If $2x = 3y$, what is the ratio of x to y?
(Hint: the answer is not 2 to 3.)

$$\frac{2x}{2} = \frac{3y}{2}$$

$$x = \frac{3}{2}y \;\; / y$$

$$\frac{x}{y} = \frac{3}{2}$$

- 380 -

TM and © 2023 PrepMatters, Inc. All rights reserved.

Ratios, Proportions, and Unit Conversions

A **ratio** is defined as the size or number of one thing in relation to another. Ratios can simply be thought of as fractions: If a and b are in a ratio of 2:3, then the fraction $\frac{a}{b}$ is equivalent to the fraction $\frac{2}{3}$. So if $a = 2$, then $b = 3$; if $a = 4$, then $b = 6$; and so on.

The simplest ratio problems will set two ratios equal to each other (forming a **proportion**) and ask you to plug in the appropriate number.

Example: *On a certain map, 2 inches represents 30 miles. How long would a distance of 450 miles appear on this map?*

$$\frac{2}{30} = \frac{x}{450}$$

To make sure everything's in the right place, read your proportion back to yourself like an analogy. For example, we could read this one as "2 inches is to 30 miles as x inches is to 450 miles." Yep, that makes sense. Now just cross-multiply to solve:

$$900 = 30x$$

$$x = \mathbf{30\ inches}$$

TIP: For a review of cross-multiplying, see p. 251.

Try It

1) If the wholesale price for 15 pounds of coffee is $28.50, what is the wholesale price, in dollars, for 24 pounds of coffee?

 $47.6

2) A rectangular photograph with a width of 4 inches and a height of 6 inches will be placed into a frame with a width of 7 inches. If the frame and the photograph are similar rectangles (their side lengths are proportional), what is the height of the frame, in inches?

 10.5 in

Math: Problem Solving and Data Analysis

The SAT loves to test you on **unit conversions**. For straightforward problems in which only one unit is changing, you might choose to use a simple proportion.

Example: *Desiree's swimming pool contains 20,800 gallons of water. If one liter is equivalent to approximately 0.26 gallons, how many liters of water are in the pool?*

$$\frac{1}{0.26} = \frac{x}{20{,}800}$$

$$20{,}800 = 0.26x$$

$$x = 80{,}000 \text{ liters}$$

For more complicated problems, though, the best approach is one you likely learned in chemistry class: set up a series of fractions so that all the extra units cancel out, and then multiply straight across.

Example: *Alicia jogs the same route every morning at an average rate of 5.1 miles per hour. If it takes her 25 minutes to complete her jog, how long is her jogging route, in <u>meters</u>? (Note: 1 mile equals approximately 1.6 <u>kilometers</u>.)*

$$\frac{25 \text{ min}}{1} \times \frac{1 \text{ hr}}{60 \text{ min}} \times \frac{5.1 \text{ mi}}{1 \text{ hr}} \times \frac{1.6 \text{ km}}{1 \text{ mi}} \times \frac{1000 \text{ m}}{1 \text{ km}}$$

$$= \frac{(25 \text{ min})(1 \text{ hr})(5.1 \text{ mi})(1.6 \text{ km})(1000 \text{ m})}{(1)(60 \text{ min})(1 \text{ hr})(1 \text{ mi})(1 \text{ km})}$$

$$= \frac{25(5.1)(1.6)(1000)}{60} \text{ m}$$

$$= 3400 \text{ meters}$$

TIP:
The test may expect you to know the basic metric system conversions (e.g., there are 1000 grams in one kilogram; there are 100 centimeters in one meter) and a few other very easy conversion rates (e.g., there are 60 seconds in one minute). If any other conversions are necessary for a problem, the conversion rates will be given (e.g., there are 5280 feet in one mile).

Try It

3) At a local gourmet store, saffron sells for $1.71 per gram. At this rate, what is the price, in dollars, for three two-ounce tins of saffron? (Note: 1 ounce = 28 grams)   *Pay attention*

$1.71(28) = 47.88 (2) = 95.76 (3)
(2-ounce tin)
= $287.28

Ratios, Proportions, and Unit Conversions

Be sure to carefully match up your units! If the units have different exponents, you have to keep multiplying those fractions enough times to cancel them all out. In other words, just because 1 foot equals 12 inches, that doesn't mean that 1 *square* foot equals 12 *square* inches.

Example: *An area of 1350 square meters is equivalent to an area of how many square kilometers?*

$$\frac{1350 \text{ m}^2}{1} \times \frac{1 \text{ km}}{1000 \text{ m}} \times \frac{1 \text{ km}}{1000 \text{ m}} = \frac{1350 \text{ km}^2}{(1000)(1000)} = \mathbf{0.00135 \text{ km}^2}$$

CHALLENGE:

If $2x = 3y$, what is the ratio of x to y?

Careful: the answer is <u>not</u> 2 to 3. Remember, the ratio we're looking for is the value of x/y. So, let's try working that out algebraically.

$$2x = 3y$$

First, divide both sides by 2:

$$x = \frac{3y}{2}$$

Next, we need to divide both sides by y. (If it's easier, you can think of this step as *multiplying* both sides by $1/y$). That gives us this:

$$\frac{x}{y} = \frac{3}{2}$$

So the ratio of x to y is backwards from what we first expected: it's **3 to 2**.

Another way to solve this problem would be to make up a value for one of the variables and plug it into the original equation. Let's say we decided to use $y = 6$:

$$2x = 3y$$
$$2x = 3(6)$$
$$2x = 18$$
$$x = 9$$
$$\text{ratio of } x \text{ to } y = \frac{9}{6} = \frac{3}{2}$$

Math: Problem Solving and Data Analysis

If there are multiple ratios in a problem, the best way to solve it may be to use substitution (plug in your own numbers).

Example: *If the ratio of a to b is 3:5 and the ratio of b to c is 3:7, what is the ratio of a to c?*

First, rewrite the ratios as fractions.

$$\frac{a}{b} = \frac{3}{5} \quad \text{and} \quad \frac{b}{c} = \frac{3}{7}$$

What makes this problem hard is the fact that b is a different number in the two equations: it's 5 in the first one and 3 in the other one. So, we plug in a new number for b so that it can be the same value in both fractions. Let's try $b = 15$:

$$\frac{a}{b} = \frac{3}{5} = \frac{9}{15} \quad \text{and} \quad \frac{b}{c} = \frac{3}{7} = \frac{15}{35}$$

This tells us that if $b = 15$, then $a = 9$ and $c = 35$. Therefore, the ratio of a to c is **9 to 35**.

TIP: To plug in numbers, start with the letter the two equations have in common. In this case, that's b.

Try It

4) If the ratio of x to y is 3 to 4 and the ratio of x to z is 4 to 5, what is the ratio of y to z?

[Student work shown:]

$\frac{x}{y} = \frac{3}{4}$ $\frac{x}{z} = \frac{4}{5}$ $\frac{y}{z} = ?$

$x = \frac{3}{4}y$ $x = \frac{4}{5}z$

$(20) \cdot \frac{3}{4}y = \frac{4}{5}z \cdot (20)$

$15y = 16z$

$4z = 5(3...)$

CHALLENGE:

If you're given a ratio of two variables and the value of their sum, you may want to use algebra to solve. For example, when two numbers in ratio 2:3 add up to 20, we can say that $2x + 3x = 20$.

Example: *At a zoo, the ratio of male reptiles to female reptiles is 3:5. There are 120 reptiles. How many male reptiles are there?*

We can't just use a proportion for this because the 120 doesn't match either category: it's not the number of male reptiles and it's not the number of female reptiles. So what do we do? Well, let's consider the possibilities. Based on the ratio, there could be exactly 3 males and 5 females (for a total of 8), or there could be exactly 6 males and 10 females (for a total of 16), and so on. Looking at that another way, there could be 3(1) males and 5(1) females, or there could be 3(2) males and 5(2) females, and so on. In other words, the number of males will be 3 times *something*, and the number of females will be 5 times *that same thing*. And we also know that the males and females have to add up to 120. We can represent that algebraically by doing this:

$$\text{\# of males} = 3x$$
$$\text{\# of females} = 5x$$

$$3x + 5x = 120$$
$$8x = 120$$
$$x = 15$$

$$\text{\# of males} = 3x = 3(15) = \mathbf{45}$$

Another way to handle this problem is to change up the relevant ratio. If hadn't been told that there are 120 total reptiles, what's the smallest total we might have? As we saw, it's eight: that's 3 males and 5 females. That means that out of every 8 reptiles, 3 of them are males. Therefore, while the ratio of males to *females* is 3 to 5, the ratio of males to *total reptiles* is 3 to 8. And now we can do a proportion!

$$\frac{3}{8} = \frac{x}{120}$$

$$x = \frac{3}{8}(120) = \mathbf{45}$$

Chapter Answer Key

Try It
1) $45.60
2) 10.5 inches
3) $287.28
4) 16:15

Ratios, Proportions, and Unit Conversions

Practice Set 1: Easy-Medium

1

Of the last 32 emails Joe received, 15 were spam. What is the ratio of non-spam emails to spam emails?

A. 15:32
B. 17:32
C. 15:17
D. 17:15

2

At a bake sale, the ratio of the number of cookies sold to the number of brownies sold is 3 to 4. If 24 brownies were sold at the bake sale, how many cookies were sold?

3

A mass of 0.28 kilograms is equivalent to a mass of how many grams?

(Note: 1 kilogram = 1000 grams)

4

A gardener needs to buy enough mulch to cover 6 cubic feet of her lawn. If 50 pounds of mulch can cover $2\frac{1}{2}$ cubic feet, how many pounds of mulch does the gardener need to buy?

A. 90
B. 100
C. 120
D. 130

5

In the line segment shown below, the ratio of the length of $\overline{FG}$ to the length of $\overline{GH}$ is 2:5.

What is the ratio of the length of $\overline{GH}$ to the length of $\overline{FH}$?

A. 2:7
B. 3:5
C. 2:3
D. 5:7

6

In a recent survey, residents of counties A, B, C, and D were asked whether they plan to vote in an upcoming mayoral election. The numbers of "Yes" and "No" responses for each county are shown in the table below.

County	Yes	No	Total
A	25	92	117
B	78	61	139
C	45	18	63
D	51	24	75
Total	235	232	467

Based on the data in the table, in which county was the ratio of "Yes" responses to "No" responses the *greatest*?

A. A
B. B
C. C
D. D

7

At a bookstore, 30% of the books are currently on sale. What is the ratio of the number of books that are currently on sale to the total number of books at the bookstore?

A. 3:10
B. 3:7
C. 3:5
D. 7:3

Math: Problem Solving and Data Analysis

8. Bob will drive a distance of 180 miles at an average speed of 45 miles per hour. What is the total amount of time required for the journey, in *minutes*?

A. 60
B. 120
C. 180
D. 240

9. Yesterday, a university dining hall served 540 students, 36 of whom requested a vegetarian meal. At 1:00 yesterday, the study group for a physics class decided to take a lunch break and eat together at the dining hall. If all 15 students in the study group were served in the dining hall, and if the study group was a representative sample of all 540 students served at the dining hall that day, what is the most likely number of students in the study group who did NOT request a vegetarian meal?

A. 12
B. 14
C. 16
D. 18

10. On a recent Saturday, three friends split a "party sub" sandwich by cutting it into portions of unequal lengths. The lengths of the portions were in the ratio 1:2:3. If the original sandwich was 18 inches long, what was the length, in inches, of the largest portion?

11. In a garden, the ratio of azalea bushes to tulips is 2 to 5, and the ratio of tulips to marigolds is 5 to 8. If there are 24 marigolds in the garden, how many azalea bushes are there?

12. At Cirrus Tech, 3 out of every 5 employees are part-time, and 3 out of every 4 part-time employees work fewer than twenty hours per week. What fraction of Cirrus Tech employees are part-time employees who work fewer than twenty hours per week?

A. $\dfrac{3}{20}$
B. $\dfrac{9}{20}$
C. $\dfrac{7}{10}$
D. $\dfrac{4}{5}$

13. The ratio of the length of a rectangle, in inches, to the width of the rectangle, in feet, is 18 to 1. If the length of the rectangle is 3 <u>feet</u>, what is its width, in feet?

A. 1 foot
B. 1.5 feet
C. 2 feet
D. 3.6 feet

Ratios, Proportions, and Unit Conversions

*Can cross multiply during proportions!

Practice Set 2: Medium-Hard

1

The ratio of x to 6 is the same as the ratio y to 10. What is the value of $\frac{x}{y}$?

2

In a bag of marbles, the ratio of red to green to blue marbles is 1:3:4. Which of the following could be the number of marbles in the bag?

A. 18
B. 24
C. 26
D. 36

3

Tim makes hot chocolate by combining 14 tablespoons of hot chocolate mix with 5 cups of milk. If this makes enough hot chocolate for 6 people, how many tablespoons of hot chocolate mix will Tim need to make enough hot chocolate for 21 people?

A. 9
B. 20
C. 36
D. 49

4

If $2x = 3y$ and $2y = 3z$, then what is the ratio of x to z?

A. 2:1
B. 2:3
C. 9:4
D. 4:9

5

Based on measurements made as part of an experiment for his physics class, Algernon determined the speed of sound to be 343 meters per second. Assuming this value to be correct, which of the following is closest to the speed of sound in miles per hour?

(Note: 1 meter = 0.001 kilometer, and 1 kilometer is equivalent to approximately 0.62 miles.)

A. 13
B. 128
C. 500
D. 766

6

Three legal partners are dividing $7,500 in a 4:5:6 ratio. How much more, in dollars, does the partner with the largest share make than the partner with the smallest share?

7

The ratio of sugar to flour in a recipe is 5:2. If the amount of sugar is decreased by 30% and the amount of flour is increased by 25%, what is the new ratio of sugar to flour?

A. 1:4
B. 7:5
C. 7:3
D. 3:1

8

A saline solution is made up of 1.5 cups of salt and 5 cups of water. How many cups of water must be added so that the solution is 94% water?

9

After winning a grand prize of $60,000, Jim decides to save four times as much money as he will spend. How much money will Jim save?

A. $12,000
B. $24,000
C. $45,000
D. $48,000

10

The "escape velocity" of a planet is the minimum speed needed for an object launched from its surface to continue traveling away from the planet rather than either orbiting it or falling back down to its surface. The escape velocity from Earth's surface is about 11,186 meters per second. Which of the following is closest to is the escape velocity from Earth's surface in *miles per hour*?

(Note: 1000 meters = 1 kilometer; 1 mile = 1.609 kilometers.)

A. 417
B. 25,028
C. 40,270
D. 64,794

11

The length and width of a rectangle are in ratio 3:5. If the area of the rectangle is 135, what is the perimeter?

A. 24
B. 36
C. 48
D. 72

12

A library has 3 times as many fiction books as non-fiction books. If $\frac{1}{5}$ of all non-fiction books are biographies, what is the ratio of fiction books to biographies in this library?

A. 15:1
B. 5:3
C. 3:5
D. 1:15

13

A poll of a website's weekly visitors indicated the following data about the visitors' ages:

Age group	# of visitors
under 18	427
18-25	3,264
26-35	5,881
36-49	4,916
50-65	1,103
66 and older	812
Total	16,403

If this information was presented in a circle graph (pie chart), the degree measure for the sector representing the age group 36-49 would be closest to which of the following?

A. 30°
B. 54°
C. 72°
D. 108°

Percentages

Preview Quiz:

Solve each of the following.

1) What is 20% of 30? ____6____

2) 24 is what percent of 60? ____40%____

3) 18 is 15% of what number? ____120____

4) What price is 10% less than $80? ____72____

5) 26 is 30% more than what number? ____20____

6) 51 is what percent less than 60? ____15%____

7) 50 is what percent greater than 40? ____25%____

Both **percentages** and ratios deal with relationships between numbers. In fact, one way to solve percent problems is to think of a percentage as just another kind of ratio.

For "percent of" problems, the ratio is *part* to *whole* (or "is" to "of").

$$\frac{is}{of} = \frac{\%}{100}$$

Examples:

What is 20% of 30?

$$\frac{x}{30} = \frac{20}{100}$$
$$100x = 20(30)$$
$$x = \mathbf{6}$$

24 is what percent of 60?

$$\frac{24}{60} = \frac{x}{100}$$
$$24(100) = 60x$$
$$x = \mathbf{40}$$

18 is 15% of what number?

$$\frac{18}{x} = \frac{15}{100}$$
$$18(100) = 15x$$
$$x = \mathbf{120}$$

Another way to approach percentage problems is through word-for-word translation.

is	=
of	*
percent	$\frac{}{100}$
"what" or "what number"	x

TIP:

In the built-in calculator, you can simply type the % symbol.

Examples:

What is 20% of 30?

$$x = \frac{20}{100} * 30$$

or write this as 0.2(30)

24 is what percent of 60?

$$24 = \frac{x}{100} * 60$$

18 is 15% of what number?

$$18 = \frac{15}{100} * x$$

or write this as 0.15x

These two approaches are equally valid. Use whichever one makes the most sense to you.

Try It   Solve each of the following (using either approach).

1) What is 18% of 50?

9

2) Ten is what percent of 80?

12.5

3) Thirty is 40% of what number?

75

Some percentage problems deal with the percent by which something has **changed.** For example, consider the question "What is 70% less than 200?" Here, it's not that the problem is asking us to find 70% *of* 200—it's asking us to find what the result is when 200 is *reduced* by that value.

To increase or decrease a number by p percent, you find $p\%$ of the number and then either add that to or subtract it from the original. In other words:

$$\text{Original} \pm \text{Percent}(\text{Original}) = \text{Final}$$

Examples: *What price is 10% less than $80?*

$80 - 0.10(80) = x$
$80 - 8 = x$
$x = \$72$

26 is 30% more than what number?

$x + 0.30(x) = 26$
$x + 0.3x = 26$
$1.3x = 26$
$x = \mathbf{20}$

TIP:

The "Original" is the value after the word "than" in the problem.

TIP:

Percent increases and decreases, step by step:

1. Write the percent value as a decimal.

    25% → 0.25

2. For "percent more than," *add* that decimal value to 1; for "percent less than," *subtract* it from 1.

    "25% more than"   "25% less than"
    = 1.25   = 0.75

3. Multiply the result by the original number.

    "25% more than 40"   "25% less than 40"
    1.25(40)   0.75(40)
    = 50   = 30

Try It   Solve each of the following.

4) What is 20% more than 50?

5) If 34 is 15% less than x, what is x?

Math: Problem Solving and Data Analysis

You can also use the Original & Final formula for problems in which the percent is unknown.

Examples:

51 is what percent less than 60?

$60 - x(60) = 51$
$60x = 9$
$x = 0.15 = \mathbf{15\%}$

50 is what percent greater than 40?

$40 + x(40) = 50$
$40x = 10$
$x = 0.25 = \mathbf{25\%}$

CHALLENGE:

For a shortcut for the percent change problems in which the percent is unknown, you can use a ratio approach. This time, instead of *is* to *of*, set up your ratio as *amount of change* to the *base* (the number after the word "than").

Examples: 40 is what percent less than 64?

$$\frac{64-40}{64} = \frac{x}{100}$$
$x = \mathbf{37.5\%}$

50 is what percent greater than 40?

$$\frac{50-40}{40} = \frac{x}{100}$$
$x = \mathbf{25\%}$

For scenarios involving time, you can think of this as $\frac{|\text{new} - \text{old}|}{\text{old}}$.

Try It

6) A company had $800 in sales last year and $900 in sales this year. By what percent did sales increase?

$\frac{900-800}{800} \quad \frac{100}{800} = \frac{x}{100}$

$.125 = \frac{x}{100}$

$x = 12.5\%$

TIP:

Many percent change problems are great for **back-solving**.

Chapter Answer Key

Try It	1)	9
	2)	12.5%
	3)	75
	4)	60
	5)	40
	6)	12.5%

FROM THE BLOG

The literature on sleep deprivation is pretty darned stark: nearly everything one can measure from verbal retrieval to emotional control to blood pressure can be roughed up by sleep deprivation. Even worse, self-analysis suffers too. In one study, researchers found that their sleep-deprived subjects thought they had done great on the tasks they'd been given, when in fact their performance had tanked. They simply didn't realize it – their self-analysis was way off.

I encourage you to file that nugget away. If you were surprised by a test score that came back lower than you expected, it may be that on that test, it was your post-test assessment that missed the mark. Doing better next time may involve nothing more than taking the test again after you've caught a few more Z's.

Math: Problem Solving and Data Analysis

Practice Set 1: Easy-Medium

1
What is 30% of 15?

2
What is 0.4% of 800?
A. 3.2
B. 32
C. 320
D. 3,200

3
Fifteen is what percent of twenty?
A. 3%
B. 25%
C. 75%
D. 80%

4
Forty percent of what number is 24?

5
If 150% of x is 24, what is the value of x?
A. 16
B. 18
C. 20
D. 36

6
What number is 30% more than 40?
A. 43
B. 52
C. 64
D. 68

7
What number is 44% less than 60?
A. 16
B. 26.4
C. 33.6
D. 48

8
$36.00 is 120% of what price?
A. $22.00
B. $26.10
C. $30.00
D. $43.20

9
15 is what percent less than 20?
A. 25%
B. 30%
C. $33\frac{1}{3}\%$
D. 75%

10
20 is what percent greater than 15?
A. 25%
B. 30%
C. $33\frac{1}{3}\%$
D. 75%

Percentages

11

If a price is $36 after a 25% discount, what was the price before the discount?

A. $45
B. $48
C. $52
D. $60

12

14 is 30% less than which of the following numbers?

A. 18.2
B. 20
C. 23.8
D. 26.4

13

If 70% of x is 42, what is 30% of x?

A. 3
B. 6
C. 12
D. 18

14

Of the 60 problems on a math test, a student answered 12 of the problems incorrectly and the rest correctly. If the student answered p% of the problems correctly, what is the value of p?

15

When 25% of x is rounded to the nearest whole number, the result is 55. Which of the following could be the value of x?

A. 215
B. 221
C. 222
D. 223.5

16

On Wednesday, 160 students took a standardized test consisting of multiple-choice questions with five possible responses (A, B, C, D, and E). The table below shows the distribution of responses for the first two questions on the test.

Choice	#1	#2	Total
A	12	117	129
B	10	5	15
C	125	9	134
D	6	3	9
E	7	26	33
Total	160	160	320

Out of all the responses recorded for the first two questions, approximately what percent of the answers were C?

A. 39%
B. 42%
C. 50%
D. 78%

17

The length of a circle's radius, in inches, is approximately what percent of the circle's circumference, in inches?

(Note: the circumference C of a circle with radius r is equal to $C = 2\pi r$).

A. 1.57%
B. 15.9%
C. 31.8%
D. It cannot be determined from the given information.

18

If Leslie has 20% more books than she had last week and she currently has 150 books, how many books did Leslie have last week?

A. 75
B. 120
C. 125
D. 200

Math: Problem Solving and Data Analysis

Practice Set 2: Medium-Hard

1. Mike has 20 red shirts and 30 black shirts. 15% of the red shirts and 30% of the black shirts are striped. If p percent of all of Mike's shirts are striped, what is the value of p?

2. Daniel works as a waiter. He earns $3 an hour plus a 15% tip on all the food he sells. If he earns $45 in 6 hours, how many dollars' worth of food did he sell?

A. 180
B. 200
C. 280
D. 300

3. Kieran purchased several items at a wholesale price, then sold them all for $102.87. This amount was 35% greater than the wholesale price he paid for the items. What was the wholesale price?

A. $66.87
B. $76.20
C. $83.48
D. $183.87

4. What is 0.06% of $\frac{4}{5}$ of 3.2×10^5?

5. Ezekiel received some money for his birthday and decided to use part of it to buy a new pair of headphones. At the store, he handed 60% of his birthday money to the cashier and received $1.80 in change. If the change he received was 6% of the total amount of money he had handed to the cashier, how much money did Ezekiel receive for his birthday?

A. $30
B. $40
C. $50
D. $60

6. A leather jacket is sold at a 40% discount. After a 5% sales tax, the total price is $176.40. To the nearest dollar, what was the original pre-tax price of the jacket?

A. $120
B. $238
C. $280
D. $392

7. On Monday, a store received a delivery of b bushels of apples. The store sold 20% of the bushels on Monday and 20% of the remaining bushels on Tuesday. Which of the following represents the number of bushels from the delivery that were sold on Tuesday?

A. $0.2b$
B. $0.2(0.2b)$
C. $0.2(0.8b)$
D. $b - 0.2b$

Mean, Median, and Mode

Preview Quiz:

Define each term:

1) mean: _____

2) median _____

3) mode _____

4) range _____

Fill in the blank:

5) The standard deviation is a measure of _____
_____

Solve:

6) What is the average (arithmetic mean) of 4, 9, and 5?

7) What is the median of the set {5, 1, 9, −7, 2}?

8) What is the median of the set {10, 2, 1, 4, 8, −3}?

9) What is the mode of the set {1, 3, 4, 4, 10}?

10) What is the range of the set {1, 3, 4, 4, 10}?

11) A squad of 5 soldiers has an average weight of 182 pounds. After a sixth soldier joins the squad, the new average weight is 179 pounds. How much does the sixth soldier weigh?

Math: Problem Solving and Data Analysis

To find the **mean** of a set of numbers, add them up and divide by how many numbers there are. The result, commonly called the **average**, is technically the **arithmetic mean**.

Example: What is the average (arithmetic mean) of 4, 9, and 5?

$$\text{mean} = \frac{4+9+5}{3} = \frac{18}{3} = \mathbf{6}$$

The **median** is the center of the data. To find it, first put the numbers in order from smallest to largest, and then cross off the numbers from both ends. If the set had an odd number of values, the median is the number left standing in the middle. If the set had an even number of values, there will be two numbers left in the middle; the median is the average (the arithmetic mean) of those two.

Example: What is the median of the set $\{5, 1, 9, -7, 2\}$?

$\{-\cancel{7}, \cancel{1}, 2, \cancel{5}, \cancel{9}\}$: The median is **2**.

Example: What is the median of the set $\{10, 2, 1, 4, 8, -3\}$?

$\{-\cancel{3}, \cancel{1}, 2, 4, \cancel{8}, \cancel{10}\}$: $\text{median} = \dfrac{2+4}{2} = \mathbf{3}$

TIP: Remember to put the terms in order first!

However, because of the SAT's built-in calculator, you'll rarely need to actually calculate the mean or median in this way. Just type in the word `mean` or `median`, and then follow that command with the list of numbers in parentheses:

1. mean(4, 9, 5) = 6

2. median(5, 1, 9, −7, 2) = 2

Mean, Median, and Mode

The **mode** is the number that repeats the most.

*Example: In the set {1, 3, 4, 4, 10}, the mode is **4**.*

To find the **range** of a data set, just subtract the smallest value from the biggest value.

*Example: In the set {1, 3, 4, 4, 10}, the range is $10 - 1 = $ **9**.*

Try It   A class of 9 students received the following scores on a recent exam:

82, 77, 65, 92, 97, 93, 82, 88, and 71

1) What is the mean of the scores?

2) What is the median?

3) What is the mode?

4) What is the range?

Math: Problem Solving and Data Analysis

The SAT loves to trick you by taking a topic that you are very familiar with and asking you "backward" questions. For example, instead of giving you the sum of a group of numbers and asking you to solve for the average, they will generally give you the average and ask you to solve for the sum. When in doubt, just keep coming back to the same equation:

$$\text{mean} = \frac{\text{sum}}{\#}$$

Example: A squad of 5 soldiers has an average weight of 182 pounds. After a sixth soldier joins the squad, the new average weight is 179 pounds. How much does the sixth soldier weigh?

First, let's tackle the 182. Write out the mean equation and plug in what you know.

$$\text{First five soldiers: } 182 = \frac{\text{sum}}{5} \rightarrow \text{sum} = 182(5) = 910$$

The problem then gives us another mean: 179. So we write out the equation again:

$$\text{All six soldiers: } 179 = \frac{\text{sum}}{6} \rightarrow \text{sum} = 179(6) = 1{,}074$$

So the total weight of the squad is 1,074 pounds, and the weights of the first five soldiers added up to 910 pounds. Therefore, the weight of that last soldier must be $1074 - 910 =$ **164 pounds**.

Try It

5) The average budget for the last ten weddings held at the Astor Ballroom was $25,000. If the most recent wedding is excluded from the list, the average budget for the remaining nine weddings is $23,500. What was the budget for the most recent wedding?

TIP:

You can rearrange the formula for mean to make a handy acronym: **S**(um) = **A**(verage) * **T**(hings)

You may be asked to find the mean, median, mode, or range based on a **frequency distribution**. Remember this example from p. 370?

To find the mean, first multiply each value by its frequency and add up all those products: this gives you the sum of all the values. Next, add up all the frequencies: this gives you the total number of values in the set. Finally, divide the first sum by the second one.

$$\text{mean} = \frac{1(3) + 2(5) + 3(6) + 4(6) + 5(3)}{3 + 5 + 6 + 6 + 3} = \frac{70}{23}$$

To find the median, first consider how many values there are (add up all the frequencies). In this case, there are 23 values, so what's the term in the middle? Well, $23/2 = 11.5$, so the median is the 12th term (since that leaves 11 terms before it and 11 terms after it). Now look at the figure. There are a total of 8 terms in the first two bars, so that's not enough to get us to the median. But if we add in the third bar, we have a total of 14 terms. Therefore, the median is in that third bar: the median of this set is **3**.

TIP:

To find the median of an odd number of terms, divide the number of terms by 2 and round up. For example, say there are 47 terms. Since $47/2 = 23.5$, the median is the 24th term.

Try It Fifty families were asked how many television sets they had in their homes. The responses are shown in the table below.

Number of TVs	Frequency
0	5
1	11
2	15
3	12
4	6
5	1

6) What is the average (arithmetic mean) number of TVs per family?

7) What is the median number of TVs per family?

CHALLENGE:

The **standard deviation** is a measure of how spread out a set of data is from the mean. The size of the numbers doesn't matter—all that matters is how far away they are, on average, from the mean of the set.

Example: Set A = {1, 5, 20}   Set B = {100, 101, 102}

The numbers in Set B are larger, but they're more closely grouped around the mean, so **Set A has the greater standard deviation**.

Example 2: Set C = {20, 20, 80, 80}   Set D = {30, 50, 70}

Here, both sets have the same mean (50), and set C has some repeating terms, while set D doesn't. None of that matters. In set C, the terms are all 30 away from the mean, while the terms in D are all closer than that. It's the spread from the mean that matters, not the distance from the other terms. **Set C's standard deviation is greater**.

Try It   8) If Set E = {2, 9, 10} and Set F = {10, 11, 12}, which set has the greater standard deviation?

TIP:

In the built-in calculator, use the command `stddev()` to find the standard deviation.

Mean, Median, and Mode

Chapter Answer Key

Try It		
	1)	83
	2)	82
	3)	82
	4)	32
	5)	$38,500
	6)	2.12
	7)	2
	8)	Set E

Math: Problem Solving and Data Analysis

Practice Set 1: Easy-Medium

1

A group of friends recently contributed to a food drive. Youssef and Brian each donated 4 cans of food, Sal donated 8 cans of food, and Alysha and Lou each donated 7 cans of food. For these five friends, what was the average number of cans of food donated per person?

A. 5
B. 6
C. 7
D. 8

2

What is the positive difference between the median and the mean of the list of numbers below?

3, 17, 5, 2, 7, 7, 1

A. 1
B. 2
C. 3
D. 4

3

Jamal has an average test score of 92. What is the sum of his test scores if he has taken 5 tests?

4

The mean age of 10 infants in a research study is 8.6 months. If infant A were withdrawn from the study, the new mean of the remaining 9 infants would be 9 months. What is infant A's age, in months?

A. 4
B. 5
C. 6
D. 7

5

The table below lists the number of members of Reilly High's men's and women's swim teams who are 15, 16, 17, or 18 years old. No one on either team is below 15 or over 18 years of age.

Age	Men's Team: # of members	Women's Team: # of members
15	4	2
16	4	4
17	10	8
18	6	5

What is the average (arithmetic mean) age of the men's team?

6

If the 10 and 11 in the list below were replaced with 9 and 9, which of the following would increase?

8, 6, 9, 8, 7, 10, 11

A. the mean of the list
B. the median of the list
C. the mode of the list
D. the range of the list

7

If the average (arithmetic mean) of x, $x + 1$, and $2x - 5$ is 12, then what is the median of these three integers?

A. 10
B. 11
C. 12
D. 15

Practice Set 2: Medium-Hard

1

Ben has two brothers: a younger brother, Roger, and an older brother, Howard. Roger is three years younger than Ben. The range of the three siblings' ages, in years, is 5. If Howard is 15 years old, how old is Ben?

A. 10
B. 11
C. 12
D. 13

2

If Maya averages 0.6 goals per game during the first 10 games of the season, how many goals does she need to score in the 11th game in order to raise her average to 1 goal per game?

3

In a charity walkathon, 100 athletes each walked 1, 2, 3, 4, or 5 miles, as shown in the table below.

Miles Walked	Number of Athletes
1	10
2	13
3	18
4	35
5	24

If a represents the median number of miles walked and b represents the mode of miles walked, what is the value of $a - b$?

A. -1
B. 0
C. 1
D. 2

4

If $2z = 2x + 2y - 6$, then what is the average (arithmetic mean) of x and y?

A. $\dfrac{z+6}{2}$
B. $\dfrac{z+3}{2}$
C. $\dfrac{z+6}{3}$
D. $z + 3$

5

Sets A and B are defined as follows:
$$A = \{2, 3, 5, 8, 9\}$$
$$B = \{2, 2, 10, 10, 300\}$$

Which of the following statements about sets A and B is true?

A. The range of Set A is greater than the range of Set B.
B. Set A has exactly one mode.
C. The median of Set A is one half the median of Set B.
D. The standard deviation of Set A is equal to the standard deviation of Set B.

6

At a certain gymnastics competition, the contestants receive scores from a panel of seven judges. To determine a contestant's final score, the computer deletes the highest and lowest of the seven scores and calculates the average (arithmetic mean) of the remaining scores. Felicia received the following scores from the panel: 15.73, 16.21, 19.34, 15.82, 18.14, 19.40, and 15.99. What was Felicia's final score?

A. 16.87
B. 17.10
C. 17.23
D. 17.78

Math: Problem Solving and Data Analysis

7
Mrs. Johnson's 1st period class has 21 students with an average grade of 84. Her 2nd period class has 28 students with an average grade of 91. What is the average of both classes combined?

8
The average (arithmetic mean) of a list of integers is 53. Three of the integers are 12, 108, and 36. If the average of the remaining integers on the list is 54, what is the total number of integers on the list?

A. 4
B. 5
C. 6
D. 7

9
Which of the following lists of numbers has the smallest standard deviation?

A. 2, 4, 6, 8, 10
B. 4, 4, 50, 90, 90
C. 5, 6, 7, 8, 9
D. 10, 20, 30, 40, 100

10
The average (arithmetic mean) of a, b, and c is 12. If a is increased by 1, b is decreased by 4, and c remains unchanged, what will be the new average of a, b, and c?

A. 11
B. 12
C. 13
D. It cannot be determined.

11
If $x + y = z$ and $z = 6$, what is the average (arithmetic mean) of $x, y,$ and z?

12
Peng has 5 more marbles than Ali, Raj has twice as many marbles as Peng, and Kaimana has 16 fewer than triple the number of marbles that Raj has. If Kaimana has 26 marbles, then what is the average number of marbles per person for Ali, Peng, Raj, and Kaimana?

A. 12.25
B. 12.5
C. 13.25
D. 14

13
Data set A consists of 35 positive integers with a mean of 26.4. Data set B is created by adding 2 to each of the integers in data set A. Data set C is created by multiplying each of the integers in data set A by 2. Which of the following statements must be true?

A. The standard deviation of data set A is equal to the standard deviation of data set B.
B. The standard deviation of data set A is equal to the standard deviation of data set C.
C. The median of data set A is equal to the median of data set B.
D. The median of data set A is equal to the median of data set C.

Probability

Preview Quiz:

1) A box contains 32 oranges and tangerines. If Elsa picks a piece of fruit at random from the box, the probability that she will pick an orange is equal to $\frac{3}{4}$. How many oranges are in the box?

	Undergraduate students	Graduate students	Total
On campus	3562	184	3746
Off campus	986	671	1657
Total	4548	855	5403

2) The table above represents the number of undergraduate and graduate students in a particular program at Bethesda University and whether those students live on campus or off campus. What is the probability that a randomly chosen student who lives on campus is a graduate student?

3) If Adele flips a coin twice, what is the probability that the coin will land heads-up both times?

4) If Adele randomly selects two coins from a purse containing three quarters, three dimes, and three nickels, what is the probability that both of the coins she selects will be quarters?

Math: Problem Solving and Data Analysis

The **probability** of a single event happening is defined as the ratio $\frac{part}{whole}$, where the "part" is the number of favorable outcomes (i.e., outcomes that give you what you're seeking) and the "whole" is the total number of possible outcomes.

Example: A box contains 32 oranges and tangerines. If Elsa picks a piece of fruit at random from the box, the probability that she will pick an orange is equal to $\frac{3}{4}$. How many oranges are in the box?

$$\frac{\text{oranges}}{\text{total fruits}} = \frac{x}{32} = \frac{3}{4}$$

$$x = \frac{3}{4}(32) = \mathbf{24}$$

Be sure to **read carefully** so that the numbers in the problem end up in the right spots in the fraction.

Example: A toy bag contains 3 red marbles, 4 green marbles, 6 blue marbles, and 7 other toys. If an object is drawn at random from the bag, what is the probability that the object is a marble that is NOT green?

$$\frac{\text{non-green marbles}}{\text{total \# of items}} = \frac{3+6}{3+4+6+7} = \frac{\mathbf{9}}{\mathbf{20}}$$

Try It

1) What is the probability that a card drawn at random from a standard deck of 52 playing cards is a face card? (Note: a standard deck of playing cards contains a total of 12 face cards: 6 red and 6 black.)

2) What is the probability that a card drawn at random from a standard deck of 52 playing cards is a seven that is NOT black? (Note: a standard deck of playing cards contains a total of four sevens: two red and two black.)

Many probability problems on the SAT will be based on a table of data. For these, be very careful to line up which category is the "part" and which is the "whole" (it may not be the total represented by the entire table).

Example:

	Undergraduate students	Graduate students	Total
On campus	3562	184	3746
Off campus	986	671	1657
Total	4548	855	5403

The table above represents the number of undergraduate and graduate students in a particular program at Bethesda University and whether those students live on campus or off campus. What is the probability that a randomly chosen student who lives on campus is a graduate student?

$$\frac{\text{on-campus grad students}}{\text{all on-campus students}} = \frac{184}{3746} = 0.0491$$

TIP:
The word "given" indicates the *whole*. For example, the campus problem could have been rewritten this way: *If a student is chosen at random, what is the probability that she lives on campus, given that she is a graduate student?*

Try It   For the questions below, use the table shown in the example above.

3) What is the probability that a student chosen at random is an undergraduate student who lives off campus?

4) If an undergraduate student is chosen at random, what is the probability that he lives off campus?

(Hint: these two questions do <u>not</u> have the same answer.)

Some probability problems involve **multiple events**. Solve "and" problems by multiplying the individual probabilities of each of the events.

Example: If Adele flips a coin twice, what is the probability that the coin will land heads-up both times?

Probability of heads on 1st flip = $\frac{1}{2}$

Probability of heads on 2nd flip = $\frac{1}{2}$

$$\frac{1}{2} * \frac{1}{2} = \frac{1}{4}$$

Be sure to consider whether the outcomes of early events will affect the probabilities of the later events.

Example: If Adele randomly selects two coins from a purse containing three quarters, three dimes, and three nickels, what is the probability that both of the coins she selects will be quarters?

The first time she selects a coin, there are 3 quarters out of a total of 9 coins, so the probability of selecting a quarter is 3/9. Now there are 2 quarters left out of 8 remaining coins, so the probability of selecting a quarter the second time is 2/8. Therefore:

$$\frac{3}{9} * \frac{2}{8} = \frac{6}{72} = \frac{1}{12}$$

Try It A bag contains 3 green marbles, 2 red marbles, and 5 black marbles.

5) If Malik draws a marble at random, returns it to the bag, and then draws a marble again, what is the probability that he will select a green marble both times?

6) If Malik draws a marble at random and then draws a second marble at random (without replacing the first one), what is the probability that he will select a green marble both times?

CHALLENGE:

Solve "or" problems either by writing out all of the possibilities or by calculating the probability of the event not happening at all and then subtracting that probability from 1.

Example: *If Adele flips a coin twice, what is the probability that the coin will land heads-up at least once?*

There are only four possible outcomes for two flips of a coin: heads-heads, heads-tails, tails-heads, or tails-tails. In three of those four outcomes, the coin has landed heads-up at least once. So the answer is

$$\frac{\text{\# of outcomes with at least one heads}}{\text{total \# of outcomes}} = \frac{3}{4}.$$

Alternatively, we can take advantage of the rule that the probability of something happening and the probability of it *not* happening will always add up to 1. Start by calculating the probability of the opposite outcome from the one we want: that is, what is the probability that the coin never lands heads-up at all? Since she's flipping the coin twice, that's the same thing as asking this: what's the probability that the coin will land tails-up twice in a row? That's easy: $\frac{1}{2} * \frac{1}{2} = \frac{1}{4}$. Therefore, the probability that this outcome *doesn't* happen (that is, the probability that the coin *does* land heads-up at least once) is $1 - \frac{1}{4} = \frac{3}{4}$.

Math: Problem Solving and Data Analysis

Chapter Answer Key

Try It	1)	12/52 or 0.231
	2)	2/52 or 0.038
	3)	986/5403 or 0.182
	4)	986/4548 or 0.217
	5)	9/100 or 0.09
	6)	6/90 or $0.0\overline{66}$

Practice Set 1: Easy-Medium

1

At a teachers' conference, a committee consists of 3 Spanish language teachers, 2 French language teachers, 6 math teachers, 5 history teachers, and 4 science teachers. If a committee member is chosen at random, what is the probability that the member chosen is NOT a language teacher?

A. 0.05
B. 0.25
C. 0.60
D. 0.75

2

A gift store sells 12 t-shirts and x tote bags in one day. If one of these products is selected at random, what is the probability that the product selected is a tote bag?

A. $\dfrac{x}{x+12}$
B. $\dfrac{12}{x+12}$
C. $\dfrac{x}{12}$
D. $\dfrac{12}{x}$

3

A bowl contains red, yellow, and purple lollipops. There are 18 yellow lollipops and 22 red lollipops. The probability of choosing a purple lollipop is $\dfrac{3}{7}$. How many purple lollipops are there in the bowl?

4

There are 720 juniors and seniors at a certain high school. A representative from either the junior or senior class is to be chosen at random. If the probability that a junior is chosen is 5/16, how many <u>seniors</u> are there at this school?

A. 200
B. 225
C. 312
D. 495

5

Liam rolls two standard dice. What is the probability that he rolls a double six?

A. $\dfrac{1}{36}$
B. $\dfrac{1}{12}$
C. $\dfrac{1}{6}$
D. $\dfrac{1}{3}$

6

The table below gives the results of a study of two groups of mice, Group A and Group B. The scientist recorded how many mice in each group were able to solve a puzzle in 1-2 attempts, 3-5 attempts, or 6 or more attempts and how many never solved it.

	1-2	3-5	6+	Never
Group A	9	14	6	2
Group B	13	11	7	0

If a mouse is chosen at random from those that solved the puzzle in 3-5 minutes, what is the probability that the mouse belongs to Group B?

A. 0.23
B. 0.35
C. 0.44
D. 0.56

Practice Set 2: Medium-Hard

1

A fair six-sided die will be rolled three times. Which of the following gives the probability that the outcome of the rolls will be a 2, then a 3, then a 4?

A. $\left(\frac{1}{6}\right)\left(\frac{1}{6}\right)\left(\frac{1}{6}\right)$

B. $\left(\frac{2}{6}\right)\left(\frac{3}{6}\right)\left(\frac{4}{6}\right)$

C. $\left(\frac{1}{6}\right)\left(\frac{1}{5}\right)\left(\frac{1}{4}\right)$

D. $\frac{1}{6} + \frac{1}{6} + \frac{1}{6}$

2

The bar graph below shows the distribution of ages among the 50 participants in a summer pre-college program.

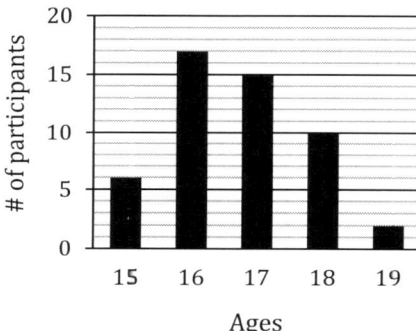

What is the probability that the age of a participant chosen at random was either 16 or 17?

A. $\frac{(15)(17)}{50}$

B. $\frac{(16)(17)}{50}$

C. $\frac{15 + 17}{50}$

D. $\frac{16 + 17}{50}$

3

If the probability that event X will occur twice is 0.84, what is the probability that event X will NOT occur twice?

A. 0
B. 0.16
C. 0.26
D. 0.71

4

Next year, Emma and Zoe will attend a school that has 4 different lunch periods. If each girl has an equal chance of being assigned to each lunch period, what is the probability that both will be assigned to the same lunch period?

5

Mr. Vega has to go through a certain intersection once a day on his way to work. Each time he goes through the intersection, the probability that he will hit a red light is 50%. What is the probability that Mr. Vega will hit a red light at least one day of a 5-day workweek?

A. 10%
B. 50%
C. 70%
D. 97%

Statistics

Preview Quiz:

Solve each of the following.

1) A random sample of 100 students was surveyed from a 500-student senior class. If 80 of the students surveyed planned to attend the homecoming dance, approximately how many seniors plan to attend?

2) In a random sample of 1000 dog owners in the United States, 75% were homeowners. Which of the following is an appropriate conclusion?

   A) Most US homeowners are dog owners.
   B) Most US dog owners are homeowners.
   C) Most people in the US own a dog, a home, or both.

3) A random sample of 500 voters was surveyed from a district of 2 million voters. 72% of those surveyed support Johnson for mayor, with a margin of error of 4%. Of the 2 million voters in the district, the percent that support Johnson for mayor is very likely to be between _____ and _____.

4) The mean GPA of a random sample of 200 students at a middle school was 3.1. The margin of error was 0.1. Which of the following is the best conclusion?

   A) It is likely that all students at the school have GPAs between 3.0 and 3.2.
   B) The mean GPA of the students at the school is likely to be between 3.0 and 3.2.
   C) No student at the school has a GPA below 3.0.

Math: Problem Solving and Data Analysis

A common statistical technique when dealing with large populations is to study a smaller **sample** of the population and then extrapolate from those findings.

The simplest of these problems can be answered with a simple proportion.

Example: *A random sample of 100 students was surveyed from a 500-student senior class. If 80 of the students surveyed planned to attend the homecoming dance, approximately how many seniors plan to attend?*

$$\frac{80}{100} = \frac{x}{500}$$

$$x = 500\left(\frac{80}{100}\right)$$

$$x = \mathbf{400} \text{ seniors}$$

TIP:

For a review of proportions, see p. 352.

In order for the findings to be applicable to the larger group, the sample should be **random**. A **biased** sample is one that is not random.

What do we mean by random? Say we have a sample of 100 people. This sample is random if *every possible sample* of 100 people has an equal chance of being selected. Consider *who* was surveyed, *where* they were found, *how* they were approached, and any other methodology that might cause a particular subgroup to have a greater or lesser chance of inclusion than any other subgroup.

TIP:

The word "bias" in this context is distinct from its everyday usage. It simply means that the sample is not random; it does *not* imply that the people involved in the sampling have some sort of intentional prejudice against the group that's not adequately represented.

Try It   Are these random samples?

1) A mayor seeking information about his constituents puts a poll on the city website.

2) A company wants information about its workforce. Every worker whose employee ID number ends in 2 receives an interview.

3) A university wants to measure the level of interest its students have in the school's football team. It offers free tickets to the homecoming game to the first 100 students who volunteer to participate.

If the sample is random, we can draw a conclusion about the larger population that it's drawn from. But take care to identify precisely which group that is. That's the *only group* that we can use the sample to make reliable predictions about. Watch out for questions that apply the data to another population, even an apparently similar one.

Example: In a random sample of 1000 dog owners in the United States, 75% were homeowners. Which of the following is an appropriate conclusion?

A) Most US homeowners are dog owners.
B) Most US dog owners are homeowners.
C) Most people in the US own a dog, a home, or both.

The sample is drawn from dog owners in the United States, so that's the only population we can draw conclusions about. The answer is **B**.

Try It   4) A survey was mailed out to all 1200 people who earned a bachelor's degree from PM university in 2010. Two hundred of the responses came from physics majors, 146 of whom had gone on to grad school. If these 200 responses are a representative sample of the physics majors, what can be concluded?

A) Most PM graduates go on to grad school.
B) Most PM graduates from the class of 2010 went on to grad school.
C) Most PM graduates from the class of 2010 who majored in physics went on to grad school.

The **margin of error** is a way of estimating how close the sample's response is likely to be to the response of the population as a whole. The sample response, plus or minus the margin of error, is the range of the likely responses from the overall population.

Example: 60% of a sample answered "yes" to a survey question, where the margin of error was 3%. Therefore, the percent of the population as a whole who would answer "yes" to that question is very likely to be between 57% and 63%.

> **TIP:**
> When in doubt, check the strength of language of the answer choice. A choice that uses weaker language is more likely to be the right answer. For example, "X is associated with Y" is a better bet than "X causes Y," and "X *may* be associated with Y" is even better.

The smaller the sample size, the greater the margin of error.
Note that the size of the total population is *irrelevant* to the margin of error.

Example: A random sample of 500 voters was surveyed from a district of 2 million voters. 72% of those surveyed support Johnson for mayor, with a margin of error of 4%.

1. Of the 2 million voters in the district, the percent that support Johnson for mayor is very likely to be between _____ and _____.

   The actual percent should be 72 plus or minus 4: between **68%** and **76%.**

2. If 1000 voters had been surveyed instead of 500, the margin of error would have been:

   A) less than 4%.
   B) greater than 4%.
   C) equal to 4%.

   A *larger* sample size yields a *smaller* margin of error. The answer is **A**.

> **TIP:**
> Between sample size and bias, bias is generally the bigger deal. Think of it this way: if the sample is too small, the conclusion we can reliably draw about the larger population will be less precise than it could have been. But if the sample is not random, no reliable conclusion can be drawn at all.

The **type of conclusion** drawn from the sample also matters, because it's the only type of conclusion we can draw about the population as a whole. For example, if the result from the random sample was a mean, we can draw a conclusion about the mean of the larger population. Don't go beyond that to draw other kinds of conclusions.

Example: The mean GPA of a random sample of 200 students at a middle school was 3.1. The margin of error was 0.1. Which of the following is the best conclusion?

A) It is likely that all students at the school have GPAs between 3.0 and 3.2.
B) The mean GPA of the students at the school is likely to be between 3.0 and 3.2.
C) No student at the school has a GPA below 3.0.

The answer is **B**.

Chapter Answer Key

Try It	1)	No
	2)	Yes
	3)	No
	4)	C

FROM THE BLOG

One of the best tools we have on the SAT is the ability to answer questions in the way that works best for us. Very often, students will spend 5-6 minutes answering a single challenging question, foregoing 2-3 other questions they could answer correctly and quickly. Nobody likes to feel that she's "quitting," but it is vital to congratulate yourself on making strategic choices, promising yourself you'll go back at the end, and moving on to more easily solved questions.

Math: Problem Solving and Data Analysis

Practice Set 1: Easy-Medium

1

A statistician interviewed a random sample of 200 Chesterton residents. Of those interviewed, 116 supported the proposed expansion of the community center. If there are a total of 35,700 Chesterton residents, which of the following is the most reasonable estimate for the number of residents who support the proposed expansion of the community center?

A. 11,600
B. 20,706
C. 23,200
D. 35,014

2

At a university, a researcher wants to evaluate the level of student satisfaction with the writing center. Which of the following study designs is most likely to result in a random sample of students at the university?

A. Survey the 100 students with the highest GPAs and the 100 students with the lowest GPAs
B. Survey 500 randomly selected English majors
C. Select 50 student ID numbers at random and then survey each student selected
D. On a randomly selected day, survey the first 200 students who enter the writing center

3

If a random sample of employees is selected from the shoe department of a Virginia department store and surveyed, which of the following is the largest population to which the results of the survey can be applied?

A. The employees in the sample
B. All shoe department employees at the department store
C. All employees at the department store
D. All shoe department employees in Virginia

4

In a survey conducted of a random sample of California residents, a researcher found that 19% of respondents had been born outside the state. The survey's margin of error was 3%. Which of the following is the best interpretation of these results?

A. The researcher is between 16% and 22% sure that the survey was accurate.
B. The percentage of California residents who were born outside the state cannot exceed 22%.
C. It is unlikely that the percentage of California residents who were born outside the state is less than 16% or more than 22%.
D. It is likely that between 16% and 22% of Americans were born outside the state in which they reside.

5

A statistician hypothesized that the general public's confidence in their own mathematics abilities varies widely from person to person. To test her theory, she surveyed 300 randomly selected pedestrians on the campus of an elite university. She found that 70% of those surveyed reported a moderate to high degree of confidence in their own mathematics abilities. Which of the following is the most accurate assessment of this survey?

A. The survey's results demonstrate that most people are at least moderately confident in their own mathematics abilities.
B. Because the survey's sample was not representative of the general public, it can be concluded that less than 70% of the general population are confident in their own mathematics abilities.
C. The survey design was inappropriate because the sample size was too small.
D. The survey's results may not be reliable because the sample was biased.

Practice Set 2: Medium-Hard

1

Holistic Healing Inc. wanted to research the effects of their new supervitamin, Supplement X, which is believed to reduce acne in young adults. A random sample of 1,200 young adults with acne was divided into two groups: half received Supplement X and half received a sugar pill. After six months, all participants from both groups were evaluated to measure any decreases in acne. Compared to the participants who had received the sugar pill, 60% more of the participants who had received Supplement X showed such a decrease. Which of the following is the most appropriate conclusion?

A. Supplement X decreases acne.
B. Supplement X decreases acne at least in young adults, but it may not have such an effect on other populations.
C. 60% of young adults with acne who take Supplement X are likely to experience a decrease in their acne within six months.
D. For young adults with acne, Supplement X use is associated with decreased acne, but it may not directly cause the decrease.

2

In a random sample of 50 action figures available for sale at a toy store, the mean selling price was $12.20, with a margin of error of $1.16. Which of the following can be inferred from these findings?

A. All action figures in the sample have a selling price between $11.04 and $13.36.
B. Most action figures at the store have a selling price between $11.04 and $13.36.
C. Any value between $11.04 and $13.36 is a plausible mean selling price of the action figures in the sample.
D. Any value between $11.04 and $13.36 is a plausible mean selling price of the action figures at the store.

3

A random sample of varsity athletes at Greendale High School was surveyed about their sleep habits. The sample included 50 soccer players, 65% of whom reported getting at least 8 hours of sleep per night. Which of the following can most reliably be inferred?

A. Most varsity athletes at Greendale High School get at least 8 hours of sleep per night.
B. Less than 35% of varsity soccer players at Greendale High School are sleep-deprived.
C. Most varsity soccer players at Greendale High School get at least 8 hours of sleep per night.
D. No students at Greendale High School get more than 8 hours of sleep per night.

4

In a survey of a random sample of 500 dog owners, 84% of respondents reported that they take their dog to the veterinarian once a year. Which of the following must be true?

 I. 84% of dog owners take their dog to the veterinarian once a year.
 II. If another randomly selected sample of 500 dog owners were surveyed, 84% would report that they take their dog to the veterinarian once a year.
 III. If a random sample of 500 cat owners were surveyed, 84% would report that they take their cat to the veterinarian once a year.

A. None
B. II only
C. I and II only
D. I and III only

Geometry and Trigonometry
Area and Volume

Preview Quiz:

Solve each of the following.

1) A rectangle with a length of 4 centimeters has an area of 14 square centimeters. What is the width of the rectangle?

$A = L \cdot W$
$14 = 4 \cdot W$ $W = 3.5 cm$

2) In the figure below, all edges intersect at right angles. What is the area of the shape?

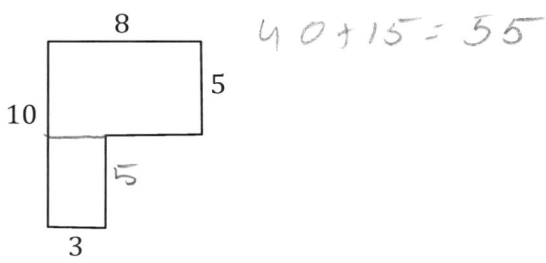

$40 + 15 = 55$

3) The figure below shows a rectangular prism with a length of 12 centimeters (cm), a width of 4 cm, and a height of 7 cm. What is the volume and what is the surface area of the prism?

$L \cdot W \cdot H = V$
$12 \cdot 4 \cdot 7 = V$
$366 \, cm^3 = V$
$A = 2(lw + wh + hl)$ $A = 320 \, cm^2$

Area and Volume

Are you groaning at the thought of re-learning long-forgotten formulas? Good news: the SAT provides them for you at the beginning of each math module. Here's an advance look at the specific information that is provided:

REFERENCE

     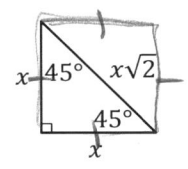

$A = \pi r^2$ $A = lw$ $A = \frac{1}{2}bh$ $a^2 + b^2 = c^2$ Special right triangles
$C = 2\pi r$

$V = lwh$ $V = \pi r^2 h$ $V = \frac{4}{3}\pi r^3$ $V = \frac{1}{3}\pi r^2 h$ $V = \frac{1}{3}lwh$

The number of degrees of arc in a circle is 360.
The number of radians of arc in a circle is 2π.
The sum of the measures in degrees of the angles of a triangle is 180.

(handwritten notes: double check radian/degree w/ sin, cos, tan of an angle)

TIP:

On the SAT, everything is drawn to scale unless the problem tells you otherwise.

(handwritten notes: Prisms — Face Area · height)

So how do you use it?

Draw it.
If the problem hasn't provided a figure, draw one of your own. If the problem *has* provided a figure, jot down a quick copy on your scratch paper so you can draw and write on it as needed.

Trust the figures.
Everything is drawn to scale unless the problem tells you otherwise, so trust what you see. If an angle looks like it's more than 90°, it is. You can often use that as a reality check for your answer, or as a way to eliminate choices if a problem really has you stumped.

Write out the formulas.
In the testing software, look in the upper right corner of your screen for the $\boxed{x^2 \text{ Reference}}$ button. You can click that at any time to see the list of geometry formulas, always a good place to start. When attacking a word problem, check that reference screen first, and write out any formulas you see that might be relevant to the problem. (Note that some problems may involve more than one formula.)

Fill in what you know.
If the problem tells you that the height of a triangle is 5, jot that down on your sketch and plug 5 in for h in the equation you wrote down. Repeat that step for every measurement or value the problem has provided.

Take the next natural step.
At this point, you will probably see something that you can calculate, even if it's not the value the question was ultimately asking for. Go ahead and calculate it! Then just see where it takes you. Often, you'll find that taking one step leads automatically to another step, which leads to another step, and before you know it you'll have solved the problem.

Area and Volume

The **area** of a two-dimensional shape is a measure of how much space it takes up, while the **perimeter** is the length of the shape's outline. To find the perimeter of a polygon, simply add the lengths of all the sides. To find the perimeter of a circle (called the **circumference**), or to find the area of any simple two-dimensional shape, use the formulas shown in the reference section.

Example: In the figure below, the dimensions of the right triangle are given in inches (in). What is the perimeter and what is the area?

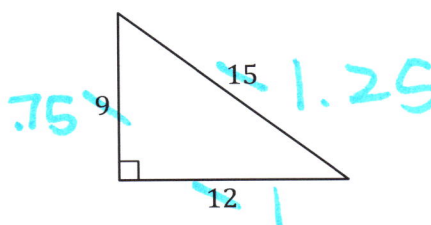

$$P = 9 + 12 + 15$$
$$P = 36 \text{ in}$$

The perimeter is **36 inches**.

$$A = \frac{1}{2}bh$$
$$A = \frac{1}{2}(12)(9)$$
$$A = 54 \text{ in}^2$$

The area is **54 square inches**.

Some problems will ask you to start with the area or perimeter and work backwards. Start by writing out the formula and plugging in whatever you know. Then use algebra to solve for the unknown values.

Example: A rectangle with a length of 4 centimeters has an area of 14 square centimeters. What is the width of the rectangle?

$$A = lw$$
$$14 = 4w$$
$$w = 14/4 = 3.5$$

The width is **3.5 centimeters**.

Math: Geometry and Trigonometry

For other problems, you'll need to use algebraic expressions to represent the dimensions or other values. Start the same way: write out the formula, plug in what you know, and solve.

Example: A certain rectangle has an area of 72. If the length is twice the width, what is the width of the rectangle?

You might start this one by drawing a rectangle. Label the width as w and the length as $2w$. Then set up your equation:

$$A = lw$$
$$72 = (2w)(w)$$
$$72 = 2w^2$$
$$36 = w^2$$
$$\mathbf{6 = w}$$

TIP:
These types of problems are also good for back-solving.

Try It Consult the formulas from p. 425 as needed as you solve. If your answer contains a π, include the π in your answer. (For example, an area of 10π should be given as 10π, not as 31.4159.)

1) What is the area, in square meters, of a circle with a radius of 9 meters?

$A = \pi r^2$
$A = \pi(9)^2$
$A = 81\pi \, m^2$

2) A rectangle has a width of 4 inches and an area of 36 square inches. What is the perimeter of the rectangle, in inches?

$36 = L \cdot 4 \quad L = 9$
$A = L \cdot W$
$P = 2L + 2W \quad 2(9) + 2(4) = 18 + 8 = \boxed{26 \text{ in}}$

3) What is the area of a square whose perimeter is 40?

100

Some problems ask how many of one shape can fit into another shape. Since area is a measure of how much space something takes up, you can solve these problems by **dividing** the area of the larger shape by the area of the smaller shape.

Try It 4) How many squares of area 25 in² can be cut out of a rectangle with length 8 in and width 400 in?

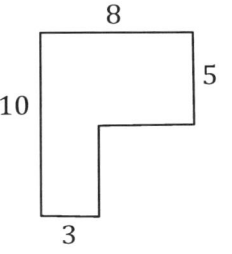

3,200 ÷ 25 = 128

The SAT will sometimes ask about a shape whose formulas are not provided in the reference section. To find the area, look to draw lines on the shape to split it into simpler shapes. Then find the areas of each of those and add them together.

Example: In the figure below, all edges intersect at right angles. What is the area of the shape?

We can draw a single line on this figure to divide it into two rectangles. Draw it that way, and be sure to adjust the dimensions accordingly:

15 + 11 = 36

The area of the left rectangle is $10(3) = 30$. The area of the right rectangle is $5(5) = 25$. Therefore, the area of the shape is $30 + 25 = \mathbf{55}$.

Try It 5) What is the perimeter of the shape used in the example above?

36

Math: Geometry and Trigonometry

The **volume** of a three-dimensional shape is a measure of the three-dimensional shape it takes up. Its **surface area** is the sum of the areas of all its faces.

Example: The figure below shows a rectangular prism with a length of 12 centimeters (cm), a width of 4 cm, and a height of 7 cm. What is the volume and what is the surface area of the prism?

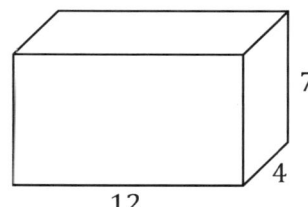

Start by writing out the formula for volume of a rectangular prism (provided in the reference section):

$$V = lwh$$
$$V = (12)(4)(7)$$
$$V = 336 \text{ cm}^3$$

The volume is **336 cubic centimeters**.

To find the surface area, we'll need the areas of the six rectangles that make up this prism. Take them one matching pair at a time. The front and the back are each a 12×7 rectangle:

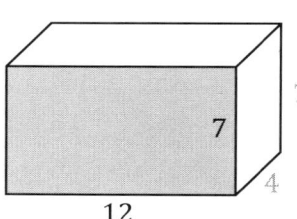

The top and the bottom are each a 12×4 rectangle:

And the left and right ends are each a 7×4 rectangle:

So the total surface area will be the sums of the areas of two 12×7 rectangles, two 12×4 rectangles, and two 7×4 rectangles:

$$SA = 2(12*7) + 2(12*4) + 2(7*4)$$
$$SA = 2(84) + 2(48) + 2(28)$$
$$SA = 320$$

The surface area is **320 square centimeters**.

Try It   Consult the formulas from p. 425 as needed as you solve.

6) What is the volume of a cylinder with a radius of 3 and a height of 10?

$V = \pi r^2 h \qquad V = 90\pi$
$V = \pi (3)^2 (10)$

7) What is the surface area of a cube whose volume is 1000?

$SA = 6(10)^2 \qquad SA = 600$

$V = L \cdot W \cdot H$

8) A cone with a volume of 32π has a height of 6. What is the radius of the cone's base?

$32\pi = \frac{1}{3}\pi r^2 (6) \qquad 96 = (r^2)(6)$
$16 = r^2$
$r = 4$

9) How many cubes of side length 2 cm would fit into a rectangular prism with dimensions 6 cm by 4 cm by 10 cm?

$V = x^3 \qquad V = 8 cm^3 \qquad V = lwh \qquad V = 240 cm^3$

×30

Math: Geometry and Trigonometry

Chapter Answer Key

Try It	1)	81π
	2)	26
	3)	100
	4)	128
	5)	36
	6)	90π
	7)	600
	8)	4
	9)	30

Practice Set 1: Easy-Medium

1

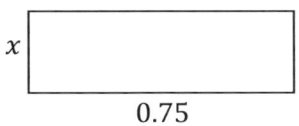

Note: figure not drawn to scale.

If the rectangle above has an area of 1, what is the value of x?

A. $\frac{1}{2}$
B. $\frac{3}{4}$
C. $\frac{4}{3}$
D. 12

2

A rectangle with a length of 8 meters has an area of 12 square meters. What is the width, in meters, of the rectangle?

A. 1.5
B. 2
C. 2.5
D. 4

3

The picture above shows a square with side of length 3 completely enclosed within a square with side of length 4.5. What is the area of the shaded region?

4

What is the area of the pentagon shown below?

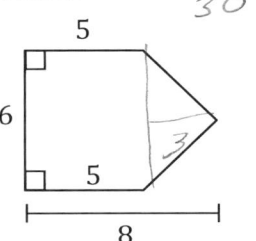

A. 25
B. 39
C. 41
D. 48

5

The volume of a certain rectangular prism is 120 cubic centimeters. If the width of the prism is 6 centimeters and the height is $\sqrt{50}$ centimeters, what is the length of the prism, in centimeters?

A. $\sqrt{7}$
B. $2\sqrt{2}$
C. 4
D. $2\sqrt{15}$

6

The figure below shows the foundation for a new building. All intersecting line segments are perpendicular, and all given dimensions are in meters.

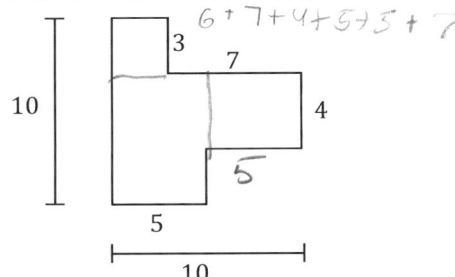

What is the perimeter of the foundation, in meters?

A. 20
B. 29
C. 34
D. 40

Math: Geometry and Trigonometry

7

What is the area of a circle with a circumference of 16π?

A. 8π
B. 16π
C. 32π
D. 64π

$16\pi = 2\pi r$
$8 = r$

8

On a garden wall, an artist creates a rectangular mosaic that is 20 feet long and 4 feet high. The mosaic is created using n individual square tiles, each 6 inches by 6 inches. What is the value of n?

(Note: 1 foot = 12 inches)

9

In the figure below, the height of the cylinder is 6 cm, and the radius of the base has length 4 cm. What is the surface area of the cylinder, in square cm?

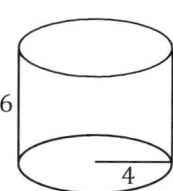

(Note: the surface area S of a cylinder with radius r and height h is given by the formula $S = 2\pi r^2 h + 2\pi r h$.)

A. 96π
B. 144π
C. 240π
D. 384π

10

In the figure below, a square is circumscribed about a circle.

If the perimeter of the square is 24, what is the area of the circle?

A. 6π
B. 9π
C. 12π
D. 16π

11

Which of the following expressions gives the volume of a rectangular solid with length $x + 3$, width $x - 3$, and height 2?

A. $2x - 6$
B. $2x + 2$
C. $2x^2$
D. $2x^2 - 18$

$(x+3)(x-3)$
$x^2 - 9$

12

In the figure below, three circles of equal size are inscribed in rectangle $ABCD$.

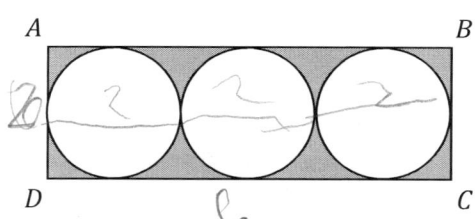

If rectangle $ABCD$ has a width of 2 and a length of 6, what is the area of the shaded region?

A. $12 - \pi$
B. $12 - 2\pi$
C. $12 - 3\pi$
D. $12 - 6\pi$

$r = 1$
π

Practice Set 2: Medium-Hard

1

Point O is the center of the circle pictured below. If the area of triangle MNO is 6, what is the area of circle O?

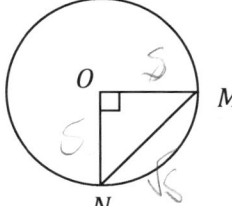

A. 3π
B. 6π
C. $4\sqrt{3}\pi$
D. 12π

2

How many small cubes with a surface area of 96 square inches can be cut from a solid wood cube whose surface area is 384 square inches?

3

In the square below, the shaded region is bounded by 4 equal arcs with centers at A, B, C, and D. If the perimeter of the square equals 24, what is the area of the shaded region?

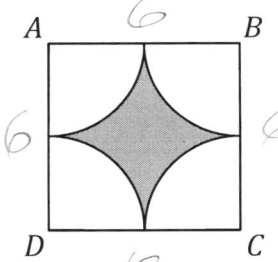

A. $36 - 6\pi$
B. $36 - 9\pi$
C. $24 - 6\pi$
D. $21 - 6\pi$

4

In the figure below, square $ABCD$ shares one vertex with triangle CEF. $\overline{AD}$ and $\overline{EF}$ are both congruent and collinear.

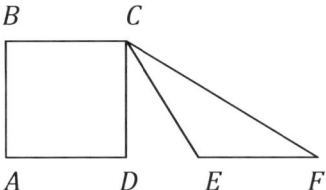

If the area of square $ABCD$ is 10, what is the area of triangle CEF?

A. 3
B. 5
C. 6
D. 12

5

An elementary school teacher has three geometric shapes: a blue rectangle, a green rectangle, and a yellow square. The blue rectangle has a length of 6 inches and a perimeter of 20 inches. The width of the green rectangle is twice the width of the blue rectangle, while the length of the green rectangle is the same as the side length of the yellow square. If the area of the yellow square is 25 square inches, what is the area of the green rectangle, in square inches?

6

A circle with diameter d has the same area as a square with side length 3. Which of the following is closest to the value of d?

A. 1.91
B. 2.86
C. 3.39
D. 5.73

Math: Geometry and Trigonometry

7

The rectangular picture frame shown below has a width of x inches and a height of $x + 2$ inches. When a picture is placed in the frame, the edges of the picture are covered by the frame's border, which has a uniform width of 1 inch on all sides. Which of the following gives the area, in square inches, of the portion of the picture NOT covered by the border?

A. $x(x - 2)$
B. $x(x + 2)$
C. $(x - 2)(x + 1)$
D. $4x$

8

Rectangle $ABCD$ has length 8 and perimeter 22. If diagonal $\overline{AC}$ is drawn, the rectangle is split into two congruent right triangles. What is the area of right triangle ABC?

9

$ABCD$ is a square with sides of length 8. Point E is the midpoint of $\overline{AD}$, and point F is the midpoint of $\overline{BC}$.

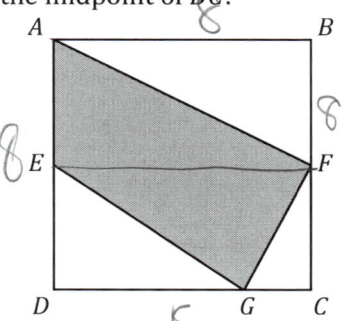

What is the ratio of the area of the shaded region to the area of the square?

A. 1:2
B. 3:4
C. 7:10
D. 9:16

10

A warehouse worker has to pack 100 small boxes of dimension 2 inches by 3 inches by 4 inches into one larger box. Which of the following could be the dimension of the larger box if all 100 boxes fit into the larger box perfectly with no space left over?

A. 20" × 30" × 40"
B. 10" × 12" × 20"
C. 10" × 15" × 24"
D. 8" × 27" × 64"

11

The side length of square A is 3 inches less than twice the side length of square B. If square B has an area of x in², which of the following gives the area of square A?

A. $0.25(x + 6\sqrt{x} + 9)$
B. $x - 6\sqrt{x} + 9$
C. $4x - 12\sqrt{x} + 9$
D. $x^2 - 6x + 9$

Angles, Lines, and Triangles

Preview Quiz:

Define each term:

1) supplementary: *complementary* – 2 angles make up 90° / 2 angles make up 180°
2) congruent: SSS, SAS, AAS, ASA, HL
3) similar: proportional SSS/SAS or AA
4) a "regular" polygon:
5) an isosceles triangle:
6) an equilateral triangle:

If two lines intersect, what is the relationship between:

7) the adjacent angles?
8) the vertical angles?

Lines l_1 and l_2 are parallel. Which angles are:

9) congruent?
10) supplementary?

Fill in the blanks:

11) The formula for the sum of the interior angles of an n-sided polygon is $180(n-2)$ or $180n - 360$

12) The third side of the triangle rule is _____

$3 < x < 11$

Math: Geometry and Trigonometry

Pick any point along a straight line, and that point can be defined as a 180-degree angle (also called a **straight angle**). If you draw new line segments out from that point, you're splitting that 180° angle into multiple pieces; thus, the newly created angles must add up to 180°.

Angles that are next to each other on a straight line, such as in the examples above, are called **adjacent** angles. Adjacent angles are always **supplementary**, meaning their degree measures add up to 180°.

When two lines intersect, the angles that are across from each other are called **opposite angles** or **vertical angles**. Opposite angles are always **congruent** (equal) to each other.

Example: In the figure, angle A is congruent to angle D, and angle B is congruent to angle C.

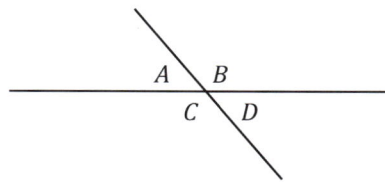

> **TIP:**
> Some other useful terms:
> - **perpendicular**: intersecting at a 90° angle
> - **bisect**: to divide into two equal parts

Parallel lines never intersect each other. When two parallel lines are intersected by another line (called a **transversal**), six angles are created; some of these are congruent to each other, while others are supplementary.

Example: If lines l_1 and l_2 are parallel in the figure below, then:
- All the even-numbered angles are congruent.
- All the odd-numbered angles are congruent.
- Each even-numbered angle is supplementary to each odd-numbered angle.

Angles, Lines, and Triangles

At some point, you probably had to memorize a bunch of these angle relationships for a math class in school: *alternate exterior angles, same-side interior angles,* etc. There's no need for all that on the SAT. Make it simple: look for angles that are in the same position as each other relative to their respective lines. These are called **corresponding angles**, and they are always congruent.

Example: For parallel lines l_1 and l_2 below, angles A and B are corresponding angles. Therefore, angle A is congruent to angle B.

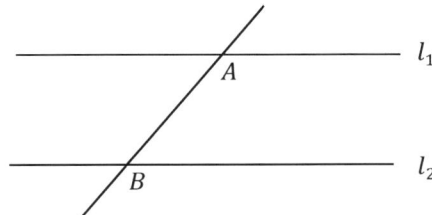

Once you find the corresponding angles, you can use them to determine lots of other angle relationships.

Example: In the figure below, $\overline{XZ}$ intersects parallel lines $\overline{AB}$ and $\overline{CD}$ at points X and Y. If the measure of $\angle AXY$ is 112°, what is the measure of $\angle DYZ$?

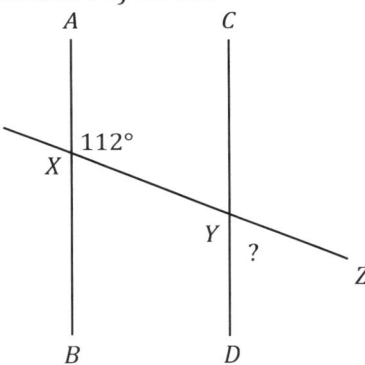

First, find the corresponding angle for the one we know. Here, that's $\angle CYZ$:

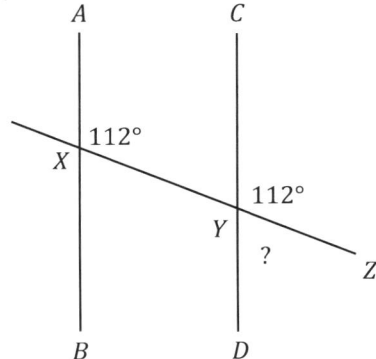

Now, what's the relationship of ∠CYZ and ∠DYZ? They're adjacent to each other, so they must add up to 180°. Therefore, the measure of ∠DYZ must be 180 − 112 = **68°**.

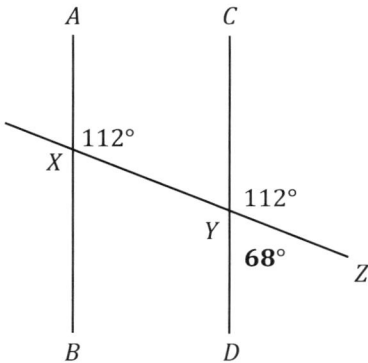

To make it easier to find those corresponding angles, try extending the lines of the figure.

Example: In parallelogram ABCD below, the measure of angle A is 155°, and point D lies on $\overline{EC}$. What is the measure of ∠ADE?

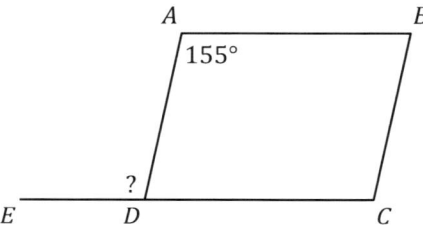

Start by redrawing the figure with lines $\overline{AD}$ and $\overline{EC}$ extended. Do you see a spot that corresponds to our 155° angle? Go ahead and fill it in.

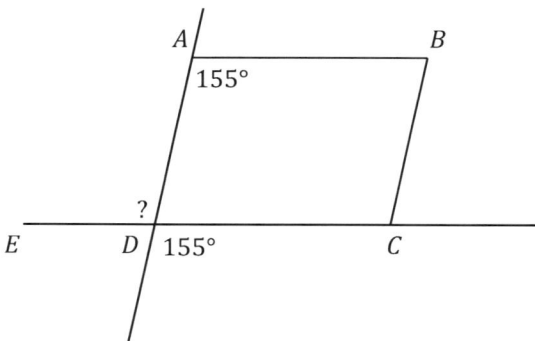

That angle is across from ∠ADE. So, since opposite angles are congruent, the measure of ∠ADE must also be **155°**.

Try It

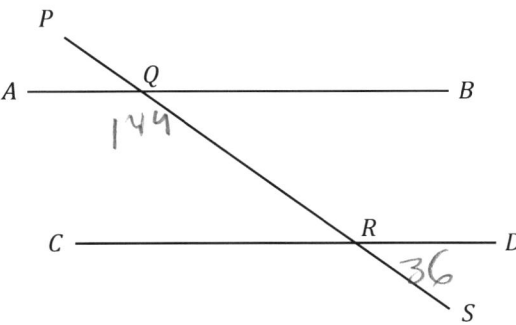

In the figure above, transversal $\overline{PS}$ intersects the parallel lines $\overline{AB}$ and $\overline{CD}$ at points Q and R, respectively.

1) Name three angles that are congruent to ∠AQP.

   RPS
   RCQ   BQR

2) If the measure of ∠AQR is 144°, what is the measure of ∠SRD?

   36

TIP:

Angles can be named with three letters or with one. In the three-letter format, the vertex is always the letter in the middle.

Example: The angle shown below could be referred to as ∠P, as ∠QPR, or as ∠RPQ. It <u>cannot</u> be referred to as ∠PQR.

Math: Geometry and Trigonometry

The interior angles of a triangle always add up to 180 degrees. For other polygons, the sum of the interior angles equals $n(180 - 2)$, where n is the number of sides.

Example: What is the sum of the interior angles of a pentagon?
$180(5 - 2) = \mathbf{540}$

In a **regular polygon**, all sides have the same length and all angles have the same degree measure.

Try It   Solve each of the following.

3) What is the sum of the interior angles of a hexagon?

720°

4) What is the degree measure of one interior angle of a regular hexagon?

120°

An **acute angle** measures less than 90 degrees, a **right angle** measures exactly 90 degrees, and an **obtuse angle** measures more than 90 degrees.

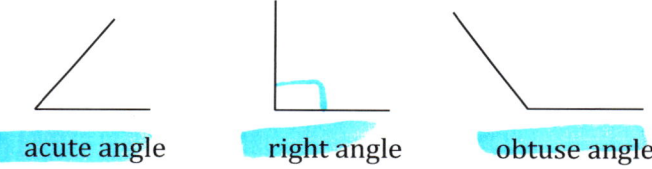

acute angle   right angle   obtuse angle

These terms also apply to triangles: an **acute triangle** contains only acute angles, a **right triangle** contains one right angle, and an **obtuse triangle** contains one obtuse angle.

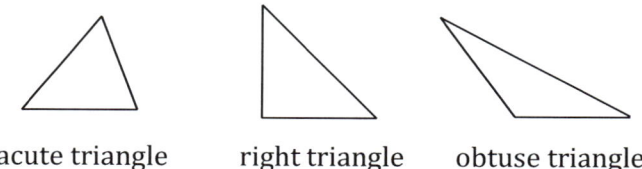

acute triangle   right triangle   obtuse triangle

TIP:

Because the interior angles of a triangle always add up to 180 degrees, these are the only possibilities. No triangle can ever have more than one obtuse angle or more than one right angle.

In a **scalene** triangle, all three sides have different lengths, and all three angles have different degree measures. In an **isosceles** triangle, two of the side lengths are the same, and two of the angles are the same (the ones across from the matching sides). In an **equilateral** triangle, all three side lengths are the same, and all three angles are the same: each angle measures 180/3 = 60 degrees.

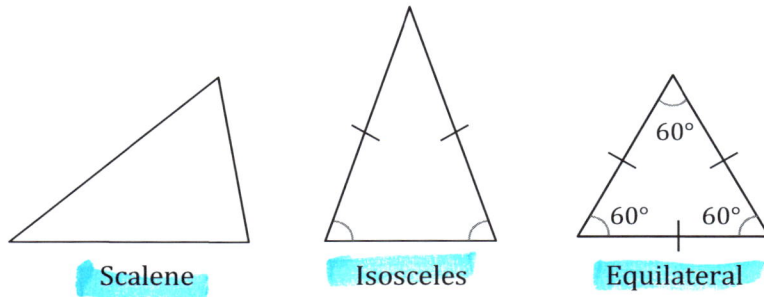

Scalene   Isosceles   Equilateral

You can make some inferences about triangle side lengths based on their angles. The sides go in order: the largest side of the triangle is always across from the largest angle, the second-largest side is across from the second-largest angle, and so on.

Try It   Solve each of the following.

5) In isosceles triangle ABC, two of the side lengths are 5 and 6. What are the two possible perimeters of triangle ABC?

16 or 17

6) The hypotenuse of right triangle XYZ has a length of 10 inches. Which of the following could be the perimeter, in inches, of triangle XYZ? **Choose all that apply.**

A) 10
B) 24
C) 30
D) 36

Math: Geometry and Trigonometry

The third side of the triangle rule is a limit on the size of an unknown side length. Each side of a triangle must be *less* than the sum of the other two sides and *greater* than the positive difference of those other two sides.

Example: Triangle XYZ has side lengths 4, 6, and x. If x is an integer, what are the possible values of x?

$6 - 4 < x < 4 + 6$
$2 < x < 10$

The remaining side length must be greater than 2 and less than 10. Since x is an integer (a whole number), the only possible values for x are **3, 4, 5, 6, 7, 8, or 9**.

Congruent triangles are identical triangles: they have the same angle measurements as each other and the same side lengths as each other. **Similar triangles** have the same angle measurements as each other but different side lengths: specifically, their side lengths are **proportional**. Solve by setting up a proportion that matches up the corresponding sides.

TIP:
For a review of proportions, see p. 352.

Example: In the figure below, the smaller triangle is similar to the larger triangle. What is the value of x?

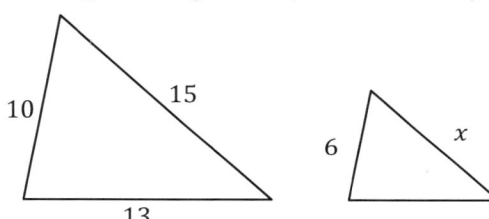

$$\frac{6}{10} = \frac{x}{15}$$

$$\frac{6}{10}(15) = x$$

$$9 = x$$

Many problems involving similar triangles will start off with a complicated diagram showing several overlapping triangles. Redraw the figure on your scratch paper and look for parallel lines, vertical angles, or any other hints that two or more angles match each other; indicate those on your drawing. Next, **redraw the figure as two separate triangles.** This will make it a lot easier to line up the sides correctly.

Example: In the figure below, $\overline{BD}$ is parallel to $\overline{AE}$. What is the value of x?

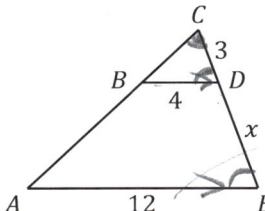

Redraw the figure as two separate triangles to make it easier to see the relationships.

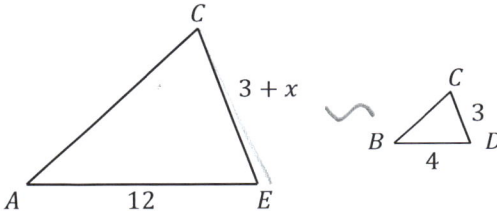

Because of the parallel lines, angle A in triangle ACE must be the same degree measure as angle B in triangle BCD, and angle E in triangle ACE must be the same degree measure as angle D in triangle BCD. Both triangles have angle C, so all the angles match: these are similar triangles. Therefore, we can set up a proportion to solve:

$$\frac{12}{4} = \frac{3+x}{3}$$

$$3(12) = 4(3+x)$$
$$36 = 12 + 4x$$
$$24 = 4x$$
$$\mathbf{6 = x}$$

Try It   Solve each of the following.

7) Triangle PQR has side lengths of 5, 6, and 7 inches. Triangle XYZ also has side lengths of 5, 6, and 7 inches. Which of the following statements is correct?

   A) PQR and XYZ are congruent triangles.
   B) PQR and XYZ are similar triangles but not necessarily congruent.
   C) PQR and XYZ are not necessarily either similar or congruent.

In the figure below, $\overline{BE}$ and $\overline{AD}$ intersect at C, and $\overline{BA}$ is parallel to $\overline{DE}$.

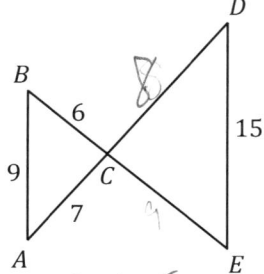

8) ∠BCA is congruent to ∠ _DCE_

9) ∠BAC is congruent to ∠ _CDE_

10) ∠ABC is congruent to ∠ _DEC_

11) What is the length of $\overline{CE}$? _10_

Chapter Answer Key

Try It
1) ∠RQB, ∠SRD, and ∠CRQ
2) 36°
3) 720°
4) 120°
5) 16 or 17
6) B only
7) A
8) ∠DCE
9) ∠CDE
10) ∠CED
11) 10

Math: Geometry and Trigonometry

Practice Set 1: Easy-Medium

1

In the figure below, a logo consists of two equilateral triangles that share one vertex. The given side lengths are in inches. What is the perimeter, in inches, of the entire logo?

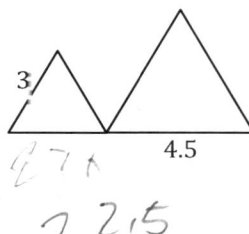

2

In the figure below, points K and L lie on line segment $\overline{JM}$.

If $JL = 10$, $JM = 13$, and $JK = 4$, what is the length of $\overline{KM}$?

A. 7
B. 8
C. 9
D. 10

3

In the figure below, $\overline{XY}$ intersects parallel line segments $\overline{AB}$ and $\overline{CD}$ at points Q and R, respectively. If the measure of $\angle CRX$ is 42°, what is the measure of $\angle AQY$?

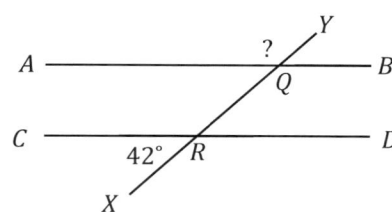

A. 42°
B. 126°
C. 138°
D. 142°

4

What is the length of $\overline{MQ}$ in triangle MPQ below?

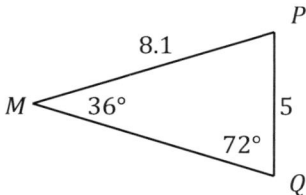

A. 5
B. 6.8
C. 7.5
D. 8.1

5

In the figure below, point R lies on $\overline{QS}$, $\angle QPR$ measures 66°, and $\angle PRS$ measures 153°. What is the measure of $\angle PQR$?

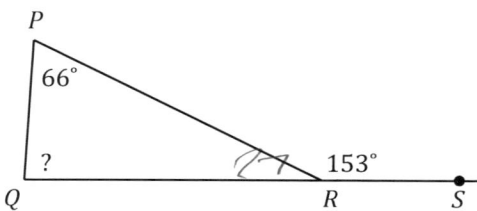

A. 24°
B. 72°
C. 87°
D. 114°

6

Andre uses a computer to draw a regular nonagon (a 9-sided polygon). What is the measure, in degrees, of one interior angle of the nonagon?

7

What is the perimeter of parallelogram WXYZ?

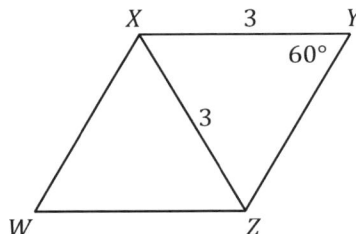

A. 12
B. $6\sqrt{3}$
C. 9
D. $3\sqrt{3}$

8

In the figure below, a circle has been divided into 8 congruent sectors by lines that all pass through the circle's center, creating 8 central angles that each measure $x°$. What is the value of x?

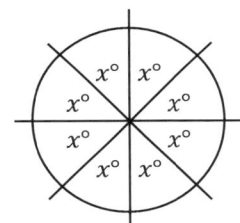

9

In the parallelogram below, what is the value of x?

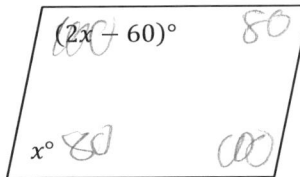

A. 40
B. 60
C. 80
D. 90

10

In the figure below, $\overline{BD}$ is parallel to $\overline{AE}$, point B lies on $\overline{AC}$, and point D lies on $\overline{CE}$. The lengths given are in centimeters. What is the length, in centimeters, of $\overline{CE}$?

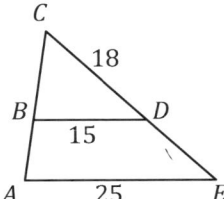

A. 20
B. 24
C. 27
D. 30

11

In triangle ACD, shown below, $\overline{AC} \cong \overline{AD}$, $\overline{AC} \perp \overline{AD}$, $\overline{BE}$ bisects $\overline{AD}$, and $\overline{BE} \parallel \overline{CD}$. What is the measure of $\angle BED$?

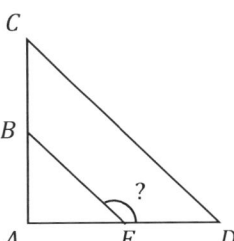

A. 45°
B. 75°
C. 105°
D. 135°

12

Points A, B, C, and D lie on a line segment in that order, such that B bisects $\overline{AC}$ and C bisects $\overline{BD}$. If the length of $\overline{BC}$ is 4, what is the length of $\overline{AD}$?

A. 4
B. 6
C. 8
D. 12

Math: Geometry and Trigonometry

Practice Set 2: Medium-Hard

1

The town of Bellmore is 8 miles from the town of Cedarhurst and 2 miles from the town of Farmingdale. Which of the following could NOT be the distance between Cedarhurst and Farmingdale?

A. 5 miles
B. 6 miles
C. 7 miles
D. 9 miles

2

If line l is parallel to line m, what is the value of x?

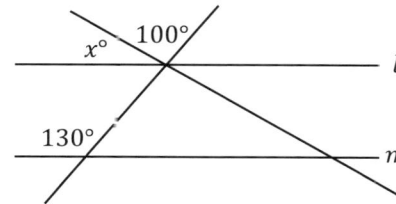

3

In the figure below, $\overline{BD}$ is a diagonal of trapezoid $ABCD$, where $\overline{AD}$ and $\overline{BC}$ are parallel. If $\angle BAD$ measures 43° and $\angle DBC$ measures 65°, what is the measure of $\angle ABD$?

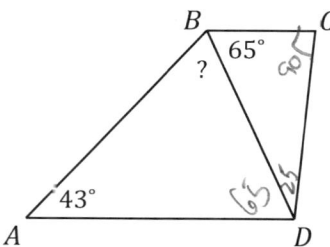

A. 25°
B. 47°
C. 65°
D. 72°

4

In the figure below, $ABCDE$ is a regular pentagon. If A, E, and F are collinear, what is the measure of $\angle DEF$, in degrees?

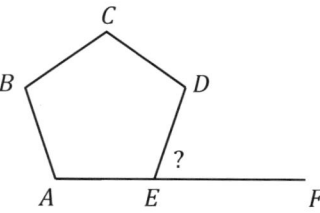

5

In the figure below, points P and Q lie on one side of rectangle $MNRS$.

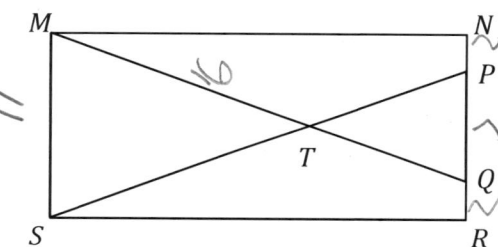

If the length of $\overline{MS}$ is 11, the length of $\overline{PQ}$ is 7, and the length of $\overline{MT}$ is 16, what else can be concluded?

A. The length of $\overline{TQ}$ is $\dfrac{112}{11}$.

B. The length of $\overline{TP}$ is $\dfrac{112}{11}$.

C. The length of $\overline{ST}$ is $\dfrac{77}{16}$.

D. The length of $\overline{ST}$ is $\dfrac{176}{7}$.

TM and © 2023 PrepMatters, Inc. All rights reserved.

6

In the figure below, triangle ABC is similar to triangle DEF, where each side of triangle DEF is 3 times the length of the corresponding side of triangle ABC.

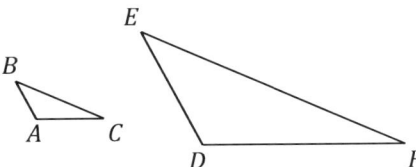

If the smallest angle in triangle DEF measures $24°$, what is the measure of the smallest angle in triangle ABC?

A. $8°$
B. $24°$
C. $66°$
D. $72°$

7

In the figure below, the horizontal bases of the two triangles are parallel.

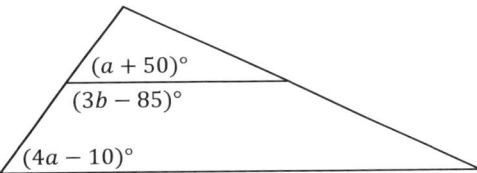

What is the value of $a + b$?

8

In the figure below, what is the average (arithmetic mean) of a and b?

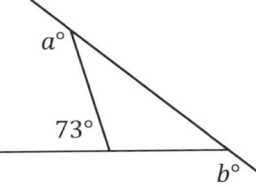

A. $36.5°$
B. $86°$
C. $107°$
D. $143.5°$

9

Which of the following statements, if true, is independently sufficient to prove that $l \parallel p$ in the figure below?

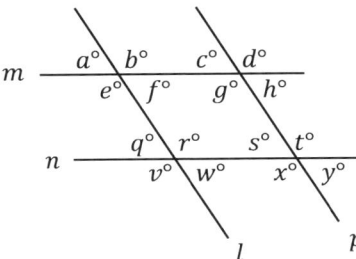

A. $c = h$
B. $f = w$
C. $q = s$
D. $d = y$

10

If two of the angles of a triangle measure $42°$ and $48°$, the triangle must be which of the following?

A. scalene right
B. scalene acute
C. isosceles acute
D. isosceles obtuse

11

Skew lines are lines that neither intersect nor lie in the same plane. In the prism shown below, each of the six rectangular faces is perpendicular to both hexagonal bases. Which of the following line segments is skew to $\overline{AB}$?

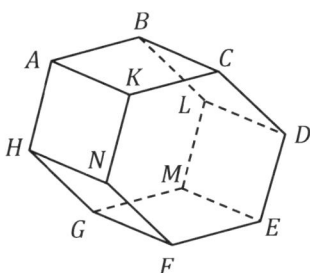

A. $\overline{AH}$
B. $\overline{GM}$
C. $\overline{FE}$
D. $\overline{ME}$

Math: Geometry and Trigonometry

Right Triangles and Trigonometry

The relevant provided formulas:

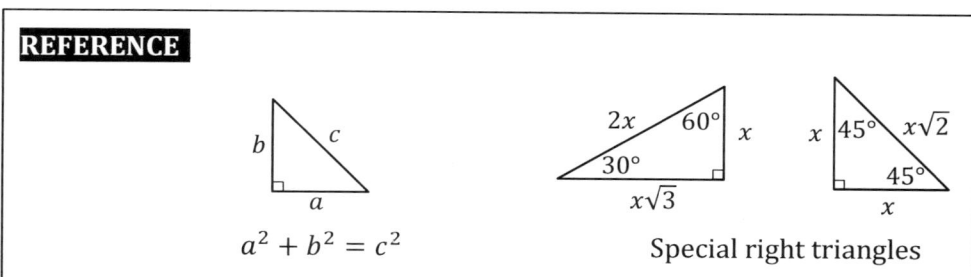

Preview Quiz:

Solve:

1) A right triangle has the side lengths shown. What is the value of x?

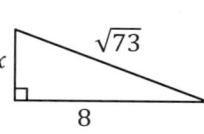

3

2) Name three common Pythagorean triples:

3, 4, 5   5, 12, 13   8, 15, 17

3) What is the length of the hypotenuse of a 45-45-90 triangle with a leg of length 5?

$5\sqrt{2}$

4) What is the perimeter of a 30-60-90 triangle with a hypotenuse of 8?

$12 + 4\sqrt{3}$

Fill in the blanks:

5) $\sin = \dfrac{O\ pposite}{H\ ypotenuse}$

6) $\cos = \dfrac{A\ djacent}{H}$

7) $\tan = \dfrac{O}{A}$

8) How do you use the inverse trig functions $\sin^{-1}$, $\cos^{-1}$, and $\tan^{-1}$? find based on known trig

9) If $\cos 81° = 0.156$, then $\sin 9° =$ 0.156

A **right triangle** consists of two **legs**, each of which is across from an acute angle, and one **hypotenuse**, which is across from a right angle.

For any right triangle with legs of lengths a and b and a hypotenuse of length c, the **Pythagorean Theorem** states that $a^2 + b^2 = c^2$.

Example: What is the length of the shorter leg in the right triangle shown?

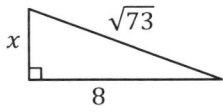

$(x)^2 + (8)^2 = (\sqrt{73})^2$
$x^2 + 64 = 73$
$x^2 = 9$
$x = 3$

TIP:

Because the largest angle in a triangle is always across from the largest side, the hypotenuse is always the longest side in any right triangle.

Try It

1) What is the area of the right triangle shown?

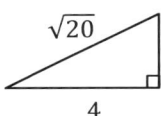

4

2) Which of the following gives the length of the hypotenuse of a right triangle with legs of length k and n?

A) $k^2 + n^2$
B) $\sqrt{k^2 + n^2}$
C) $k^2 - n^2$
D) $\sqrt{k^2 - n^2}$

You can save yourself some time by memorizing a few **Pythagorean triples**, which are sets of three whole numbers that happen to satisfy the Pythagorean theorem. For example, $\{3, 4, 5\}$ is a Pythagorean triple, because $3^2 + 4^2 = 5^2$. Some other helpful triples are $\{5, 12, 13\}$ and $\{8, 15, 17\}$. Note that multiples of these patterns work too.

Example: What is the hypotenuse of the triangle shown below?

This is a multiple of a 3-4-5 triangle. Because the legs are $4(3) = 12$ and $4(4) = 16$, the hypotenuse must be $4(5) = \mathbf{20}$.

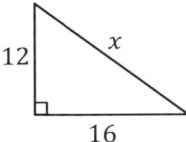

Included in the reference section are the unique patterns of side lengths for the **special right triangles**. You can use these as a shortcut to quickly answer many questions involving 30-60-90 triangles or 45-45-90 triangles.

Example: What is the hypotenuse of the triangle shown?

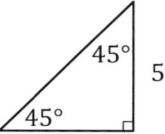

See the reference triangle on the left: the sides of a 45-45-90 triangle, from smallest to largest, are x, x, and $x\sqrt{2}$. Therefore:

$$x = 5$$
$$\text{hypotenuse} = x\sqrt{2} = \mathbf{5\sqrt{2}}$$

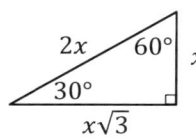

Example: What is the perimeter of the triangle shown?

See the reference triangle on the left: the sides of a 30-60-90 triangle, from smallest to largest, are x, $x\sqrt{3}$, and $2x$. Therefore:

$$\text{hypotenuse} = 2x = 8$$
$$x = 4 = \text{shorter leg}$$
$$x\sqrt{3} = 4\sqrt{3} = \text{longer leg}$$
$$\text{Perimeter} = 8 + 4 + 4\sqrt{3} = \mathbf{12 + 4\sqrt{3}}$$

Try It

3) What is the area of an isosceles right triangle with hypotenuse $6\sqrt{2}$?

18

4) The equilateral triangle below has side length 4 and height h. What is the value of h?

$2\sqrt{3}$

The trigonometric functions **sine**, **cosine**, and **tangent** can be defined as ratios of specific side lengths in a right triangle. The acronym **SOH-CAH-TOA** is a way to remember the relationships. For example, the TOA portion means that the tangent of any angle is equal to the length of the opposite leg (the leg across from that angle) divided by the length of the adjacent leg (the other leg in the triangle).

Here are all the ratios:

SOH	CAH	TOA
$\sin = \dfrac{\text{opposite}}{\text{hypotenuse}}$	$\cos = \dfrac{\text{adjacent}}{\text{hypotenuse}}$	$\tan = \dfrac{\text{opposite}}{\text{adjacent}}$

Be careful to line up which leg is the *opposite* and which one is the *adjacent* for the particular angle the question is asking about.

Example: *In the right triangle shown below:*

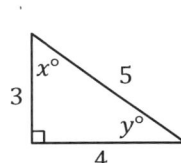

$\sin x = \dfrac{4}{5}$ $\qquad$ $\sin y = \dfrac{3}{5}$

$\cos x = \dfrac{3}{5}$ $\qquad$ $\cos y = \dfrac{4}{5}$

$\tan x = \dfrac{4}{3}$ $\qquad$ $\tan y = \dfrac{3}{4}$

TIP:
The inverse trig functions sin⁻¹, cos⁻¹, and tan⁻¹ allow you to use these values to find the degree measure of the angles.

For example, since $\sin y = 3/5$:

$y = \sin^{-1}(3/5)$
$y = 36.87°$

Make sure your calculator is in degree mode and not radians!

Try It

5) In the right triangle below, what is the value of $\cos a$?

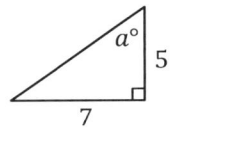

$\dfrac{5}{\sqrt{74}}$

★ $\overset{\circ}{S\!H} = \text{Ratio}$ $\dfrac{\text{opp}}{\text{hyp}}$

6) In the right triangle below, $\tan k = \dfrac{5}{4}$. What is the value of x?

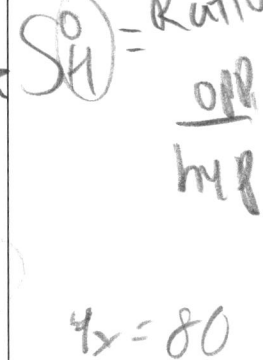

$\tan k = \dfrac{x}{16} = \dfrac{5}{4}$

$4x = 80$
$x = 20$

Math: Geometry and Trigonometry

> **CHALLENGE:**
>
> The measures of the two acute angles in a right triangle will always add up to 90°. And as you can see in the examples on p. 455, the sine of one of those angles will always be equal to the cosine of the other one. This will always work: **if $a + b = 90°$, then $\sin a = \cos b$.**
>
> *Example:* If $\cos 81° = 0.156$, *what is the value of* $\sin 9°$?
>
> Because $81 + 9 = 90$, $\cos 81°$ must equal $\sin 9°$. The answer is **0.156**.

To convert degrees into **radians**, use this relationship:

$$180° = \pi \text{ radians}$$

Example: An angle measurement of 135° is equivalent to x radians. What is the value of x?

$$\frac{135}{x} = \frac{180}{\pi}$$

$$135\pi = 180x$$

$$x = \frac{135\pi}{180}$$

$$x = \frac{3\pi}{4}$$

Try It 7) Convert $\frac{5\pi}{2}$ radians to degrees:

CHALLENGE:

The **unit circle** is a circle with a radius of 1 centered at $(0, 0)$ on the xy-plane. The coordinates of any point (x, y) on the circle are $(\cos\theta, \sin\theta)$, where θ is the angle formed between the positive x-axis and the radius connecting to that point.

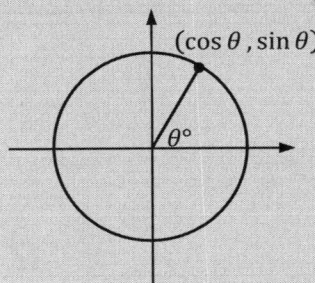

The unit circle is a convenient way to visualize and calculate trigonometric values for various angles. The quadrant that the angle falls in can quickly tell you whether the values of sin, cos, and tan will be positive or negative.

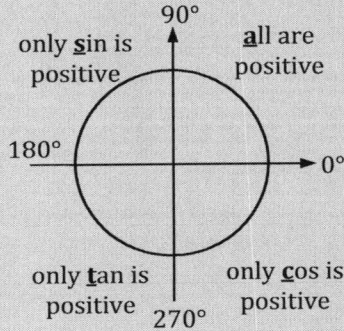

Starting in Quadrant I and moving in order through the quadrants, that sequence is **a**ll, **s**in, **t**an, **c**os. Use the mnemonic **A**ll **S**tudents **T**ake **C**alculus to remember the pattern.

Example: If $\theta = 135°$, then the corresponding point on the unit circle lies in Quadrant II. Therefore, the value of $\cos 135$ is negative, and the value of $\sin 135$ is positive.

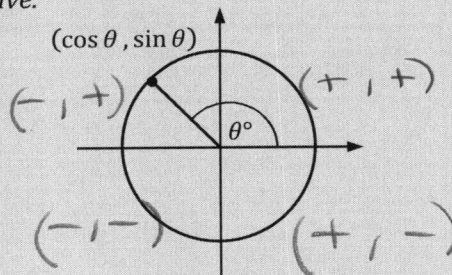

$\cos\theta = \dfrac{x}{r}$

$\sin\theta = \dfrac{y}{r}$

$\tan\theta = \dfrac{y}{x}$

Math: Geometry and Trigonometry

Chapter Answer Key

Try It
1) 4
2) B
3) 18
4) $2\sqrt{3}$
5) $\dfrac{5}{\sqrt{74}}$ or 0.581
6) 20
7) 450°

Right Triangles and Trigonometry

Practice Set 1: Easy-Medium

1

What is the length of the hypotenuse of a right triangle with legs of length 5 and 8?

A. $\sqrt{13}$
B. $\sqrt{40}$
C. $\sqrt{75}$
D. $\sqrt{89}$

2

A circle with diameter $\overline{AB}$ of length 3 is tangent to $\overline{EF}$ as shown below. If the length of $\overline{EA}$ (not shown) is equal to 6 and the length of $\overline{AF}$ (not shown) is equal to 5, what is the length of $\overline{EF}$?

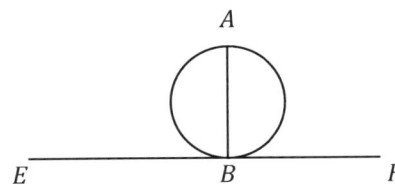

A. $4 + 3\sqrt{2}$
B. $4 + 3\sqrt{3}$
C. $7\sqrt{2}$
D. 9

3

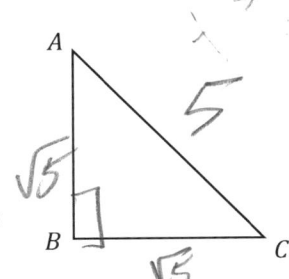

In the figure above, $\overline{AB} \perp \overline{BC}$ and $\overline{AB} \cong \overline{BC}$. If $AC = 5$, what is the area of $\triangle ABC$?

4

In the figure below, $\overline{CD}$ is a diameter of the circle, $\overline{BE}$ is a leg of right triangle ABE, and $BCDE$ is a square. What is the circumference of the circle?

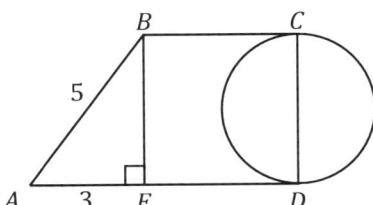

A. 2π
B. 4π
C. 12
D. 16

5

What is the value of $\cos x$ in the right triangle shown below?

6

What is the perimeter of the isosceles right triangle shown below?

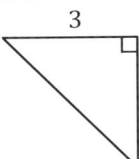

A. $3 + 3\sqrt{2}$
B. $3 + \sqrt{6}$
C. $6 + 3\sqrt{2}$
D. $6 + \sqrt{6}$

Math: Geometry and Trigonometry

7

A ladder that is 8 feet long is positioned leaning against a wall such that the measure of the angle formed between the ladder and the level ground is 60 degrees. What is the distance (on the ground) between the ladder and the wall, in feet?

A. 0.5
B. 2
C. 4
D. $4\sqrt{3}$

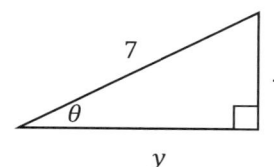

8

In the right triangle shown below, which of the following statements is true about θ?

A. $\sin\theta = \dfrac{x}{y}$

B. $\cos\theta = \dfrac{7}{y}$

C. $\cos\theta = \dfrac{7}{x}$

D. $\sin\theta = \dfrac{x}{7}$

9

If B is the largest angle in right triangle ABC, what is the measure of angle B in radians?

A. 2π
B. π
C. $\dfrac{\pi}{2}$
D. $\dfrac{\pi}{4}$

10

What is the area of the triangle shown below?

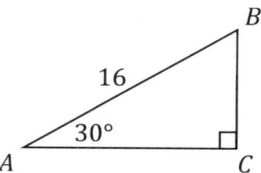

A. 8
B. $24\sqrt{2}$
C. $32\sqrt{3}$
D. 64

11

If a right triangle has a hypotenuse of length 14 and a shorter leg of length 5, what is the length of its longer leg?

A. $\sqrt{50}$
B. $\sqrt{75}$
C. $\sqrt{171}$
D. $\sqrt{221}$

12

Two ants were observed taking different routes from their anthill to a nearby food source. Ant A traveled due north for 0.8 meters, then due west for 1.5 meters, while ant B traveled in a straight line directly from the anthill to the food source. How many more meters were traveled by ant A than by ant B?

Practice Set 2: Medium-Hard

1

In right triangle PQR shown below, which of the following gives the length of $\overline{QR}$?

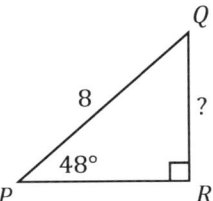

A. $\dfrac{\sin 48°}{8}$

B. $\dfrac{8}{\cos 48°}$

C. $8 \cos 48°$

D. $8 \sin 48°$

2

In quadrilateral $FGHJ$ below, angles G and J are right angles. If the lengths of $\overline{GH}$, $\overline{HJ}$, and $\overline{FJ}$ are 5, 4, and 6, respectively, which of the following is closest to the area of $FGHJ$?

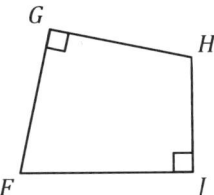

A. 20
B. 25
C. 28
D. 30

3

Equilateral triangle ABC has a perimeter of 12. What is the area of triangle ABC?

A. $2\sqrt{3}$
B. $4\sqrt{3}$
C. $6\sqrt{3}$
D. $8\sqrt{3}$

4

In a right triangle with side lengths $a, b,$ and c, where $a < b < c$, the smallest angle measures x degrees. What is the value of $\tan x$?

A. $\dfrac{a}{c}$

B. $\dfrac{a}{b}$

C. $\dfrac{b}{c}$

D. $\dfrac{c}{a}$

5

In the figure below, right triangle ABC is intersected by line l at points D and E such that line l is parallel to $\overline{AB}$. If $AB = 9, AC = 15$, the distance from line l to $\overline{AB}$ is 4, and the measure of $\angle CDE$ is $x°$, what is the value of $\cos x$?

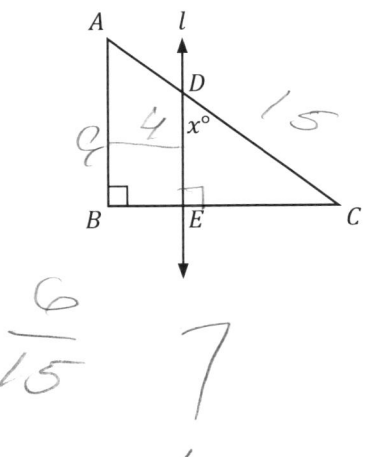

6

In triangle PQR, the lengths of $\overline{PQ}$, $\overline{QR}$, and $\overline{RP}$ are 7.5, 19.5, and 18, respectively. If the measure of angle Q is $q°$, what is the value of $\tan q$?

A. 0.417
B. 2.4
C. 2.6
D. It cannot be determined.

7

If $\cos P = \frac{r}{q}$, $q > 0$, $r > 0$, and $0 < P < \frac{\pi}{2}$, then $\tan P$ is equivalent to which of the following?

A. $\frac{q}{r}$

B. $\frac{\sqrt{q^2 - r^2}}{r}$ ⟵ (circled)

C. $\frac{\sqrt{q^2 - r^2}}{q}$

D. $\frac{q}{\sqrt{q^2 - r^2}}$

8

If $\cos \theta = 0.6$, what is the value of $\cos(90 - \theta)$?

9

The volume of a prism is equal to the product of its height and the area of tis base. In the prism shown below, each of the bases is an isosceles right triangle with a hypotenuse of $6\sqrt{2}$. If the volume of the prism is 108, what is the height of the prism?

$V = h \cdot A$

A. 3

B. $\frac{6}{\sqrt{2}}$

C. 6

D. $6\sqrt{2}$

10

If the value, to the nearest thousandth, of $\cos x$ is -0.707, which of the following could be true about x?

A. $0 \leq x \leq \frac{\pi}{6}$

B. $\frac{\pi}{3} \leq x \leq \frac{\pi}{2}$

C. $\frac{\pi}{2} \leq x \leq \frac{3\pi}{2}$

D. $\frac{3\pi}{2} \leq x \leq 2\pi$

11

If $\sin \theta = 0.45$ for the triangle shown below, then what is the value of x?

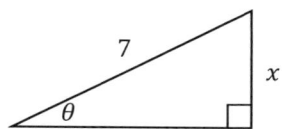

A. 0.064
B. 3.15 ⟵ (circled)
C. 3.52
D. 15.55

12

In the figure below, $\overline{YZ}$ is the hypotenuse of right triangle XYZ. If $\overline{YZ}$ has a length of 10 and the measure of angle Y is 70°, which of the following represents the length of $\overline{XZ}$?

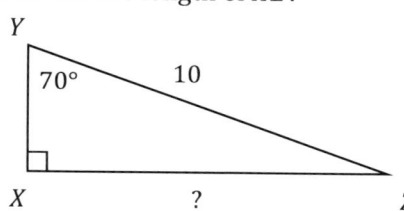

A. $10 \cos 70°$
B. $10 \tan 70°$
C. $10 \sin 20°$
D. $10 \cos 20°$

Circles

The relevant provided formulas:

REFERENCE

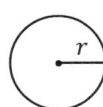

The number of degrees of arc in a circle is 360.
The number of radians of arc in a circle is 2π.

$A = \pi r^2$
$C = 2\pi r$

opps

Preview Quiz:

Define each term:

1) What is an **arc**? _____

2) What is a **sector**? _____

3) What is a **chord**? _____

4) What does it mean for a line to be **tangent** to a circle?
   _____

In the figure shown, points A, B, and C lie on the circle centered at point O, and the measure of $\angle AOC$ is 90°. The radius of the circle is 6.

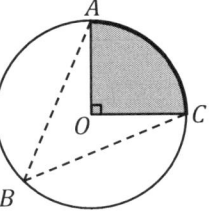

5) What is the degree measure of minor arc $\widehat{AC}$?

6) What is the degree measure of $\angle ABC$?

7) What is the length of minor arc $\widehat{AC}$?

8) What is the area of the shaded region?

If the circle given by $(x-2)^2 + (y+3)^2 = 49$ is graphed on the xy-plane:

9) What are the coordinates of the center?

10) What is the length of the radius?

11) What is the area of the circle?

Math: Geometry and Trigonometry

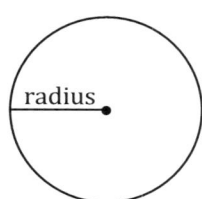
radius

All points on a circle are the same distance from the circle's center. That distance is called the **radius**.

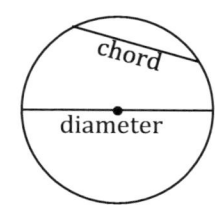
chord / diameter

A **chord** is any line segment that intersects a circle in two places. If the chord passes through the center, it is called a **diameter**. The diameter is the longest chord that can be drawn in a circle. It is twice the length of the radius.

A line that is **tangent** to a circle intersects it in exactly one place. The tangent line is perpendicular to the radius at the point of intersection.

tangent

central angle (80°, 80°)

A **central angle** is an angle with its vertex at the center of a circle. Where the radii that form the sides of the angle intersect the circle, they mark off a portion of the circumference known as an **arc**. The degree measure of the arc is equal to the degree measure of the central angle.

$m = 1/2$

An **inscribed angle** is an angle whose vertex lies on the circumference of a circle. The degree measure of the arc intercepted by an inscribed angle is twice the degree measure of the angle.

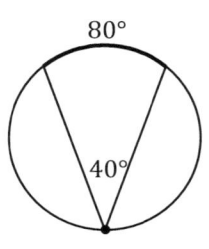
inscribed angle (80°, 40°)

$= 1/2$ central

Because an arc is just a portion of the circumference of a circle, you can use the circumference, $2\pi r$, to calculate the **length of an arc**:

$$\text{Arc length} = \frac{\text{central angle}}{360}(2\pi r)$$

Example: What is the length of minor arc AC in the circle shown?

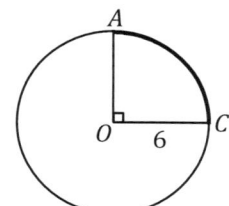

$$\text{Arc length} = \frac{90}{360}(2\pi(6))$$

$$\text{Arc length} = \frac{1}{4}(12\pi)$$

$$\text{Arc length} = 3\pi$$

The region of a circle defined by two radii and an arc is called a **sector**. Because it is a portion of the circle's area, you can use something very similar to the arc length formula to calculate the **area of a sector** based on the area of the circle, πr^2:

$$\text{Sector area} = \frac{\text{central angle}}{360}(\pi r^2)$$

Example: What is the area of the shaded region in the circle shown?

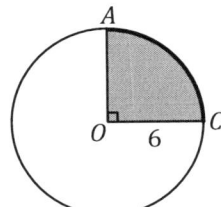

$$\text{Sector area} = \frac{90}{360}(\pi(6)^2)$$

$$\text{Sector area} = \frac{1}{4}(36\pi)$$

$$\text{Sector area} = \mathbf{9\pi}$$

Try It

1) What is the length of a 40° arc of a circle with radius 9?

2) In a circle, a sector with area 8π is intercepted by a central angle measuring $d°$. If the radius of the circle is 12, what is the value of d?

3) In the figure shown, points P, Q, and R all lie on the circle. If arc QR (shown in bold in the figure below) is a semicircle, then triangle PQR must be which of the following?

    A) an equilateral triangle
    B) a right triangle
    C) an obtuse triangle
    D) none of the above

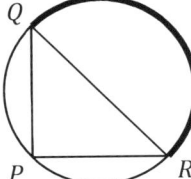

Math: Geometry and Trigonometry

In the xy-plane, the graph of $(x - h)^2 + (y - k)^2 = r^2$ is a circle centered at the point (h, k) with radius r.

Example: What is the area of the circle defined by the equation $(x - 2)^2 + (y + 3)^2 = 49$?

This equation gives a circle centered at $(2, -3)$ with a radius of 7. Now use the formula for area of a circle:

$$A = \pi r^2$$
$$A = \pi(7)^2 = \mathbf{49\pi}$$

TIP:
Don't forget to switch the signs! A $(y + 3)^2$ in the equation means the y-coordinate of the center is -3, not positive 3.

Try It

4) In the xy-plane, what are the coordinates of the center of the circle given by $(x + 1)^2 + y^2 = 4$?

5) What is the equation of the circle centered at $(-9, \ 5)$ on the xy-plane, given that the radius of the circle is 4?

6) A circle with a radius of 5 is graphed in the xy-plane with its center at $(3, 1)$. The circle passes through the point $(k, \ -3)$, where k is a positive constant. What is the value of k?

CHALLENGE:

If the test gives you the equation of a circle that is not in standard form, the easiest way to handle the problem is to simply graph the equation in the built-in calculator.

Alternatively, you can solve the problem algebraically by **completing the square.**

Example: $x^2 + y^2 - 4x + 2y - 11 = 0$

First, group the x's together and the y's together. Stand-alone numbers (constants) go on the right side of the equation.

$$x^2 - 6x + y^2 + 2y = 11$$

The x's form the first two terms of a quadratic of form $ax^2 + bx + c$, and the y's form the first two terms of a different quadratic of the form $ay^2 + by + c$. Within each of those two sets, find $(b/2)^2$; add that to both sides of the equation. For example, the b term of the x quadratic here is -6, so $(b/2)^2$ is $(-6/2)^2 = (-3)^2 = 9$. On the y side, the b term is 2, so $(b/2)^2$ is $(2/2)^2 = (1)^2 = 1$. So:

$$x^2 - 6x + \mathbf{9} + y^2 + 2y + \mathbf{1} = 11 + \mathbf{9} + \mathbf{1}$$

Now, factor both quadratics and add up the numbers on the right.

$$(x-3)^2 + (y+1)^2 = 21$$

Therefore, this is a circle centered at $(3, -1)$, with a radius of $\sqrt{21}$.

Try It   7) On the xy-plane, what is the center of the circle given by $x^2 + 4x + y^2 - 10y = 2$?

Math: Geometry and Trigonometry

Chapter Answer Key

Try It
1) 2π
2) 20
3) B
4) $(-1, 0)$
5) $(x+9)^2 + (y-5)^2 = 16$
6) 6
7) $(-2, 5)$

FROM THE BLOG

Worrying is not preparation. Don't stress; practice!

Practice Set 1: Easy-Medium

1

When graphed in the xy-plane, the circle $(x + 3)^2 + (y - 1)^2 = 16$ is centered at which of the following points?

A. $(-3, -1)$
B. $(-3, 1)$
C. $(3, -1)$
D. $(3, 1)$

2

In the figure below, the chord shown does NOT pass through the center of the circle. If the area of the circle is 49π, which of the following must be true about x, the length of the chord?

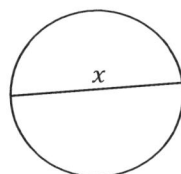

A. $x > 7$
B. $0 < x < 7$
C. $x > 14$
D. $0 < x < 14$

3

Which of the following gives the equation of a circle in the xy-plane?

A. $\dfrac{(x - 2)^2}{4} + \dfrac{(y + 8)^2}{6} = 1$
B. $(x - 1)^2 + y^2 = 1$
C. $x^2 - y^2 = 1$
D. $x + (y + 3)^2 = 1$

4

On the xy-plane, the point $(9, 0)$ lies on a circle with center $(6, -4)$. What is the radius of the circle?

5

Point C is the center of the circle of radius 18 pictured below. What is the length of arc DEF?

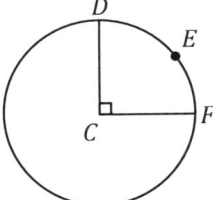

A. 6π
B. 9π
C. 12π
D. 18π

6

In the xy-plane, the graph of which of the following equations is a circle with center $(2, 5)$ and radius 9?

A. $(x - 2)^2 + (y - 5)^2 = 3$
B. $(x - 2)^2 + (y - 5)^2 = 81$
C. $(x + 2)^2 + (y + 5)^2 = 3$
D. $(x + 2)^2 + (y + 5)^2 = 81$

7

What is the length, in centimeters, of an 80° arc of a circle whose area is 81π square centimeters?

A. 2π
B. 3π
C. 4π
D. 9π

8

What is the circumference, in coordinate units, of the circle in the xy-plane given by the equation $x^2 + (y + 9)^2 = 100$?

A. 10π
B. 20π
C. 81π
D. 100π

Math: Geometry and Trigonometry

Practice Set 2: Medium-Hard

1

On the xy-plane, the circle with radius 4 and center $(2, 4)$ intersects the line $y = 8$ at which of the following points?

A. $(-4, 8)$
B. $(2, 8)$
C. $(4, 8)$
D. $(8, 14)$

2

The shaded region in the circle below is bounded by minor arc AB and by radii $\overline{OA}$ and $\overline{OB}$. If the area of the shaded region is 20% of the area of the circle, what is the degree measure of $\angle AOB$, in degrees?

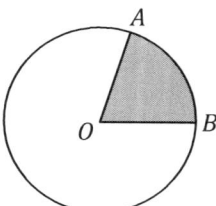

3

On the xy-plane, which of the following is an x-intercept of the circle with radius 5 and center $(3, 0)$?

A. $(-8, 0)$
B. $(2, 0)$
C. $(0, -2)$
D. $(8, 0)$

4

On the xy-plane, what is the center of the circle that has the equation $x^2 + 8x + y^2 + 18y = 10$?

A. $(3, 5)$
B. $(-5, 5)$
C. $(-4, -9)$
D. $(-8, 4)$

5

In the figure below, points A and B lie on the circle with center O, and the side lengths of triangle AOB are as shown. What is the area of the circle?

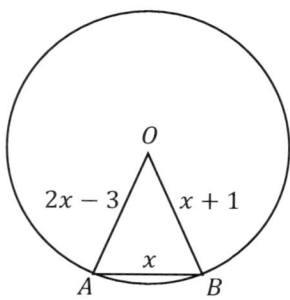

A. 4π
B. 9π
C. 16π
D. 25π

6

If all of the sides of the hexagon pictured below are congruent, and the radius of the circle is equal to 9, what is the length of arc XYZ?

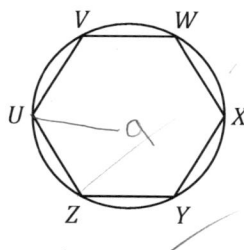

A. 3π
B. 6π
C. 9π
D. 18π

7

In the xy-plane, a circle with a radius of 4 is tangent to the lines $x = 2$ and $y = 3$. If the entire graph of the circle is located in Quadrant I, what are the coordinates of the circle's center?

A. $(6, 7)$
B. $(7, 6)$
C. $(10, 11)$
D. $(11, 10)$

Made in the USA
Middletown, DE
18 February 2024

49630985R00261